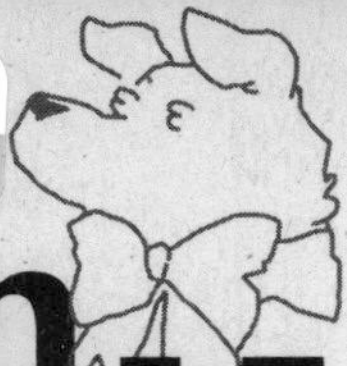

maison ikkoku 15

STORY AND ART BY RUMIKO TAKAHASHI

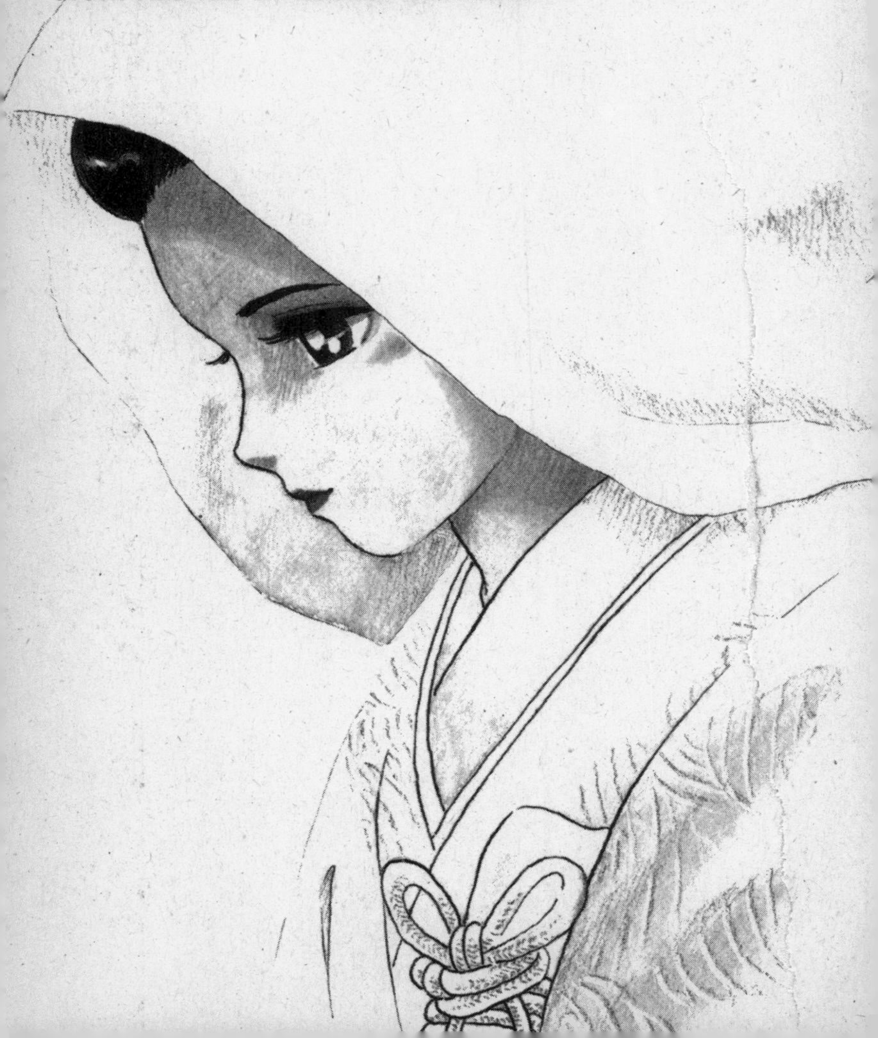

TABLE OF CONTENTS

PART ONE
THE TRUTH

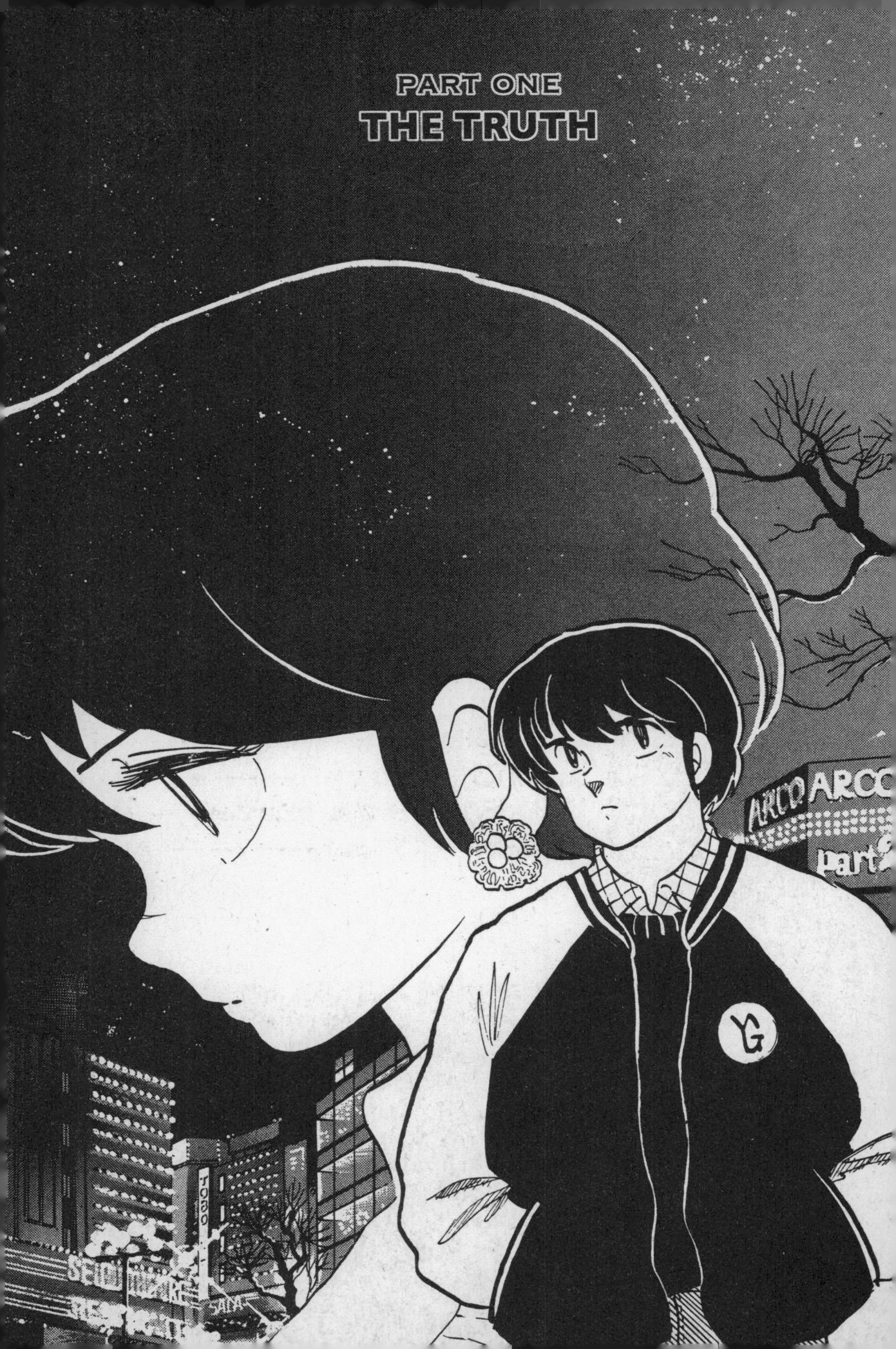
ARCO

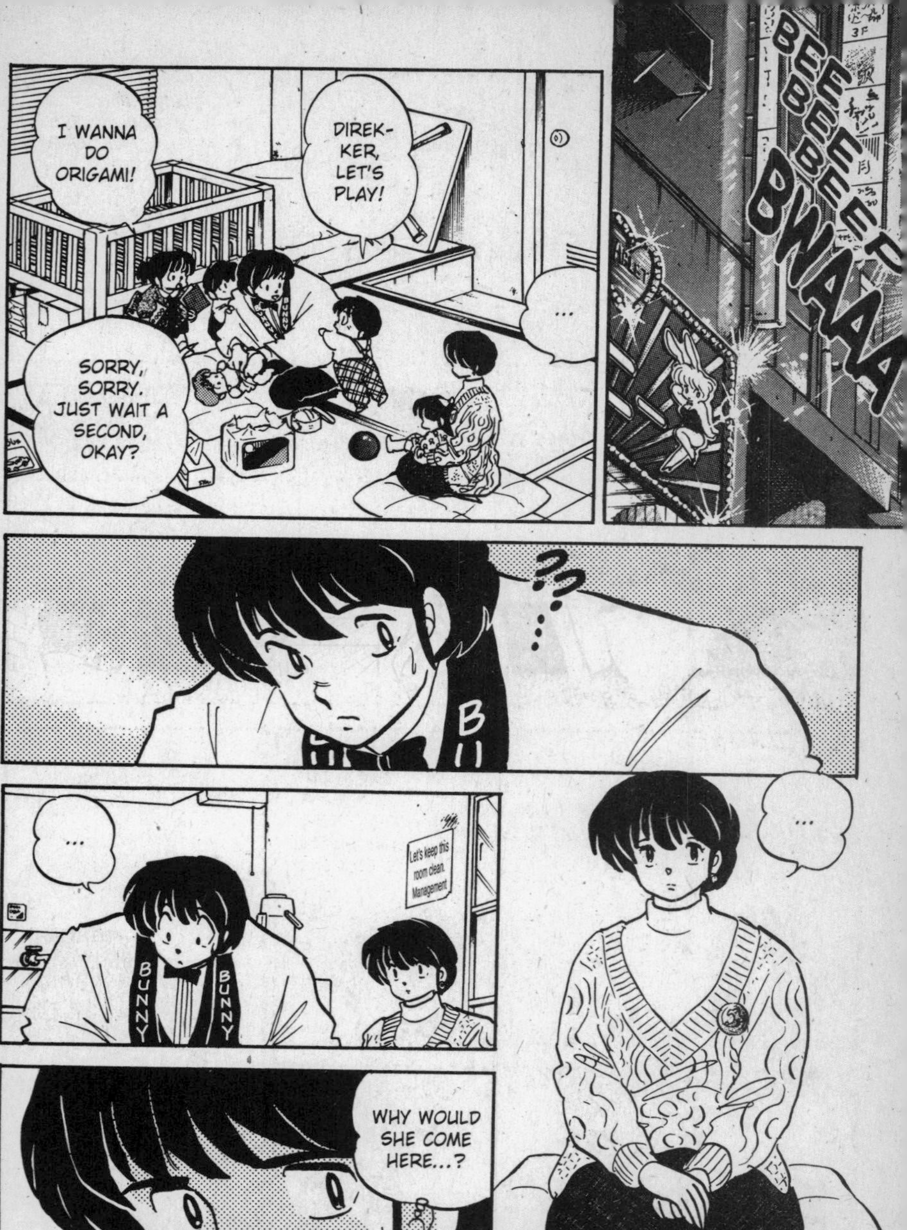
BEE
BEE
BEEP
BWAAA
DIREKKER, LET'S PLAY!
I WANNA DO ORIGAMI!
...
SORRY, SORRY. JUST WAIT A SECOND, OKAY?
??
...
...
...
Let's keep this room clean. Management
WHY WOULD SHE COME HERE...?

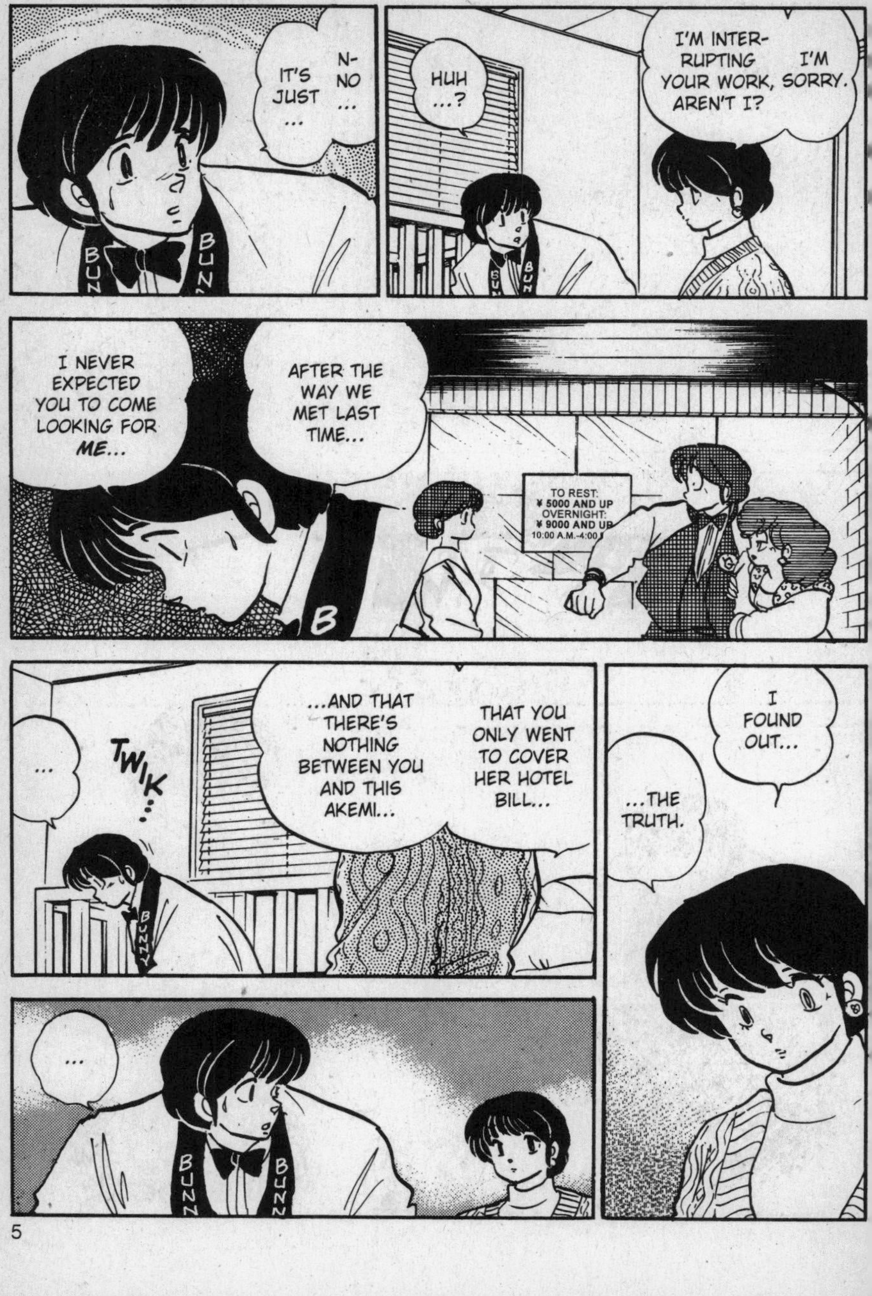
I'M SORRY.
I'M INTER-RUPTING YOUR WORK, AREN'T I?
HUH ...?
N-NO ...
IT'S JUST ...
TO REST: ¥ 5000 AND UP OVERNIGHT: ¥ 9000 AND UP 10:00 A.M.-4:00
AFTER THE WAY WE MET LAST TIME...
I NEVER EXPECTED YOU TO COME LOOKING FOR *ME*...
I FOUND OUT...
...THE TRUTH.
THAT YOU ONLY WENT TO COVER HER HOTEL BILL...
...AND THAT THERE'S NOTHING BETWEEN YOU AND THIS AKEMI...
TWIK...
...
...

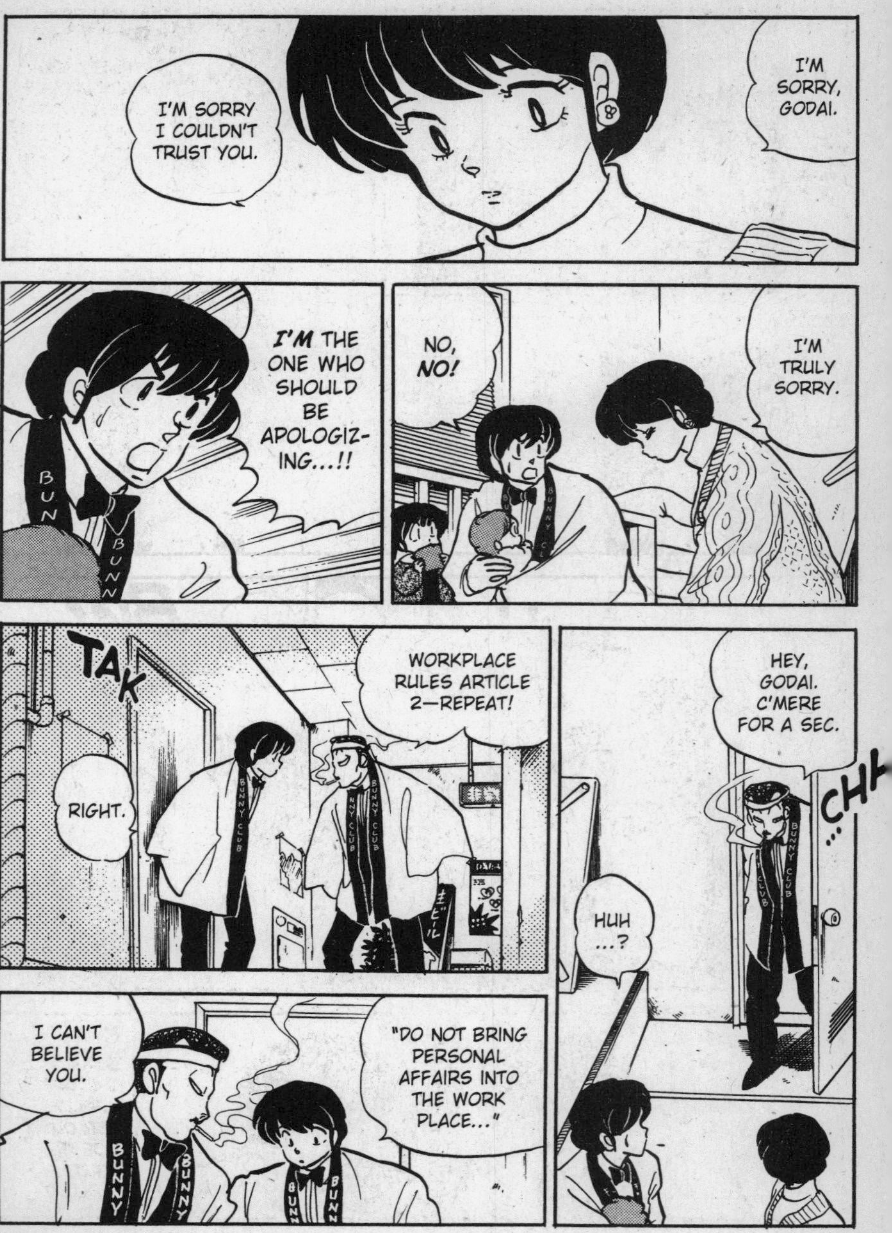
I'M SORRY, GODAI.
I'M SORRY I COULDN'T TRUST YOU.
I'M TRULY SORRY.
NO, *NO!*
I'M THE ONE WHO SHOULD BE APOLOGIZING...!!
HEY, GODAI. C'MERE FOR A SEC.
CH...
HUH ...?
WORKPLACE RULES ARTICLE 2—REPEAT!
TAK
RIGHT.
"DO NOT BRING PERSONAL AFFAIRS INTO THE WORK PLACE..."
I CAN'T BELIEVE YOU.

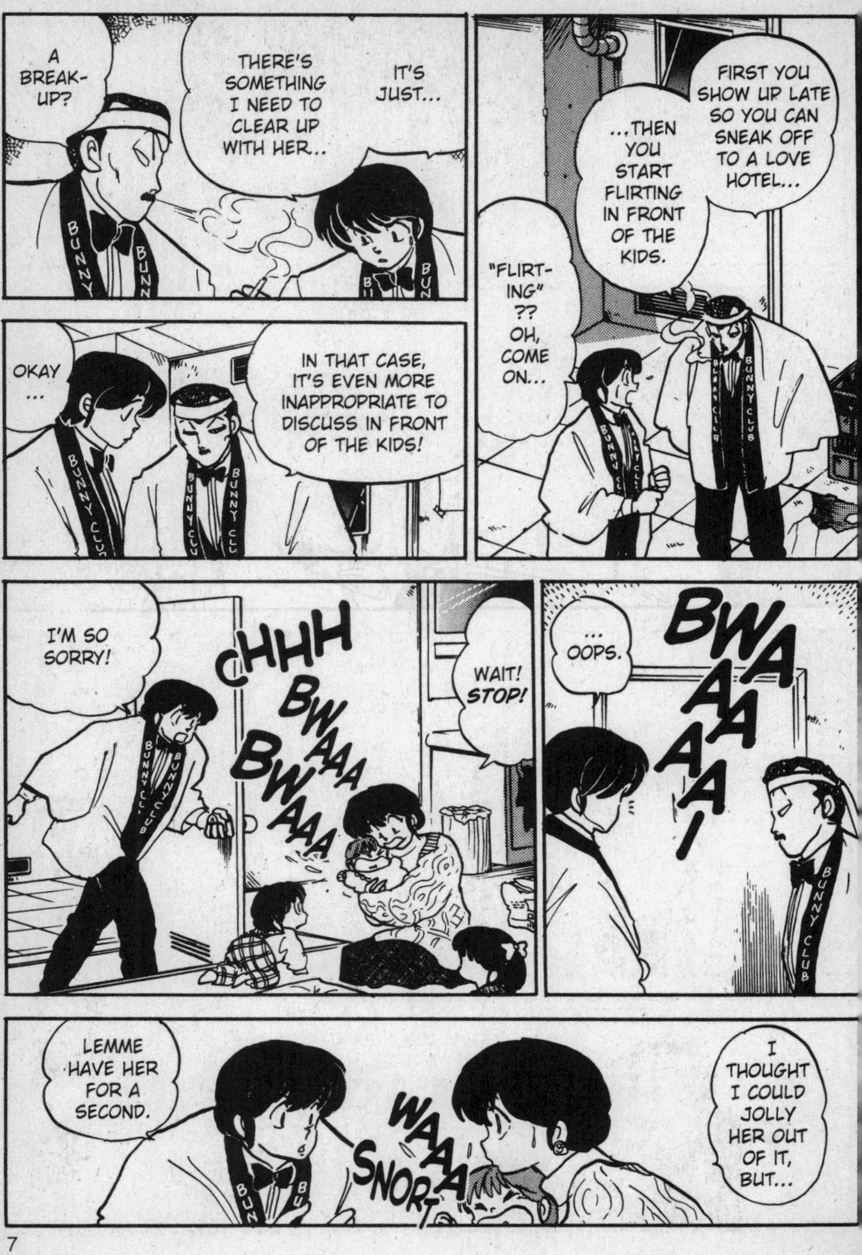
FIRST YOU SHOW UP LATE SO YOU CAN SNEAK OFF TO A LOVE HOTEL...
...THEN YOU START FLIRTING IN FRONT OF THE KIDS.
"FLIRT-ING" ?? OH, COME ON...
IT'S JUST...
THERE'S SOMETHING I NEED TO CLEAR UP WITH HER...
A BREAK-UP?
IN THAT CASE, IT'S EVEN MORE INAPPROPRIATE TO DISCUSS IN FRONT OF THE KIDS!
OKAY ...
BWAAAAAI
... OOPS.
WAIT! STOP!
CHHH
BWAAAA
BWAAAA
I'M SO SORRY!
I THOUGHT I COULD JOLLY HER OUT OF IT, BUT...
WAAAA
SNORT
LEMME HAVE HER FOR A SECOND.

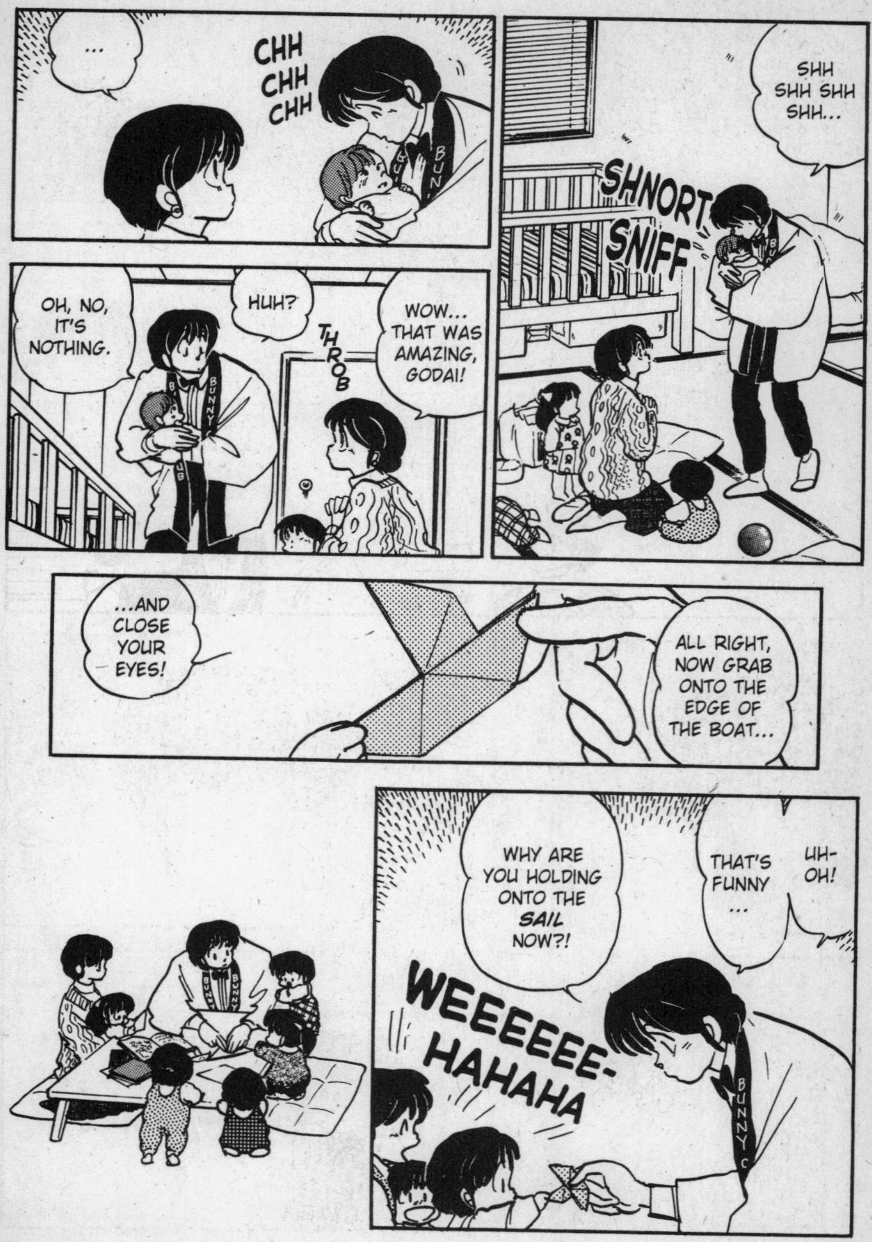
SHH SHH SHH SHH...
SHNORT SNIFF
...
CHH CHH CHH
WOW... THAT WAS AMAZING, GODAI!
THROB
HUH?
OH, NO, IT'S NOTHING.
ALL RIGHT, NOW GRAB ONTO THE EDGE OF THE BOAT...
...AND CLOSE YOUR EYES!
UH-OH!
THAT'S FUNNY ...
WHY ARE YOU HOLDING ONTO THE *SAIL* NOW?!
WEEEEEEE-HAHAHA

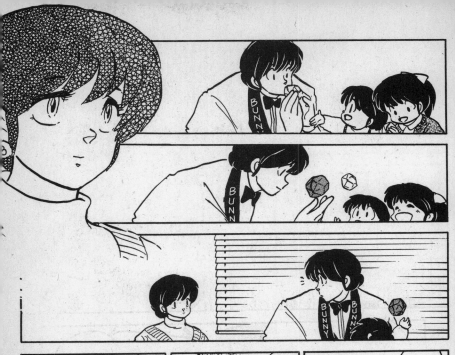

UH-HUH.

I'M GLAD.

YOU THINK—?

YOU—

YOU'RE GONNA BE A GREAT TEACHER.

SIIIIGH...

THEN... SHE REALLY CAME TO MAKE UP...?

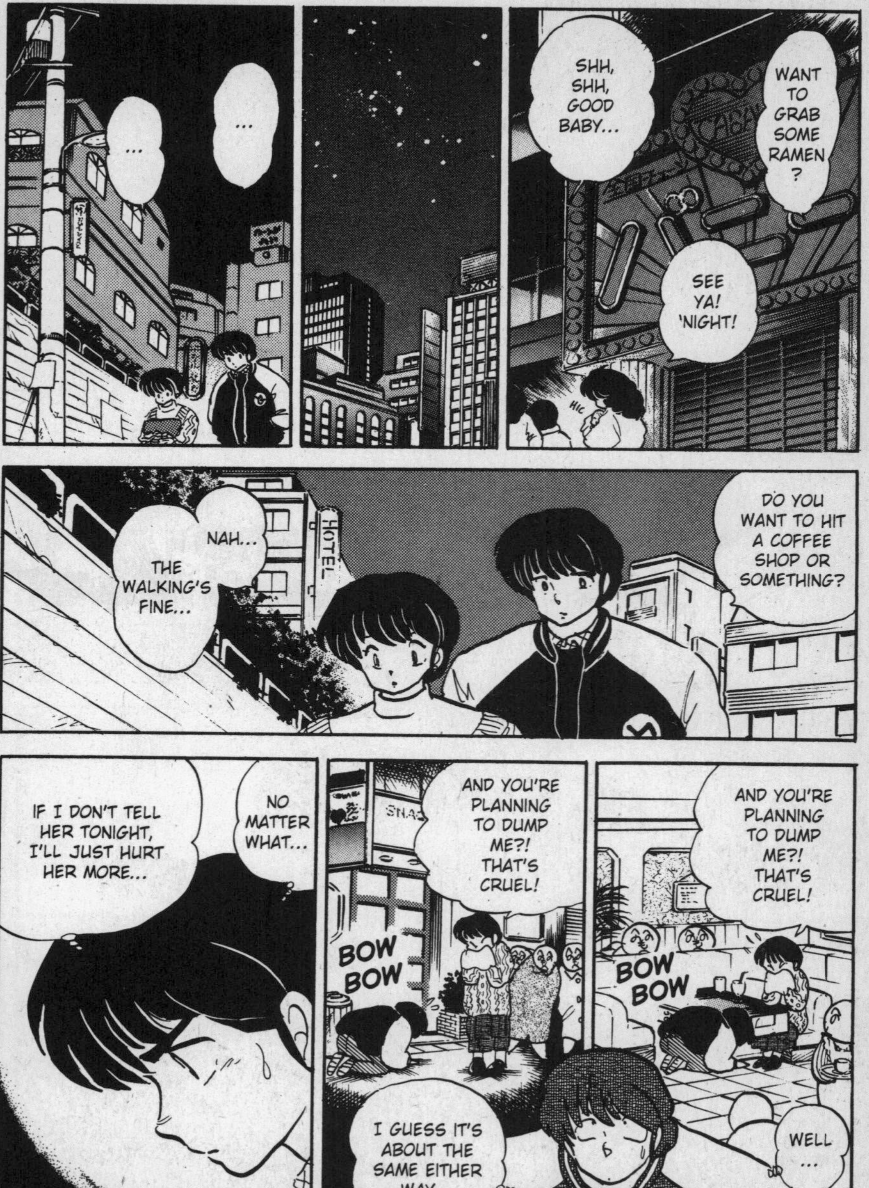
WANT TO GRAB SOME RAMEN?
SHH, SHH, GOOD BABY...
SEE YA! 'NIGHT!
HIC
...
...
DO YOU WANT TO HIT A COFFEE SHOP OR SOMETHING?
NAH... THE WALKING'S FINE...
AND YOU'RE PLANNING TO DUMP ME?! THAT'S CRUEL!
BOW BOW
WELL...
AND YOU'RE PLANNING TO DUMP ME?! THAT'S CRUEL!
BOW BOW
I GUESS IT'S ABOUT THE SAME EITHER WAY...
NO MATTER WHAT...
IF I DON'T TELL HER TONIGHT, I'LL JUST HURT HER MORE...

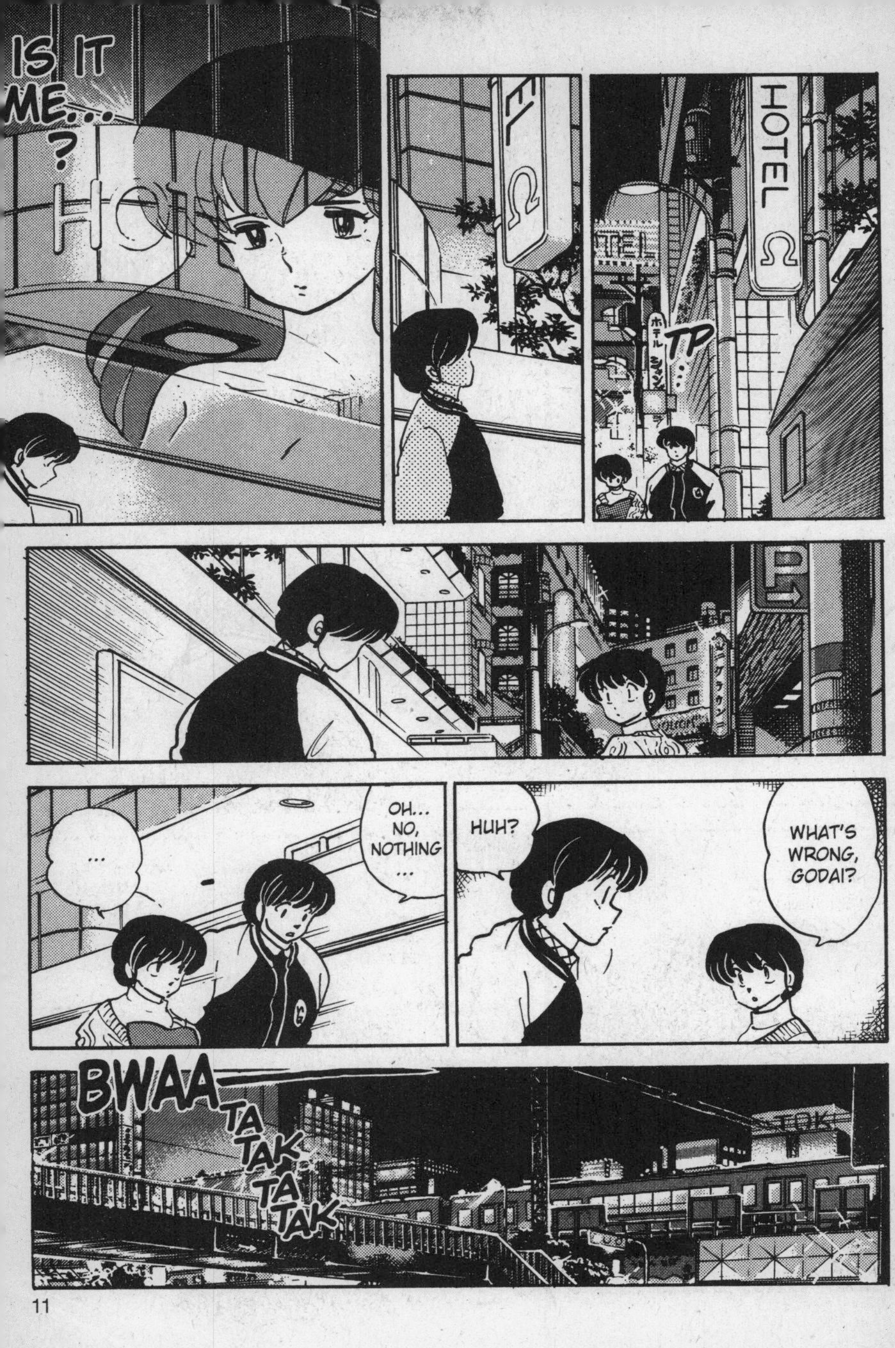
HOTEL
TP...
IS IT ME...?
WHAT'S WRONG, GODAI?
HUH?
OH... NO, NOTHING...
...
BWAA TA TAK TA TAK

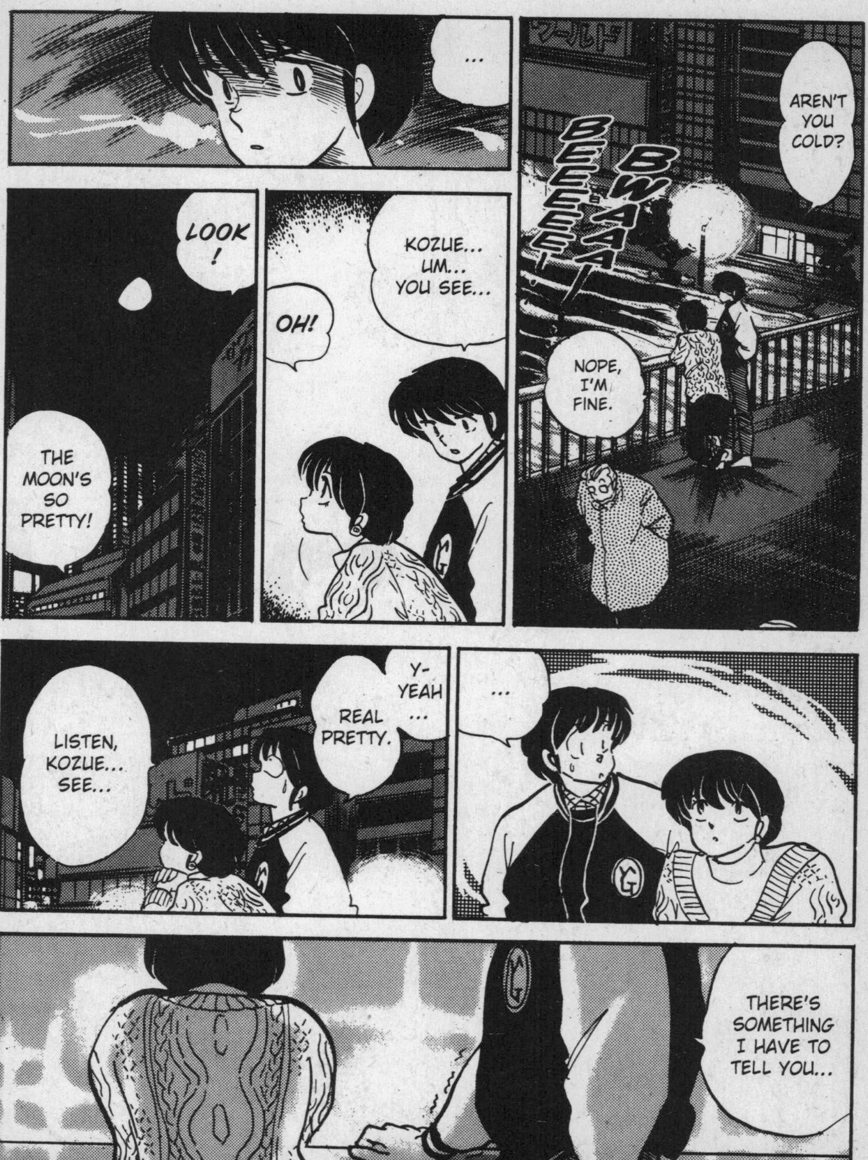

AREN'T YOU COLD?
BWAAAA
BEEEEE!
NOPE, I'M FINE.
...
KOZUE... UM... YOU SEE...
OH!
LOOK!
THE MOON'S SO PRETTY!
...
Y-YEAH... REAL PRETTY.
LISTEN, KOZUE... SEE...
THERE'S SOMETHING I HAVE TO TELL YOU...

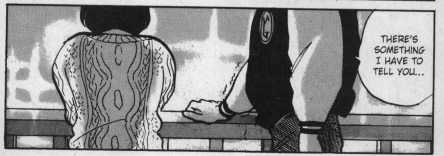

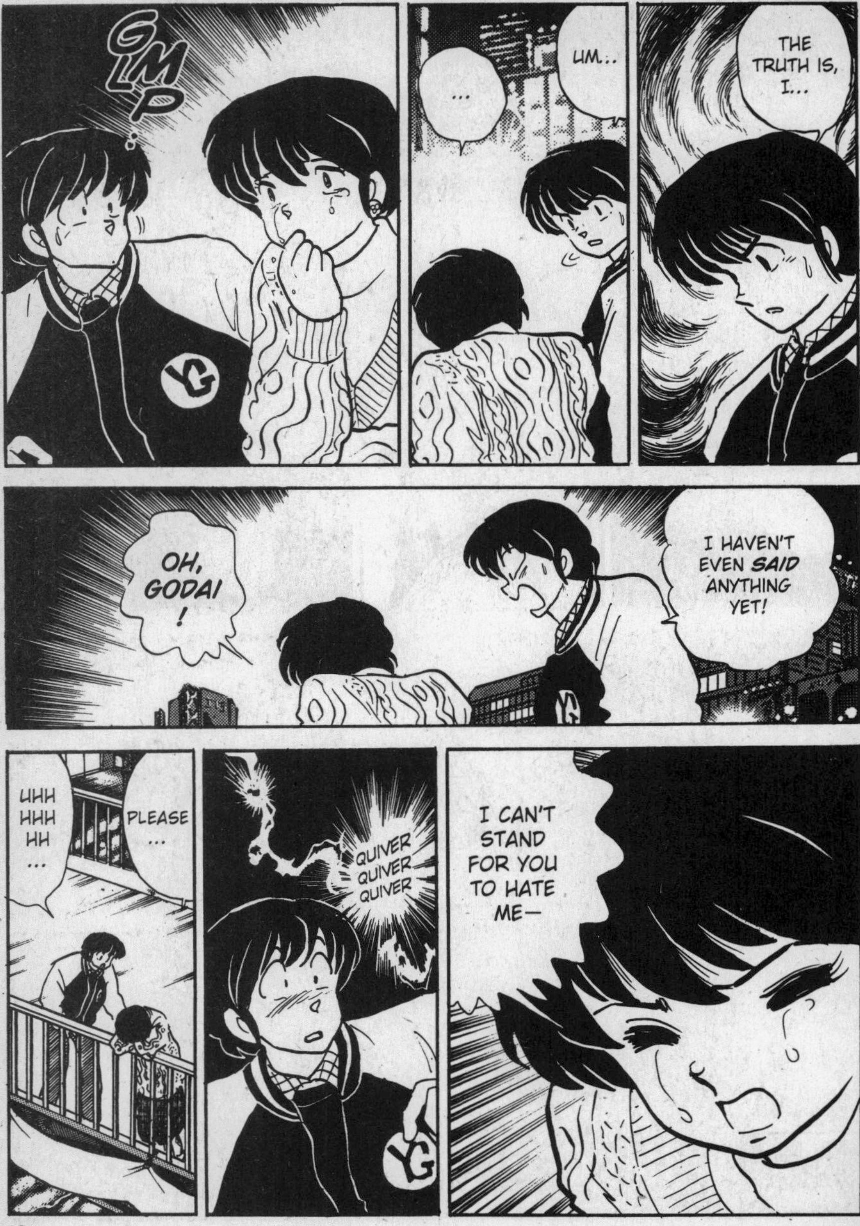
THE TRUTH IS, I...
UM...
...
GMLP
I HAVEN'T EVEN *SAID* ANYTHING YET!
OH, GODAI!
I CAN'T STAND FOR YOU TO HATE ME—
QUIVER QUIVER QUIVER
PLEASE...
UHHHHHHHH...

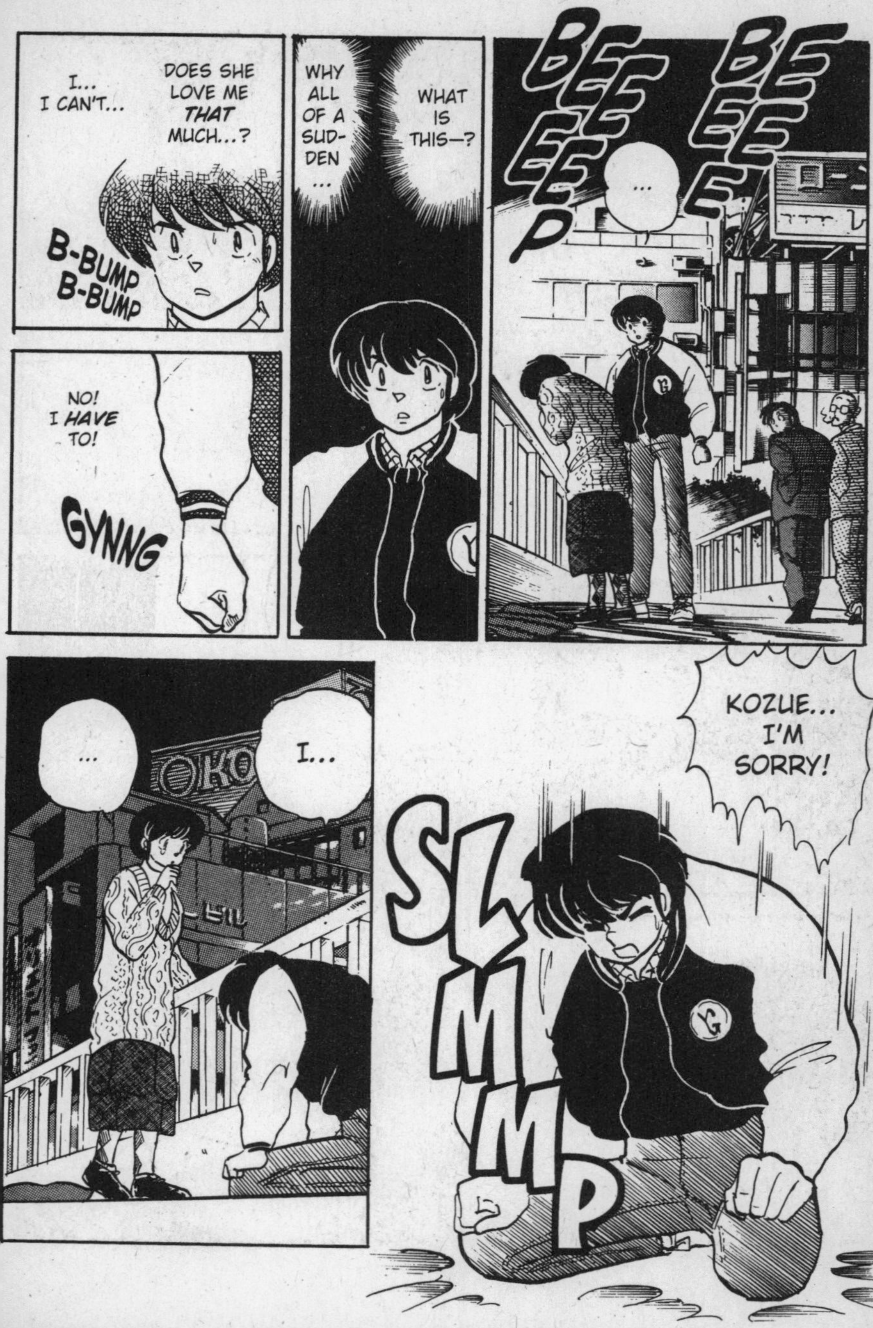
BEEEEE
BEEEEEP
...
WHAT IS THIS—?
WHY ALL OF A SUDDEN...
DOES SHE LOVE ME *THAT* MUCH...?
I... I CAN'T...
B-BUMP B-BUMP
NO! I *HAVE* TO!
GYNNG
KOZUE... I'M SORRY!
SLMMP
I...
...

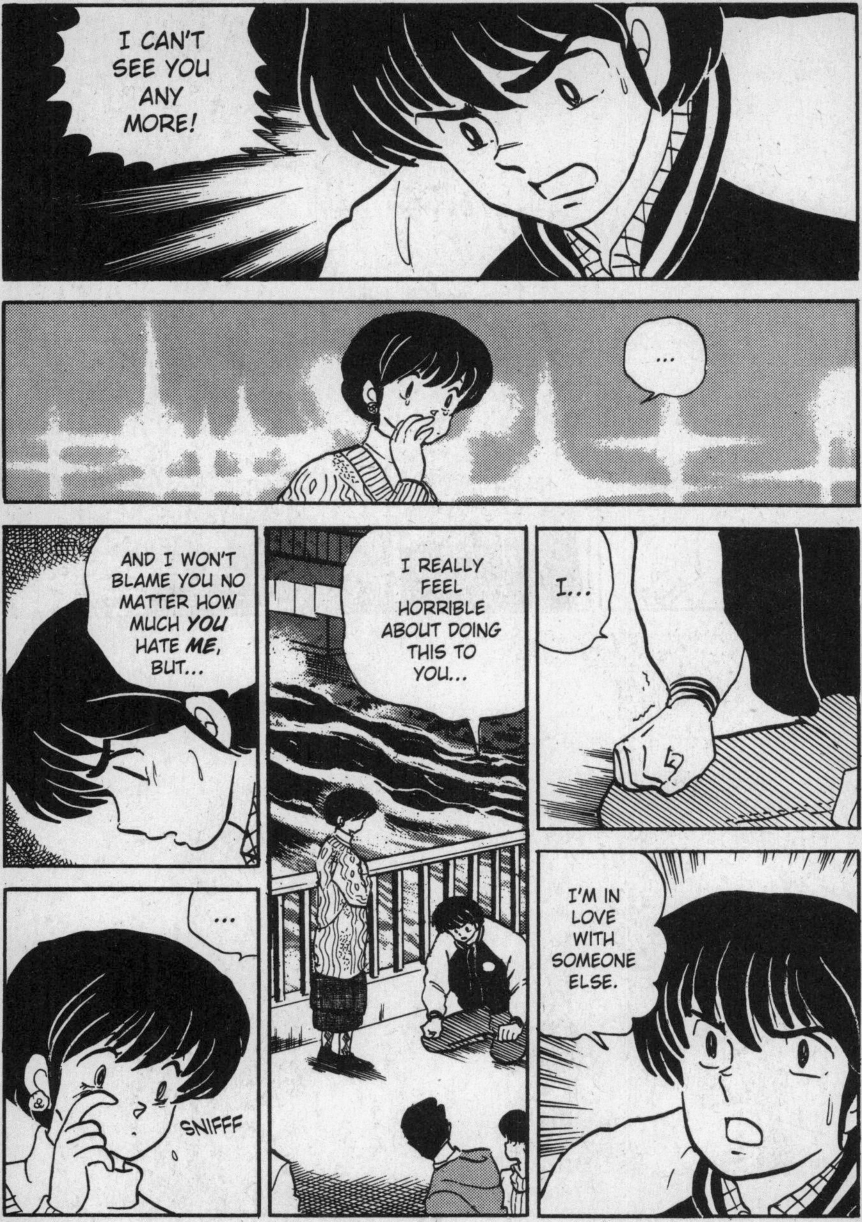
I CAN'T SEE YOU ANY MORE!
...
I...
I'M IN LOVE WITH SOMEONE ELSE.
I REALLY FEEL HORRIBLE ABOUT DOING THIS TO YOU...
AND I WON'T BLAME YOU NO MATTER HOW MUCH *YOU* HATE *ME*, BUT...
...
SNIFFF

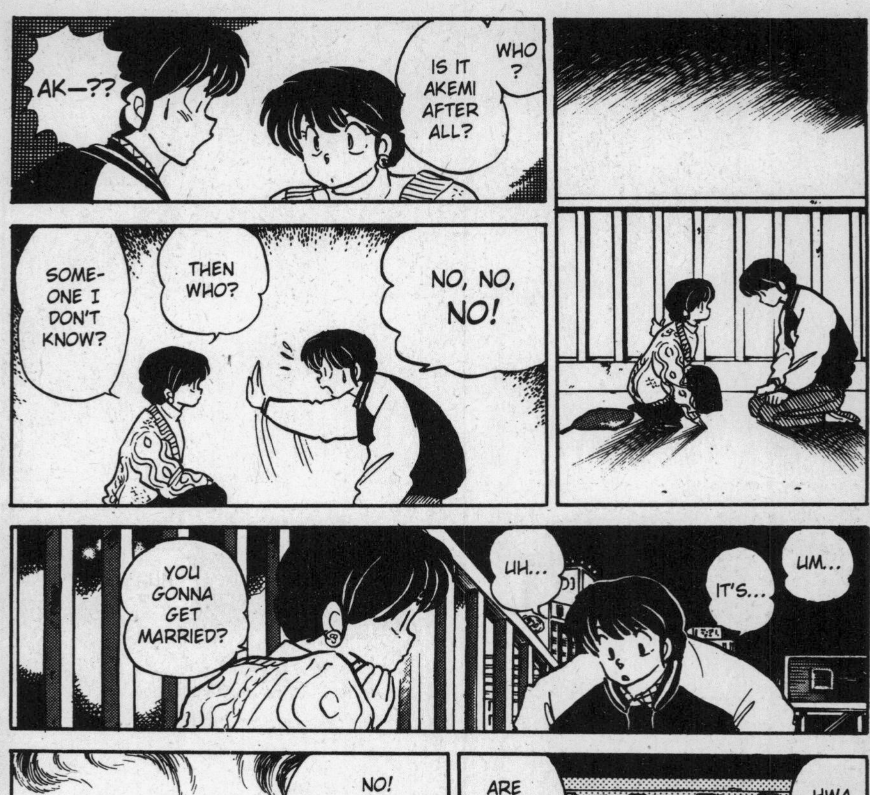
WHO ?
IS IT AKEMI AFTER ALL?
AK—??
NO, NO, NO!
THEN WHO?
SOME-ONE I DON'T KNOW?
UM...
IT'S...
UH...
YOU GONNA GET MARRIED?
HWA ??
ARE YOU GOING TO MARRY HER?
NO! I MEAN... WE'RE NOT AT THAT POINT YET...
MMMBLE MMMBLE
BUT...
I'D LIKE TO...
TH-THAT'S WHY I CAN'T GO ON WITH YOU THINKING...

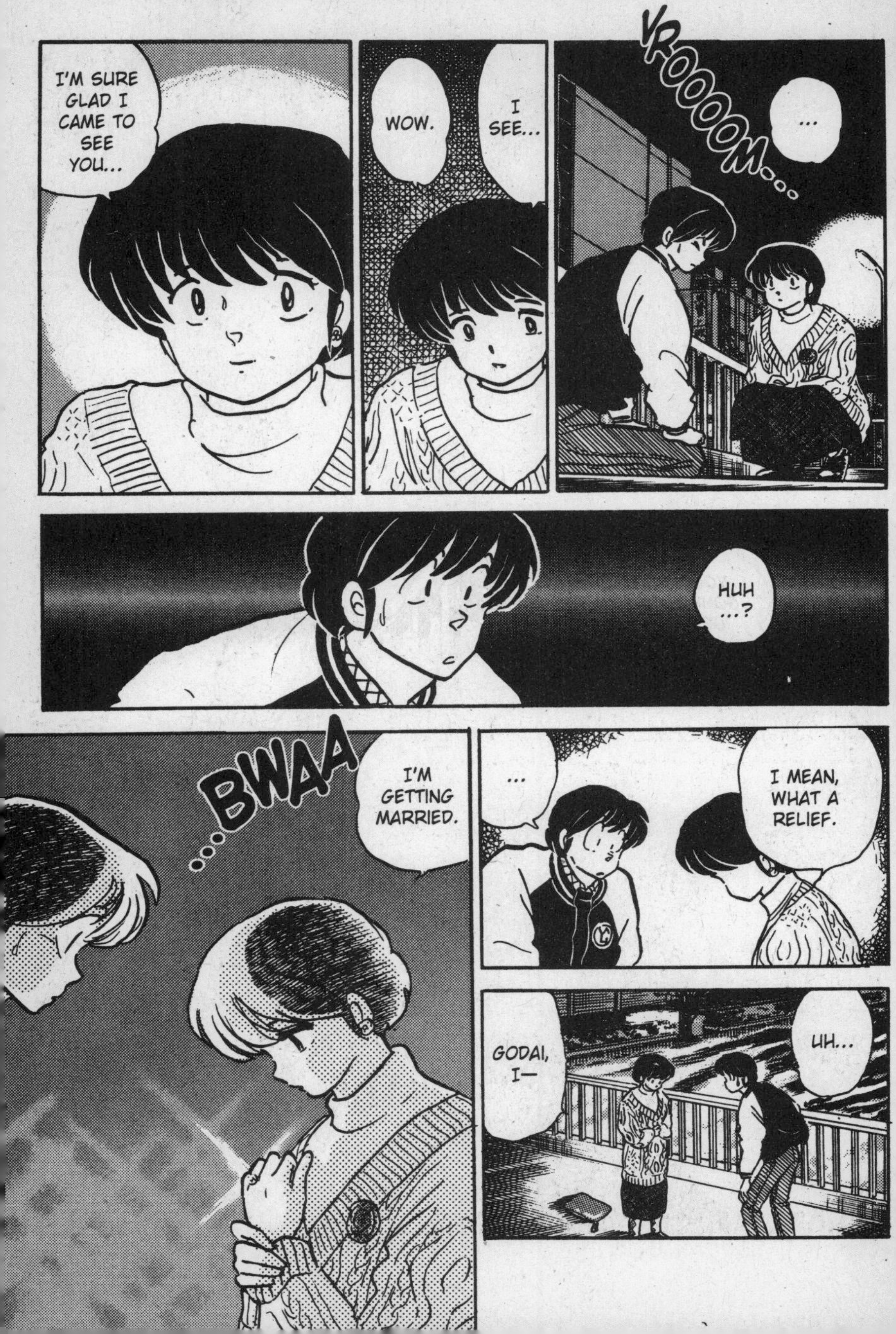
VROOOOM...
...
I SEE...
WOW.
I'M SURE GLAD I CAME TO SEE YOU...
HUH ...?
I MEAN, WHAT A RELIEF.
...
UH...
GODAI, I—
I'M GETTING MARRIED.
...BWAA

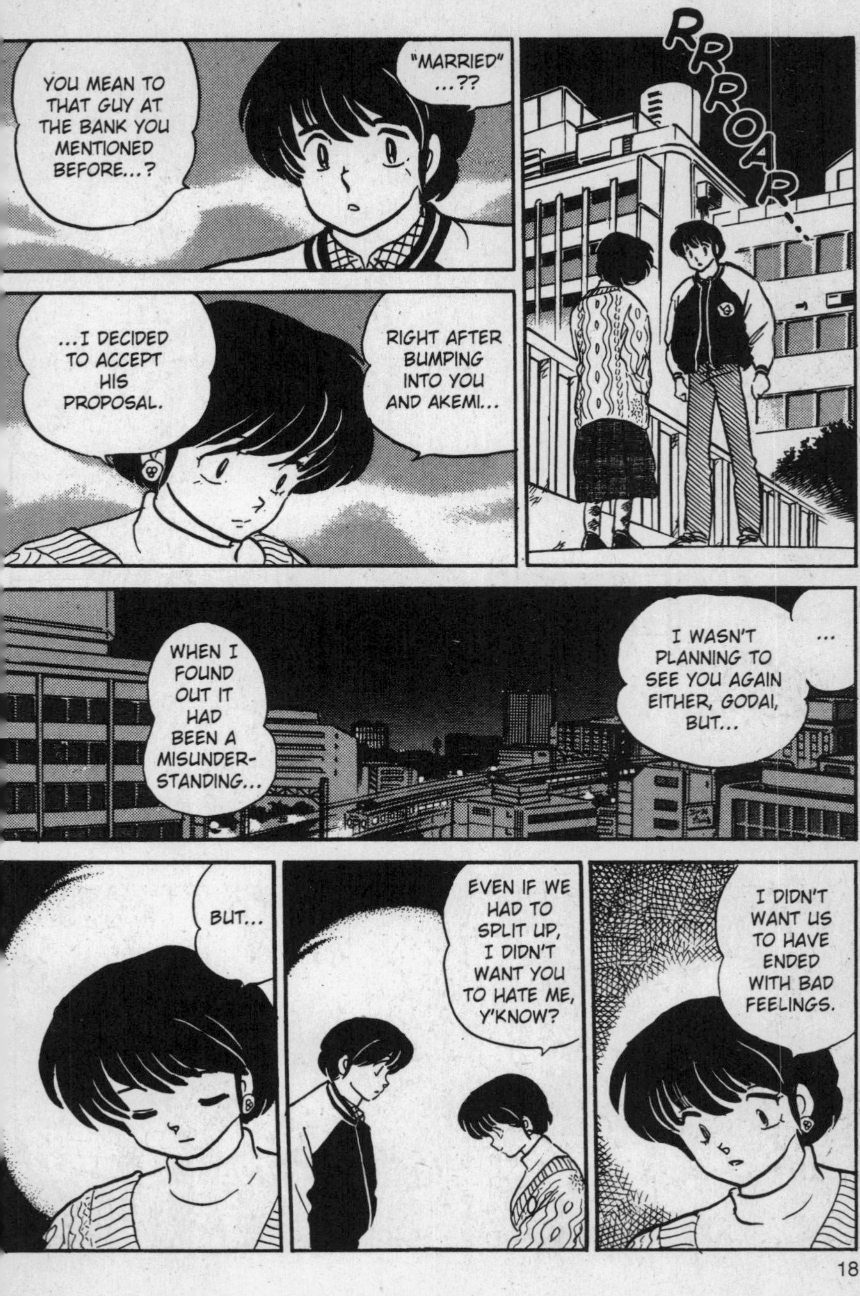
RRROAR...
"MARRIED" ...??
YOU MEAN TO THAT GUY AT THE BANK YOU MENTIONED BEFORE...?
RIGHT AFTER BUMPING INTO YOU AND AKEMI...
...I DECIDED TO ACCEPT HIS PROPOSAL.
...
I WASN'T PLANNING TO SEE YOU AGAIN EITHER, GODAI, BUT...
WHEN I FOUND OUT IT HAD BEEN A MISUNDER-STANDING...
I DIDN'T WANT US TO HAVE ENDED WITH BAD FEELINGS.
EVEN IF WE HAD TO SPLIT UP, I DIDN'T WANT YOU TO HATE ME, Y'KNOW?
BUT...

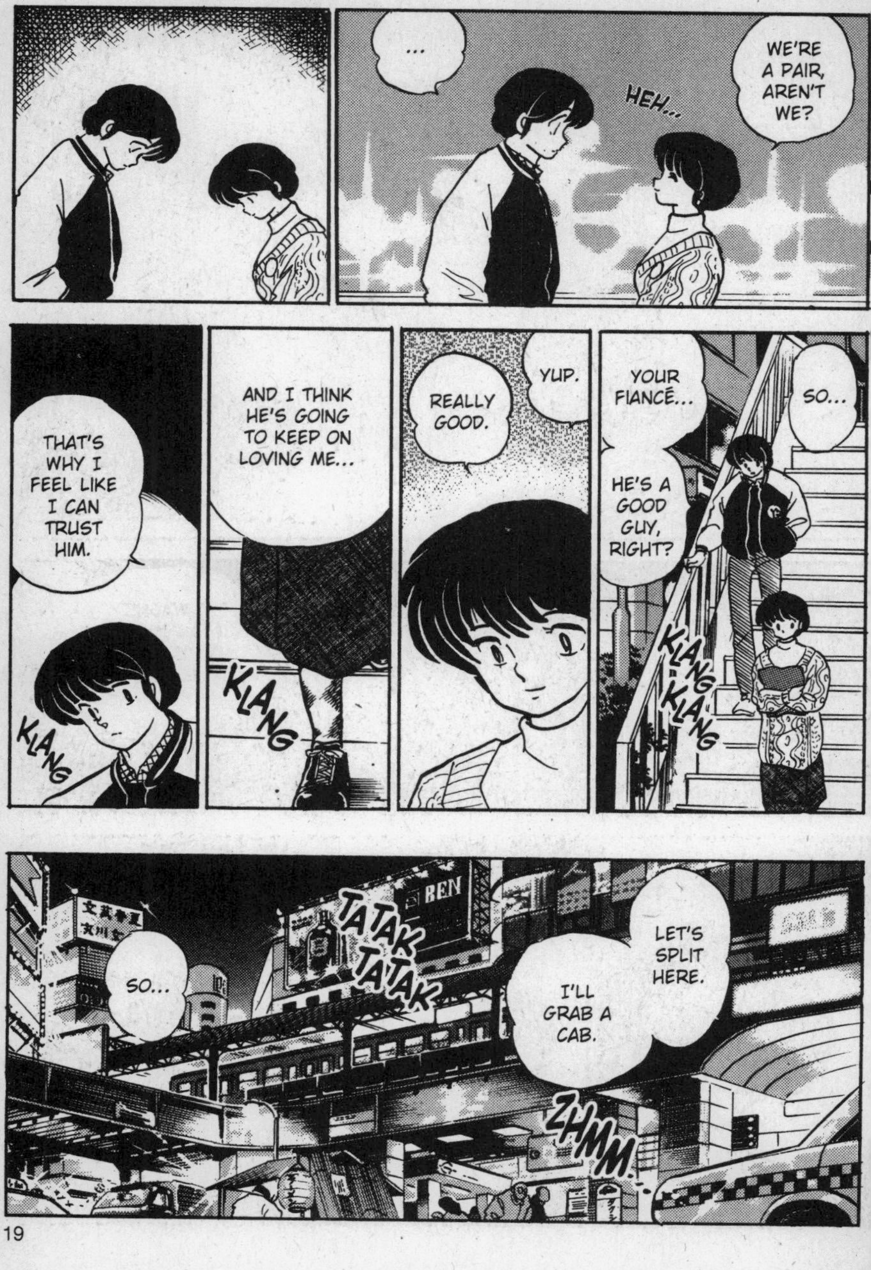
WE'RE A PAIR, AREN'T WE?
HEH...
...
SO...
YOUR FIANCÉ...
HE'S A GOOD GUY, RIGHT?
KLANG KLANG
YUP.
REALLY GOOD.
AND I THINK HE'S GOING TO KEEP ON LOVING ME...
KLANG
THAT'S WHY I FEEL LIKE I CAN TRUST HIM.
KLANG
LET'S SPLIT HERE.
I'LL GRAB A CAB.
BEN
TATAK TATAK
SO...
ZHMM.

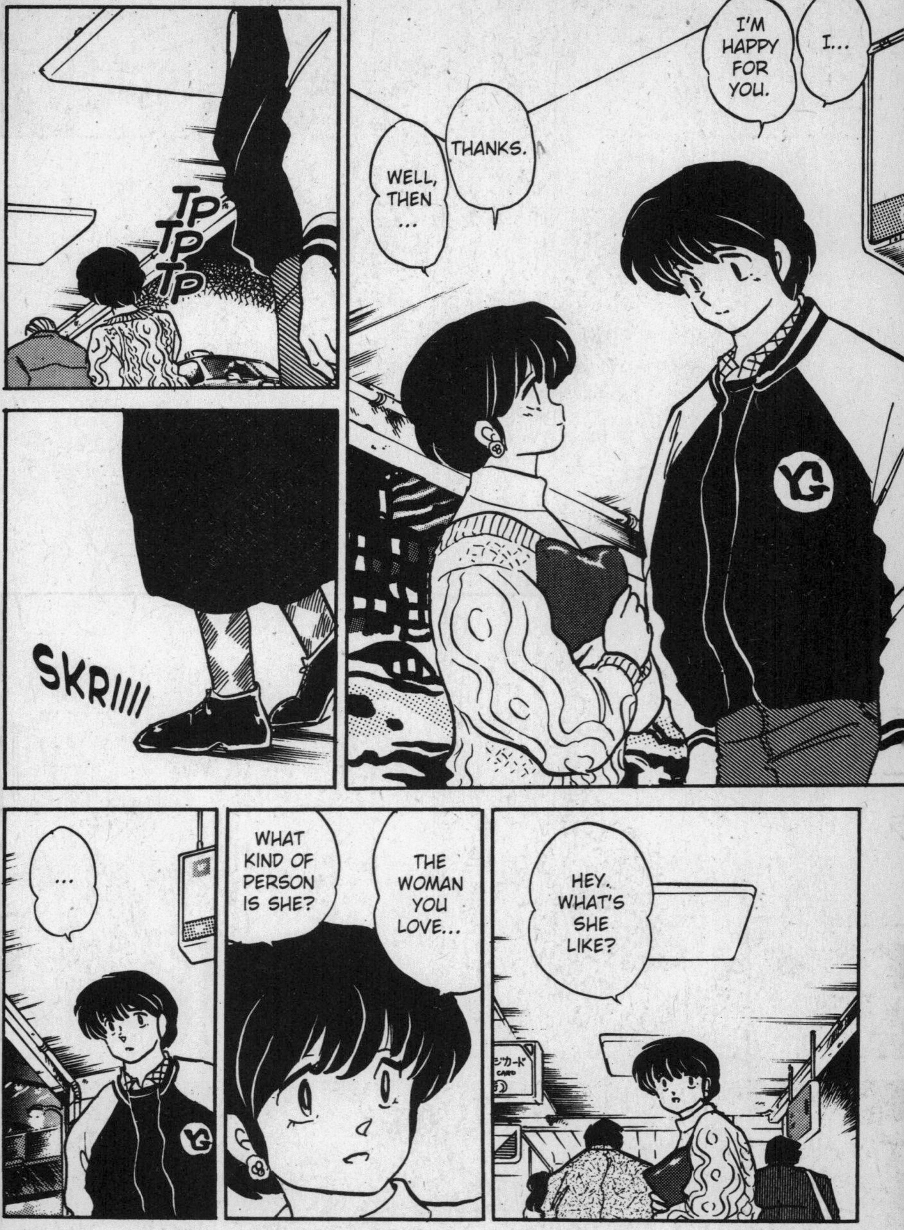
I...
I'M HAPPY FOR YOU.
THANKS.
WELL, THEN ...
TP TP TP
SKRIIIII
HEY. WHAT'S SHE LIKE?
THE WOMAN YOU LOVE...
WHAT KIND OF PERSON IS SHE?
...

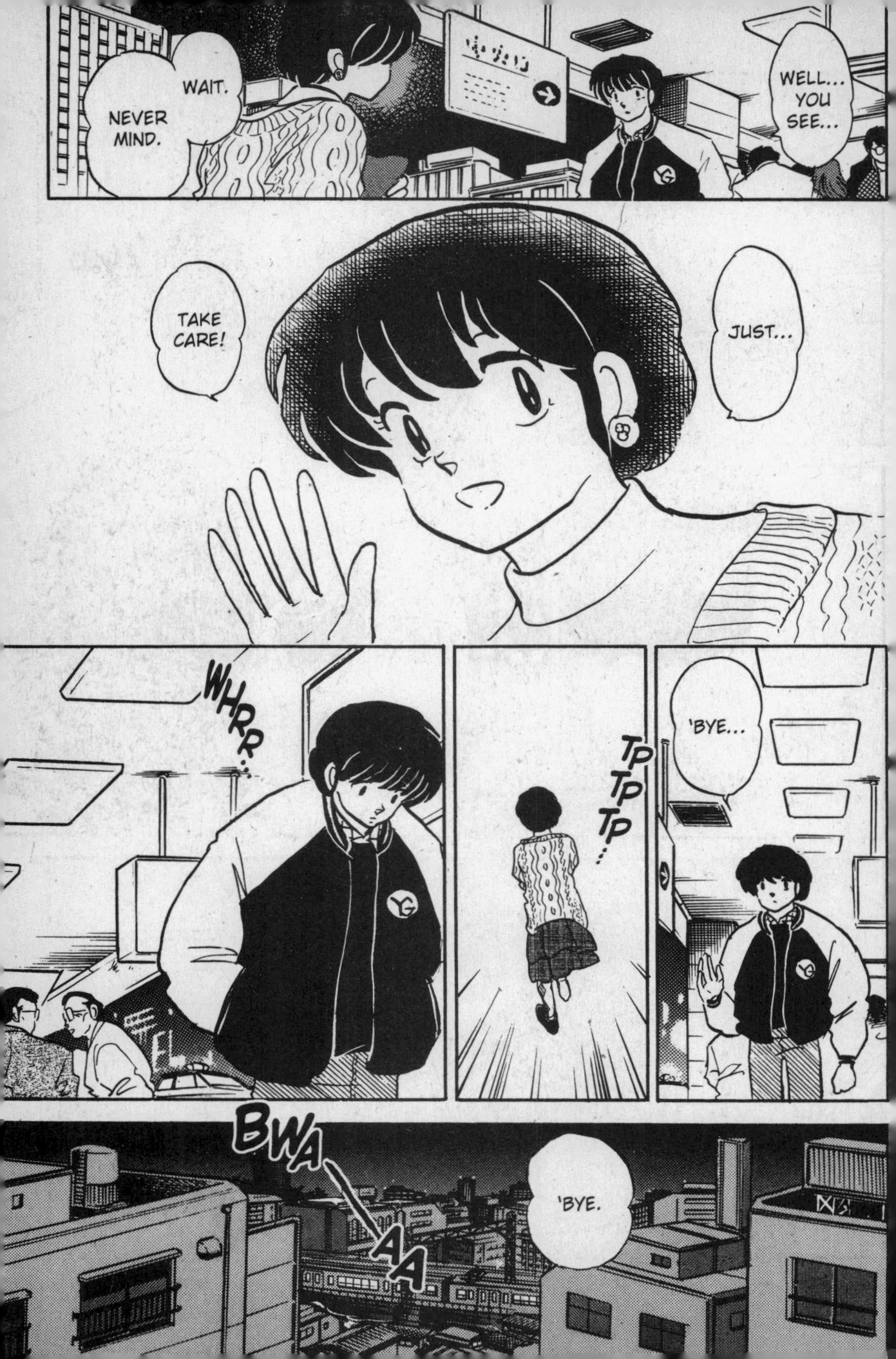
WELL... YOU SEE...
WAIT.
NEVER MIND.
JUST...
TAKE CARE!
'BYE...
TP TP TP...
WHRR...
'BYE.
BWA—AA

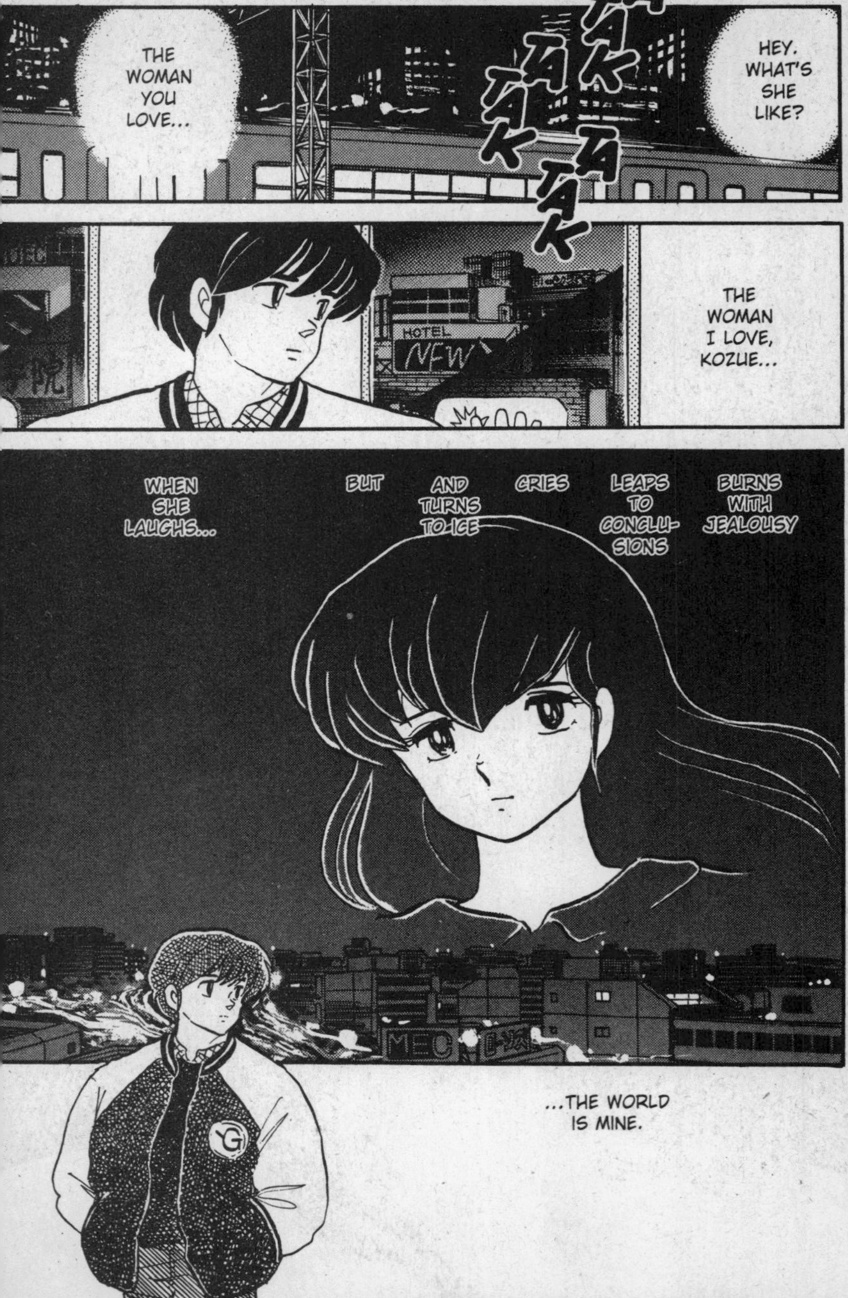
HEY. WHAT'S SHE LIKE?
TA TAK TA TAK TA TAK
THE WOMAN YOU LOVE...
THE WOMAN I LOVE, KOZUE...
BURNS WITH JEALOUSY
LEAPS TO CONCLUSIONS
CRIES
AND TURNS TO ICE
BUT
WHEN SHE LAUGHS...
...THE WORLD IS MINE.

PART TWO
SACRED VOWS

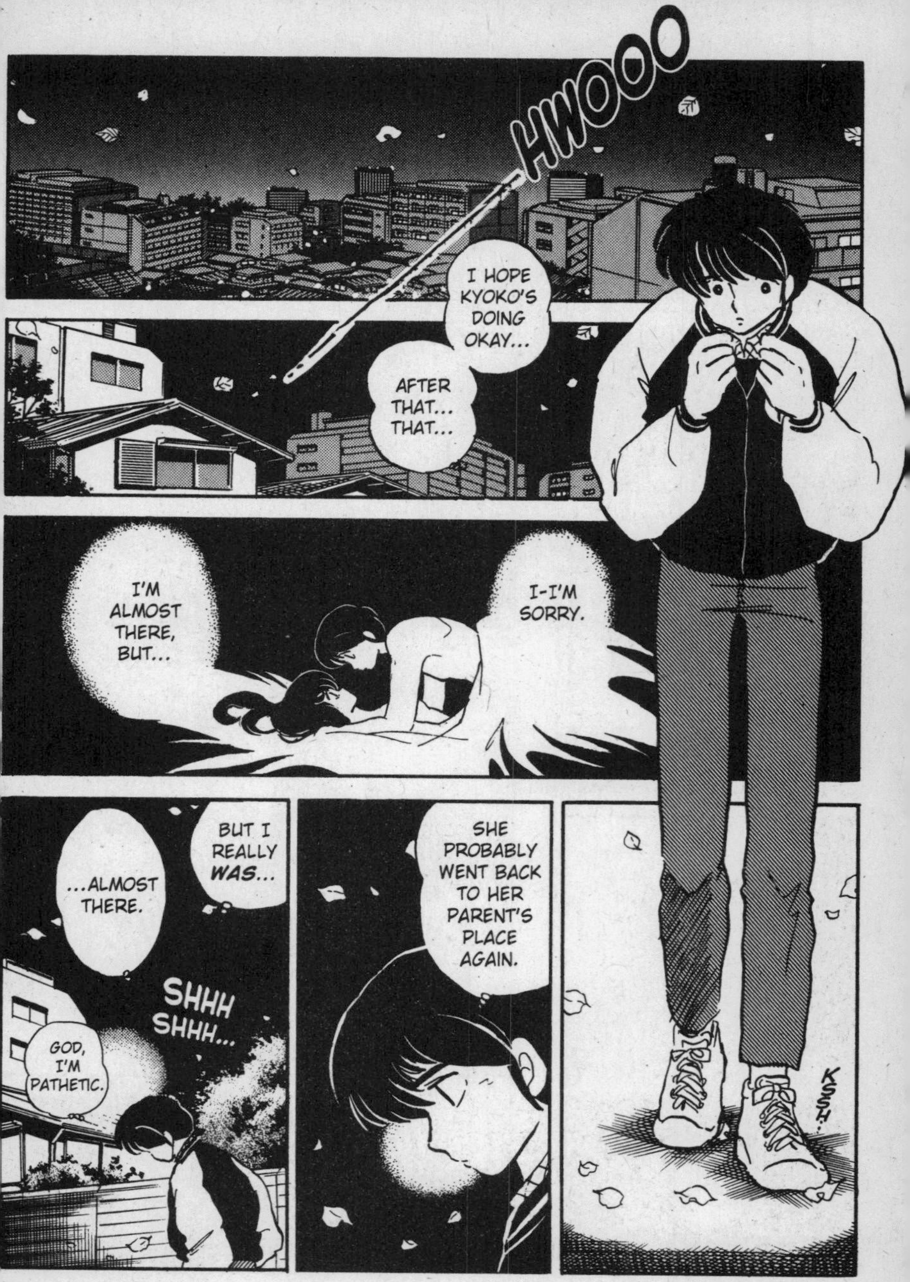
HWOOO
I HOPE KYOKO'S DOING OKAY...
AFTER THAT... THAT...
I-I'M SORRY.
I'M ALMOST THERE, BUT...
KSSH...
SHE PROBABLY WENT BACK TO HER PARENT'S PLACE AGAIN.
BUT I REALLY *WAS*...
...ALMOST THERE.
SHHH SHHH...
GOD, I'M PATHETIC.

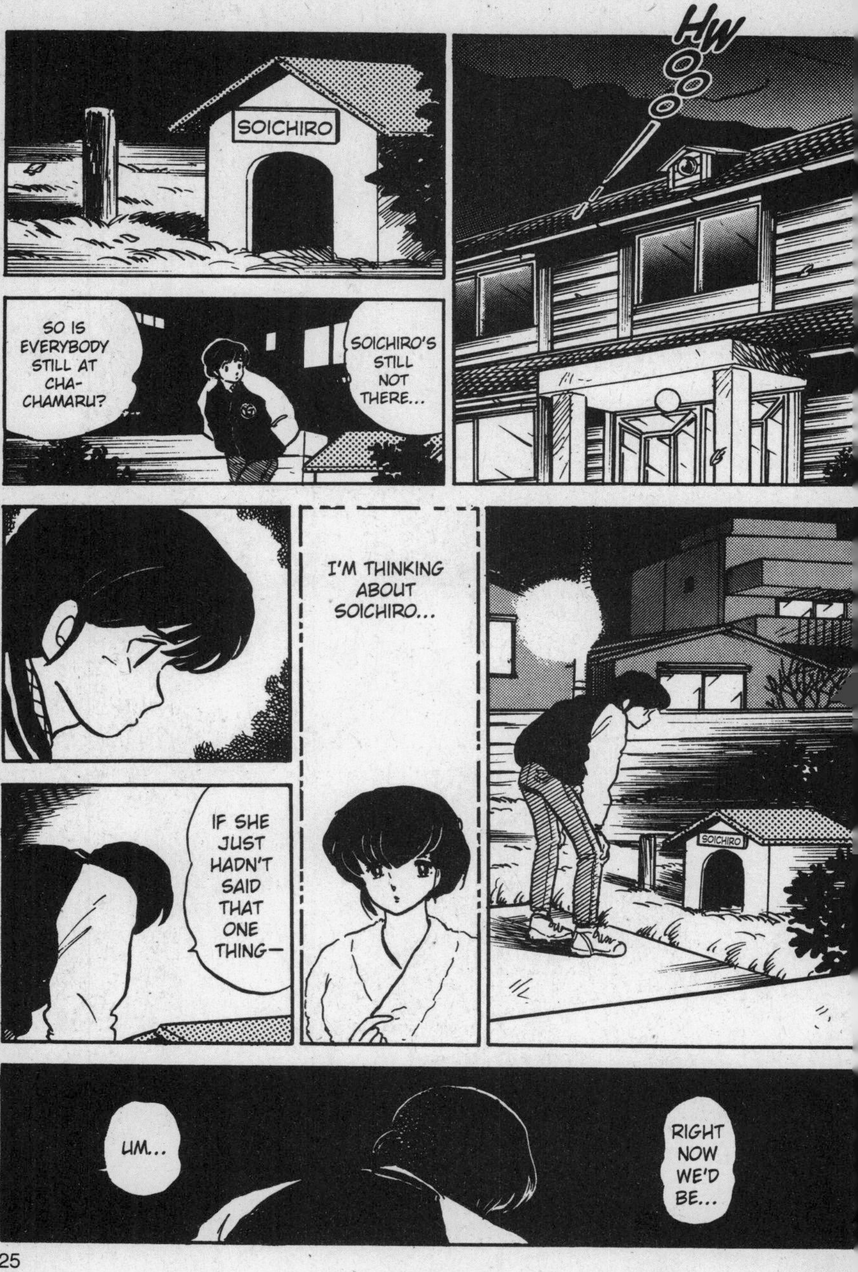
HWOOO
SOICHIRO
SOICHIRO'S STILL NOT THERE...
SO IS EVERYBODY STILL AT CHA-CHAMARU?
SOICHIRO
I'M THINKING ABOUT SOICHIRO...
IF SHE JUST HADN'T SAID THAT ONE THING—
RIGHT NOW WE'D BE...
UM...

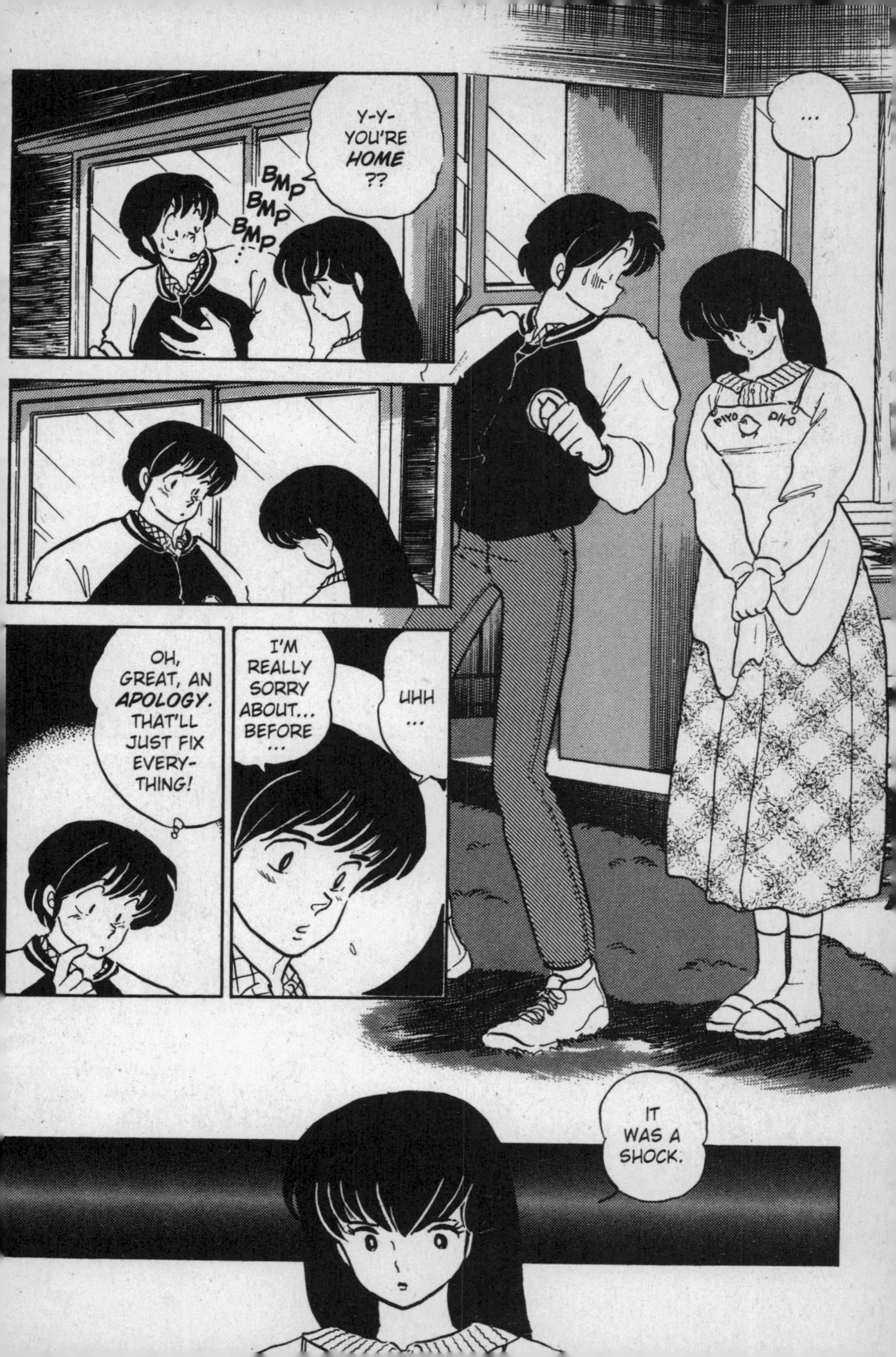
...
Y-Y- YOU'RE HOME ??
BMP BMP BMP
UHH ...
I'M REALLY SORRY ABOUT... BEFORE ...
OH, GREAT, AN APOLOGY. THAT'LL JUST FIX EVERYTHING!
IT WAS A SHOCK.

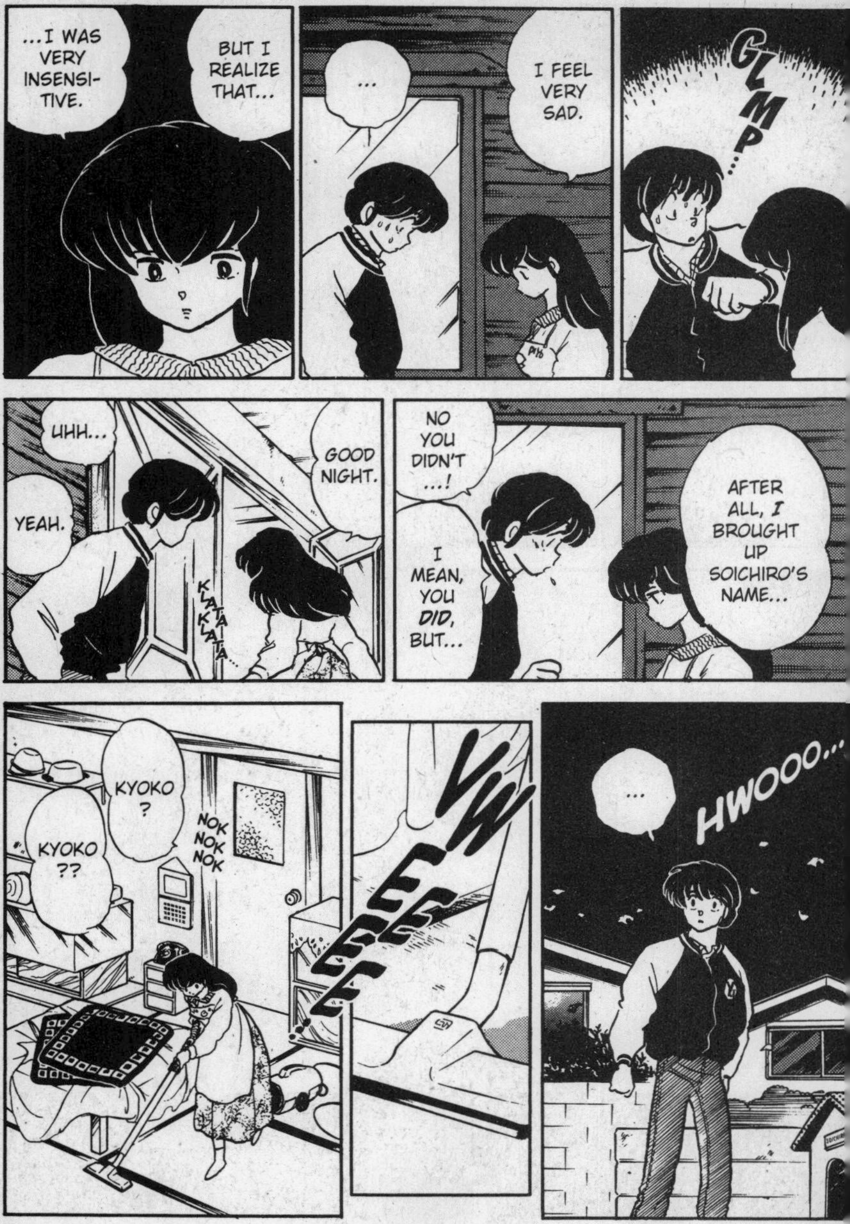
GLMP...
I FEEL VERY SAD.
...
BUT I REALIZE THAT...
...I WAS VERY INSENSITIVE.
AFTER ALL, *I* BROUGHT UP SOICHIRO'S NAME...
NO YOU DIDN'T ...!
I MEAN, YOU *DID*, BUT...
GOOD NIGHT.
UHH...
YEAH.
KLATA KLATA...
HWOOO...
...
VWEEEEE
KYOKO ?
NOK NOK NOK
KYOKO ??

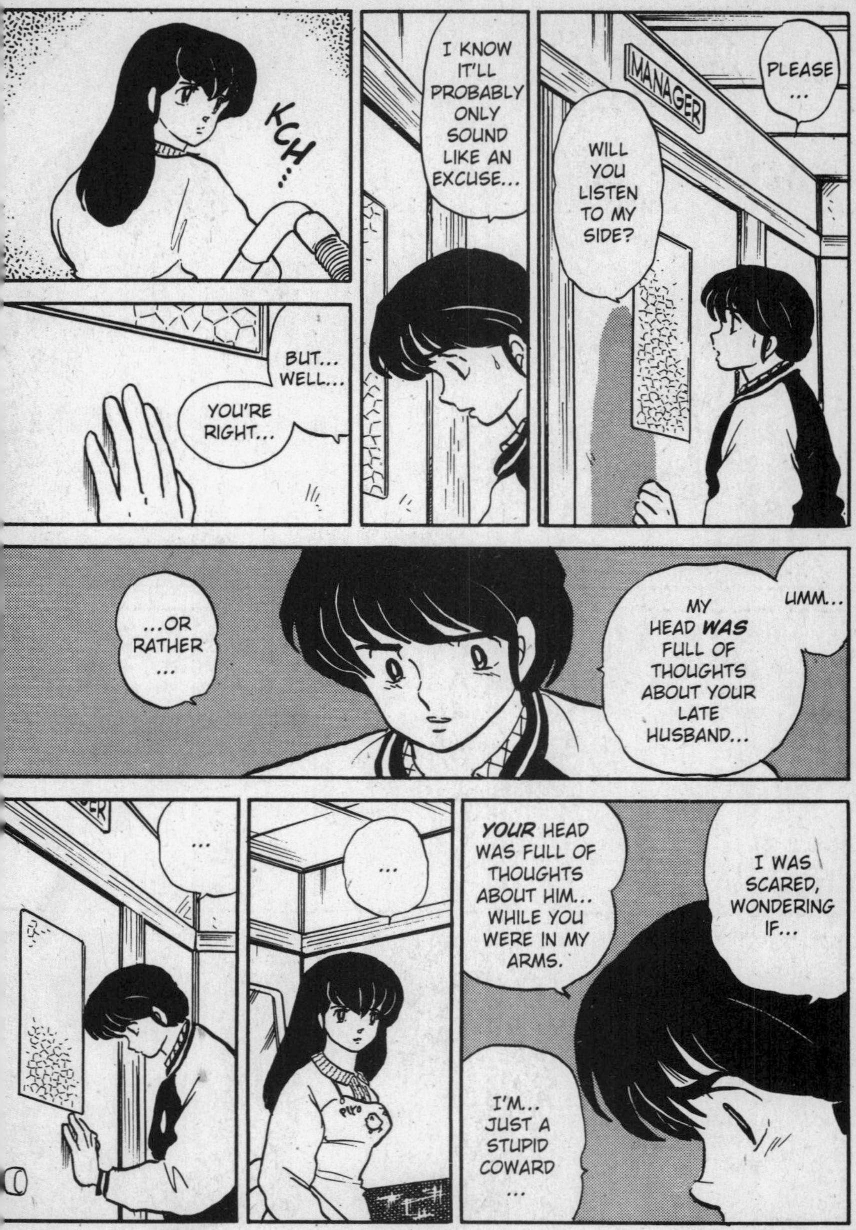
PLEASE ...
WILL YOU LISTEN TO MY SIDE?
I KNOW IT'LL PROBABLY ONLY SOUND LIKE AN EXCUSE...
KCH...
BUT... WELL...
YOU'RE RIGHT...
UMM...
MY HEAD **WAS** FULL OF THOUGHTS ABOUT YOUR LATE HUSBAND...
...OR RATHER ...
I WAS SCARED, WONDERING IF...
YOUR HEAD WAS FULL OF THOUGHTS ABOUT HIM... WHILE YOU WERE IN MY ARMS.
I'M... JUST A STUPID COWARD ...
...
...

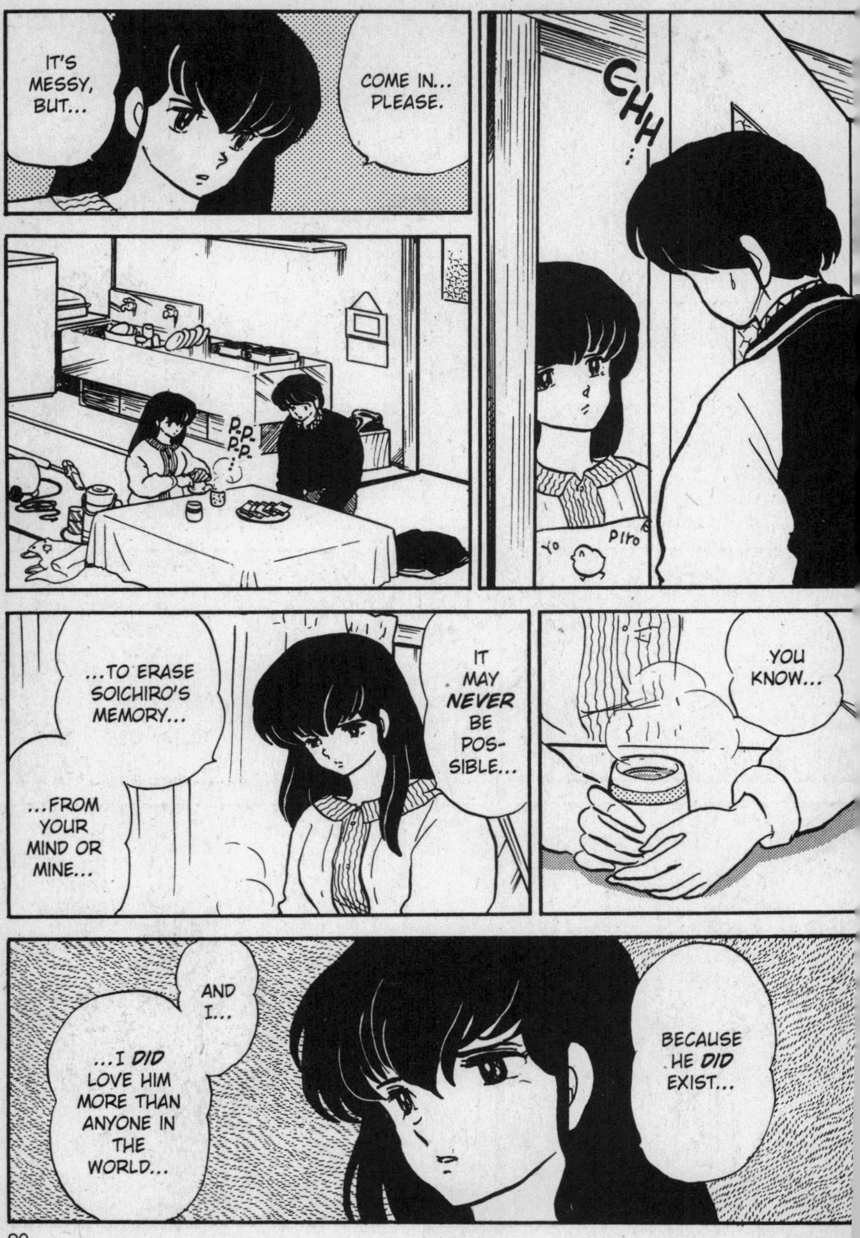
CHH...
yo
Piro
COME IN... PLEASE.
IT'S MESSY, BUT...
P-P-P-P-P...
YOU KNOW...
IT MAY *NEVER* BE POS-SIBLE...
...TO ERASE SOICHIRO'S MEMORY...
...FROM YOUR MIND OR MINE...
BECAUSE HE *DID* EXIST...
AND I...
...I *DID* LOVE HIM MORE THAN ANYONE IN THE WORLD...

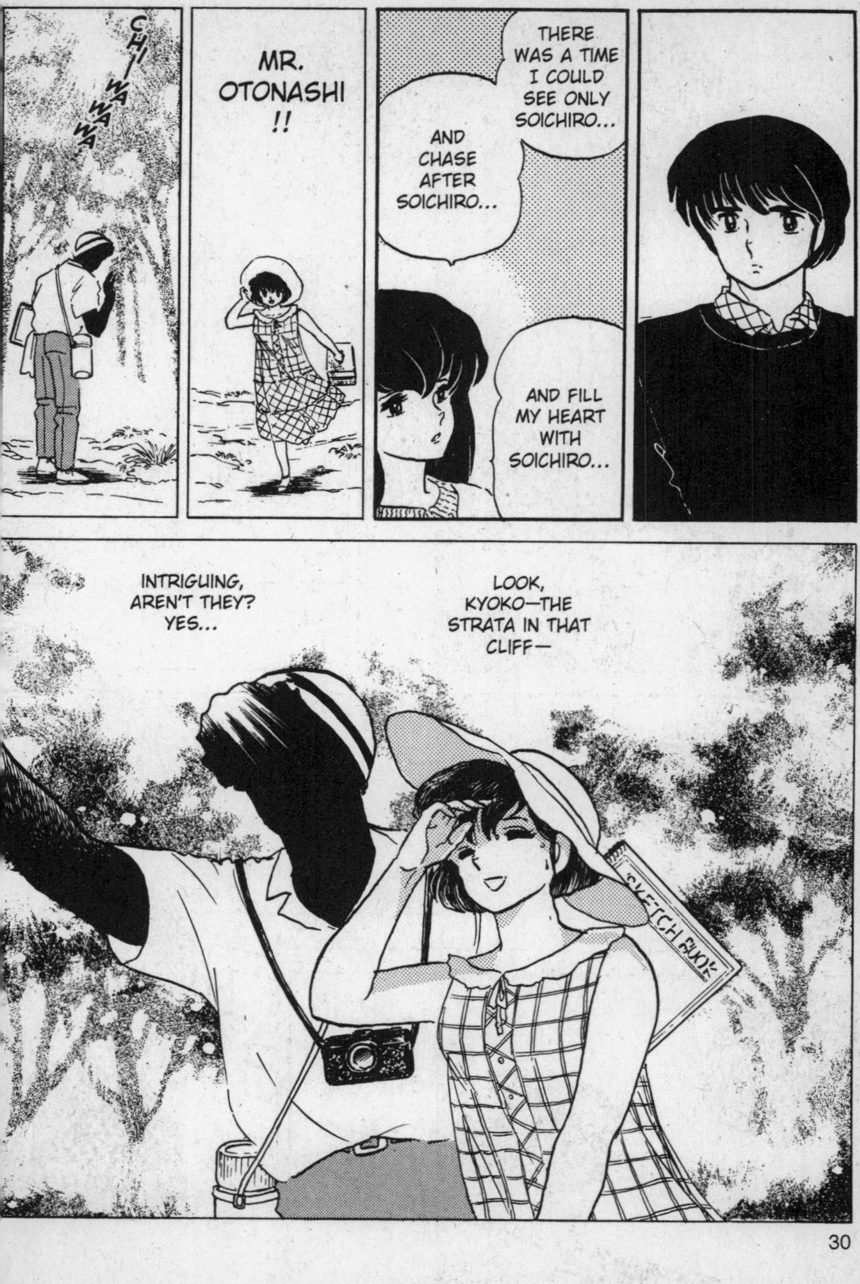
THERE WAS A TIME I COULD SEE ONLY SOICHIRO...
AND CHASE AFTER SOICHIRO...
AND FILL MY HEART WITH SOICHIRO...
MR. OTONASHI !!
CHI–WAWAWAWA
LOOK, KYOKO—THE STRATA IN THAT CLIFF—
INTRIGUING, AREN'T THEY? YES...
SKETCH BOOK

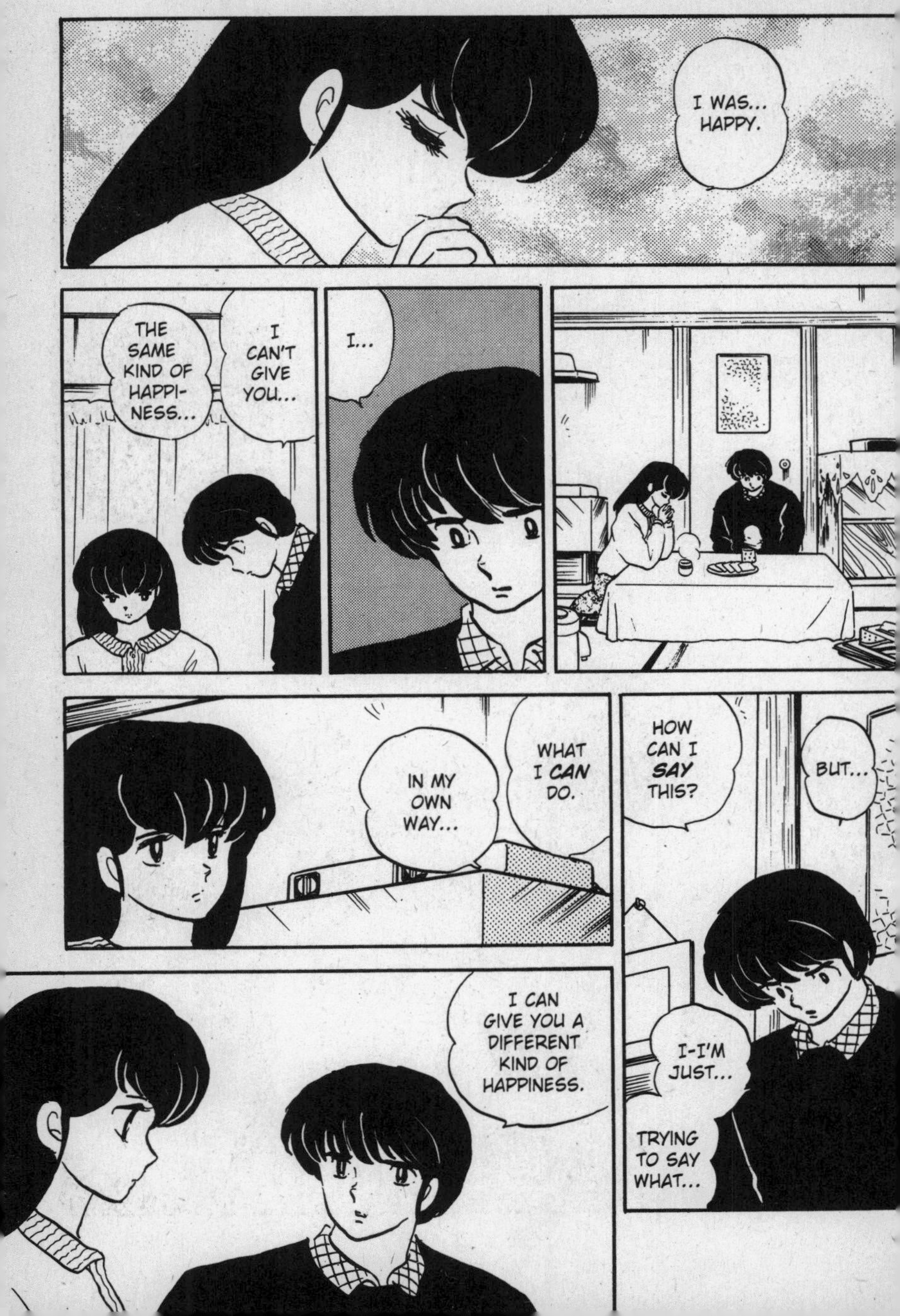
I WAS... HAPPY.
I...
I CAN'T GIVE YOU...
THE SAME KIND OF HAPPI-NESS...
BUT...
HOW CAN I *SAY* THIS?
I-I'M JUST...
TRYING TO SAY WHAT...
WHAT I *CAN* DO.
IN MY OWN WAY...
I CAN GIVE YOU A DIFFERENT KIND OF HAPPINESS.

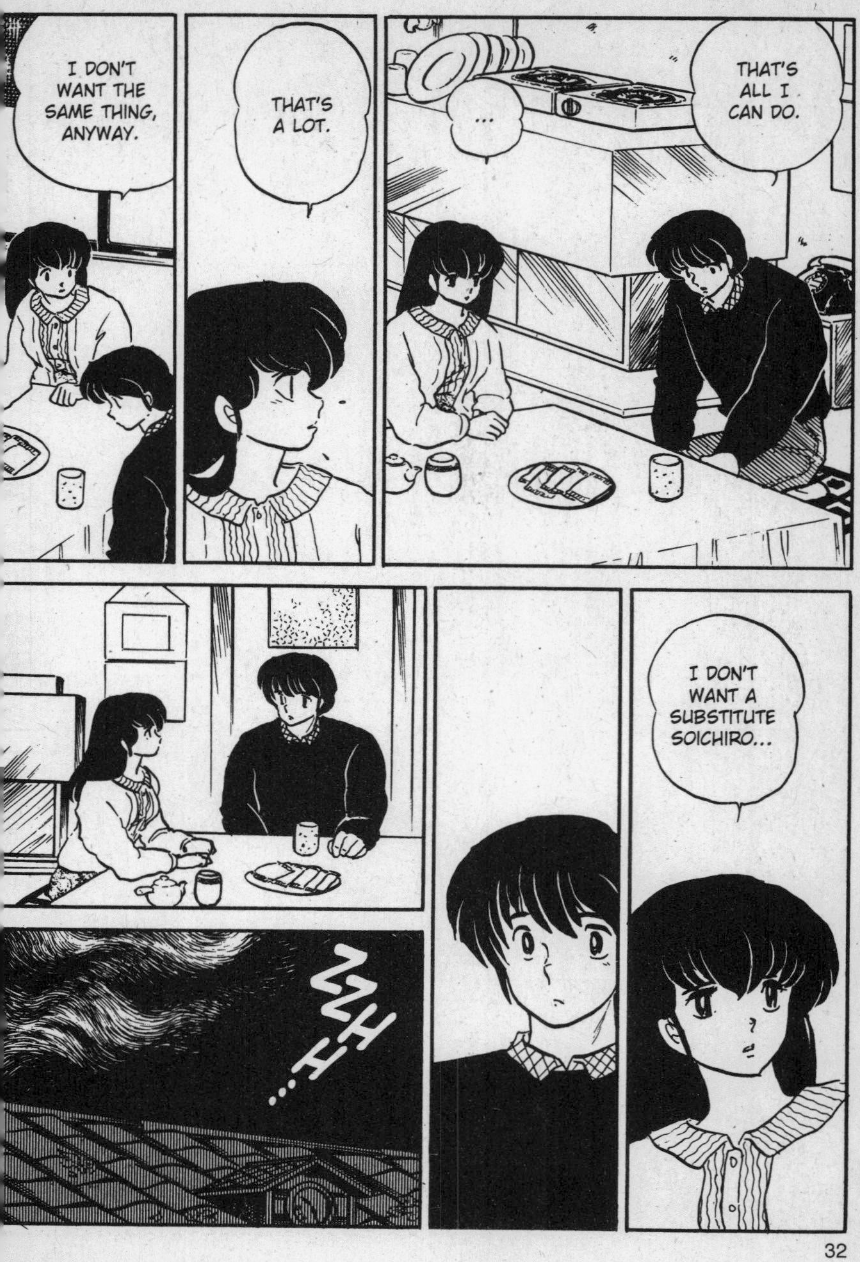
THAT'S ALL I CAN DO.
...
THAT'S A LOT.
I DON'T WANT THE SAME THING, ANYWAY.
I DON'T WANT A SUBSTITUTE SOICHIRO...
ZZHH...

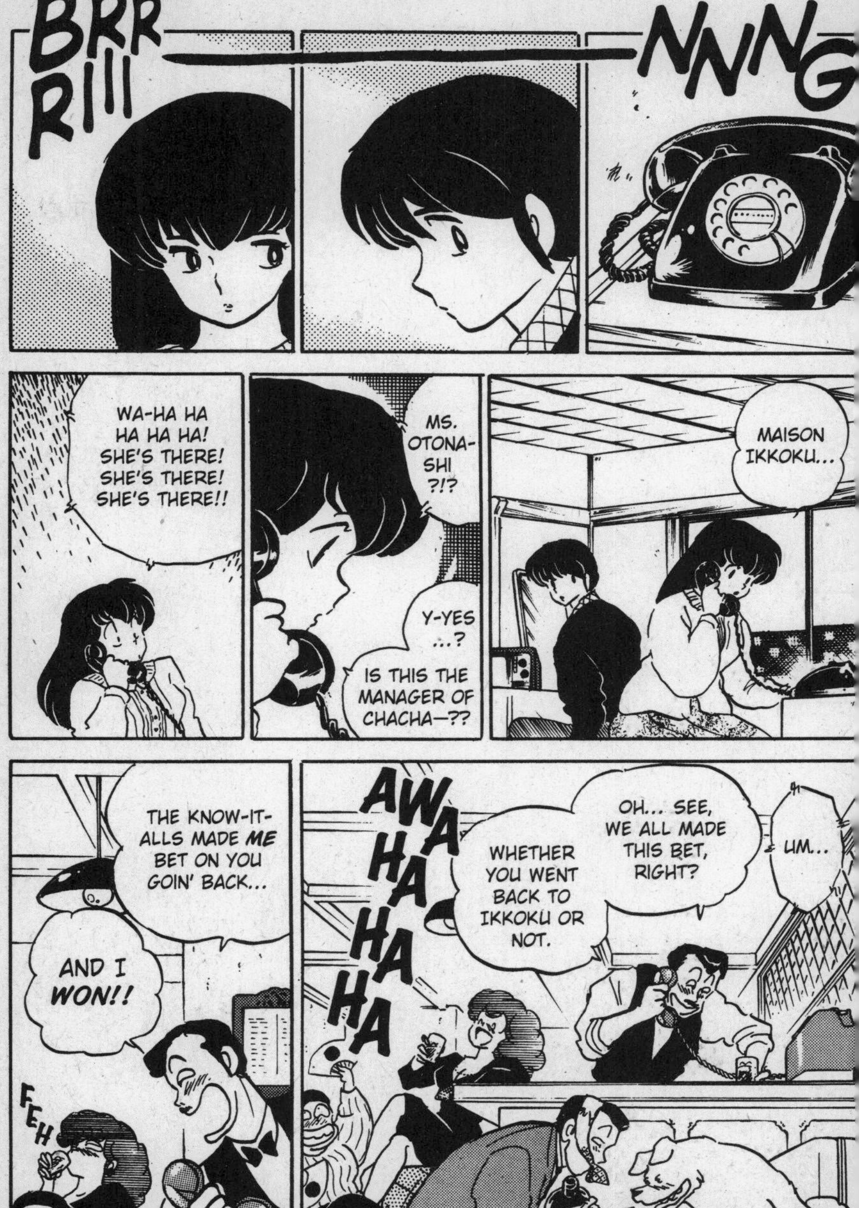
BRRRIII—NNNG
MAISON IKKOKU...
MS. OTONASHI ?!?
Y-YES ...?
IS THIS THE MANAGER OF CHACHA—??
WA-HA HA HA HA HA! SHE'S THERE! SHE'S THERE! SHE'S THERE!!
UM...
OH... SEE, WE ALL MADE THIS BET, RIGHT?
WHETHER YOU WENT BACK TO IKKOKU OR NOT.
AWAHAHAHAHAHA
THE KNOW-IT-ALLS MADE *ME* BET ON YOU GOIN' BACK...
AND I *WON!!*
FEH

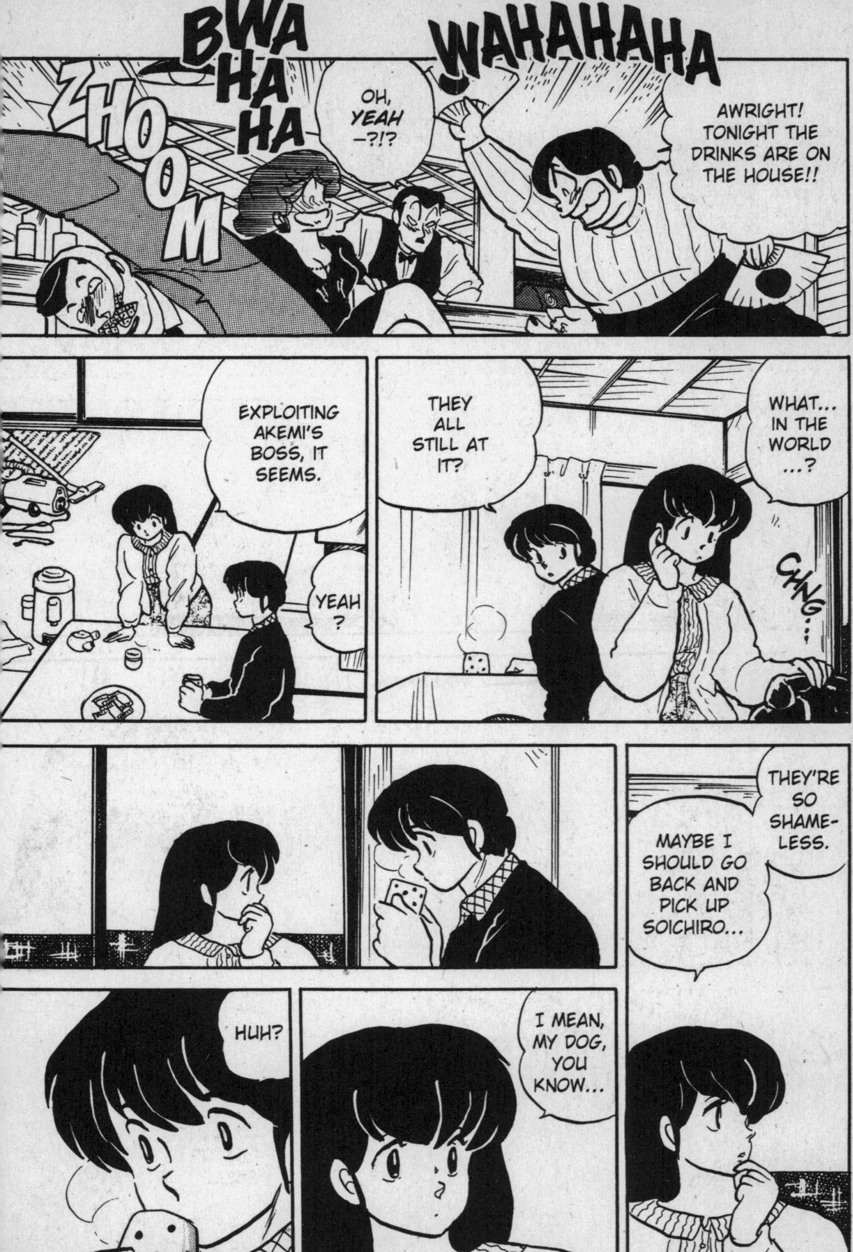
WAHAHAHAHA
AWRIGHT! TONIGHT THE DRINKS ARE ON THE HOUSE!!
OH, YEAH—?!?
BWA HA HA HA
ZHOOM
WHAT... IN THE WORLD ...?
CHNG...
THEY ALL STILL AT IT?
EXPLOITING AKEMI'S BOSS, IT SEEMS.
YEAH?
THEY'RE SO SHAME-LESS.
MAYBE I SHOULD GO BACK AND PICK UP SOICHIRO...
I MEAN, MY DOG, YOU KNOW...
HUH?

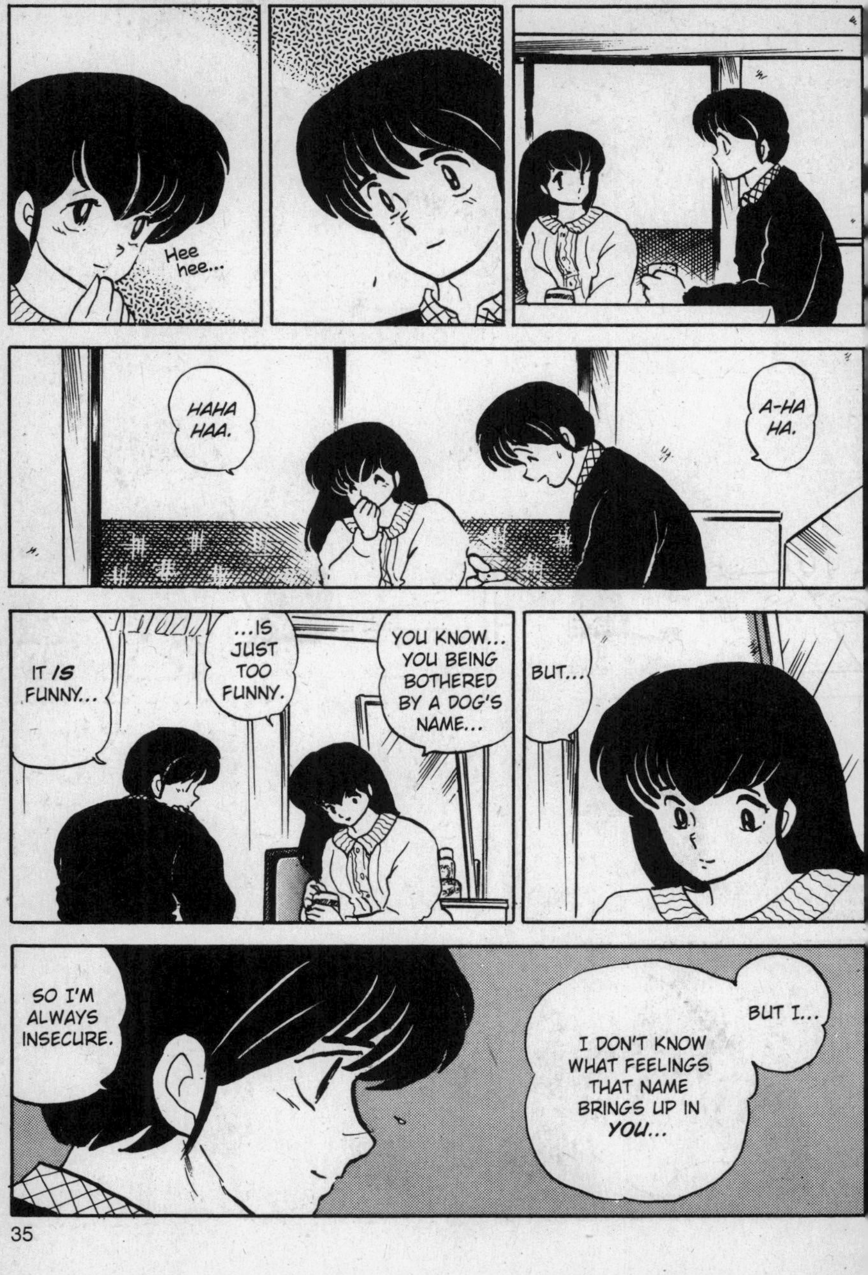
Hee hee...
A-HA HA.
HAHA HAA.
BUT...
YOU KNOW... YOU BEING BOTHERED BY A DOG'S NAME...
...IS JUST TOO FUNNY.
IT *IS* FUNNY...
BUT I...
I DON'T KNOW WHAT FEELINGS THAT NAME BRINGS UP IN *YOU*...
SO I'M ALWAYS INSECURE.

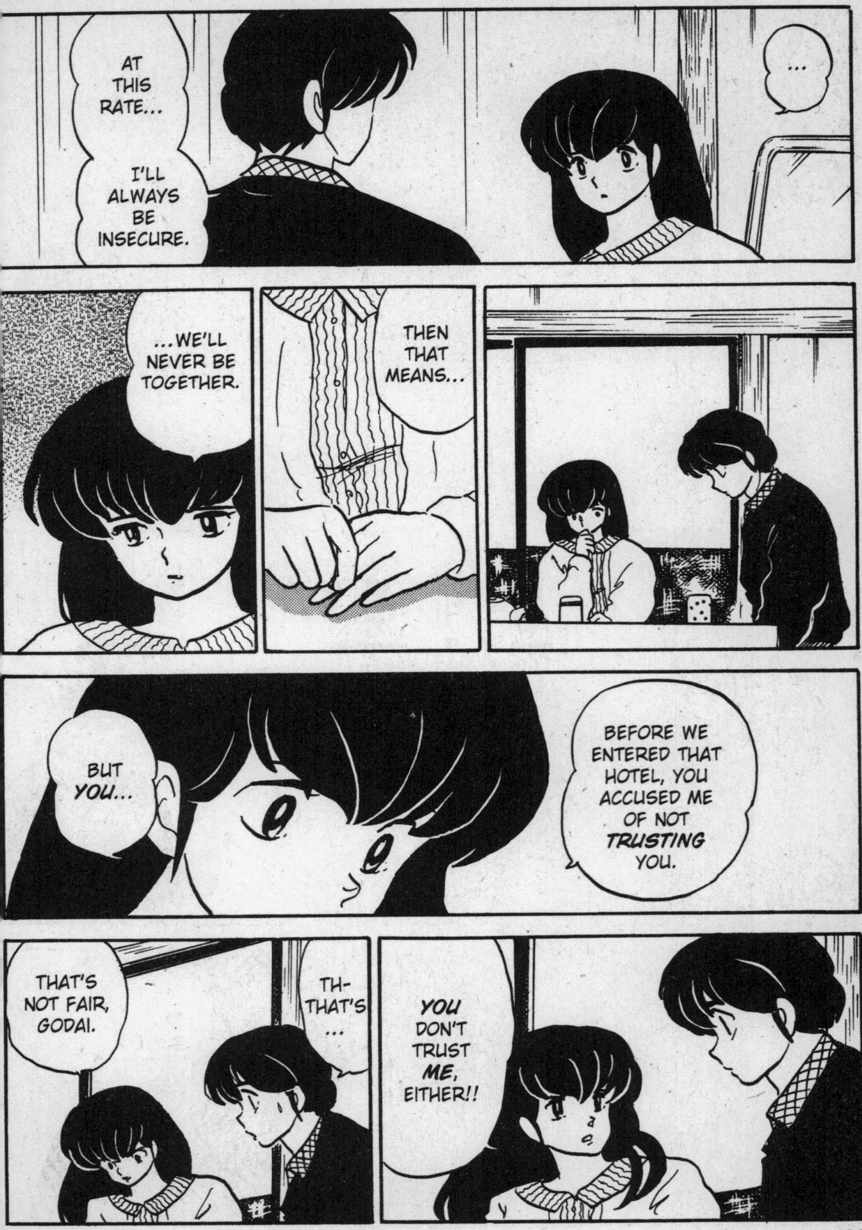
...
AT THIS RATE...
I'LL ALWAYS BE INSECURE.
THEN THAT MEANS...
...WE'LL NEVER BE TOGETHER.
BUT *YOU*...
BEFORE WE ENTERED THAT HOTEL, YOU ACCUSED ME OF NOT *TRUSTING* YOU.
YOU DON'T TRUST *ME*, EITHER!!
TH-THAT'S ...
THAT'S NOT FAIR, GODAI.

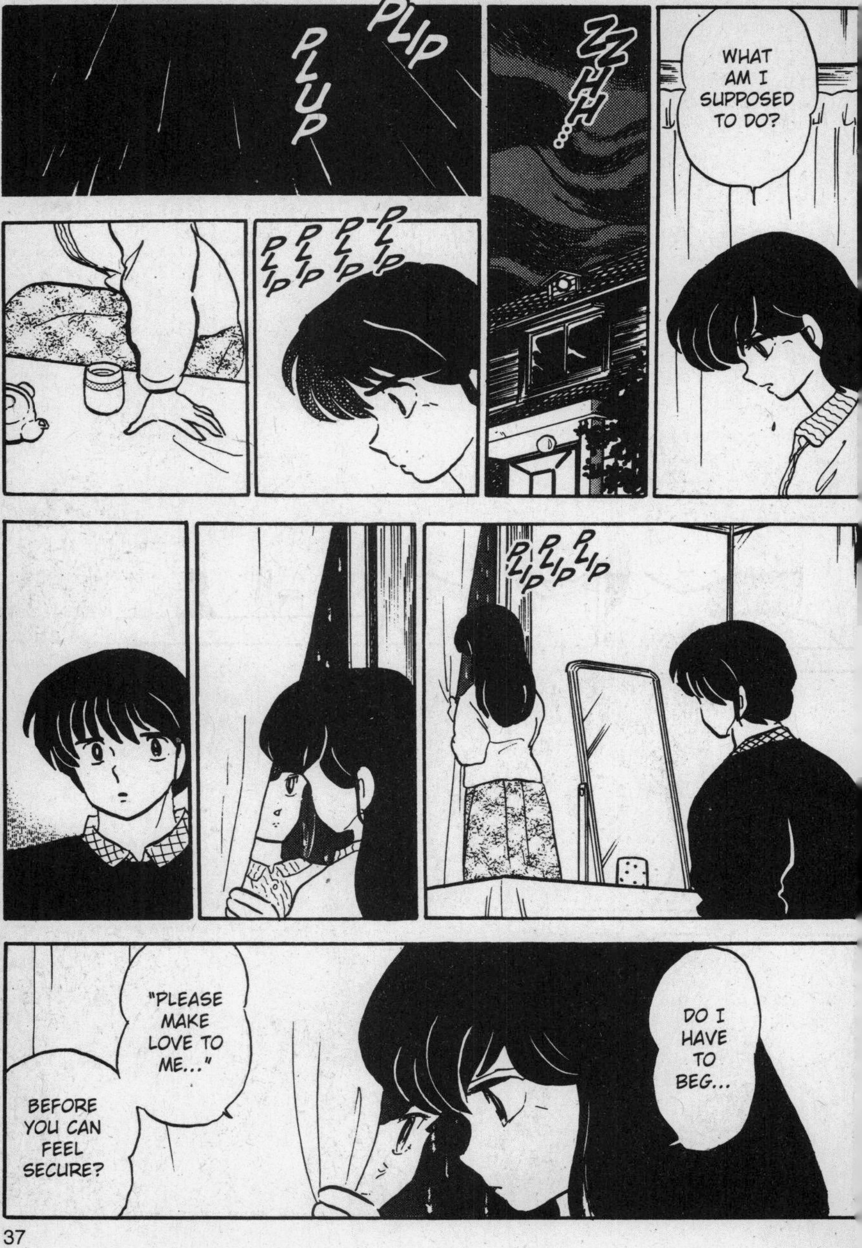
WHAT AM I SUPPOSED TO DO?
ZZHH...
PLIP
PLUP
PLIP PLIP PLIP PLIP
PLIP PLIP PLIP
DO I HAVE TO BEG...
"PLEASE MAKE LOVE TO ME..."
BEFORE YOU CAN FEEL SECURE?

ZZ HH

...DON'T KNOW WHAT TO DO ANY MORE.

I JUST...

I...

ZHH

I'M SORRY...

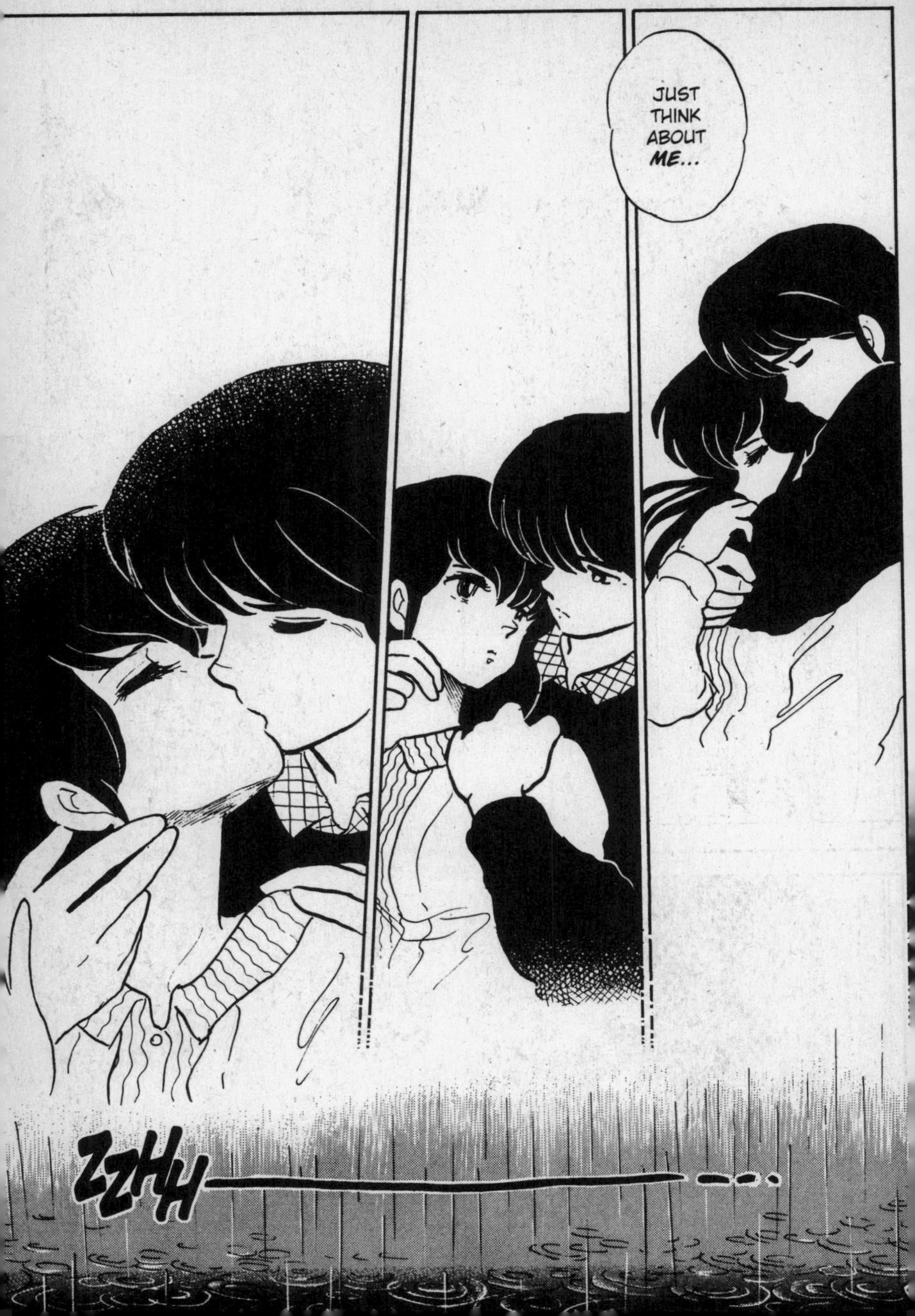
JUST THINK ABOUT *ME*...
ZZHHH—...

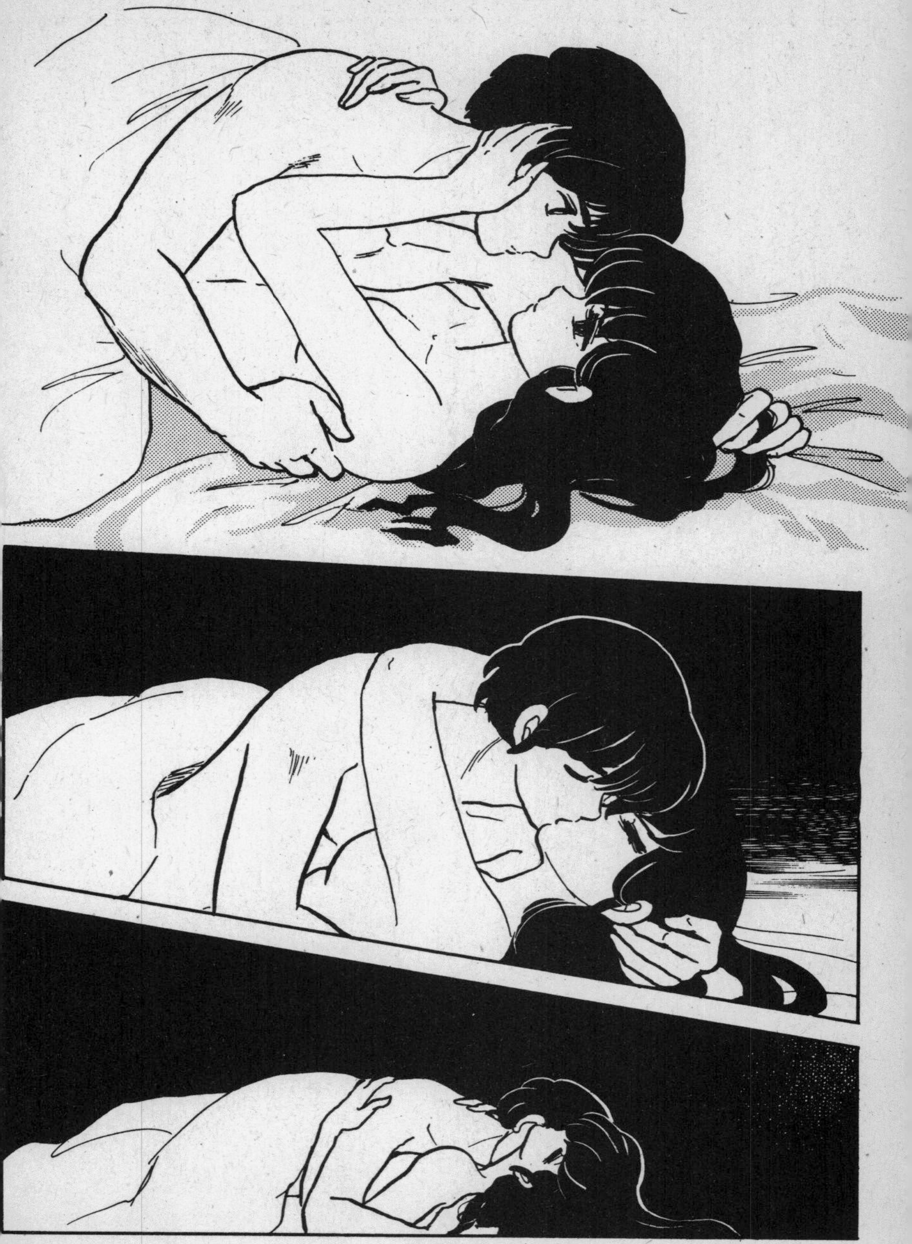

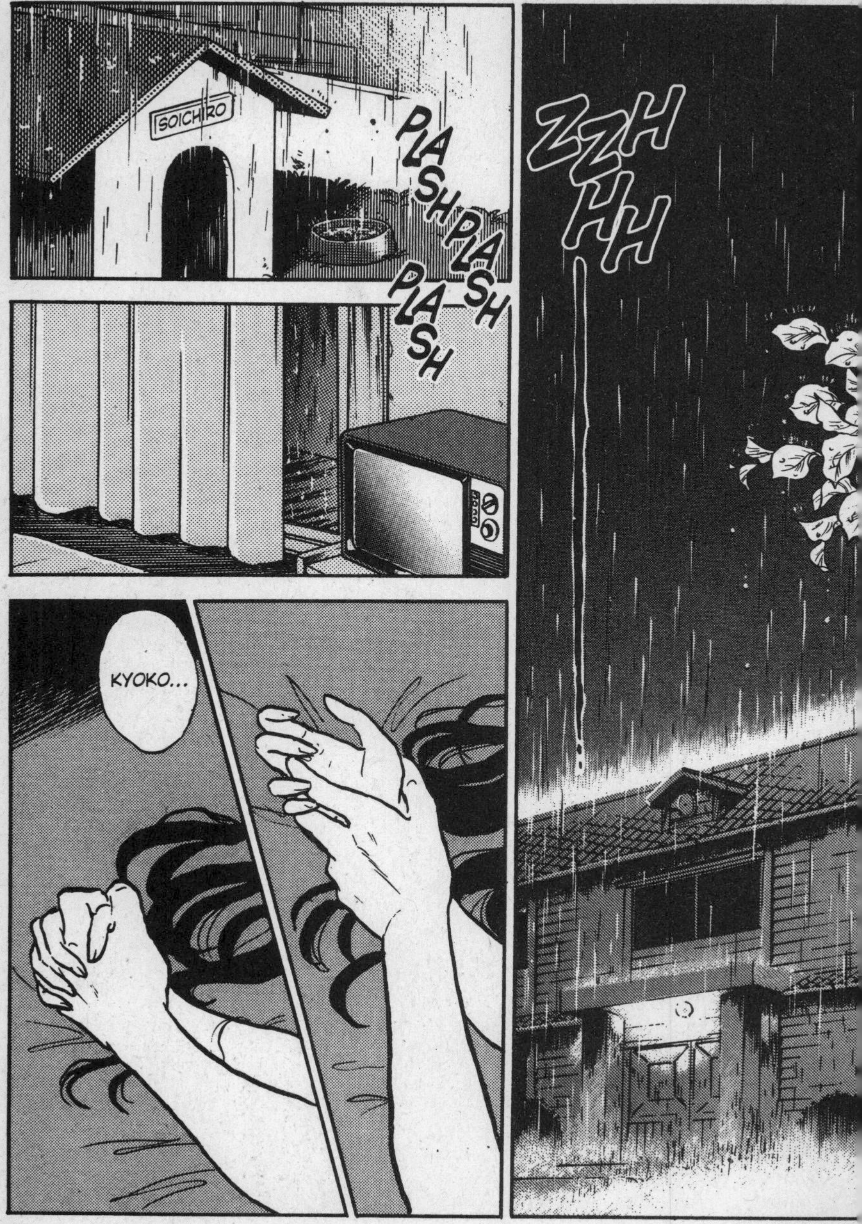
ZZHHH
SOICHIRO
PLASHPLASH
PLASH
PLASH
KYOKO...

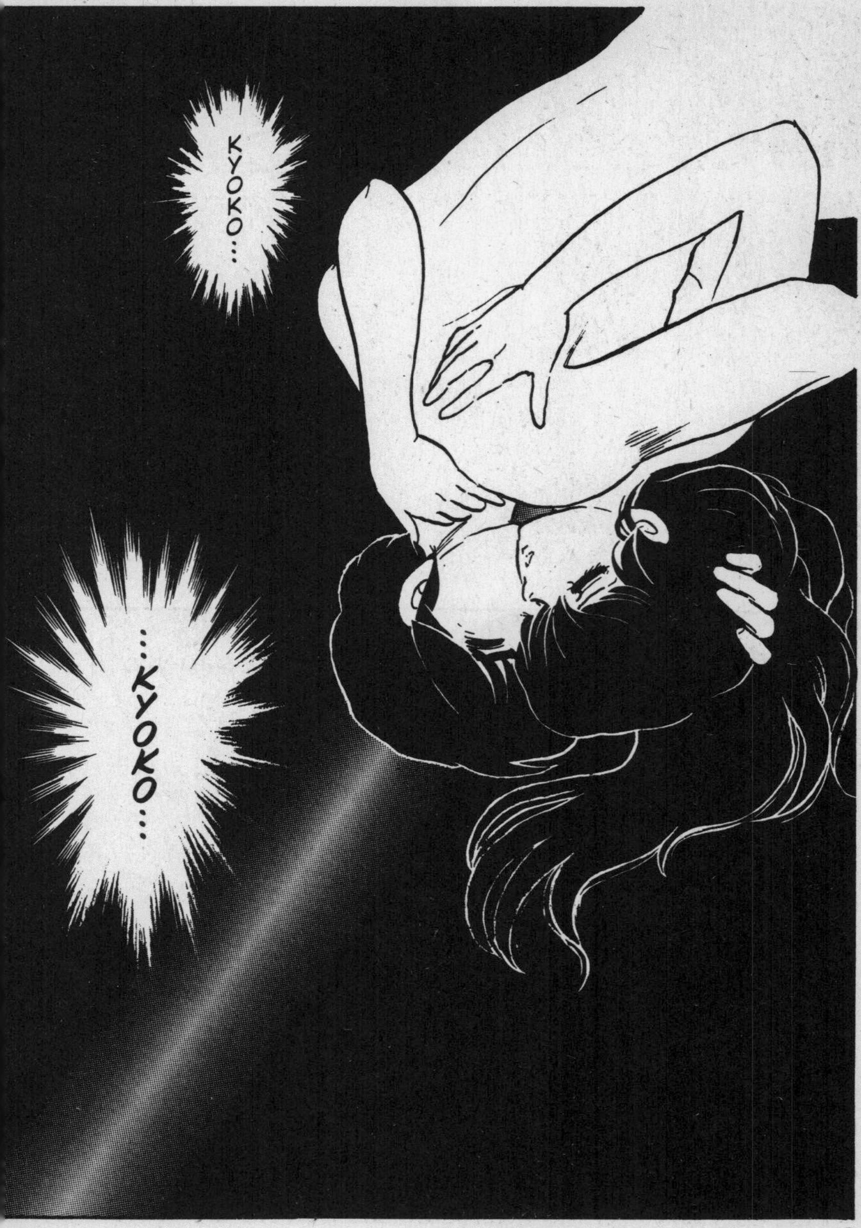
...KYOKO...
KYOKO...

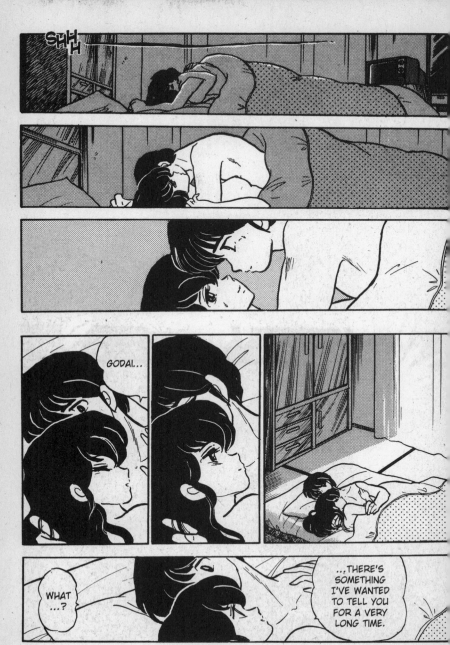

SHHH

GODAI...

WHAT...?

...THERE'S SOMETHING I'VE WANTED TO TELL YOU FOR A VERY LONG TIME.

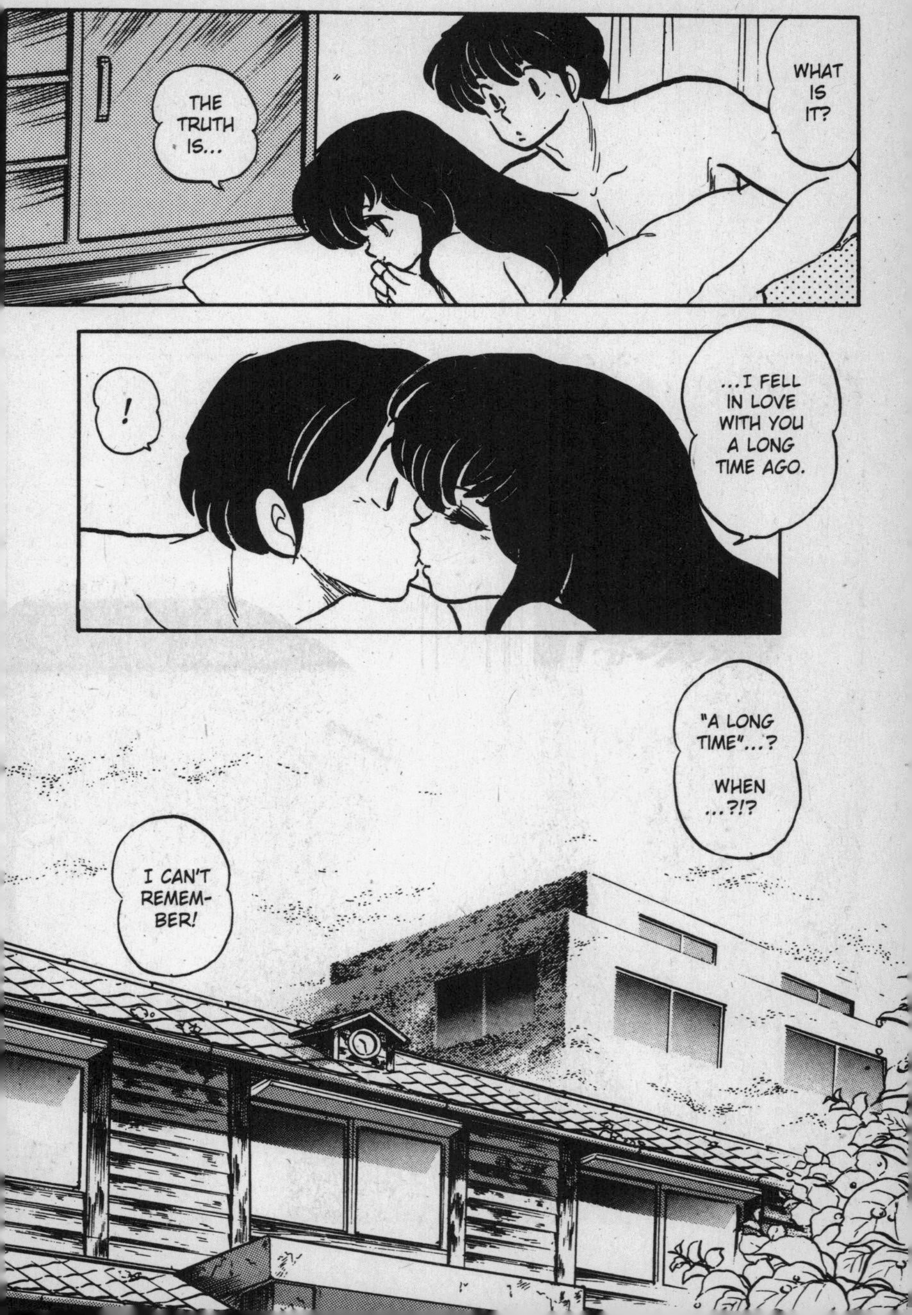
WHAT IS IT?
THE TRUTH IS...
...I FELL IN LOVE WITH YOU A LONG TIME AGO.
!
"A LONG TIME"...? WHEN ...?!?
I CAN'T REMEM- BER!

PART THREE
LOVE CALL

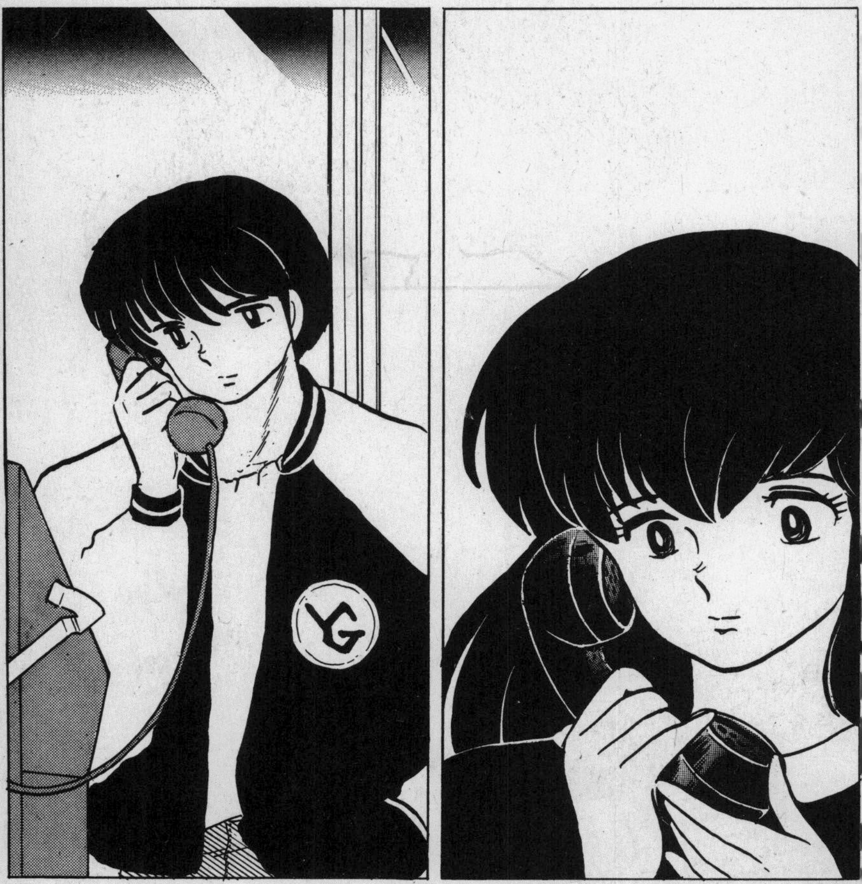

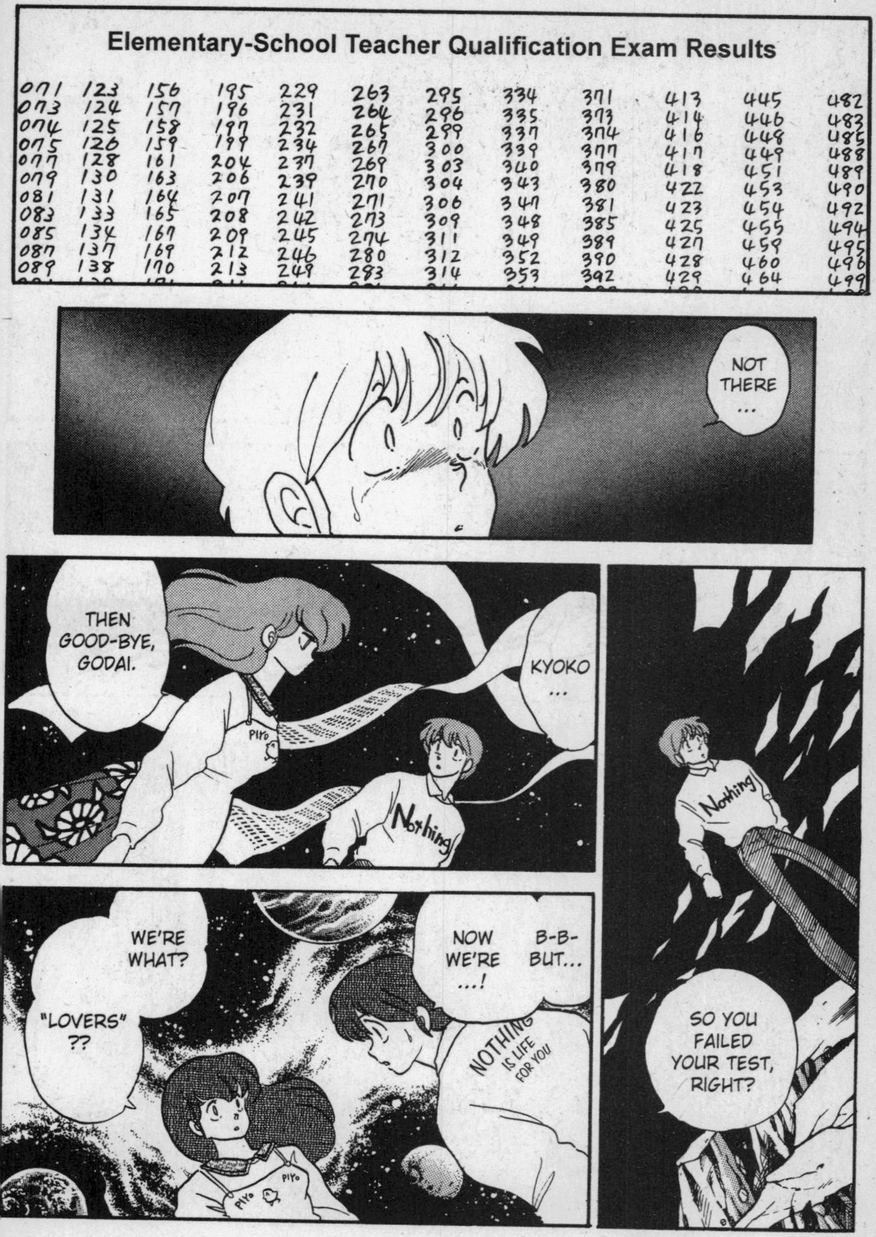
Elementary-School Teacher Qualification Exam Results
071 123 156 195 229 263 295 334 371 413 445 482
073 124 157 196 231 264 296 335 373 414 446 483
074 125 158 197 232 265 299 337 374 416 448 485
075 126 159 199 234 267 300 339 377 417 449 488
077 128 161 204 237 269 303 340 379 418 451 489
079 130 163 206 239 270 304 343 380 422 453 490
081 131 164 207 241 271 306 347 381 423 454 492
083 133 165 208 242 273 309 348 385 425 455 494
085 134 167 209 245 274 311 349 389 427 459 495
087 137 169 212 246 280 312 352 390 428 460 496
089 138 170 213 249 283 314 353 392 429 464 499
NOT THERE ...
SO YOU FAILED YOUR TEST, RIGHT?
Nothing
THEN GOOD-BYE, GODAI.
KYOKO ...
Nothing
B-B-BUT...
NOW WE'RE ...!
NOTHING IS LIFE FOR YOU
WE'RE WHAT?
"LOVERS" ??

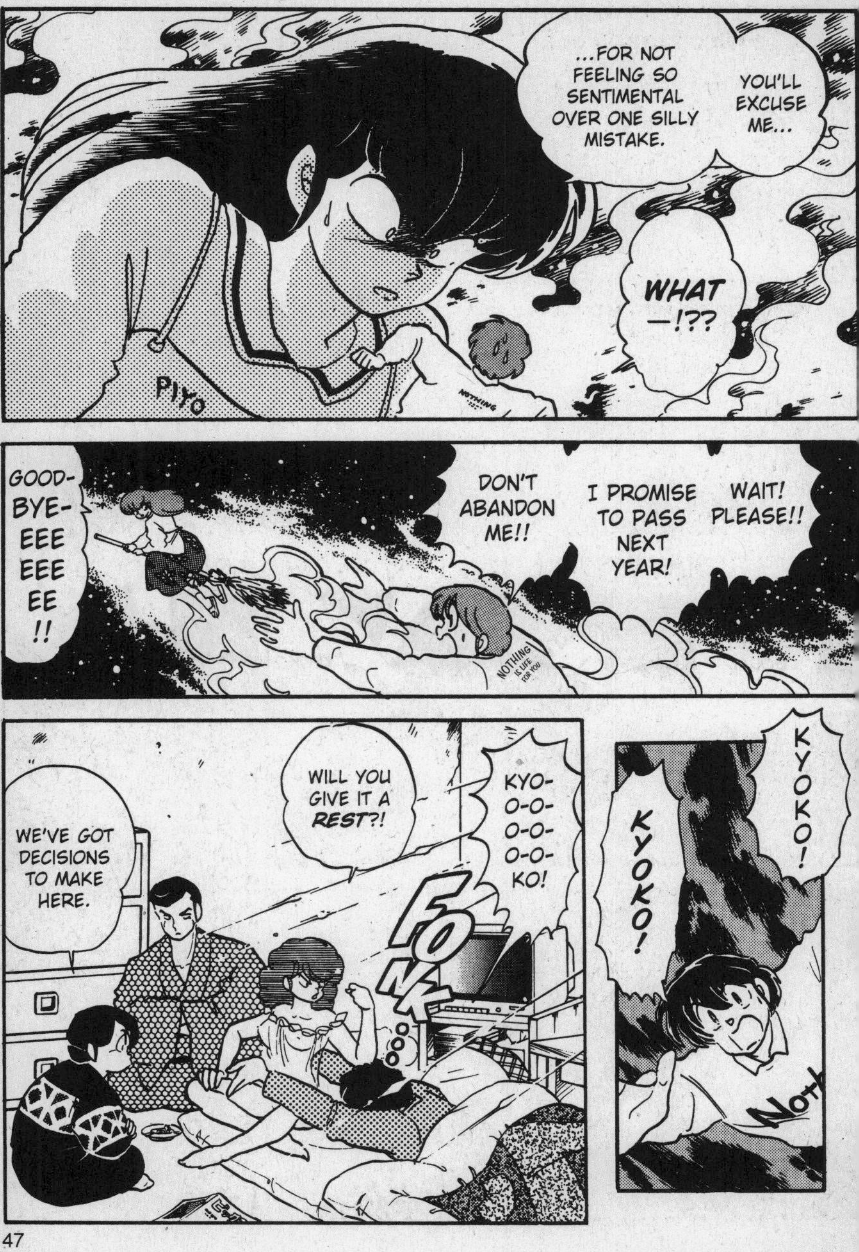
YOU'LL EXCUSE ME...
...FOR NOT FEELING SO SENTIMENTAL OVER ONE SILLY MISTAKE.
WHAT—!??
PIYO
NOTHING
WAIT! PLEASE!!
I PROMISE TO PASS NEXT YEAR!
DON'T ABANDON ME!!
GOOD-BYE-EEE EEE EE !!
NOTHING IS LIFE FOR YOU
KYOKO!
KYOKO!
KYO-O-O-O-O-O-O-KO!
FONK
WILL YOU GIVE IT A *REST*?!
WE'VE GOT DECISIONS TO MAKE HERE.

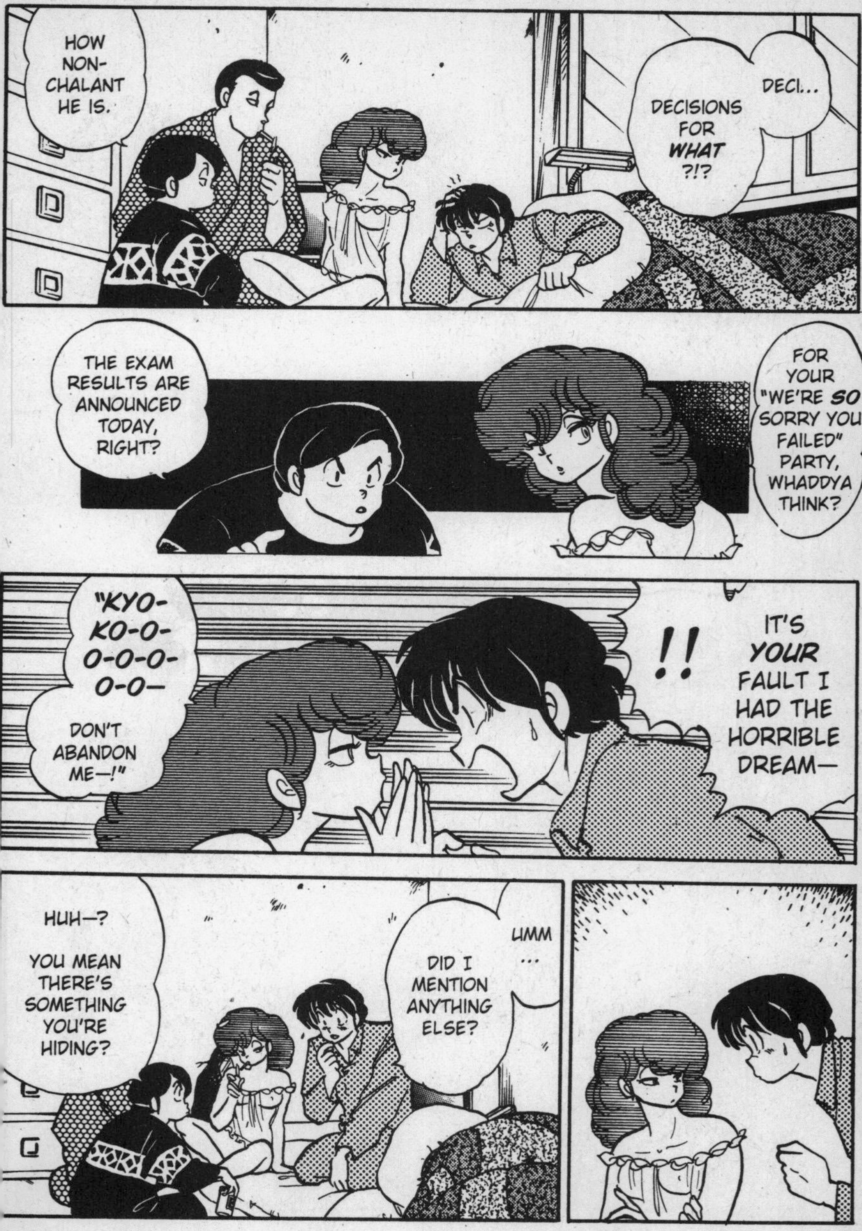
DECI...
DECISIONS FOR WHAT ?!?
HOW NON-CHALANT HE IS.
FOR YOUR "WE'RE SO SORRY YOU FAILED" PARTY, WHADDYA THINK?
THE EXAM RESULTS ARE ANNOUNCED TODAY, RIGHT?
!!
IT'S YOUR FAULT I HAD THE HORRIBLE DREAM—
"KYO-KO-O-O-O-O-O-O— DON'T ABANDON ME—!"
UMM ...
DID I MENTION ANYTHING ELSE?
HUH—?
YOU MEAN THERE'S SOMETHING YOU'RE HIDING?

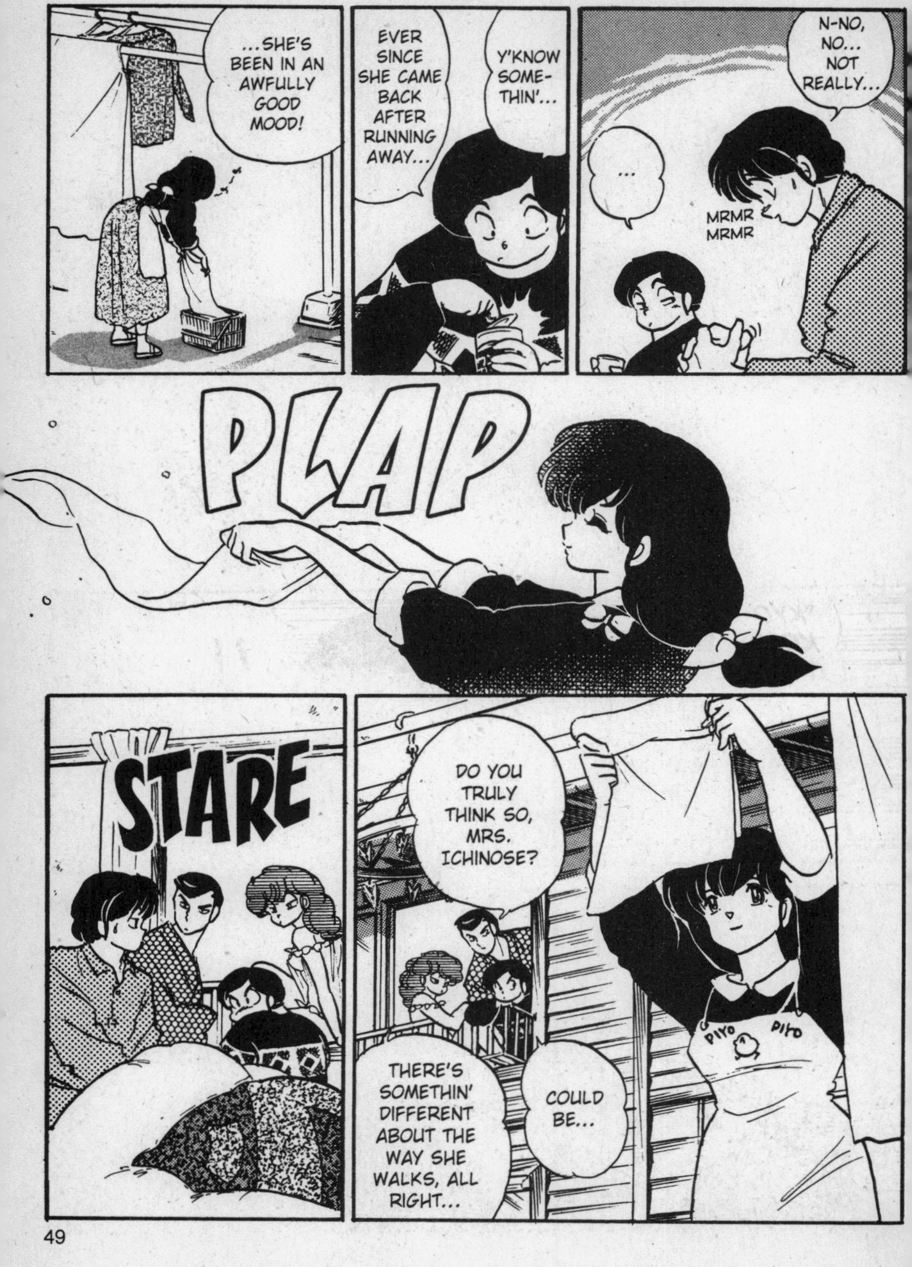
N-NO, NO... NOT REALLY...
...
MRMR MRMR
Y'KNOW SOMETHIN'...
EVER SINCE SHE CAME BACK AFTER RUNNING AWAY...
...SHE'S BEEN IN AN AWFULLY GOOD MOOD!
PLAP
DO YOU TRULY THINK SO, MRS. ICHINOSE?
COULD BE...
THERE'S SOMETHIN' DIFFERENT ABOUT THE WAY SHE WALKS, ALL RIGHT...
STARE

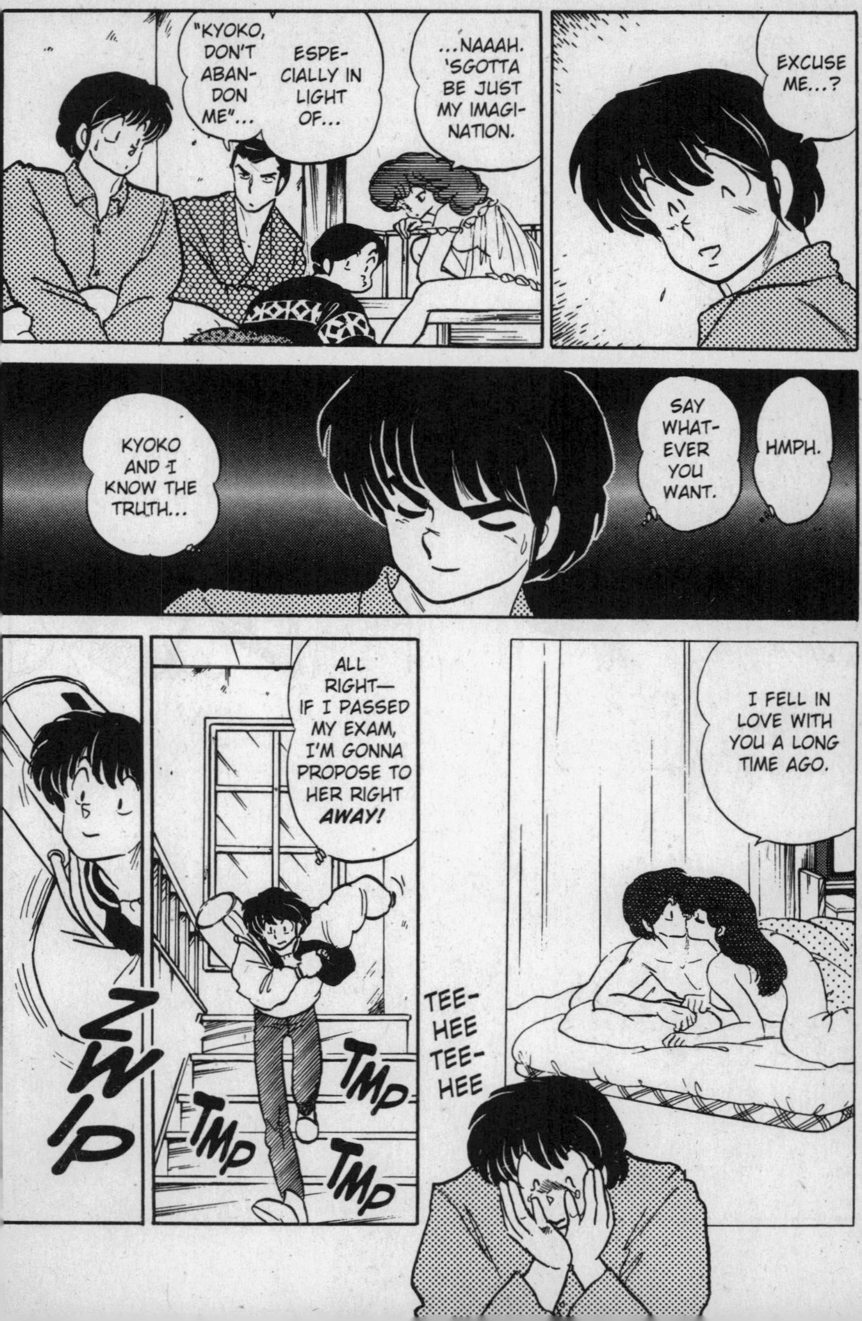
EXCUSE ME...?
...NAAAH. 'SGOTTA BE JUST MY IMAGINATION.
ESPE-CIALLY IN LIGHT OF...
"KYOKO, DON'T ABAN-DON ME"...
HMPH.
SAY WHAT-EVER YOU WANT.
KYOKO AND I KNOW THE TRUTH...
I FELL IN LOVE WITH YOU A LONG TIME AGO.
TEE-HEE TEE-HEE
ALL RIGHT— IF I PASSED MY EXAM, I'M GONNA PROPOSE TO HER RIGHT *AWAY!*
TMP
TMP
TMP
TMP
ZWIP

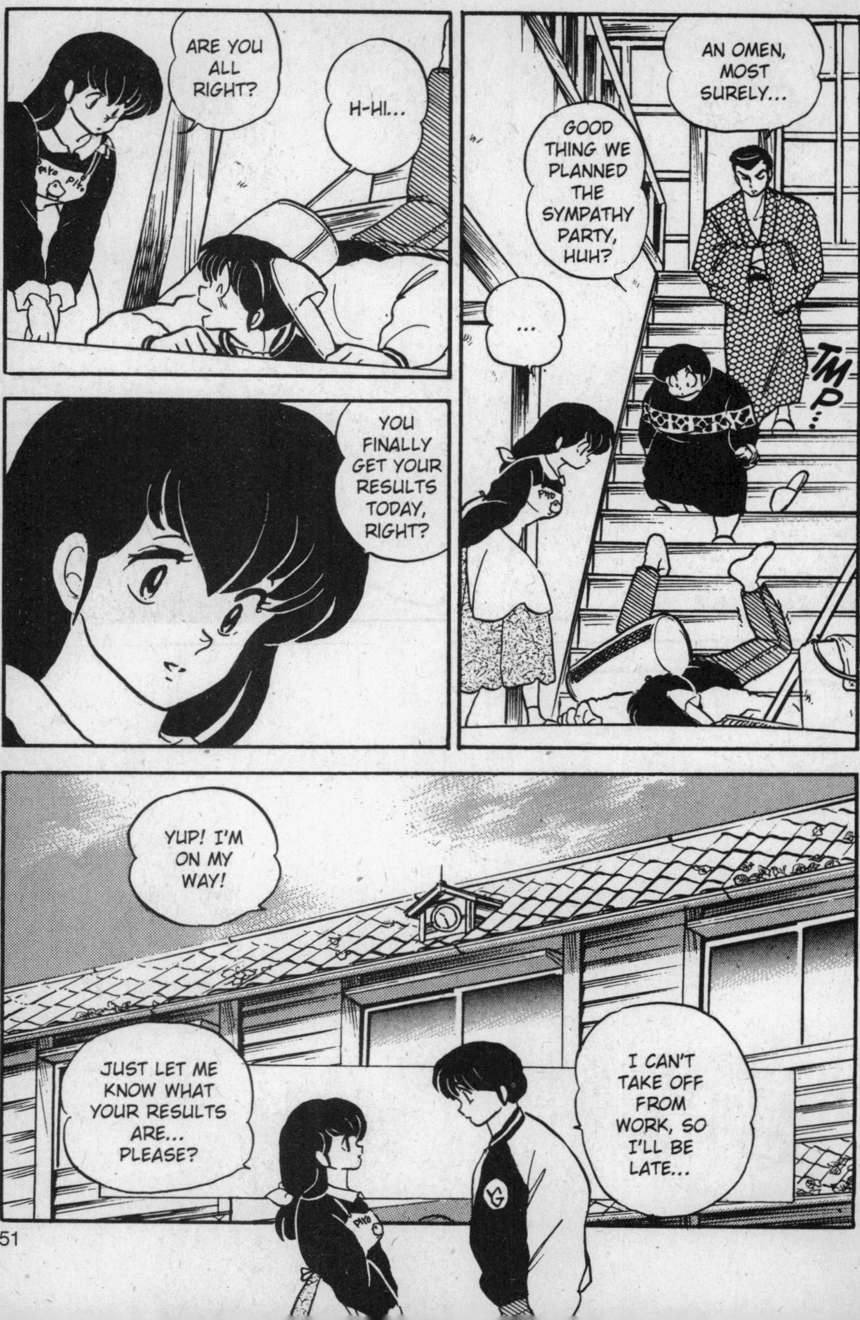
AN OMEN, MOST SURELY...
GOOD THING WE PLANNED THE SYMPATHY PARTY, HUH?
...
TMP...
H-HI...
ARE YOU ALL RIGHT?
YOU FINALLY GET YOUR RESULTS TODAY, RIGHT?
YUP! I'M ON MY WAY!
I CAN'T TAKE OFF FROM WORK, SO I'LL BE LATE...
JUST LET ME KNOW WHAT YOUR RESULTS ARE... PLEASE?

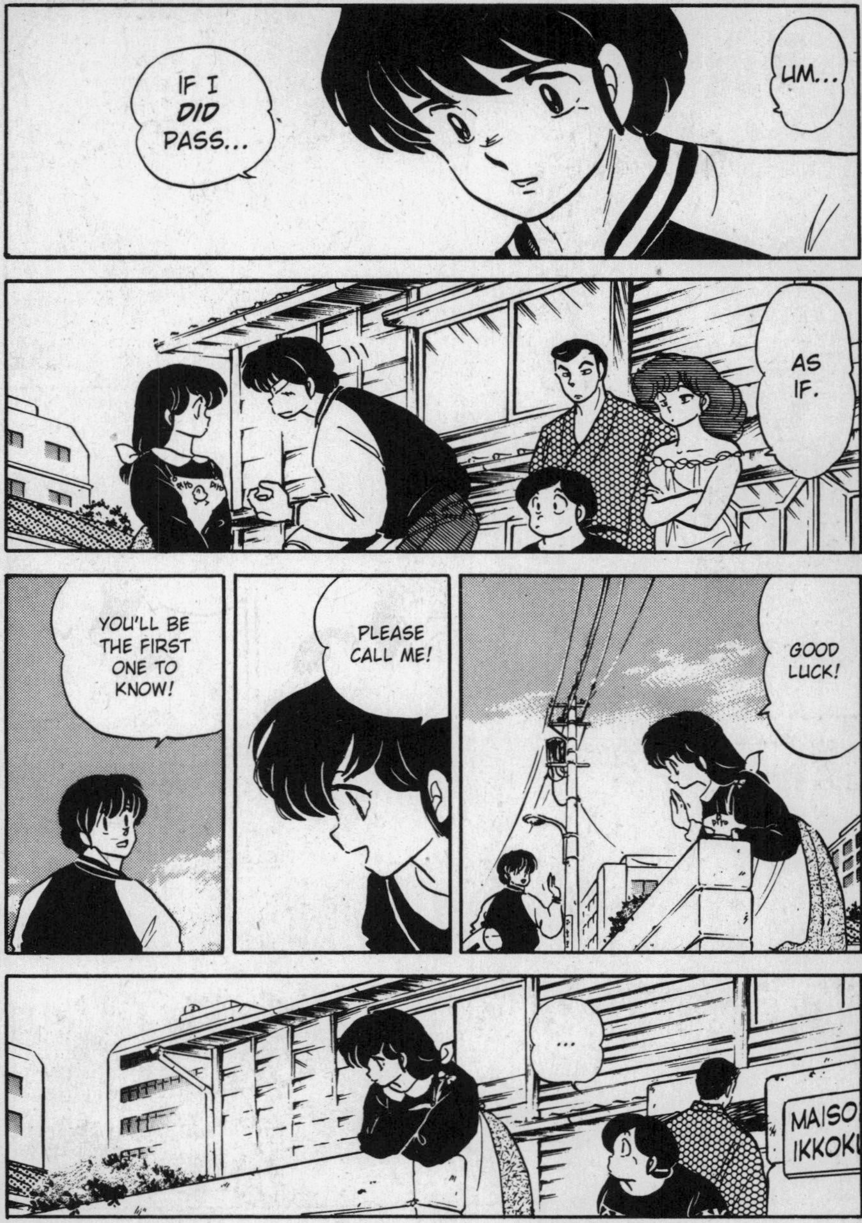
UM...
IF I DID PASS...
AS IF.
GOOD LUCK!
PLEASE CALL ME!
YOU'LL BE THE FIRST ONE TO KNOW!
...
MAISO IKKOK

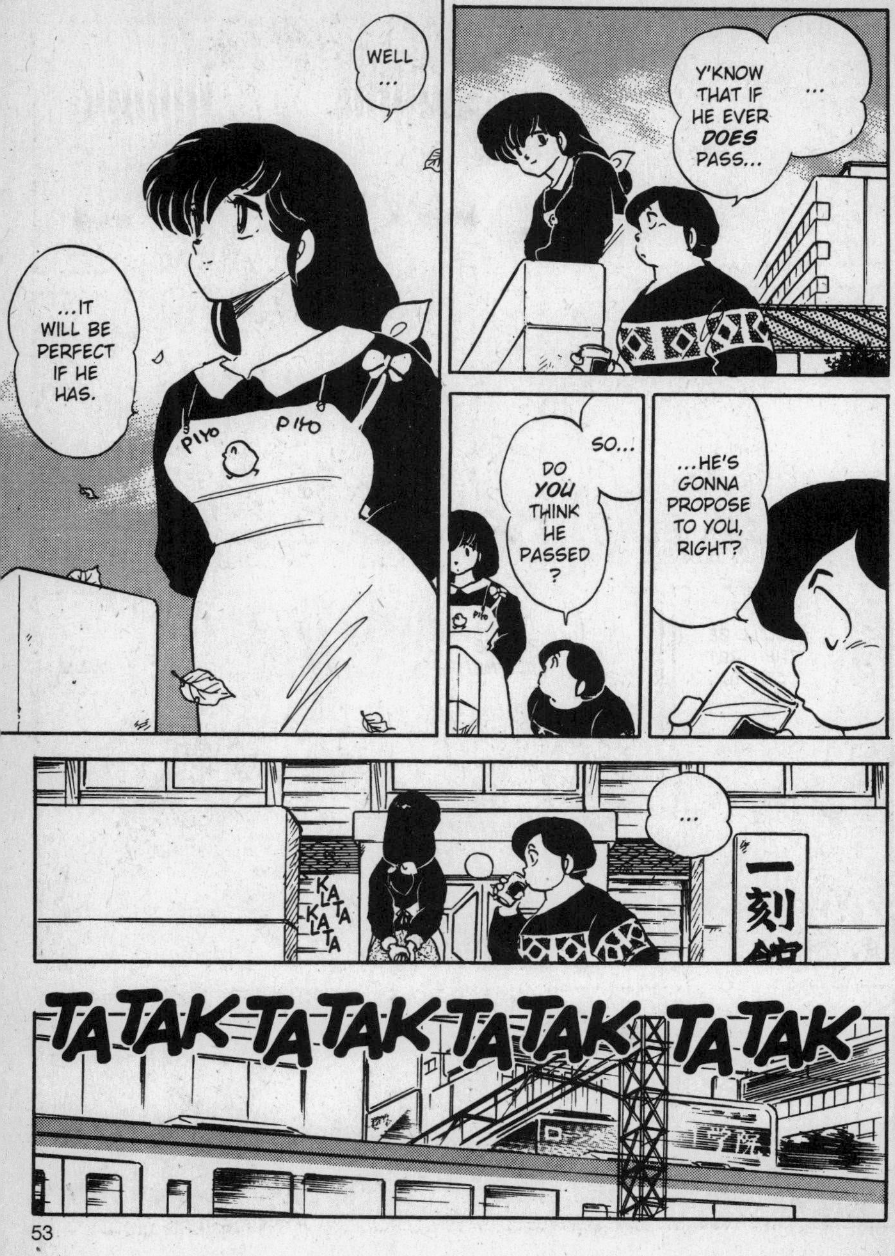
Y'KNOW THAT IF HE EVER *DOES* PASS... ...
...HE'S GONNA PROPOSE TO YOU, RIGHT?
SO... DO *YOU* THINK HE PASSED?
PIYO PIYO
WELL ...
...IT WILL BE PERFECT IF HE HAS.
...
KLATA KLATA
一刻
TA TAK TA TAK TA TAK TA TAK

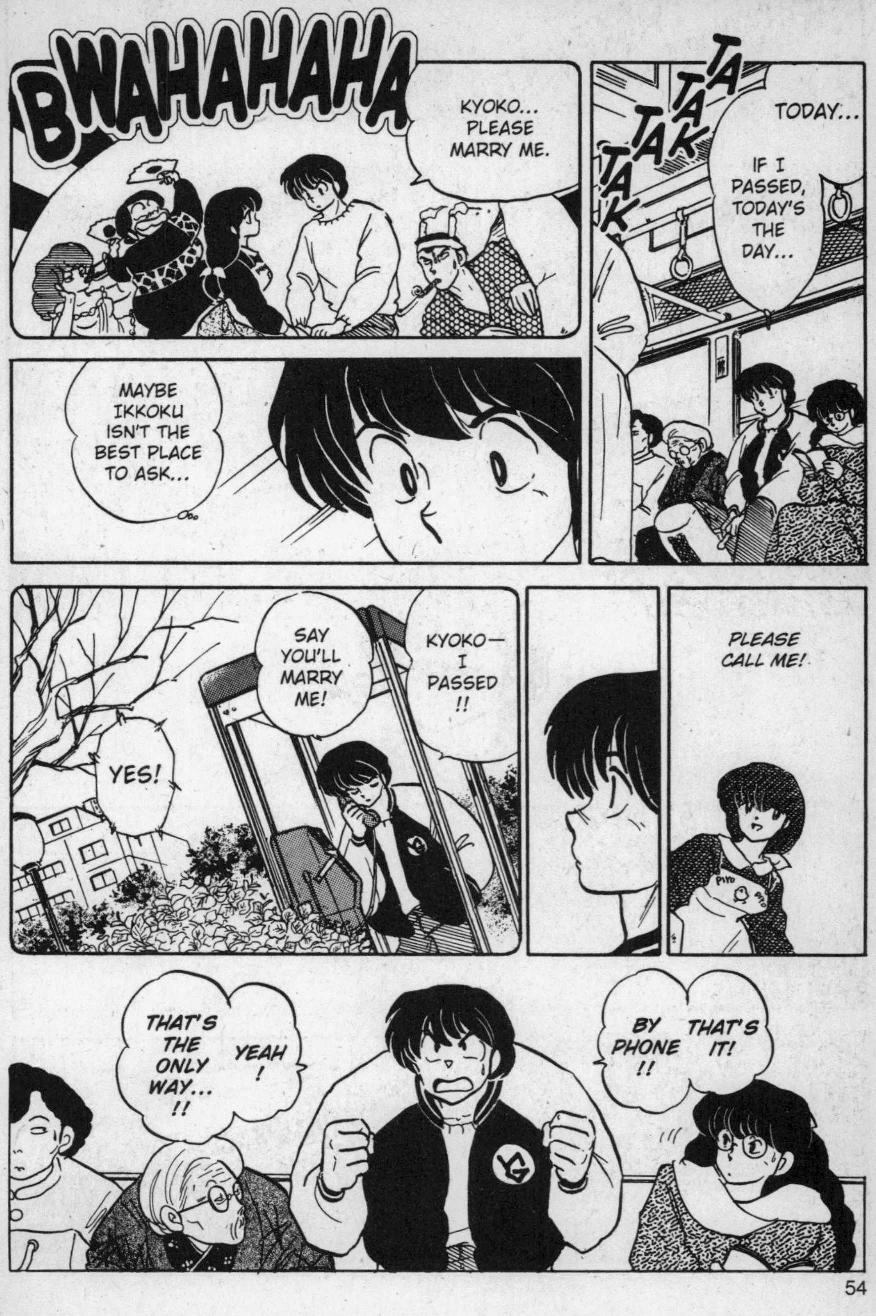
TAK TAK TAK TA
TODAY...
IF I PASSED, TODAY'S THE DAY...
BWAHAHAHAHA
KYOKO... PLEASE MARRY ME.
MAYBE IKKOKU ISN'T THE BEST PLACE TO ASK...
PLEASE CALL ME!
KYOKO— I PASSED !!
SAY YOU'LL MARRY ME!
YES!
THAT'S IT!
BY PHONE !!
YEAH !
THAT'S THE ONLY WAY... !!

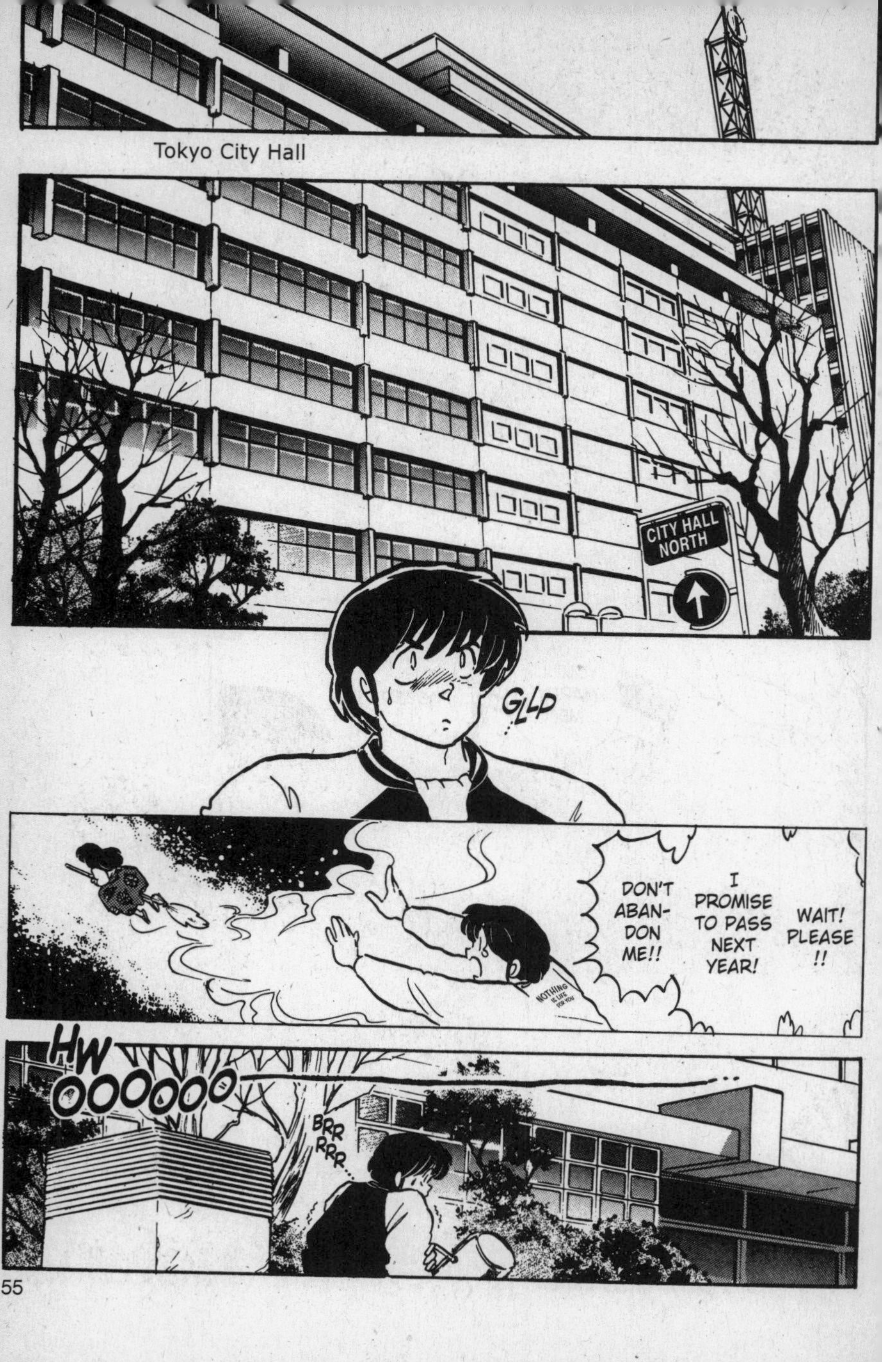
Tokyo City Hall
CITY HALL NORTH
GLLP
WAIT! PLEASE !!
I PROMISE TO PASS NEXT YEAR!
DON'T ABAN-DON ME!!
HW OOOOOO
BRR RRR...

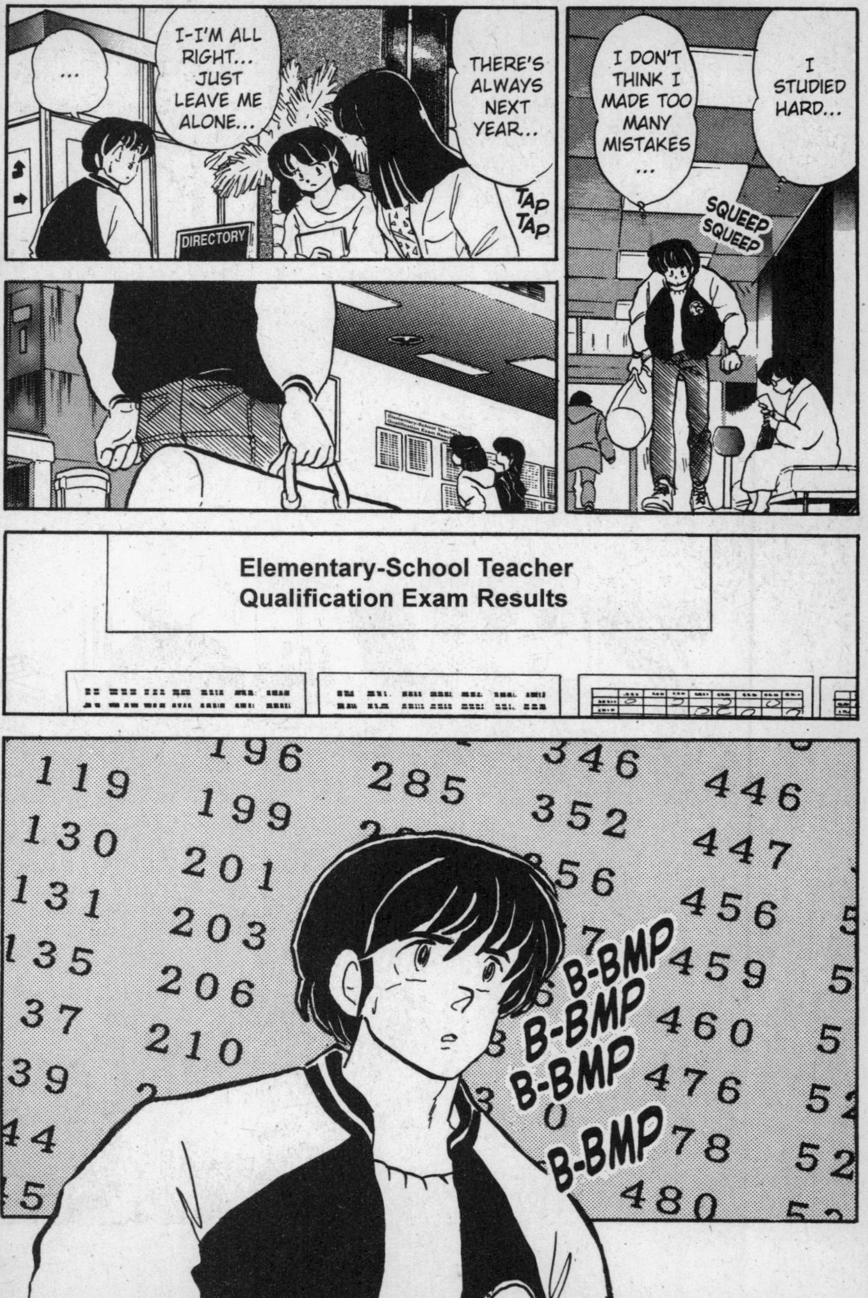
I STUDIED HARD...
I DON'T THINK I MADE TOO MANY MISTAKES ...
SQUEEP SQUEEP
THERE'S ALWAYS NEXT YEAR...
TAP TAP
I-I'M ALL RIGHT... JUST LEAVE ME ALONE...
...
DIRECTORY
Elementary-School Teacher Qualification Exam Results
196 346 119 285 446 199 352 130 447 201 131 203 456 206 459 210 460 476 480
B-BMP
B-BMP
B-BMP
B-BMP

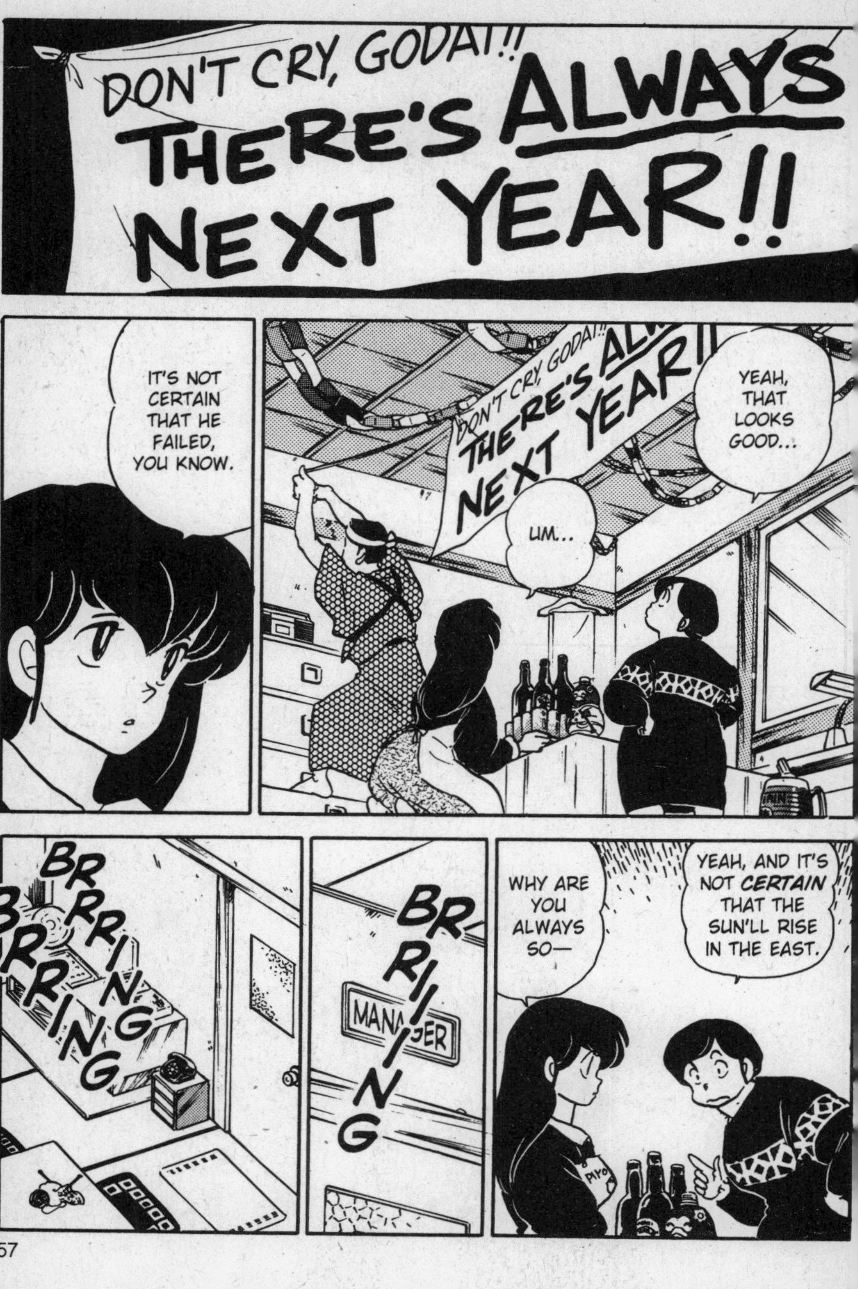
DON'T CRY, GODAI!!
THERE'S ALWAYS NEXT YEAR!!
YEAH, THAT LOOKS GOOD...
UM...
IT'S NOT CERTAIN THAT HE FAILED, YOU KNOW.
YEAH, AND IT'S NOT CERTAIN THAT THE SUN'LL RISE IN THE EAST.
WHY ARE YOU ALWAYS SO—
PIYO
BRRIIING
MANAGER
BRRRING
BRRRING

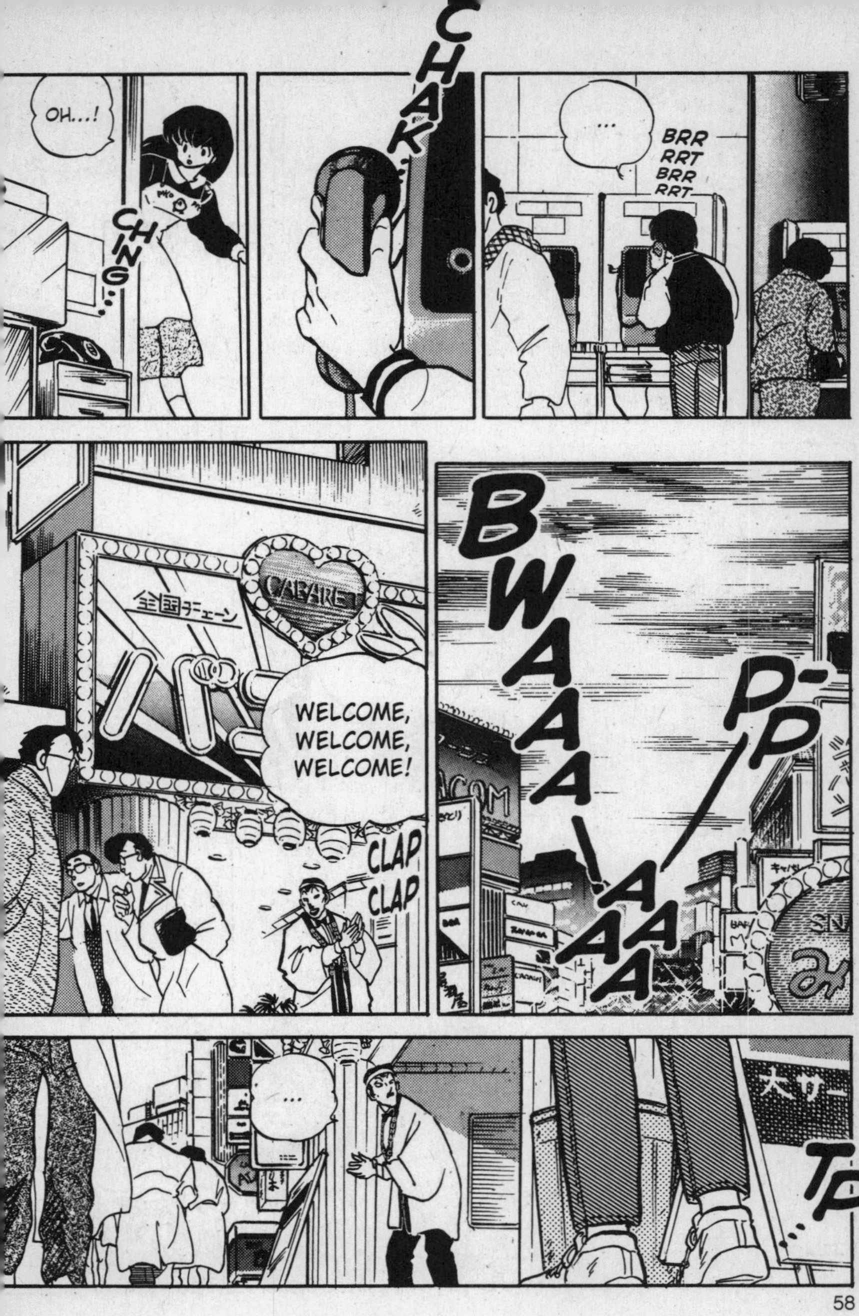
...
BRR RRT BRR RRT
CHAK
OH...!
CHING...
BWAAAA...AAA
P-P
CABARET
全国チェーン
WELCOME, WELCOME, WELCOME!
CLAP CLAP
TP...
...

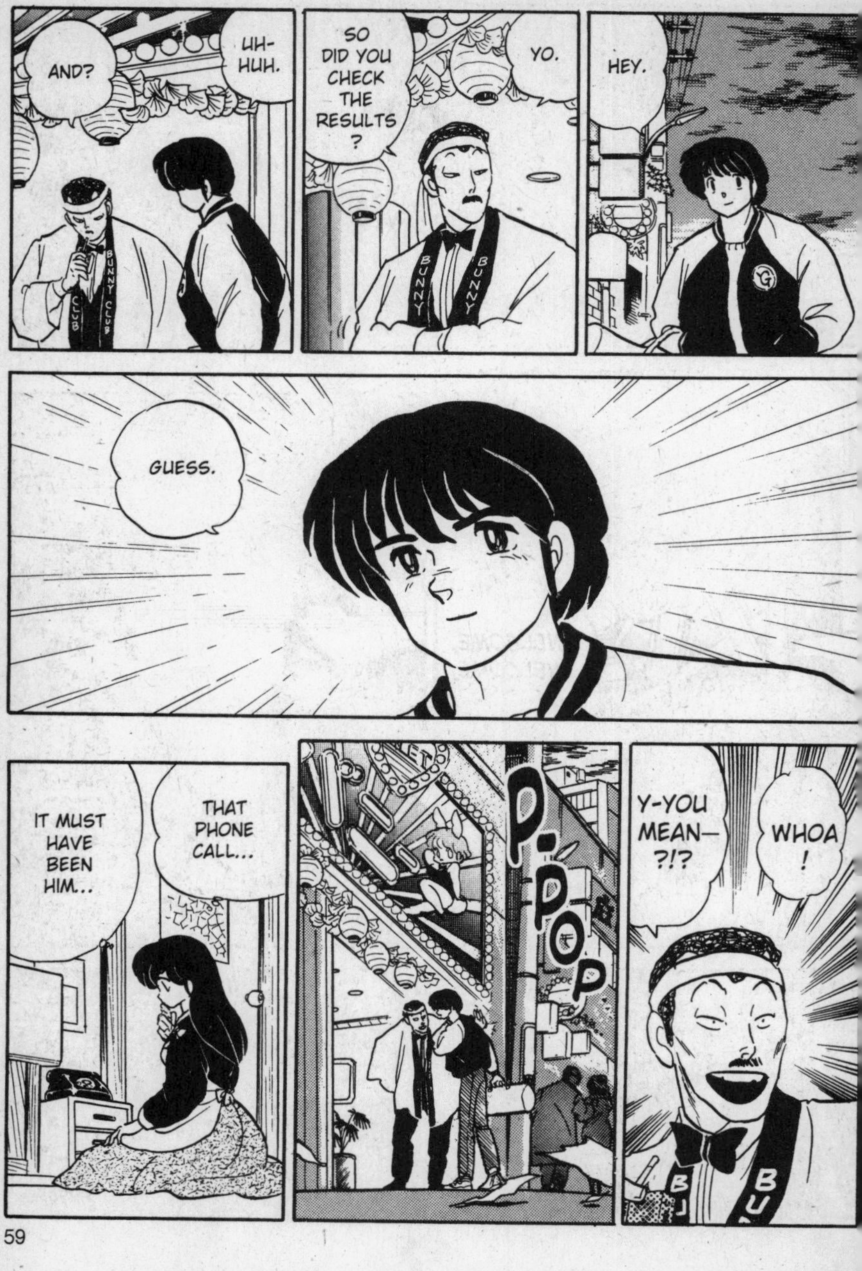
HEY.
YO.
SO DID YOU CHECK THE RESULTS?
UH-HUH.
AND?
GUESS.
WHOA!
Y-YOU MEAN—?!?
P-POP
THAT PHONE CALL...
IT MUST HAVE BEEN HIM...

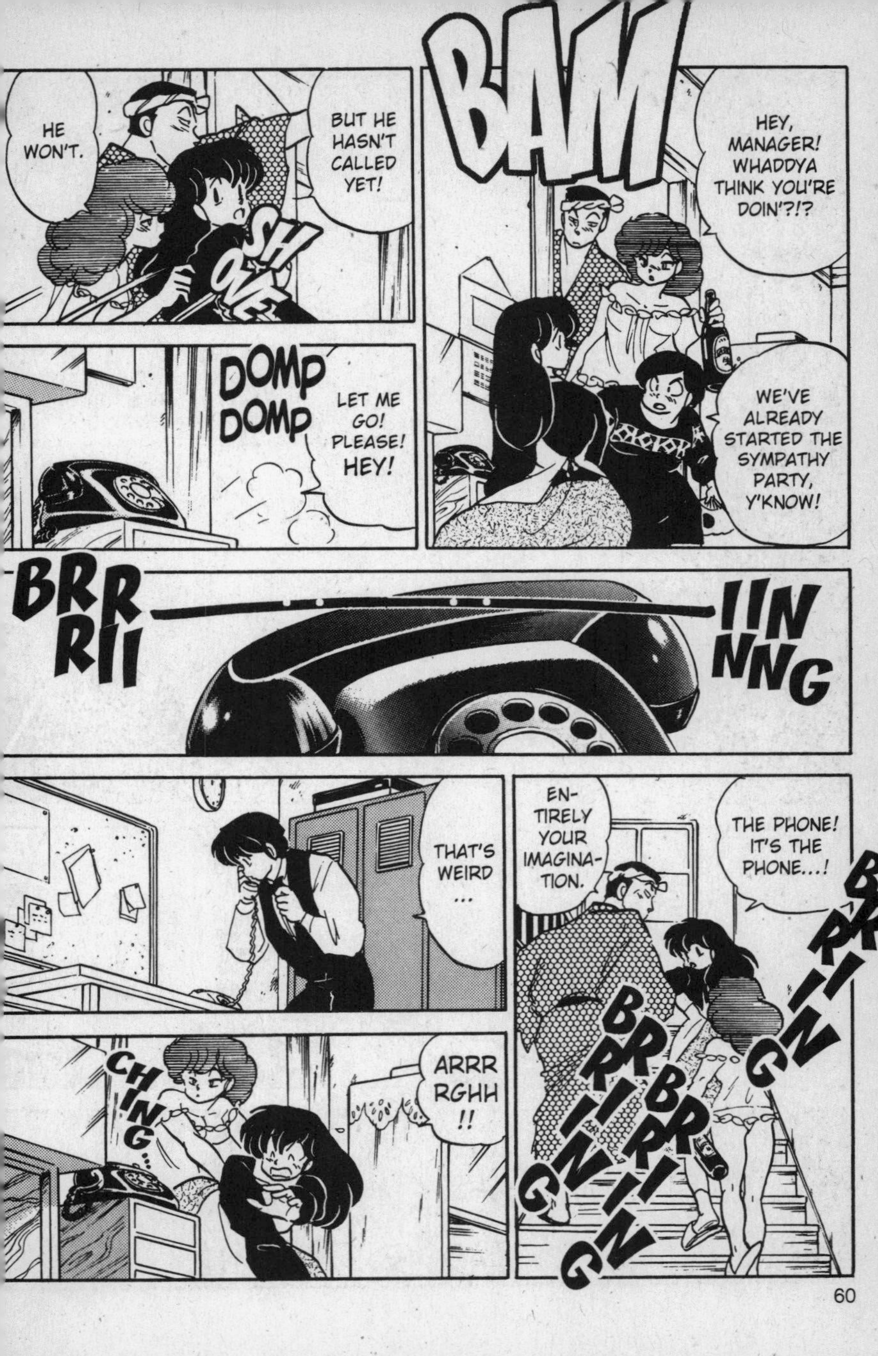
BAM
HEY, MANAGER! WHADDYA THINK YOU'RE DOIN'?!?
WE'VE ALREADY STARTED THE SYMPATHY PARTY, Y'KNOW!
BUT HE HASN'T CALLED YET!
HE WON'T.
SHOVE
LET ME GO! PLEASE! HEY!
DOMP DOMP
BRRRIIIINNNG
THE PHONE! IT'S THE PHONE...!
EN-TIRELY YOUR IMAGINA-TION.
BRRIIING
BRRIIING
BRRIIING
THAT'S WEIRD ...
ARRRRGHH !!
CHING...

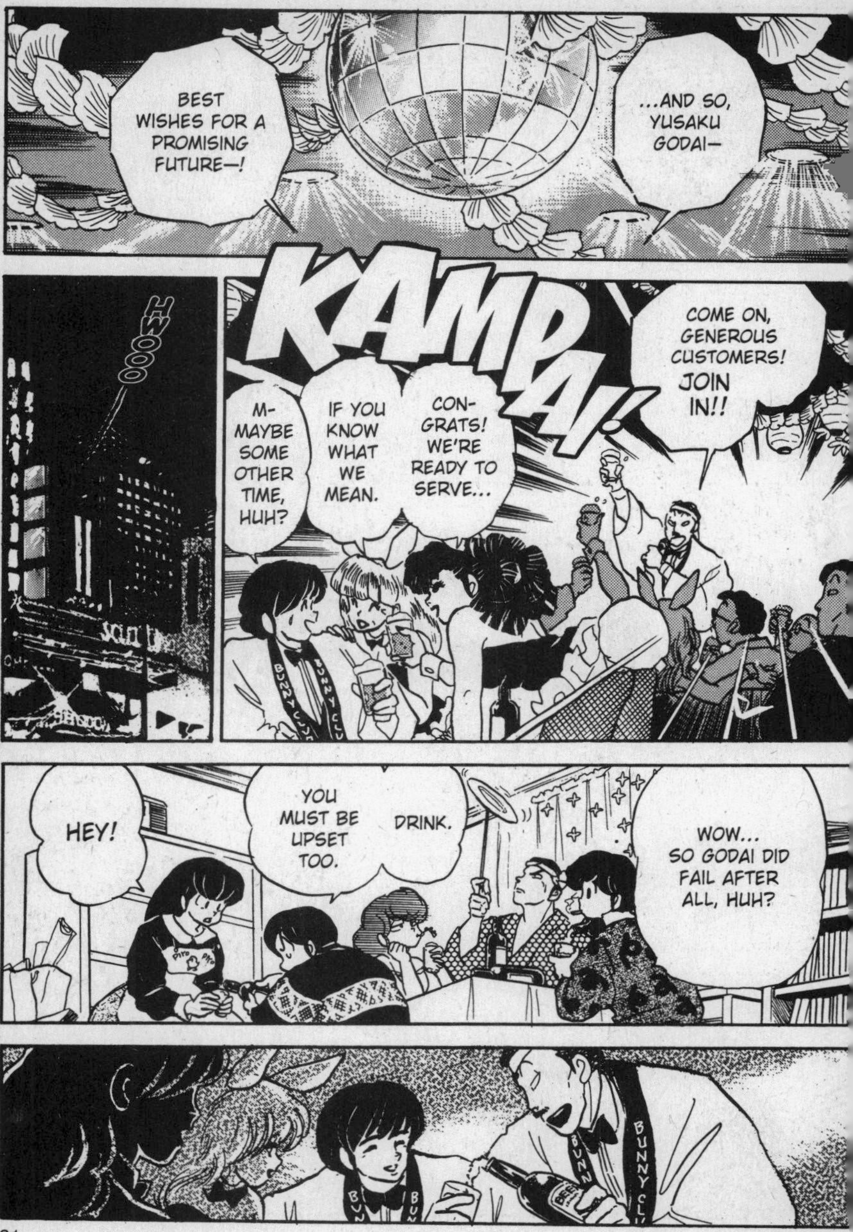
...AND SO, YUSAKU GODAI—
BEST WISHES FOR A PROMISING FUTURE—!
KAMPAI!
COME ON, GENEROUS CUSTOMERS! JOIN IN!!
CON-GRATS! WE'RE READY TO SERVE...
IF YOU KNOW WHAT WE MEAN.
M-MAYBE SOME OTHER TIME, HUH?
HWOOO
WOW... SO GODAI DID FAIL AFTER ALL, HUH?
DRINK.
YOU MUST BE UPSET TOO.
HEY!

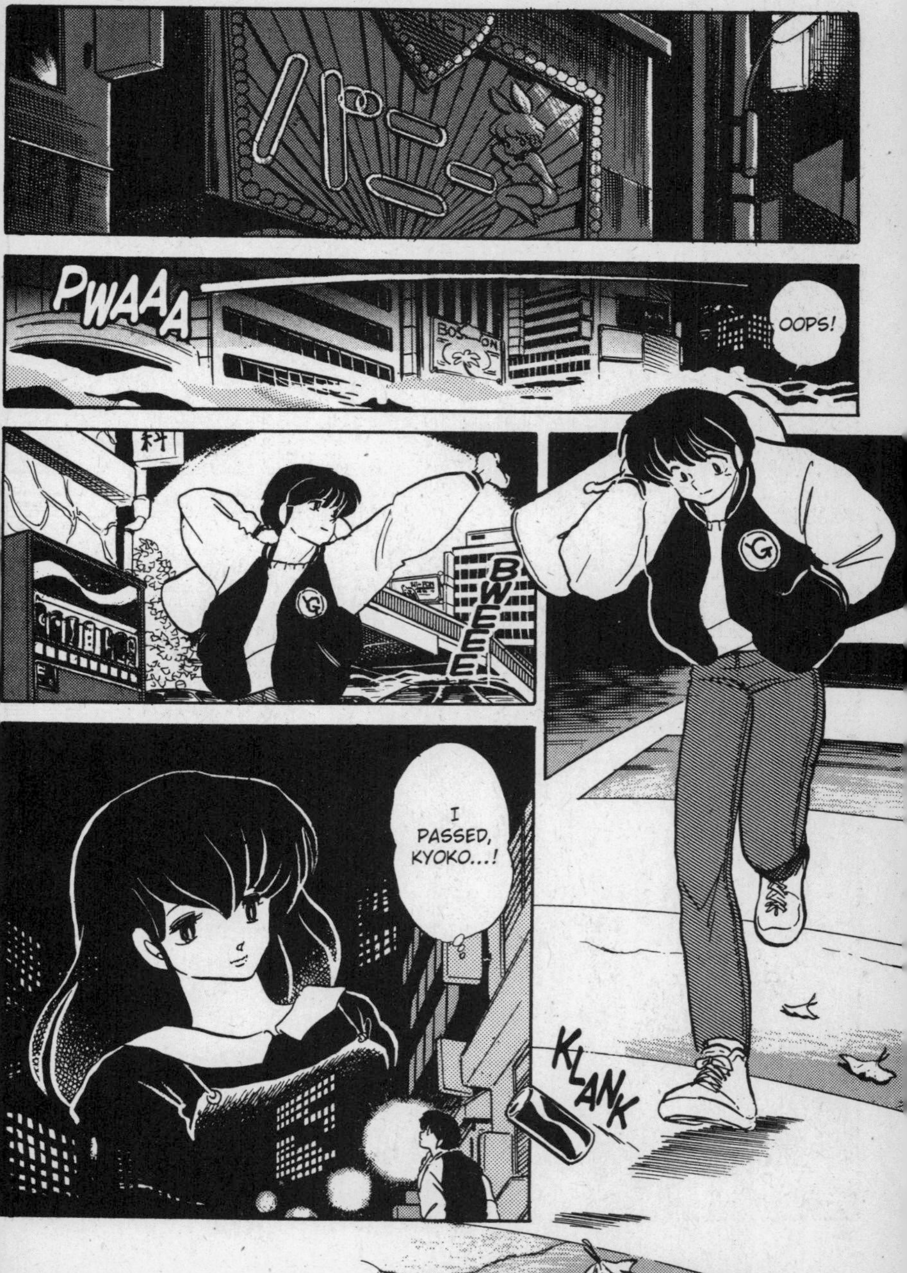
PWAAA
OOPS!
KLANK
BWEEEE
I PASSED, KYOKO...!

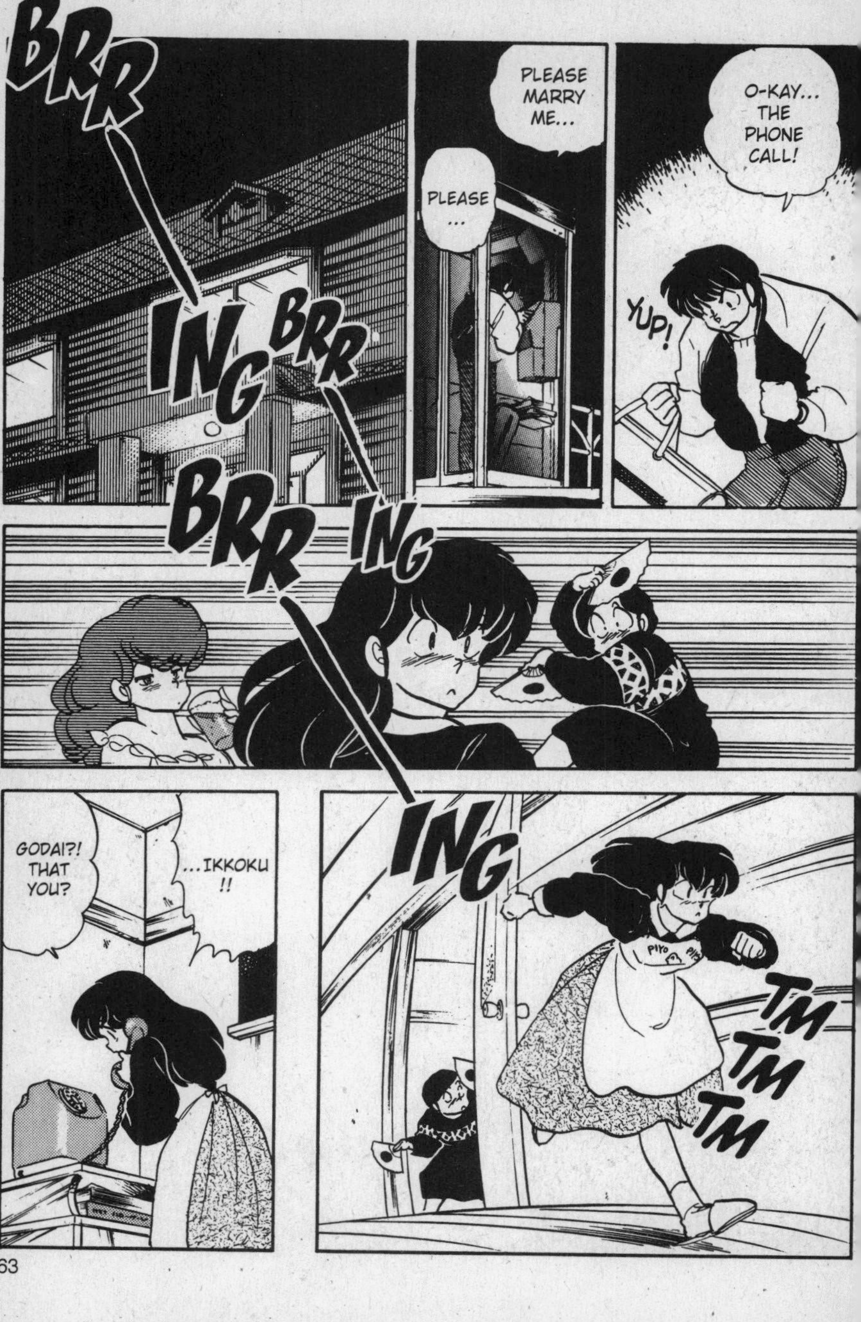
O-KAY... THE PHONE CALL!
YUP!
PLEASE MARRY ME...
PLEASE ...
BRRRING
BRRRING
BRRRING
...IKKOKU !!
GODAI?! THAT YOU?
ING
TM TM TM
PIYO PIYO

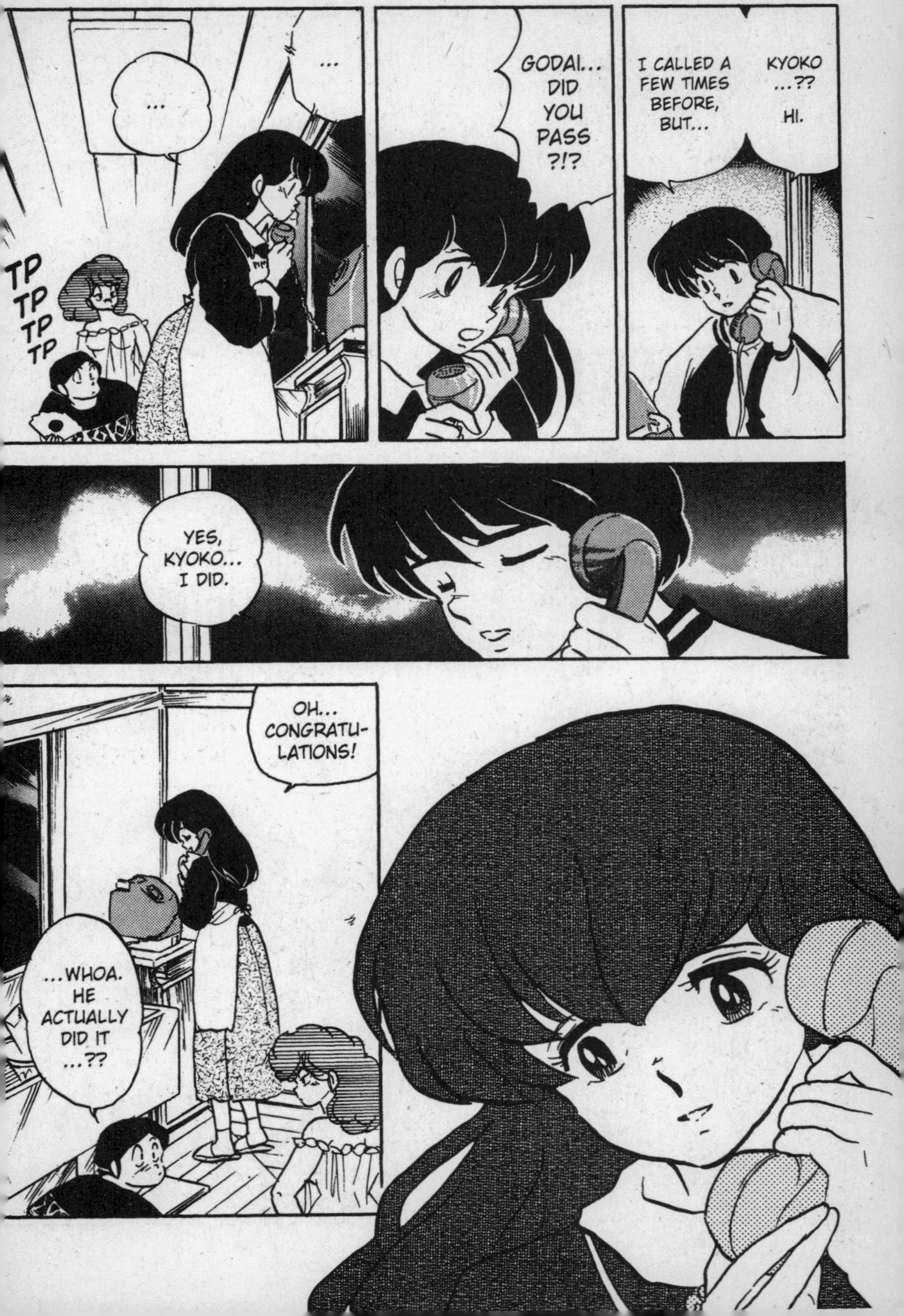
KYOKO ...??
HI.
I CALLED A FEW TIMES BEFORE, BUT...
GODAI... DID YOU PASS ?!?
...
...
TP TP TP TP
YES, KYOKO... I DID.
OH... CONGRATULATIONS!
...WHOA. HE ACTUALLY DID IT ...??

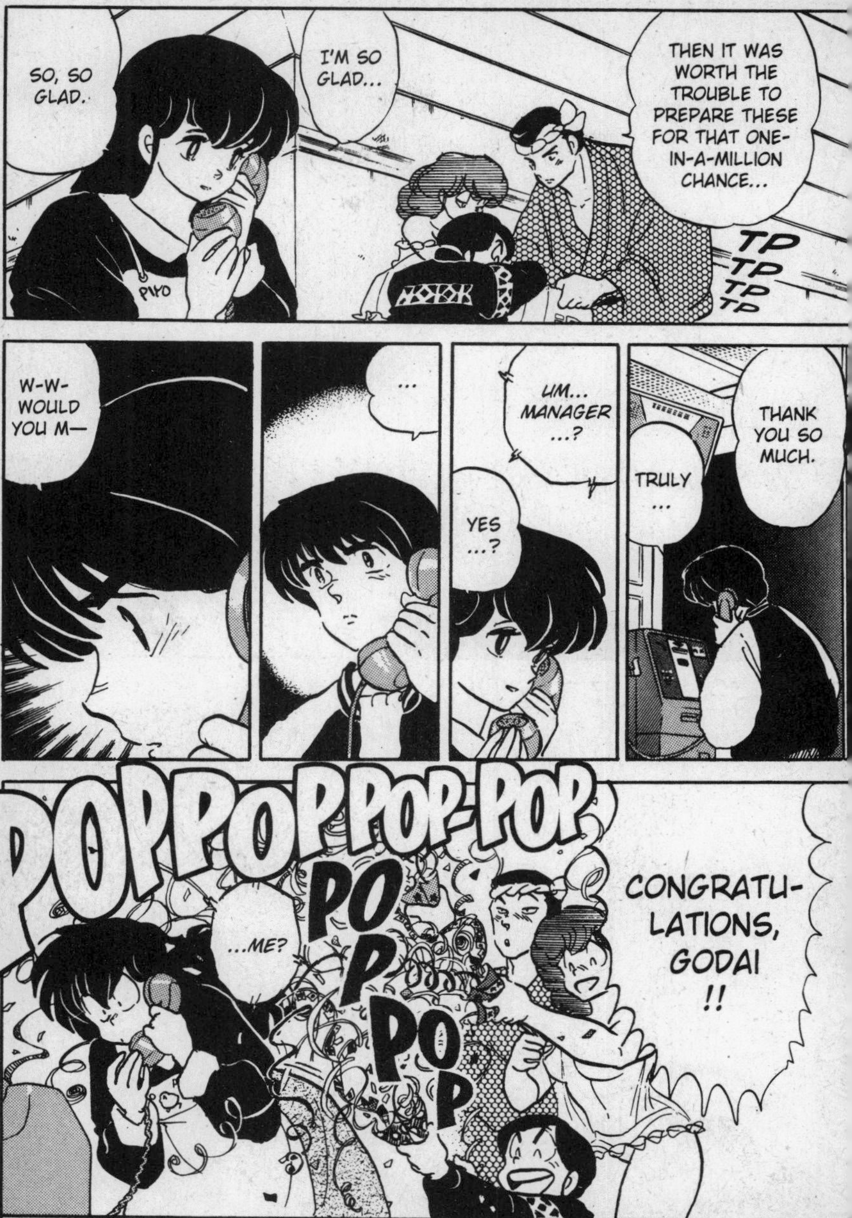
THEN IT WAS WORTH THE TROUBLE TO PREPARE THESE FOR THAT ONE-IN-A-MILLION CHANCE...
TP TP TP TP
I'M SO GLAD...
SO, SO GLAD.
PIYO
THANK YOU SO MUCH.
TRULY ...
UM... MANAGER ...?
YES ...?
...
W-W-WOULD YOU M—
CONGRATU-LATIONS, GODAI !!
POPPOPPOP-POP
PO P PO P
...ME?

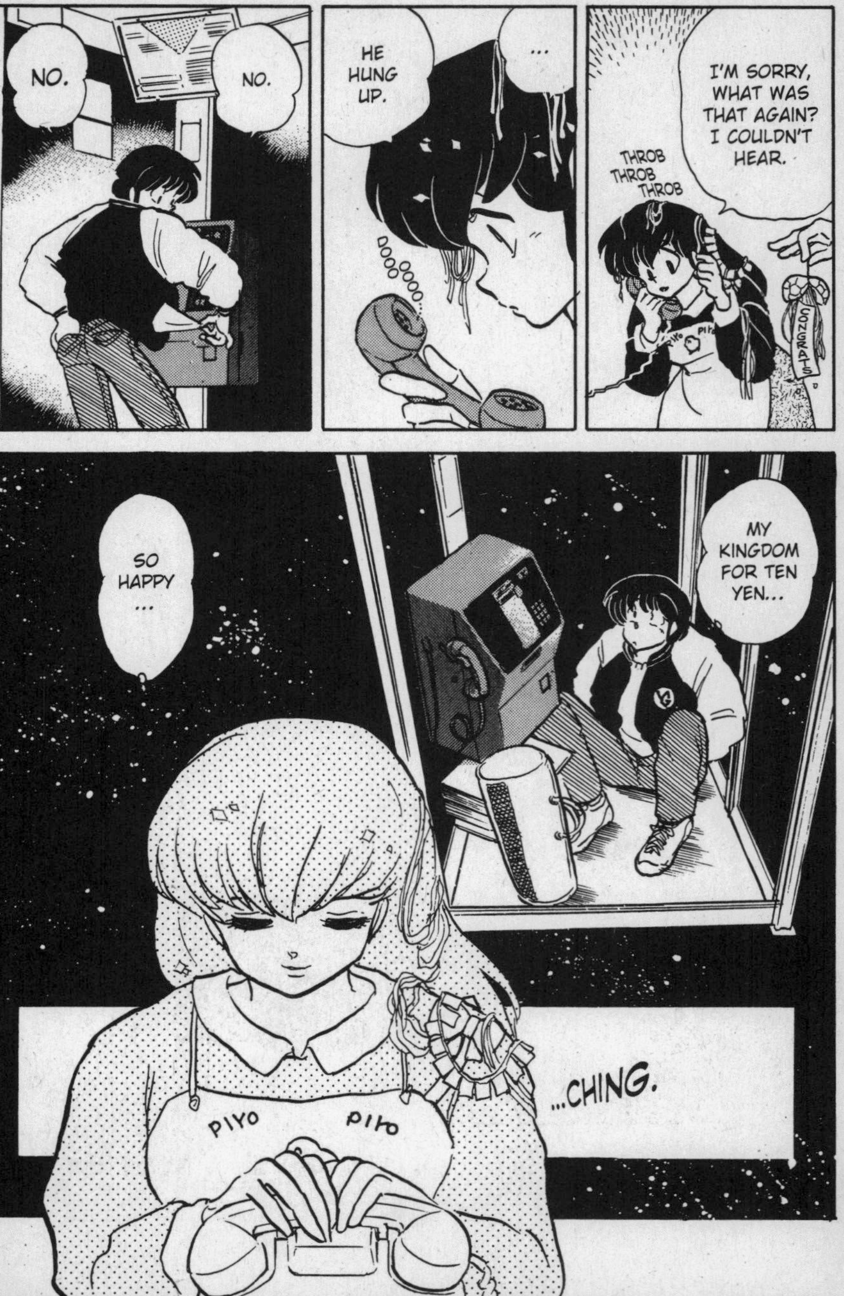
I'M SORRY, WHAT WAS THAT AGAIN? I COULDN'T HEAR.
THROB THROB THROB
PIYO PIYO
CONGRATS
...
HE HUNG UP.
NO.
NO.
MY KINGDOM FOR TEN YEN...
SO HAPPY ...
PIYO PIYO
...CHING.

PART FOUR

WAIT FOR ME TONIGHT

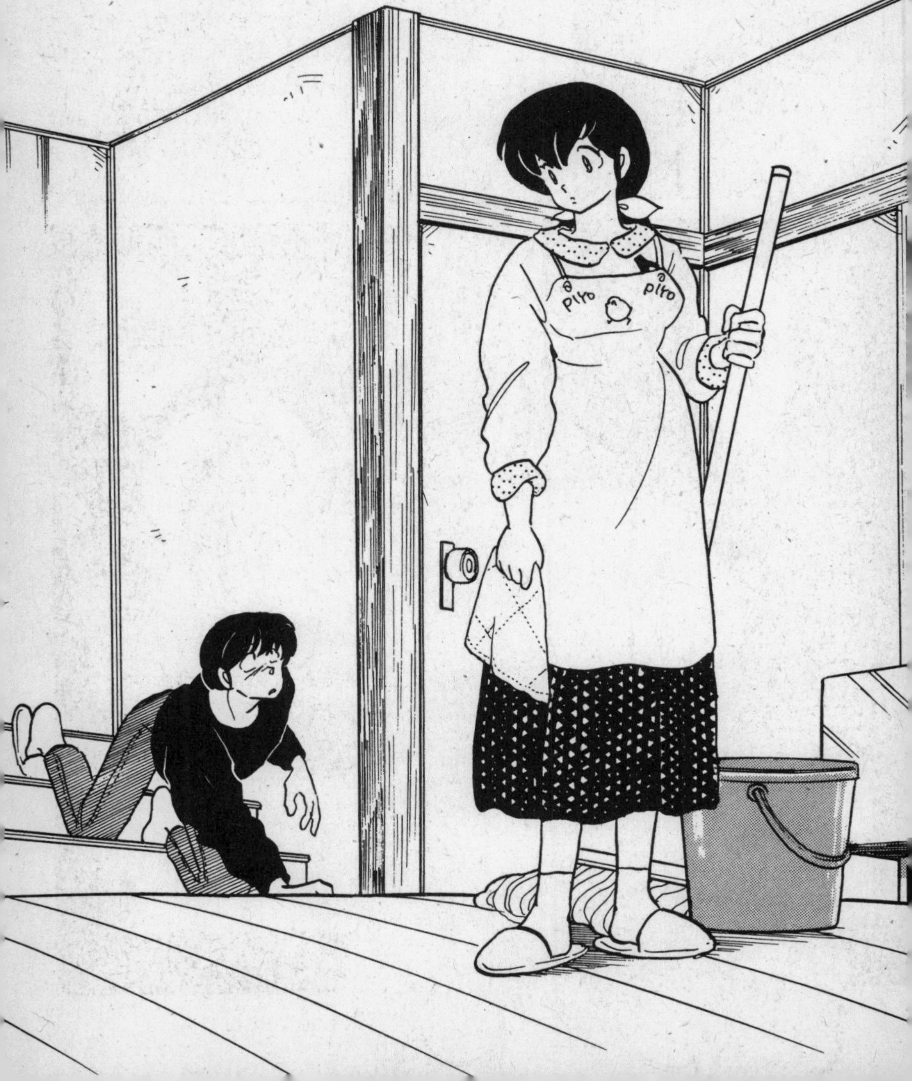
piyo
piyo

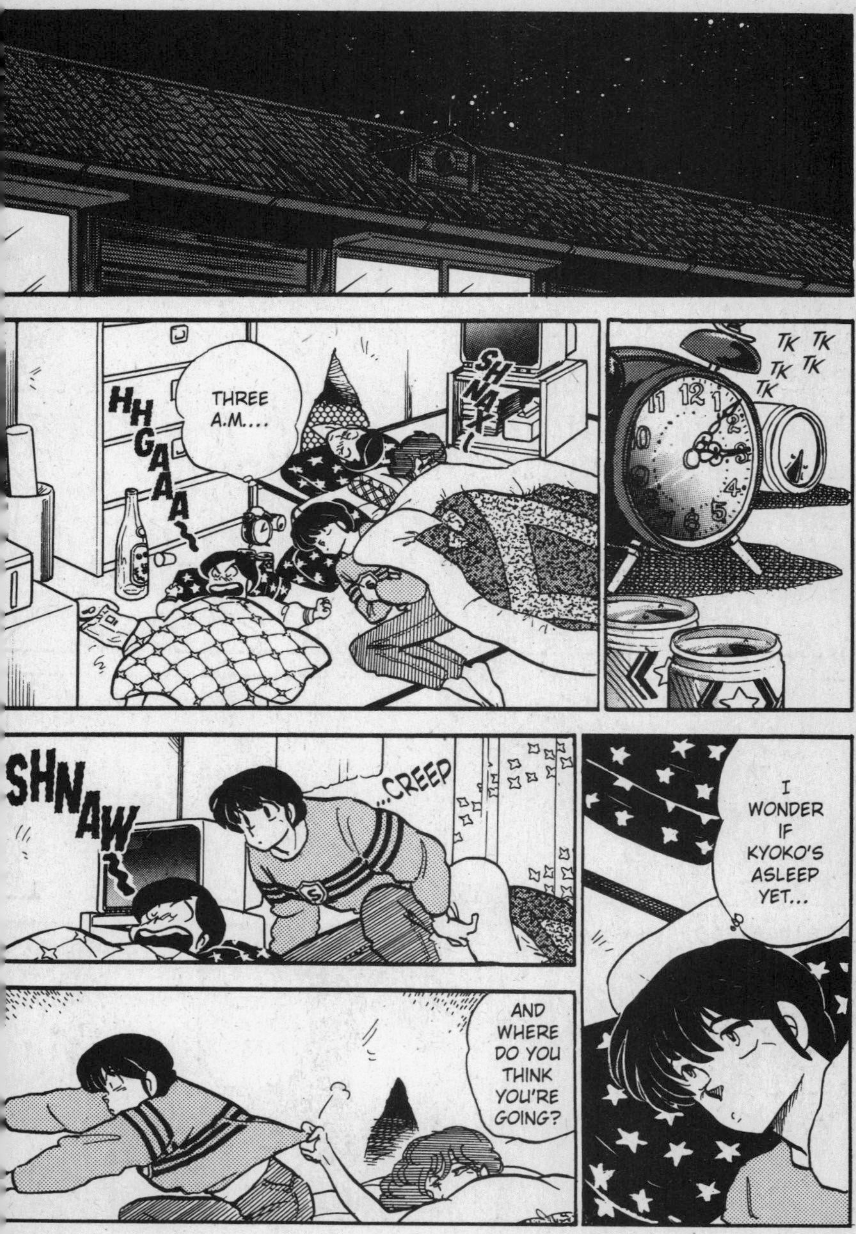
TK TK TK TK TK
THREE A.M....
SHNAX
HHGAAA
I WONDER IF KYOKO'S ASLEEP YET...
...CREEP
SHNAW
AND WHERE DO YOU THINK YOU'RE GOING?

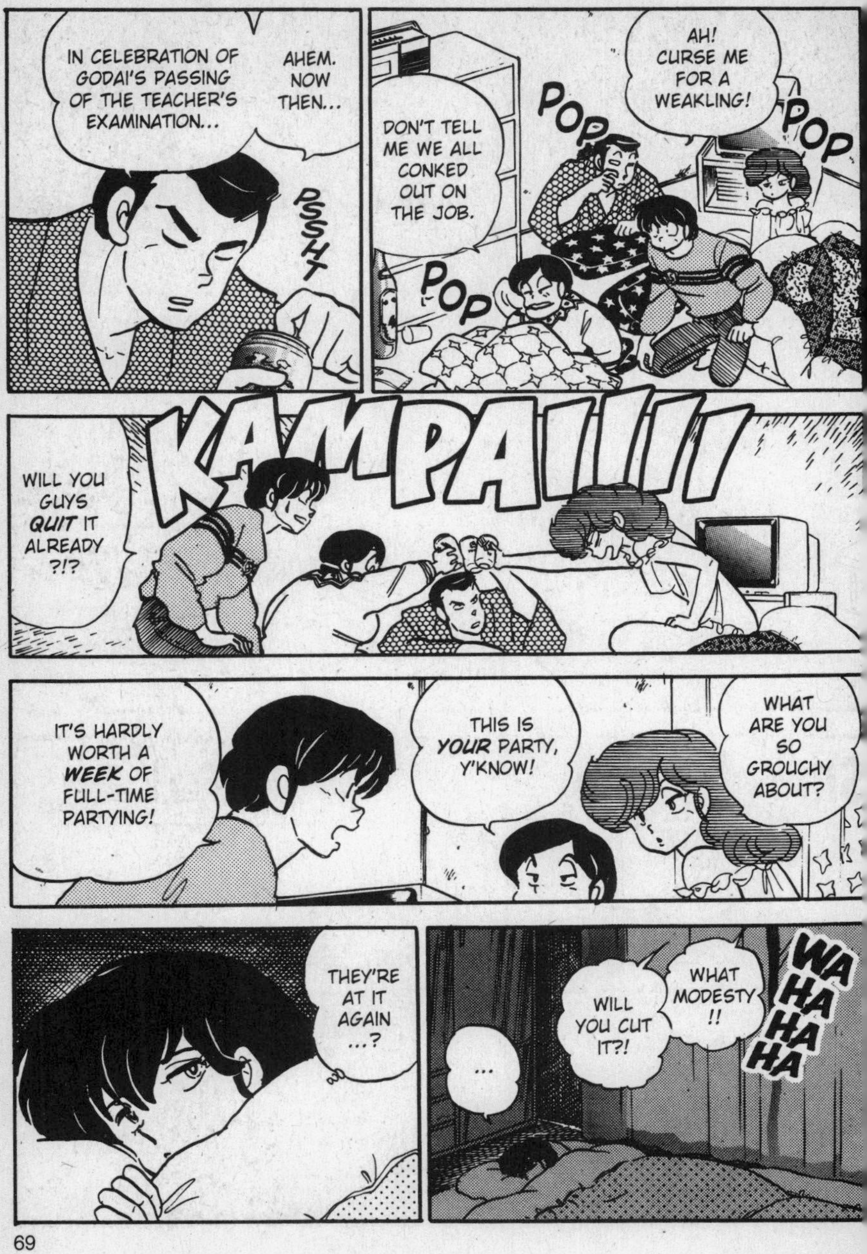

AH! CURSE ME FOR A WEAKLING!
POP
POP
DON'T TELL ME WE ALL CONKED OUT ON THE JOB.
POP
POP
AHEM. NOW THEN...
IN CELEBRATION OF GODAI'S PASSING OF THE TEACHER'S EXAMINATION...
PSSHT
KAMPAI!!!!
WILL YOU GUYS QUIT IT ALREADY?!?
WHAT ARE YOU SO GROUCHY ABOUT?
THIS IS YOUR PARTY, Y'KNOW!
IT'S HARDLY WORTH A WEEK OF FULL-TIME PARTYING!
WAHAHAHAHA
WHAT MODESTY!!
WILL YOU CUT IT?!
...
THEY'RE AT IT AGAIN...?

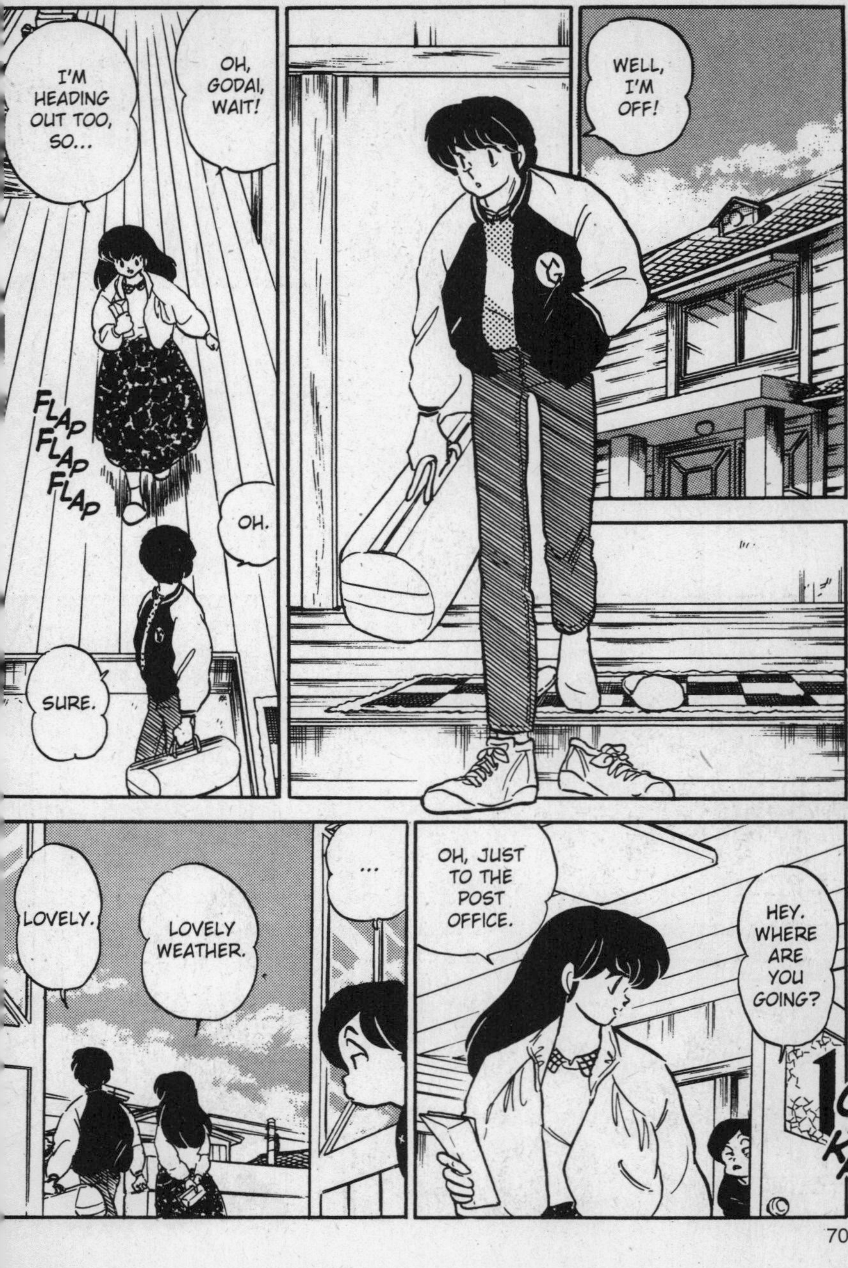
WELL, I'M OFF!
OH, GODAI, WAIT!
I'M HEADING OUT TOO, SO...
FLAP FLAP FLAP
OH.
SURE.
HEY. WHERE ARE YOU GOING?
CHKK
OH, JUST TO THE POST OFFICE.
...
LOVELY WEATHER.
LOVELY.

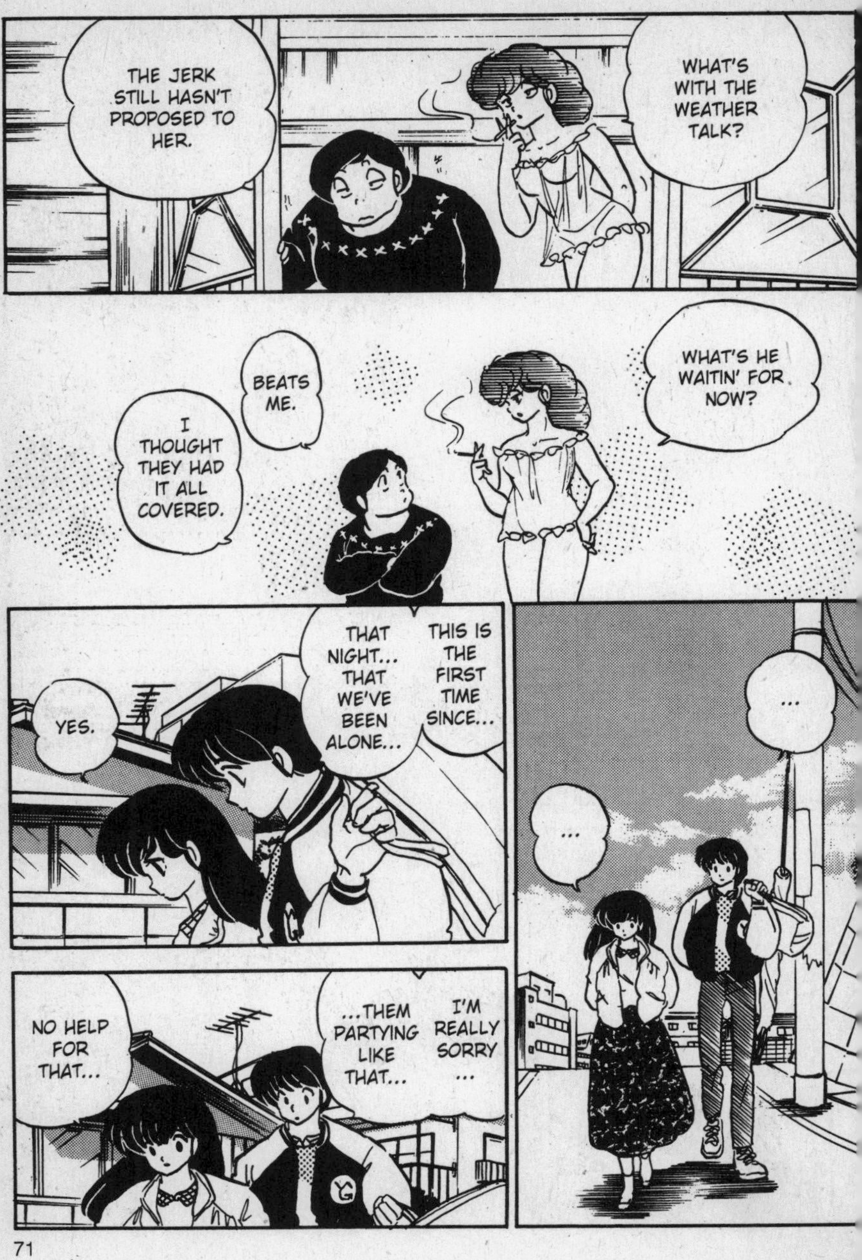
WHAT'S WITH THE WEATHER TALK?
THE JERK STILL HASN'T PROPOSED TO HER.
WHAT'S HE WAITIN' FOR NOW?
BEATS ME.
I THOUGHT THEY HAD IT ALL COVERED.
...
...
THIS IS THE FIRST TIME SINCE... THAT NIGHT... THAT WE'VE BEEN ALONE...
YES.
I'M REALLY SORRY... ...THEM PARTYING LIKE THAT...
NO HELP FOR THAT...

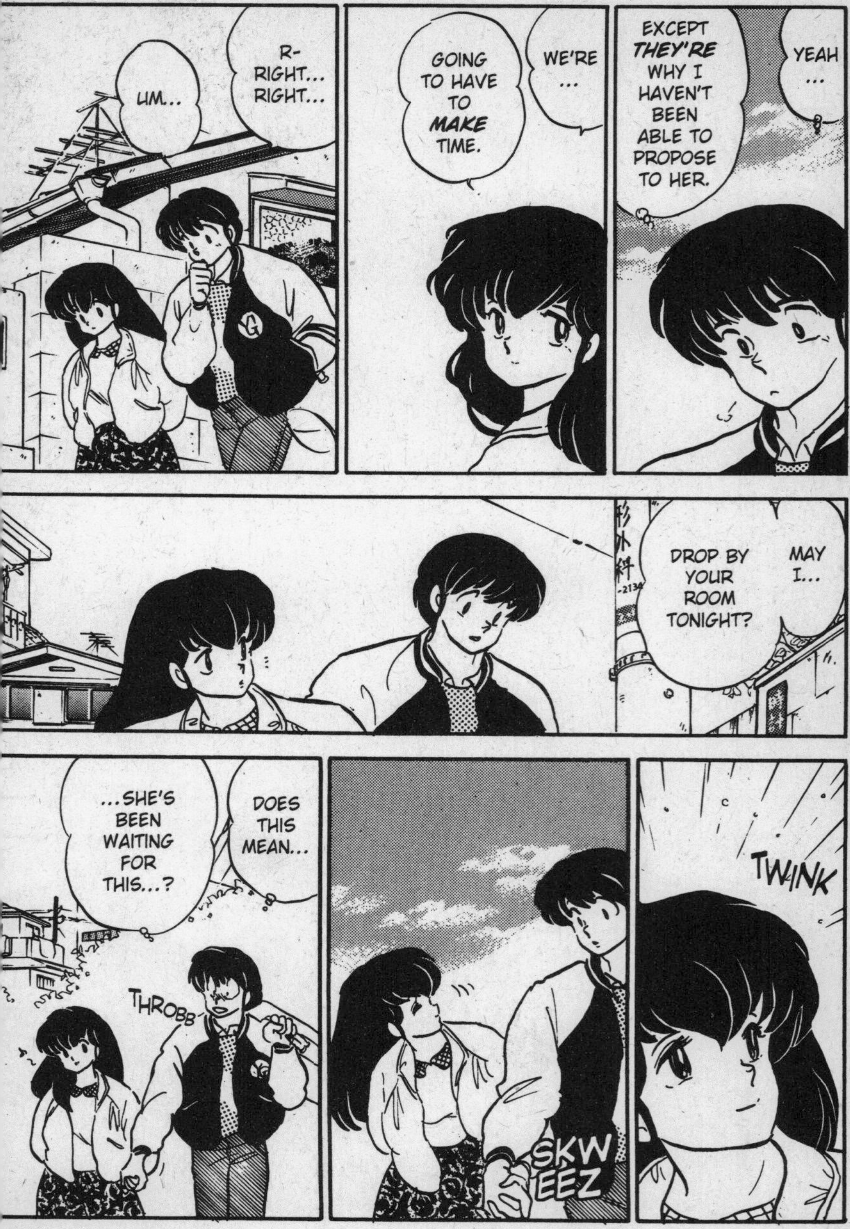
YEAH ...
EXCEPT THEY'RE WHY I HAVEN'T BEEN ABLE TO PROPOSE TO HER.
WE'RE ...
GOING TO HAVE TO MAKE TIME.
R- RIGHT... RIGHT...
UM...
MAY I...
DROP BY YOUR ROOM TONIGHT?
TWINK
SKWEEZ
DOES THIS MEAN...
...SHE'S BEEN WAITING FOR THIS...?
THROBB

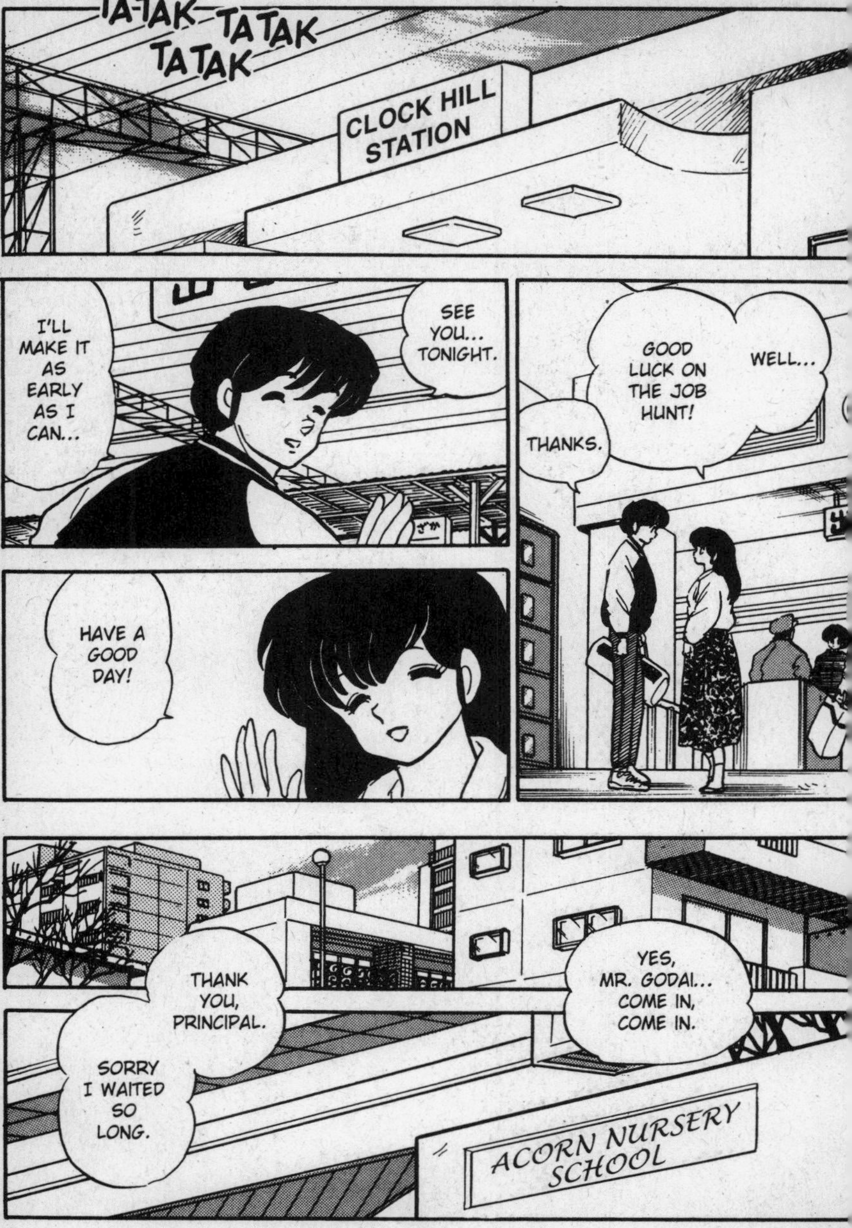
TA-TAK TATAK TATAK
CLOCK HILL STATION
WELL...
GOOD LUCK ON THE JOB HUNT!
THANKS.
SEE YOU... TONIGHT.
I'LL MAKE IT AS EARLY AS I CAN...
HAVE A GOOD DAY!
YES, MR. GODAI... COME IN, COME IN.
THANK YOU, PRINCIPAL.
SORRY I WAITED SO LONG.
ACORN NURSERY SCHOOL

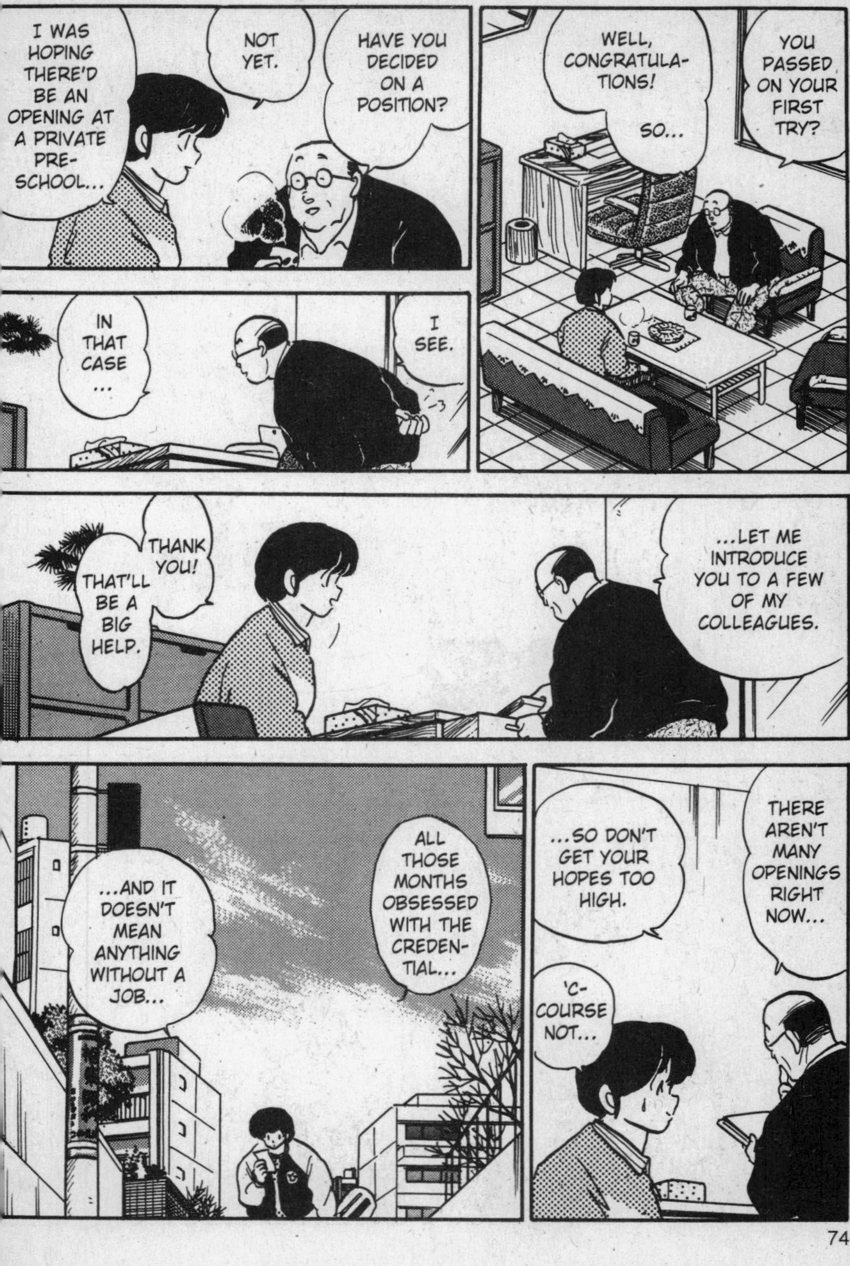
YOU PASSED ON YOUR FIRST TRY?
WELL, CONGRATULA-TIONS!
SO...
HAVE YOU DECIDED ON A POSITION?
NOT YET.
I WAS HOPING THERE'D BE AN OPENING AT A PRIVATE PRE-SCHOOL...
I SEE.
IN THAT CASE ...
...LET ME INTRODUCE YOU TO A FEW OF MY COLLEAGUES.
THANK YOU!
THAT'LL BE A BIG HELP.
THERE AREN'T MANY OPENINGS RIGHT NOW...
...SO DON'T GET YOUR HOPES TOO HIGH.
'C-COURSE NOT...
ALL THOSE MONTHS OBSESSED WITH THE CREDEN-TIAL...
...AND IT DOESN'T MEAN ANYTHING WITHOUT A JOB...

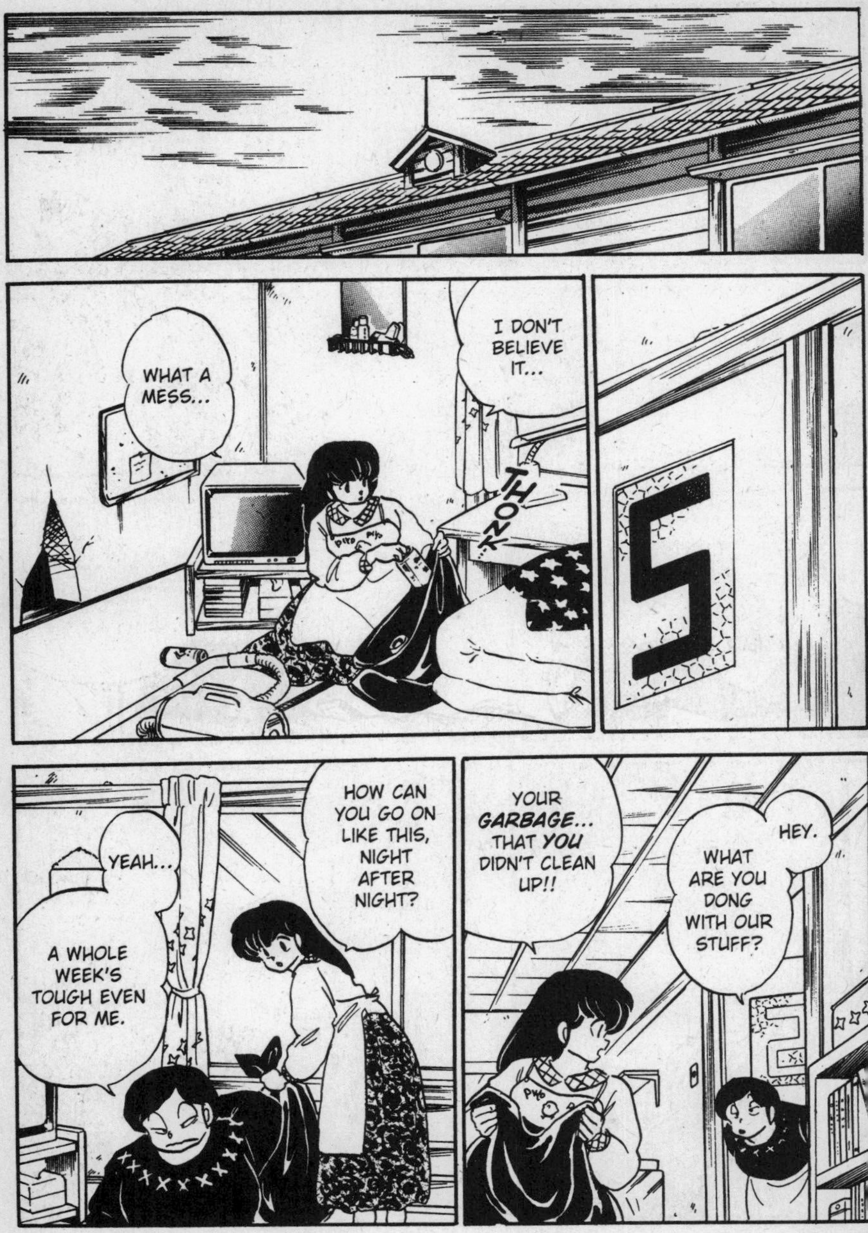
I DON'T BELIEVE IT...
WHAT A MESS...
THONK
HEY. WHAT ARE YOU DONG WITH OUR STUFF?
YOUR GARBAGE... THAT YOU DIDN'T CLEAN UP!!
HOW CAN YOU GO ON LIKE THIS, NIGHT AFTER NIGHT?
YEAH...
A WHOLE WEEK'S TOUGH EVEN FOR ME.

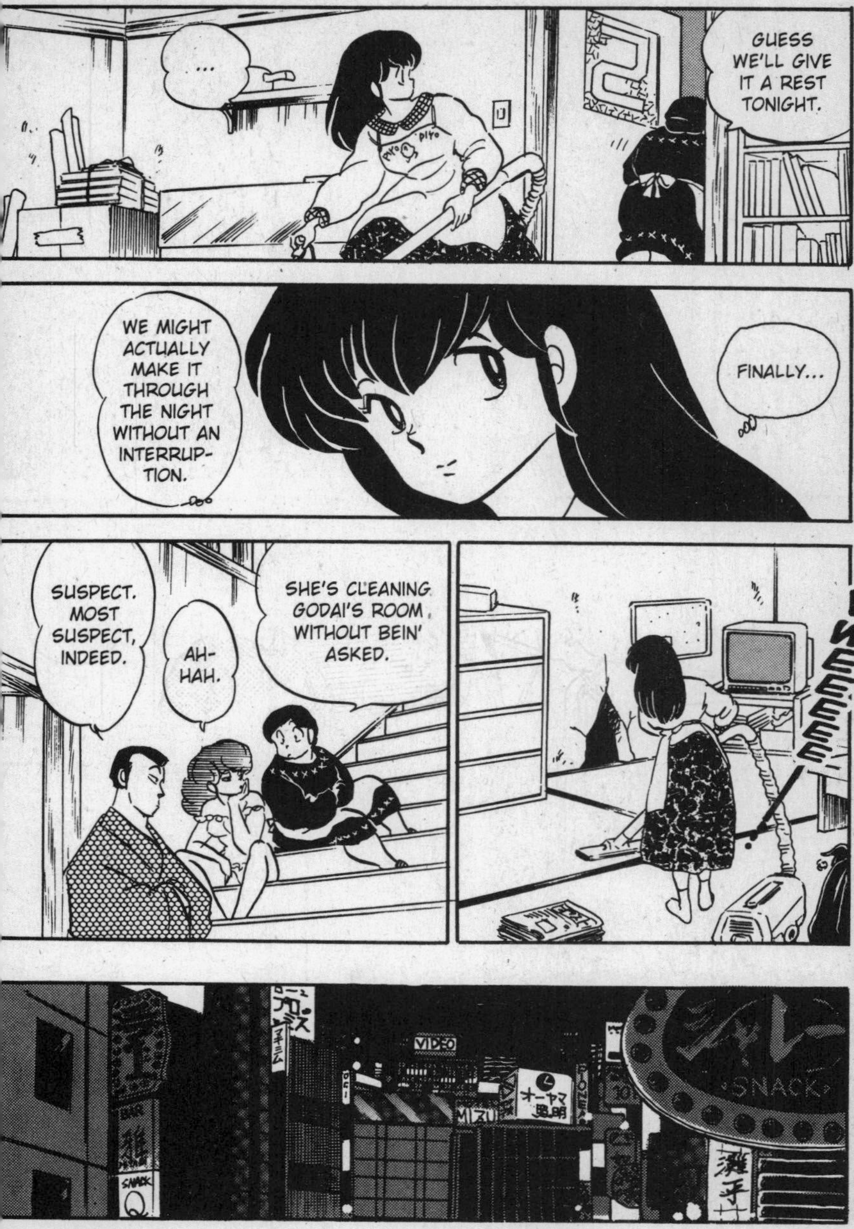
GUESS WE'LL GIVE IT A REST TONIGHT.
...
FINALLY...
WE MIGHT ACTUALLY MAKE IT THROUGH THE NIGHT WITHOUT AN INTERRUP-TION.
VWEEEEE
SHE'S CLEANING GODAI'S ROOM WITHOUT BEIN' ASKED.
AH-HAH.
SUSPECT. MOST SUSPECT, INDEED.
SNACK
VIDEO
BAR
SNACK

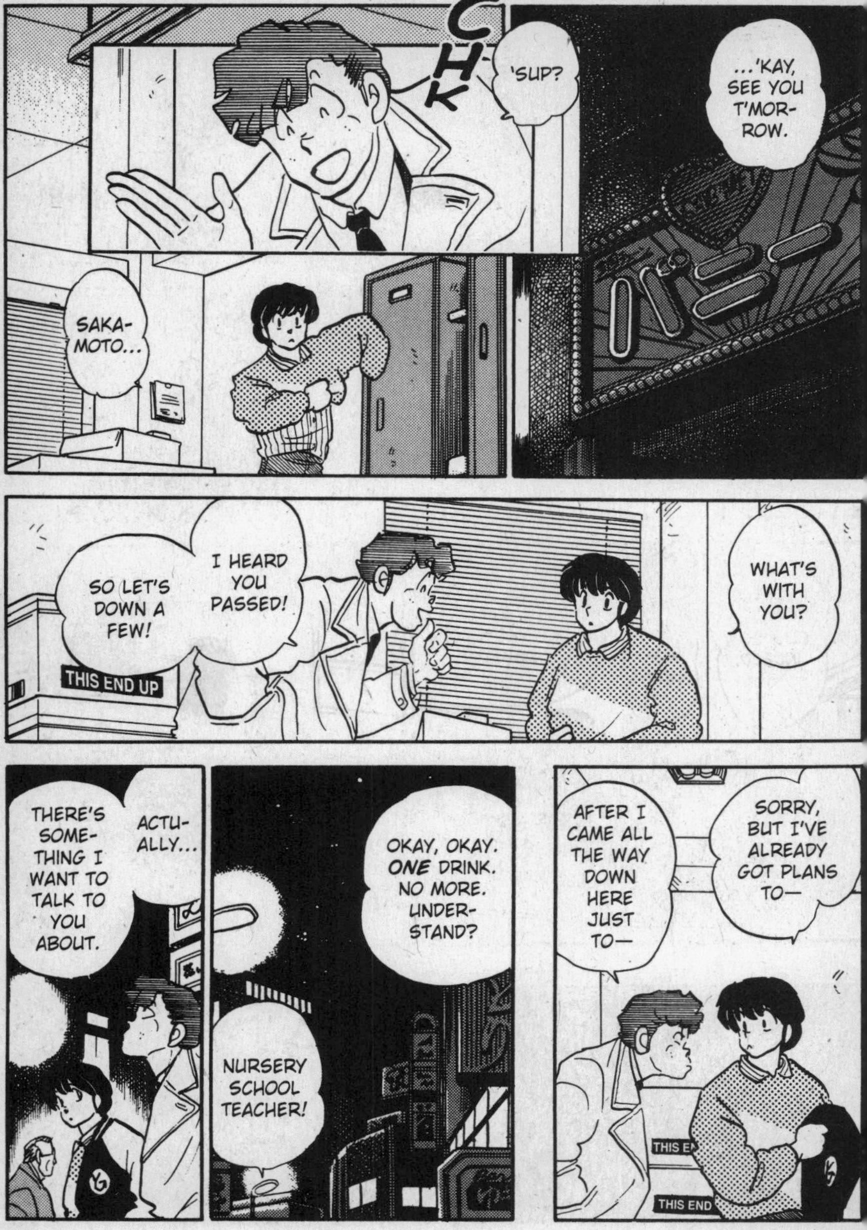
...'KAY, SEE YOU T'MOR-ROW.
CHK
'SUP?
SAKA-MOTO...
WHAT'S WITH YOU?
I HEARD YOU PASSED!
SO LET'S DOWN A FEW!
THIS END UP
SORRY, BUT I'VE ALREADY GOT PLANS TO—
AFTER I CAME ALL THE WAY DOWN HERE JUST TO—
THIS END
OKAY, OKAY. ONE DRINK. NO MORE. UNDER-STAND?
NURSERY SCHOOL TEACHER!
ACTU-ALLY...
THERE'S SOME-THING I WANT TO TALK TO YOU ABOUT.

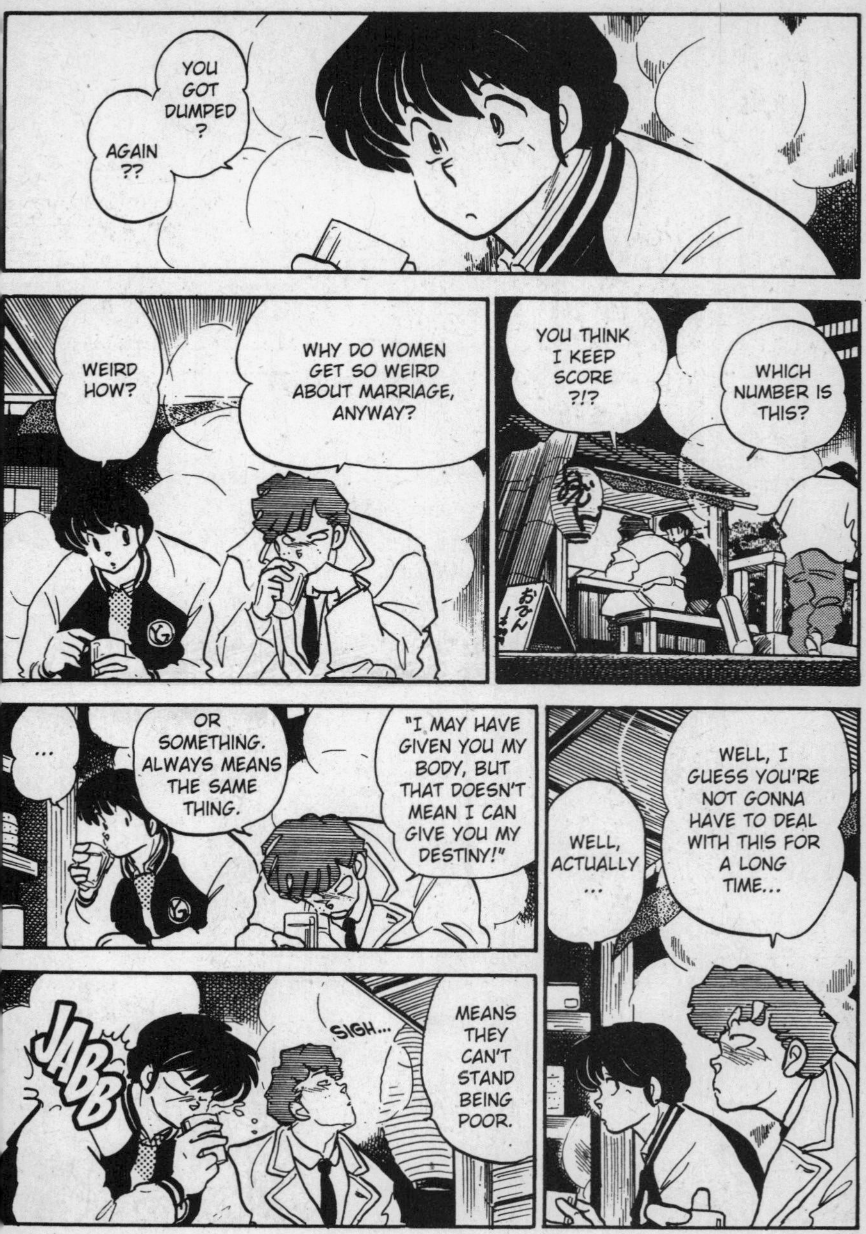

YOU GOT DUMPED?
AGAIN??
WHICH NUMBER IS THIS?
YOU THINK I KEEP SCORE?!?
WHY DO WOMEN GET SO WEIRD ABOUT MARRIAGE, ANYWAY?
WEIRD HOW?
WELL, I GUESS YOU'RE NOT GONNA HAVE TO DEAL WITH THIS FOR A LONG TIME...
WELL, ACTUALLY...
"I MAY HAVE GIVEN YOU MY BODY, BUT THAT DOESN'T MEAN I CAN GIVE YOU MY DESTINY!"
OR SOMETHING. ALWAYS MEANS THE SAME THING.
...
MEANS THEY CAN'T STAND BEING POOR.
SIGH...
JABB

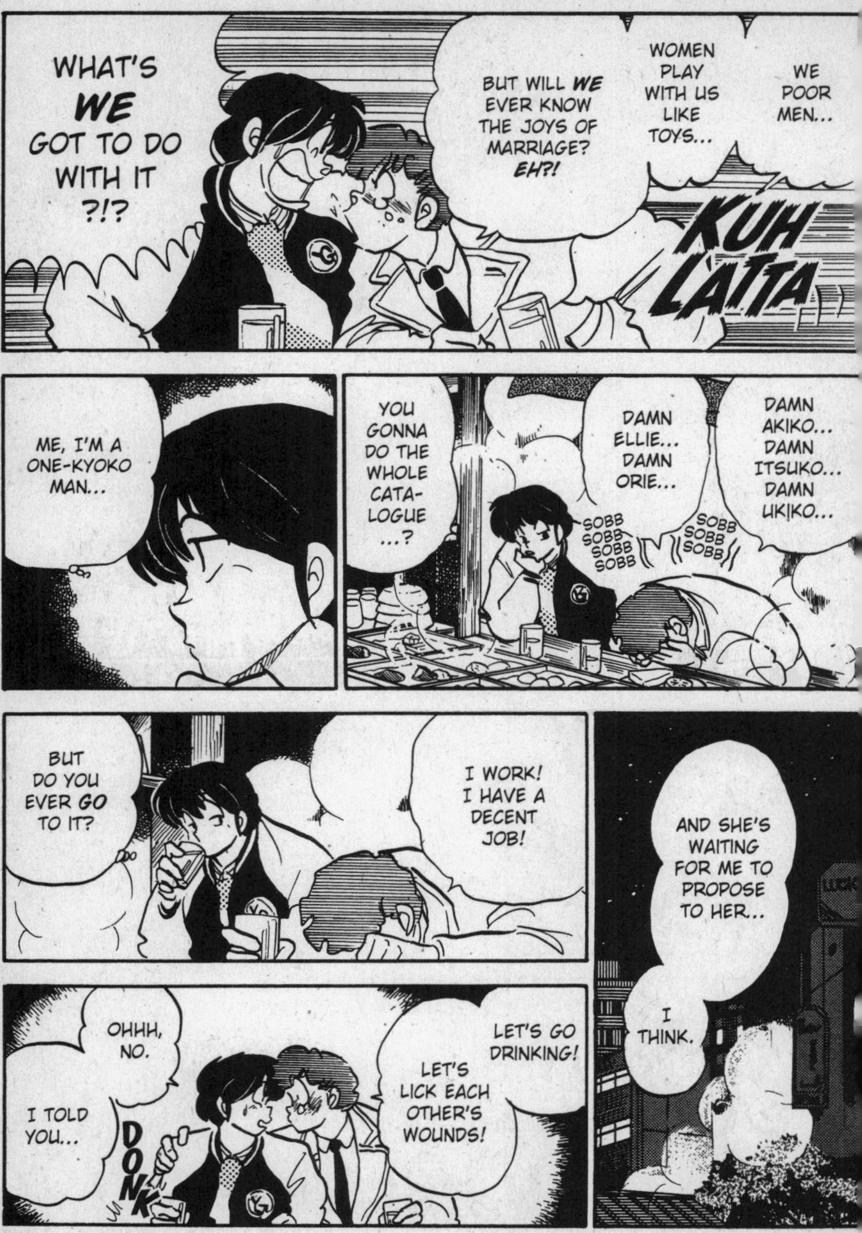
WE POOR MEN...
WOMEN PLAY WITH US LIKE TOYS...
BUT WILL **WE** EVER KNOW THE JOYS OF MARRIAGE? ***EH?!***
KUH LATTA
WHAT'S **WE** GOT TO DO WITH IT ?!?
DAMN AKIKO... DAMN ITSUKO... DAMN UKIKO...
SOBB SOBB SOBB
DAMN ELLIE... DAMN ORIE...
SOBB SOBB SOBB SOBB
YOU GONNA DO THE WHOLE CATA-LOGUE ...?
ME, I'M A ONE-KYOKO MAN...
AND SHE'S WAITING FOR ME TO PROPOSE TO HER...
I THINK.
I WORK! I HAVE A DECENT JOB!
BUT DO YOU EVER **GO** TO IT?
LET'S GO DRINKING!
LET'S LICK EACH OTHER'S WOUNDS!
OHHH, NO.
DONK
I TOLD YOU...

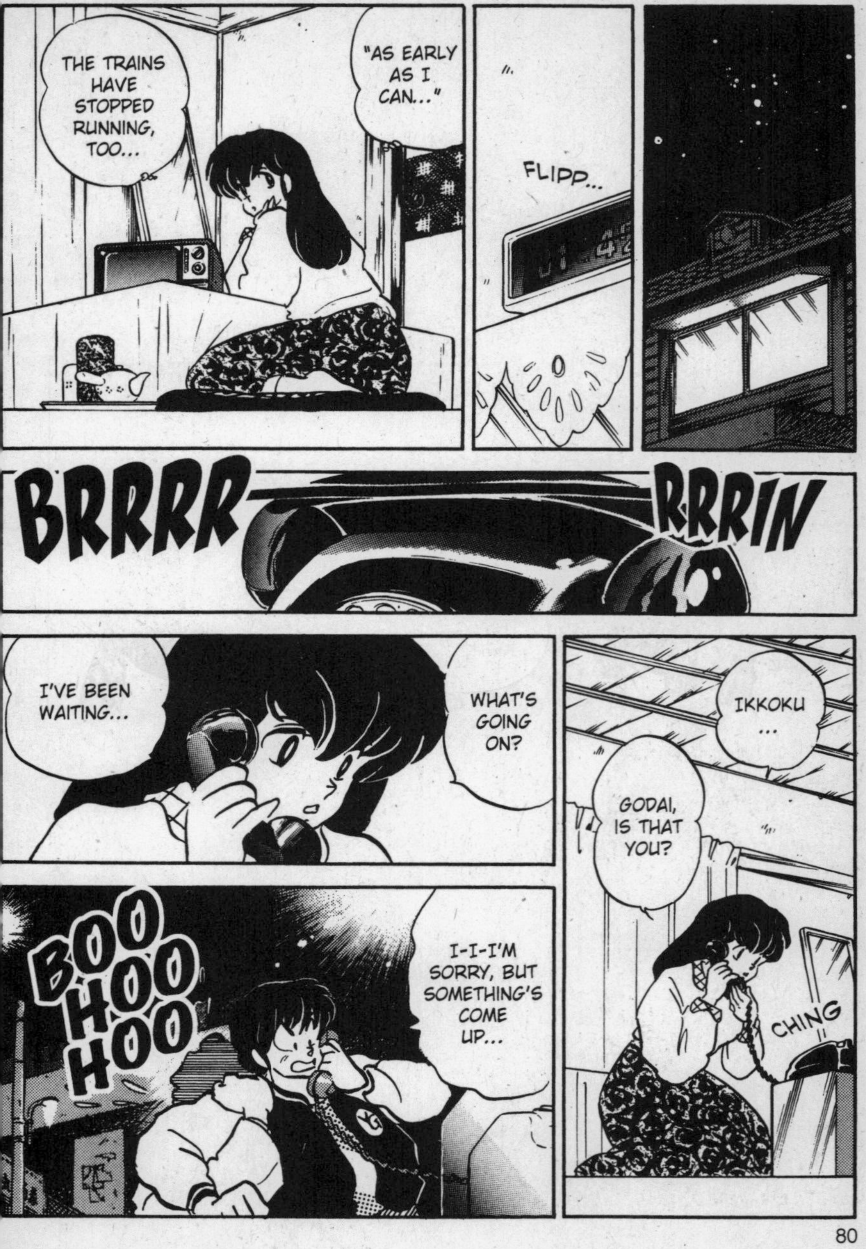
FLIPP...
"AS EARLY AS I CAN..."
THE TRAINS HAVE STOPPED RUNNING, TOO...
BRRRR
RRRIN
IKKOKU ...
GODAI, IS THAT YOU?
CHING
WHAT'S GOING ON?
I'VE BEEN WAITING...
I-I-I'M SORRY, BUT SOMETHING'S COME UP...
BOO HOO HOO

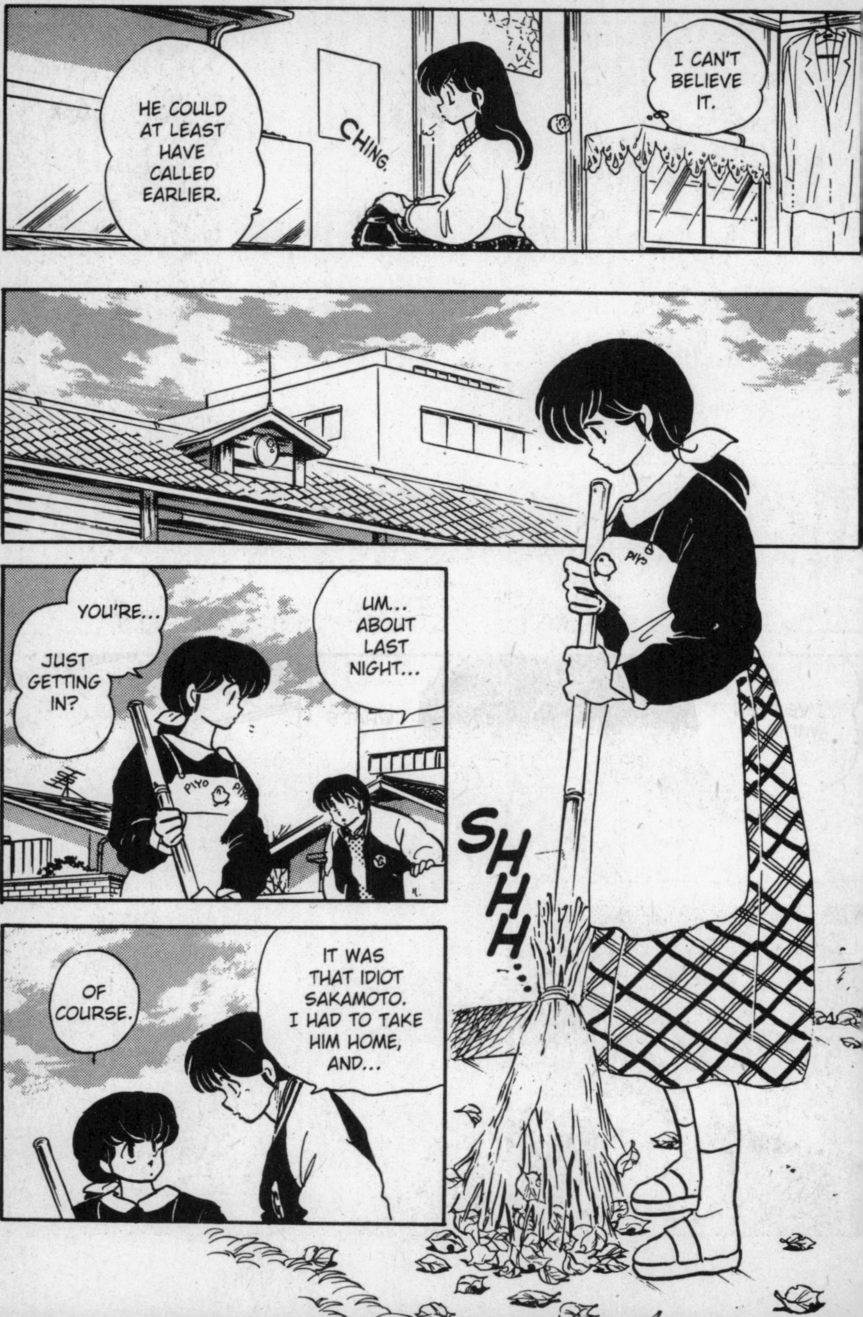
I CAN'T BELIEVE IT.
HE COULD AT LEAST HAVE CALLED EARLIER.
CHING.
SHHH...
UM... ABOUT LAST NIGHT...
YOU'RE...
JUST GETTING IN?
IT WAS THAT IDIOT SAKAMOTO. I HAD TO TAKE HIM HOME, AND...
OF COURSE.

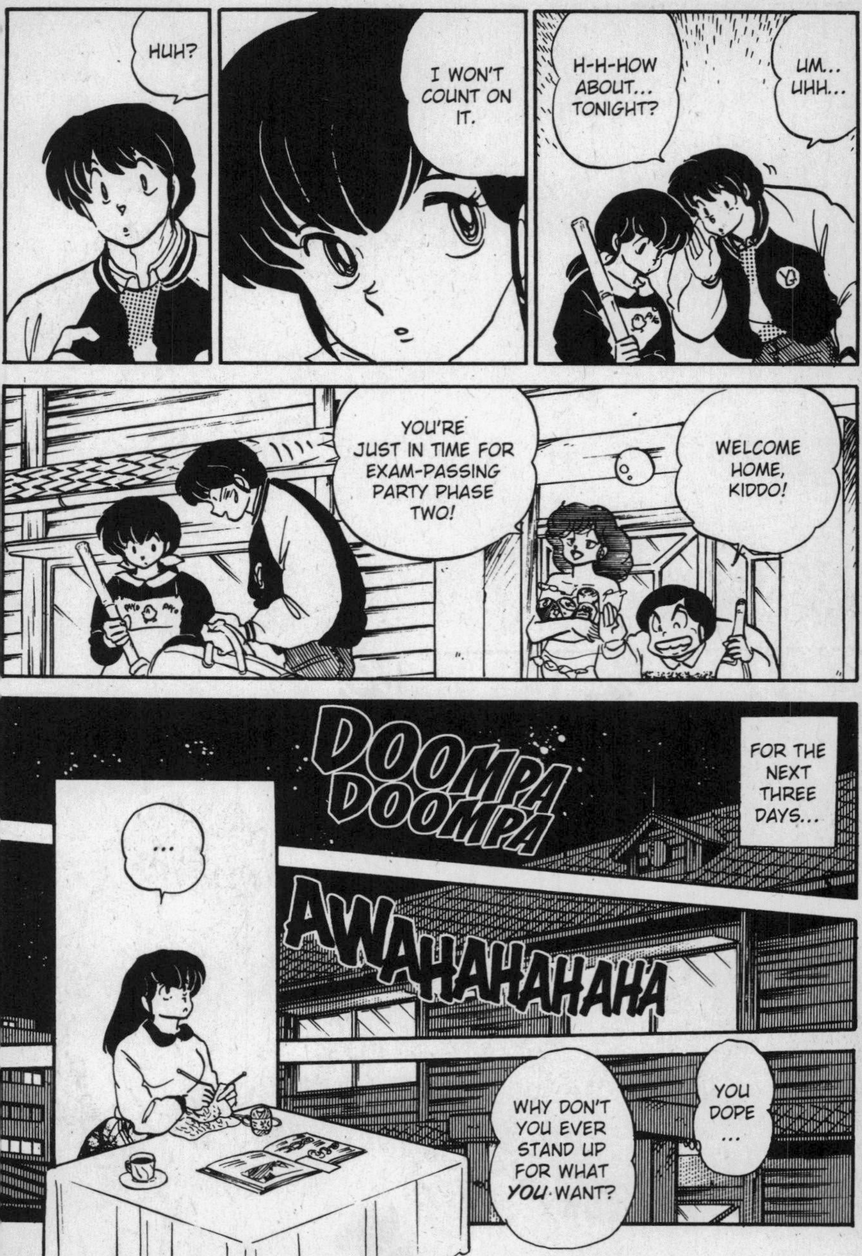
UM... UHH...
H-H-HOW ABOUT... TONIGHT?
I WON'T COUNT ON IT.
HUH?
WELCOME HOME, KIDDO!
YOU'RE JUST IN TIME FOR EXAM-PASSING PARTY PHASE TWO!
FOR THE NEXT THREE DAYS...
DOOMPA DOOMPA
AWAHAHAHAHA
YOU DOPE ...
WHY DON'T YOU EVER STAND UP FOR WHAT *YOU* WANT?
...

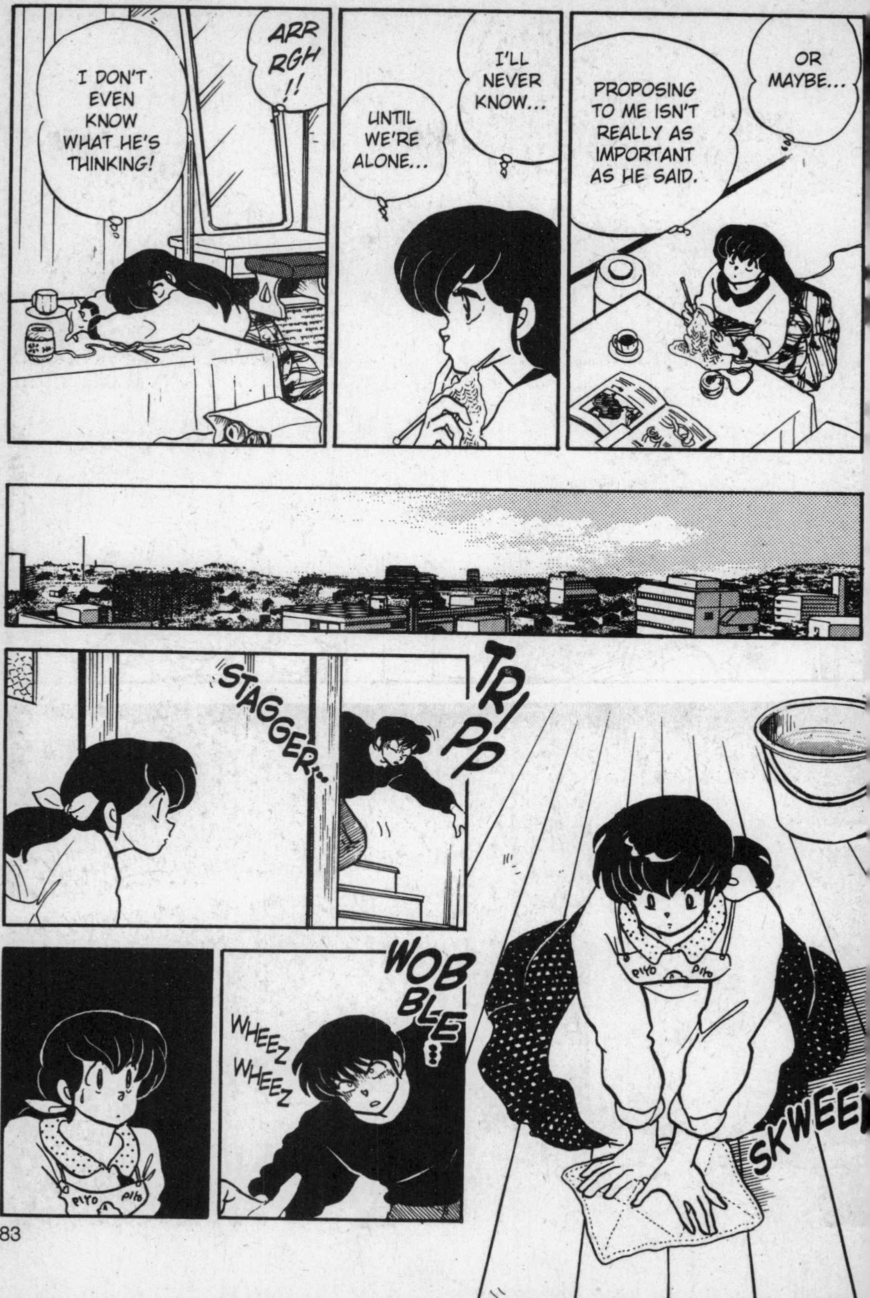

OR MAYBE...
PROPOSING TO ME ISN'T REALLY AS IMPORTANT AS HE SAID.
I'LL NEVER KNOW...
UNTIL WE'RE ALONE...
ARRRGH!!
I DON'T EVEN KNOW WHAT HE'S THINKING!
SKWEE
PIYO PIYO
TRIPP
STAGGER...
WOBBLE...
WHEEZ WHEEZ
PIYO PIYO

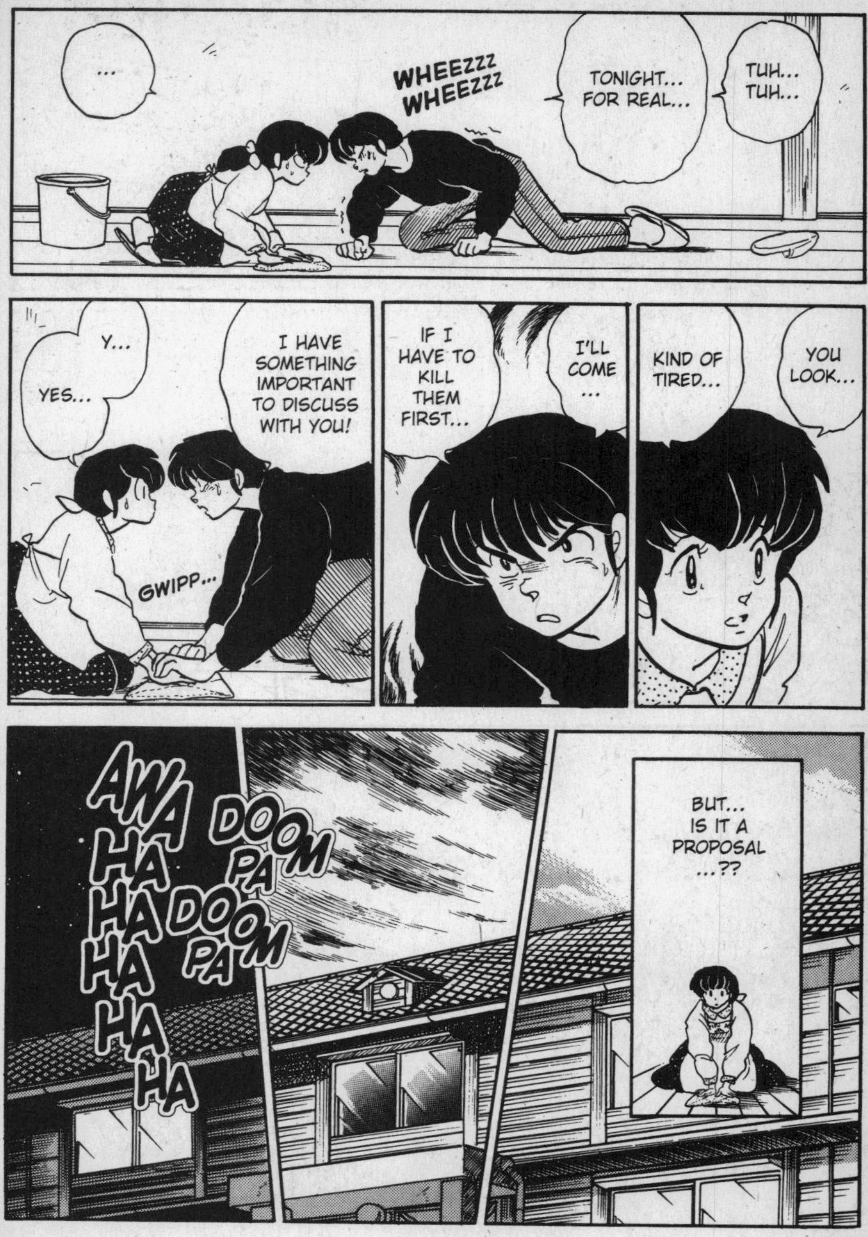
TUH... TUH...
TONIGHT... FOR REAL...
WHEEZZZ WHEEZZZ
...
YOU LOOK...
KIND OF TIRED...
I'LL COME ...
IF I HAVE TO KILL THEM FIRST...
I HAVE SOMETHING IMPORTANT TO DISCUSS WITH YOU!
Y... YES...
GWIPP...
BUT... IS IT A PROPOSAL ...??
DOOM PA DOOM PA
AWA HA HA HA HA HA HA

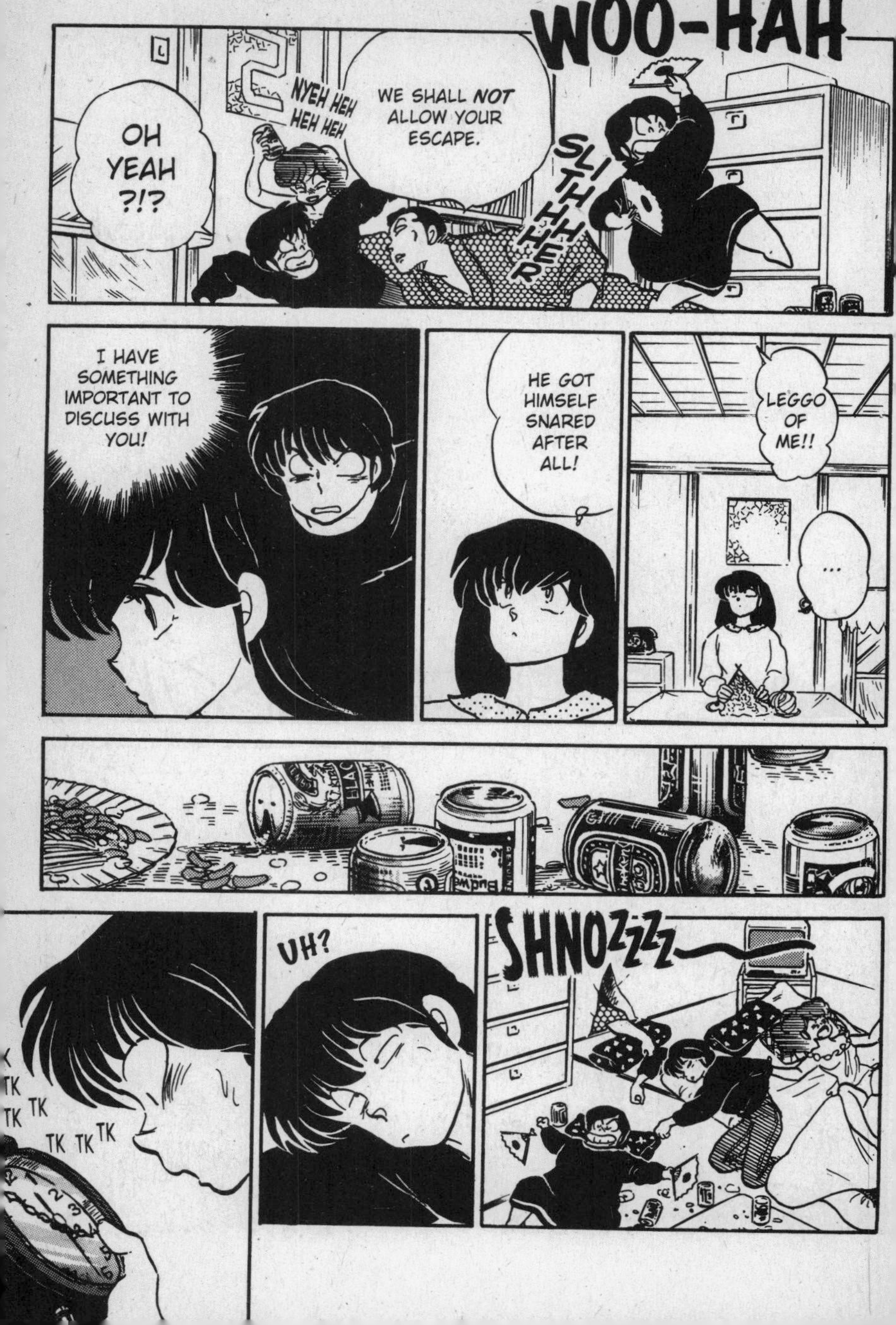
WOO-HAH
SLITHHHHER
WE SHALL NOT ALLOW YOUR ESCAPE.
NYEH HEH HEH HEH
OH YEAH ?!?
LEGGO OF ME!!
...
HE GOT HIMSELF SNARED AFTER ALL!
I HAVE SOMETHING IMPORTANT TO DISCUSS WITH YOU!
SHNOZZZZ
UH?
TK TK TK TK TK TK

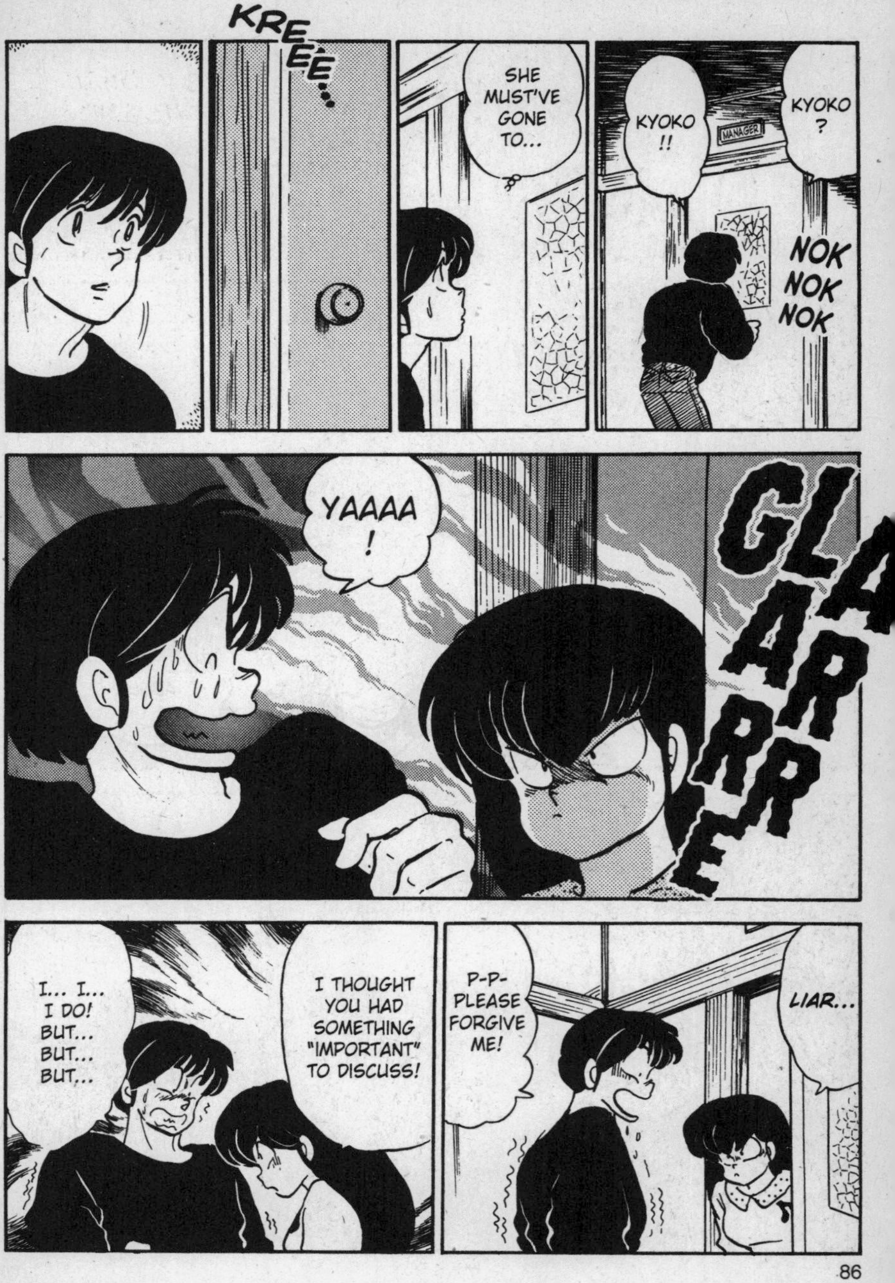
KYOKO ?
KYOKO !!
MANAGER
NOK NOK NOK
SHE MUST'VE GONE TO...
KREEEE...
GLAARRRE
YAAAA !
LIAR...
P-P-PLEASE FORGIVE ME!
I THOUGHT YOU HAD SOMETHING "IMPORTANT" TO DISCUSS!
I... I... I DO! BUT... BUT... BUT...

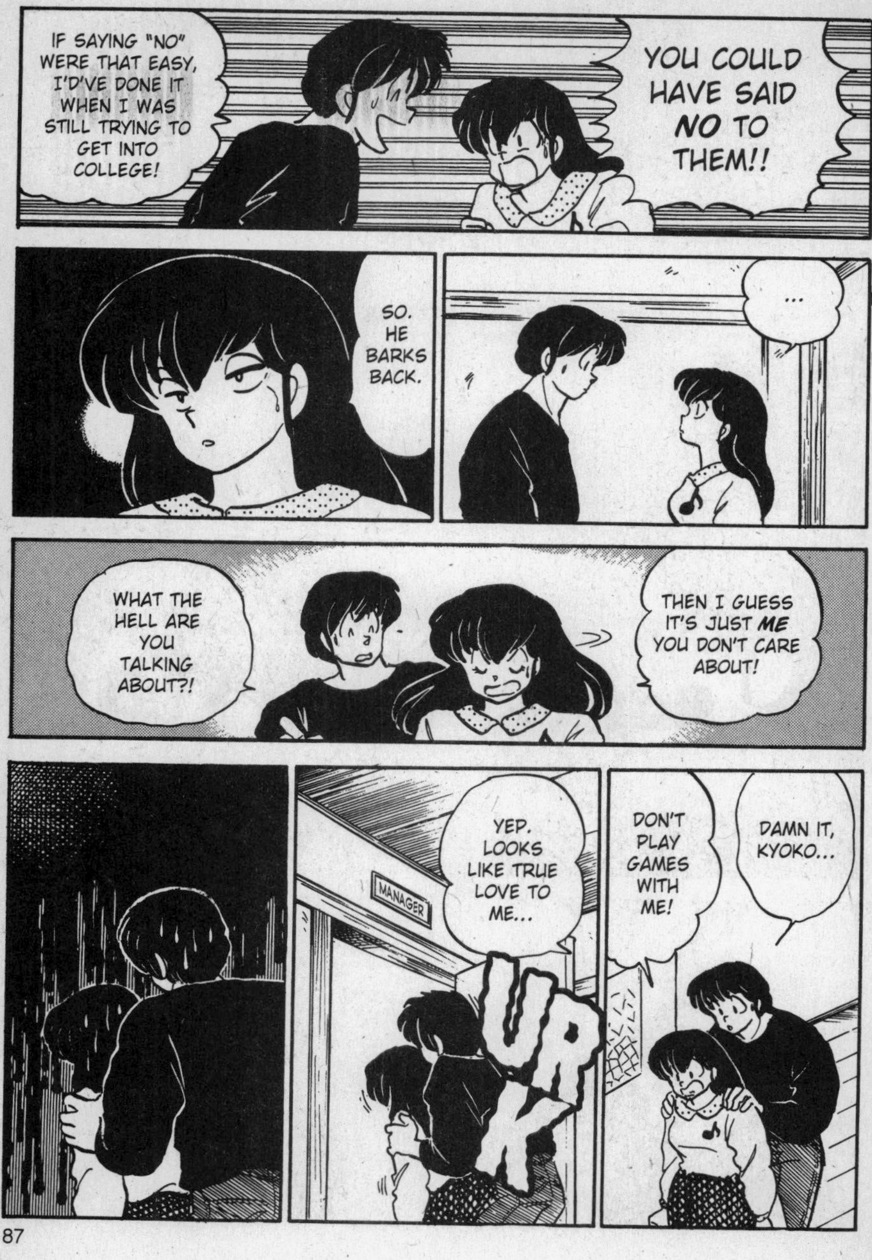
YOU COULD HAVE SAID *NO* TO THEM!!
IF SAYING "NO" WERE THAT EASY, I'D'VE DONE IT WHEN I WAS STILL TRYING TO GET INTO COLLEGE!
...
SO. HE BARKS BACK.
THEN I GUESS IT'S JUST *ME* YOU DON'T CARE ABOUT!
WHAT THE HELL ARE YOU TALKING ABOUT?!
DAMN IT, KYOKO...
DON'T PLAY GAMES WITH ME!
YEP. LOOKS LIKE TRUE LOVE TO ME...
MANAGER

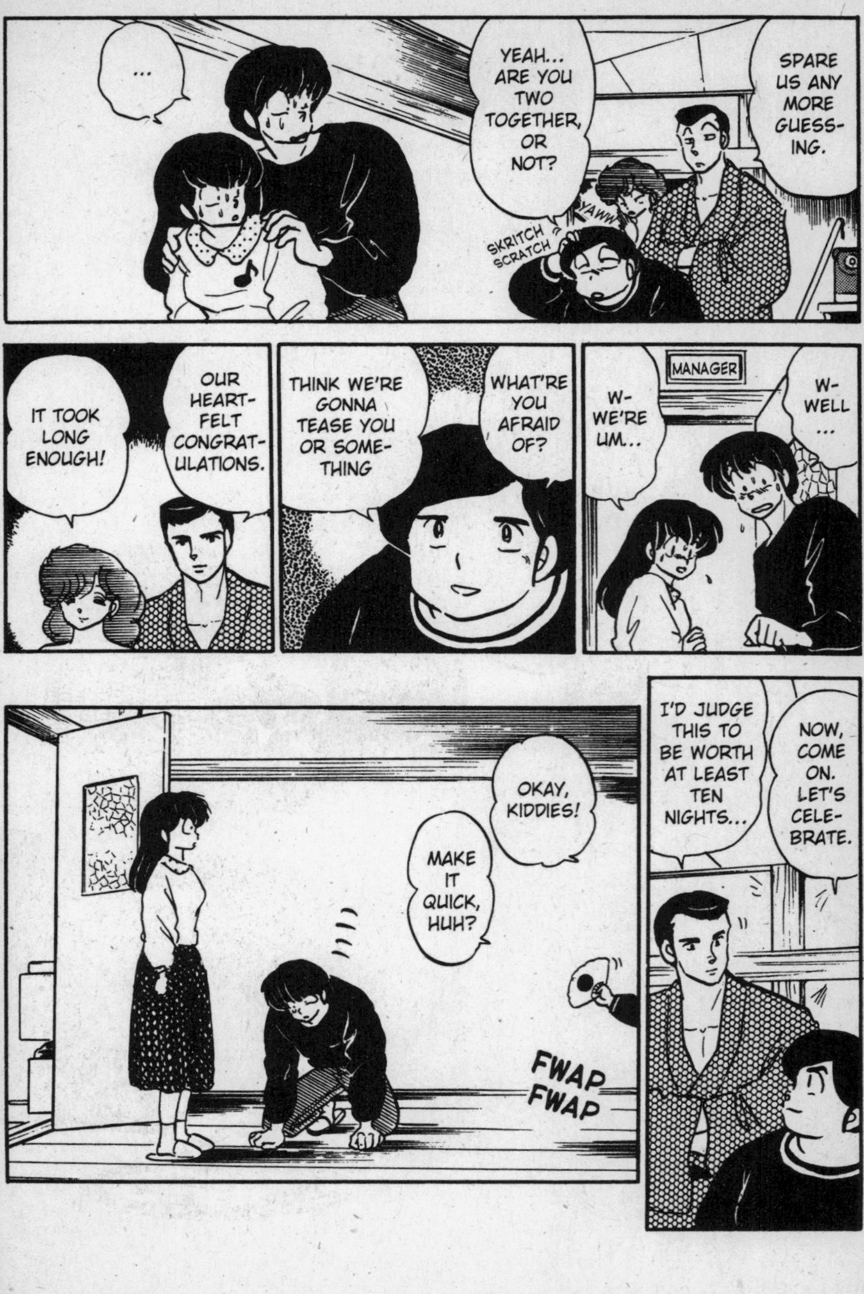
SPARE US ANY MORE GUESS-ING.
YEAH... ARE YOU TWO TOGETHER, OR NOT?
SKRITCH SCRATCH
...
W-WELL ...
MANAGER
W-WE'RE UM...
WHAT'RE YOU AFRAID OF?
THINK WE'RE GONNA TEASE YOU OR SOME-THING
OUR HEART-FELT CONGRAT-ULATIONS.
IT TOOK LONG ENOUGH!
NOW, COME ON. LET'S CELE-BRATE.
I'D JUDGE THIS TO BE WORTH AT LEAST TEN NIGHTS...
OKAY, KIDDIES!
MAKE IT QUICK, HUH?
FWAP FWAP

PART FIVE
SYMPATHY

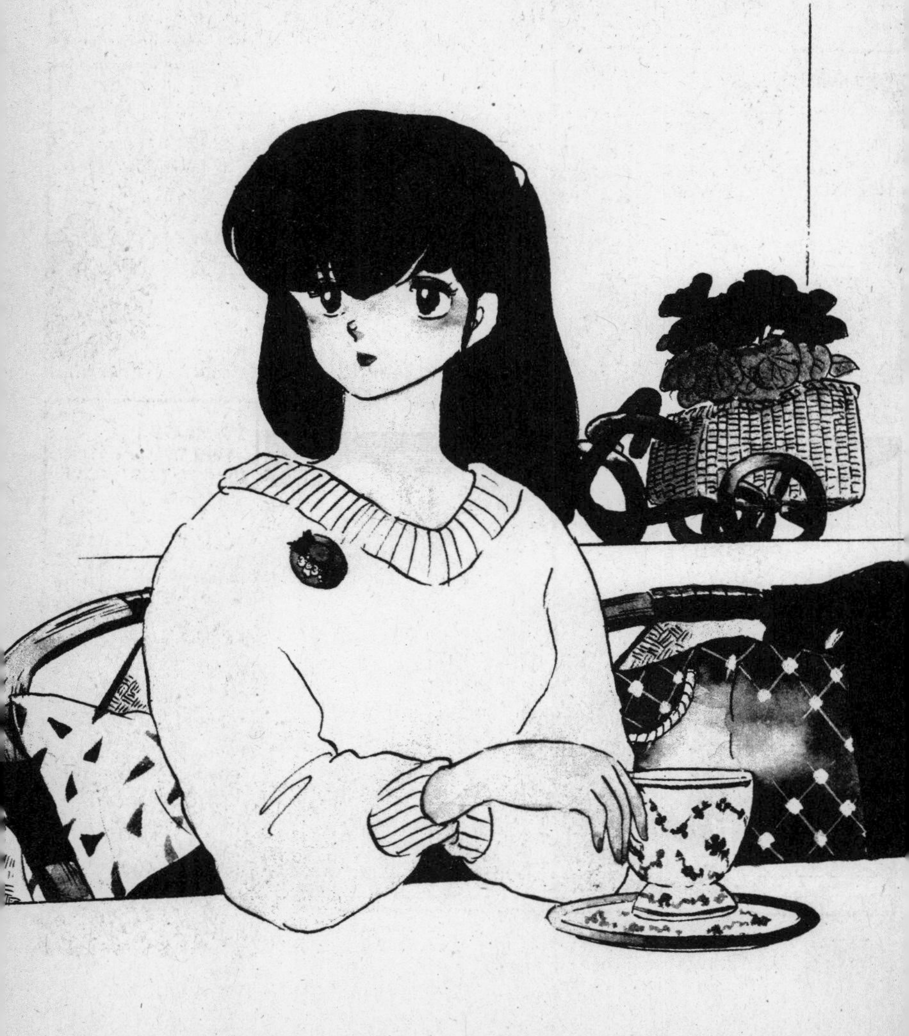

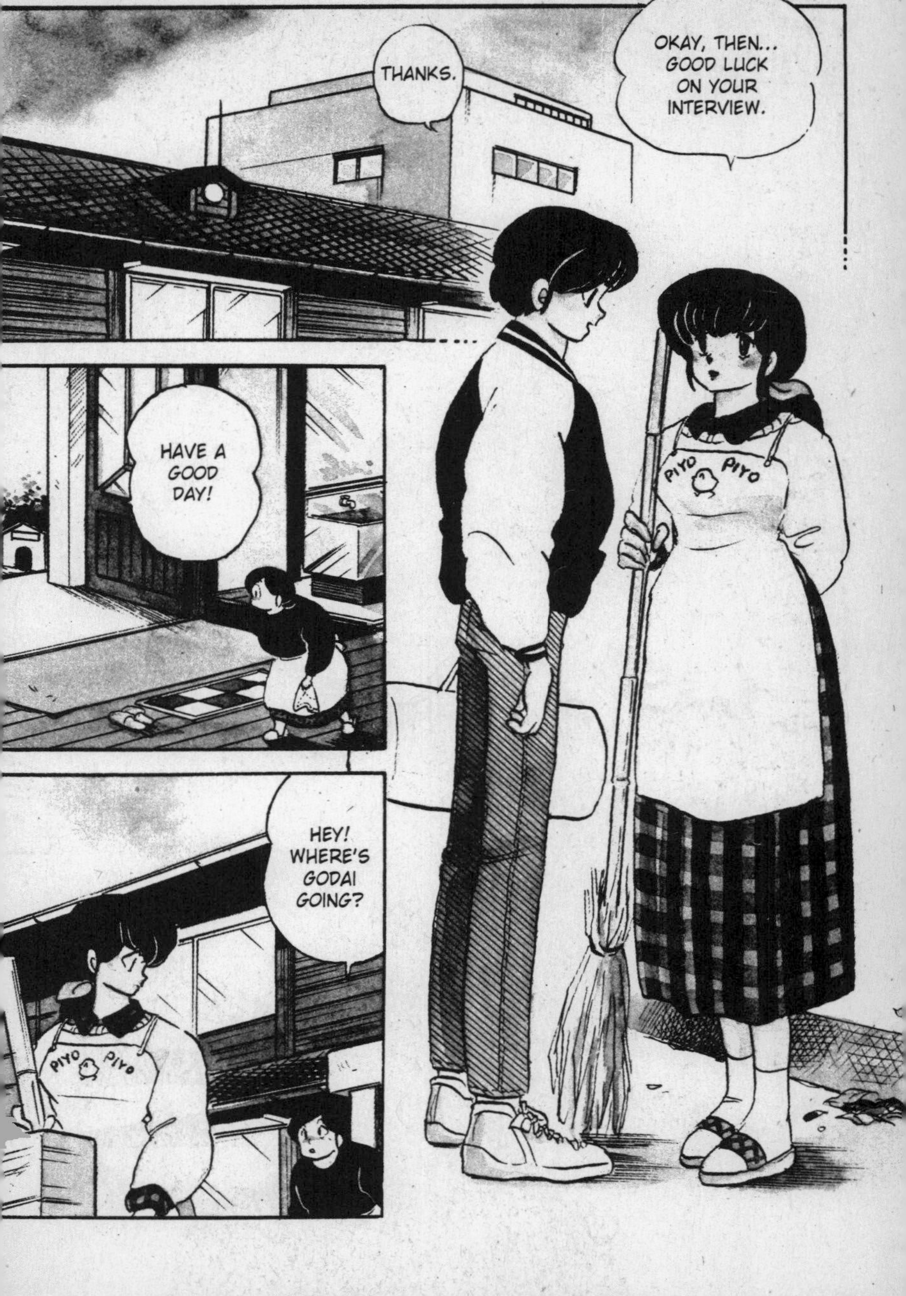
OKAY, THEN... GOOD LUCK ON YOUR INTERVIEW.
THANKS.
HAVE A GOOD DAY!
HEY! WHERE'S GODAI GOING?

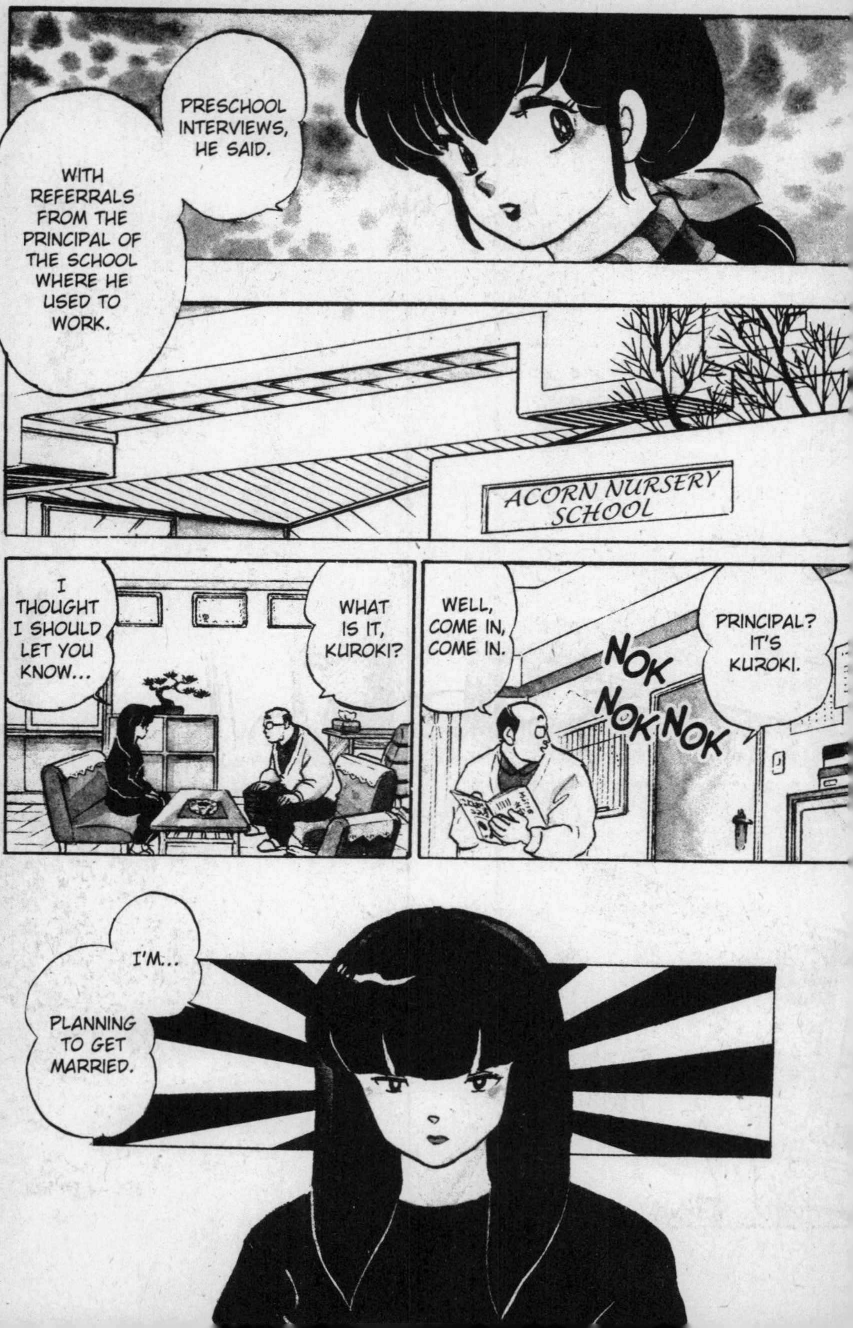
PRESCHOOL INTERVIEWS, HE SAID.
WITH REFERRALS FROM THE PRINCIPAL OF THE SCHOOL WHERE HE USED TO WORK.
ACORN NURSERY SCHOOL
PRINCIPAL? IT'S KUROKI.
NOK NOK NOK
WELL, COME IN, COME IN.
WHAT IS IT, KUROKI?
I THOUGHT I SHOULD LET YOU KNOW...
I'M...
PLANNING TO GET MARRIED.

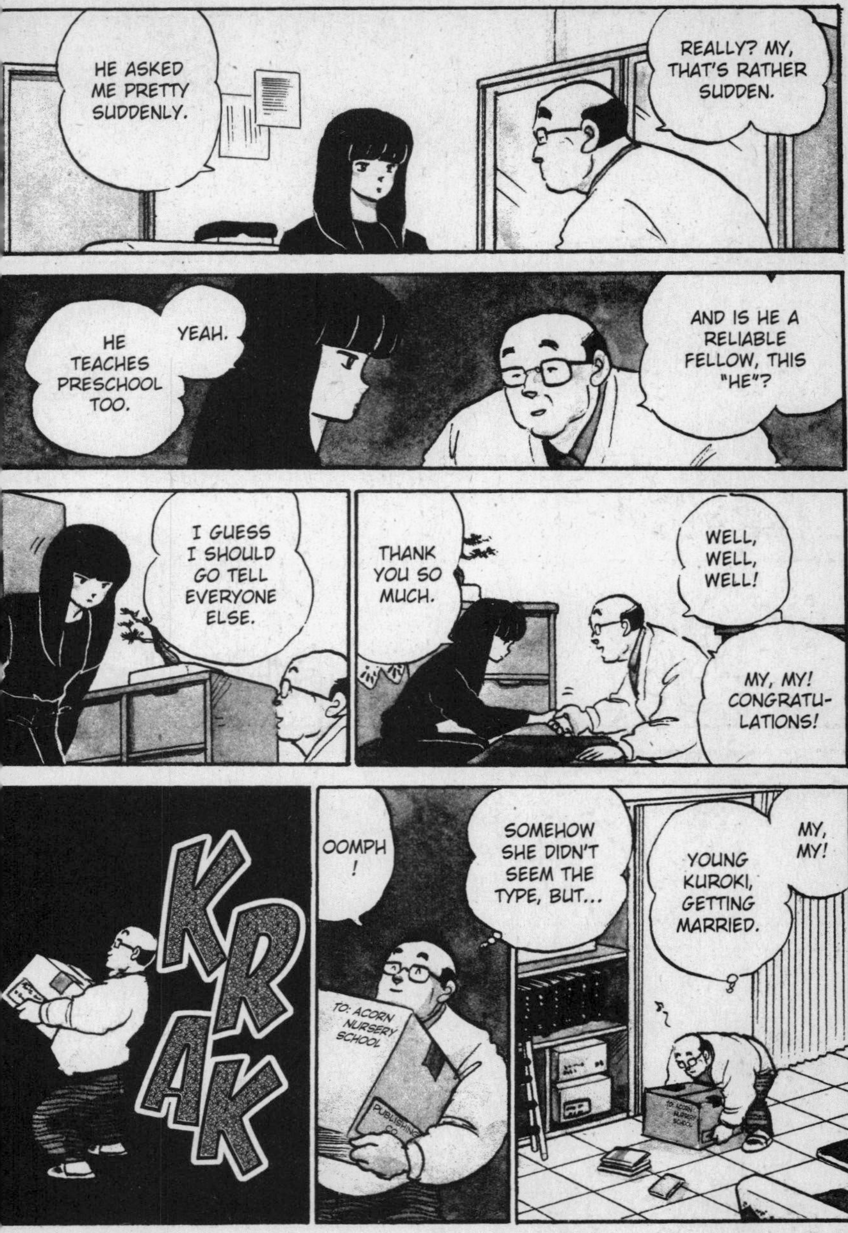
REALLY? MY, THAT'S RATHER SUDDEN.
HE ASKED ME PRETTY SUDDENLY.
AND IS HE A RELIABLE FELLOW, THIS "HE"?
YEAH.
HE TEACHES PRESCHOOL TOO.
WELL, WELL, WELL!
MY, MY! CONGRATULATIONS!
THANK YOU SO MUCH.
I GUESS I SHOULD GO TELL EVERYONE ELSE.
MY, MY!
YOUNG KUROKI, GETTING MARRIED.
SOMEHOW SHE DIDN'T SEEM THE TYPE, BUT...
OOMPH!
TO: ACORN NURSERY SCHOOL
PUBLISHING CO.
KRAK

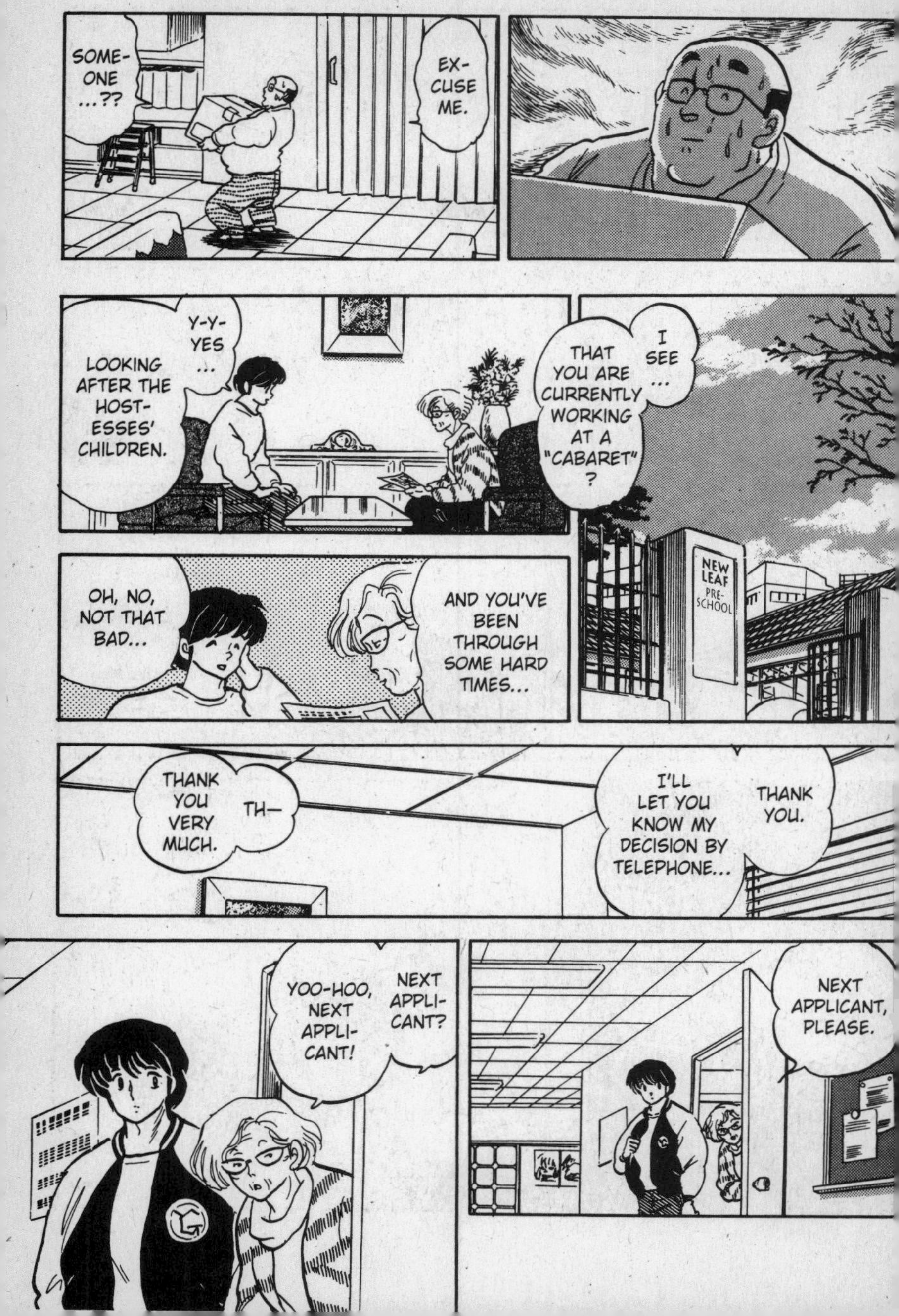

EX-CUSE ME.
SOME-ONE ...??
I SEE ...
THAT YOU ARE CURRENTLY WORKING AT A "CABARET"?
NEW LEAF PRE-SCHOOL
Y-Y-YES ...
LOOKING AFTER THE HOST-ESSES' CHILDREN.
AND YOU'VE BEEN THROUGH SOME HARD TIMES...
OH, NO, NOT THAT BAD...
THANK YOU.
I'LL LET YOU KNOW MY DECISION BY TELEPHONE...
TH—
THANK YOU VERY MUCH.
NEXT APPLICANT, PLEASE.
NEXT APPLI-CANT?
YOO-HOO, NEXT APPLI-CANT!

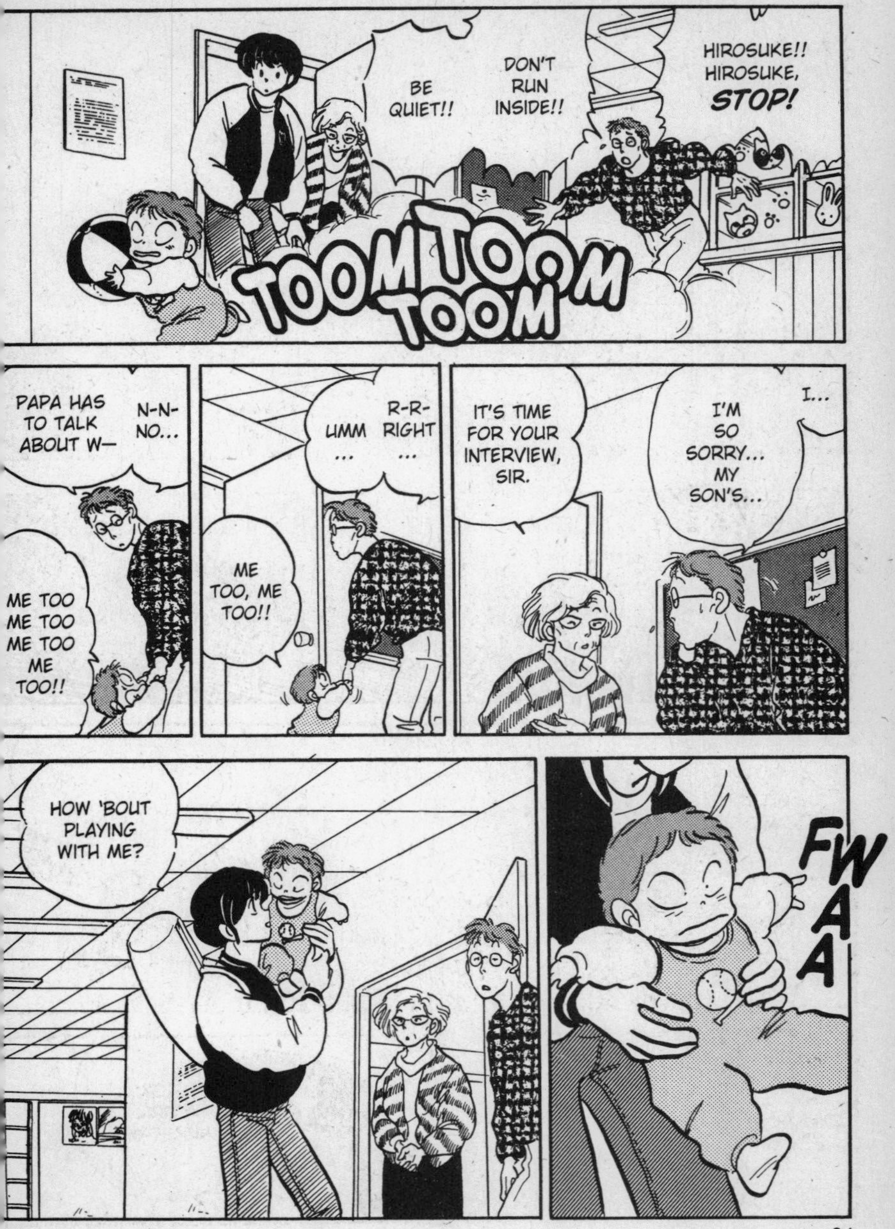
HIROSUKE!! HIROSUKE, STOP!
DON'T RUN INSIDE!!
BE QUIET!!
TOOM TOOM TOOM
I...
I'M SO SORRY... MY SON'S...
IT'S TIME FOR YOUR INTERVIEW, SIR.
R-R-RIGHT...
UMM...
ME TOO, ME TOO!!
N-N-NO...
PAPA HAS TO TALK ABOUT W—
ME TOO ME TOO ME TOO ME TOO!!
FWAA
HOW 'BOUT PLAYING WITH ME?

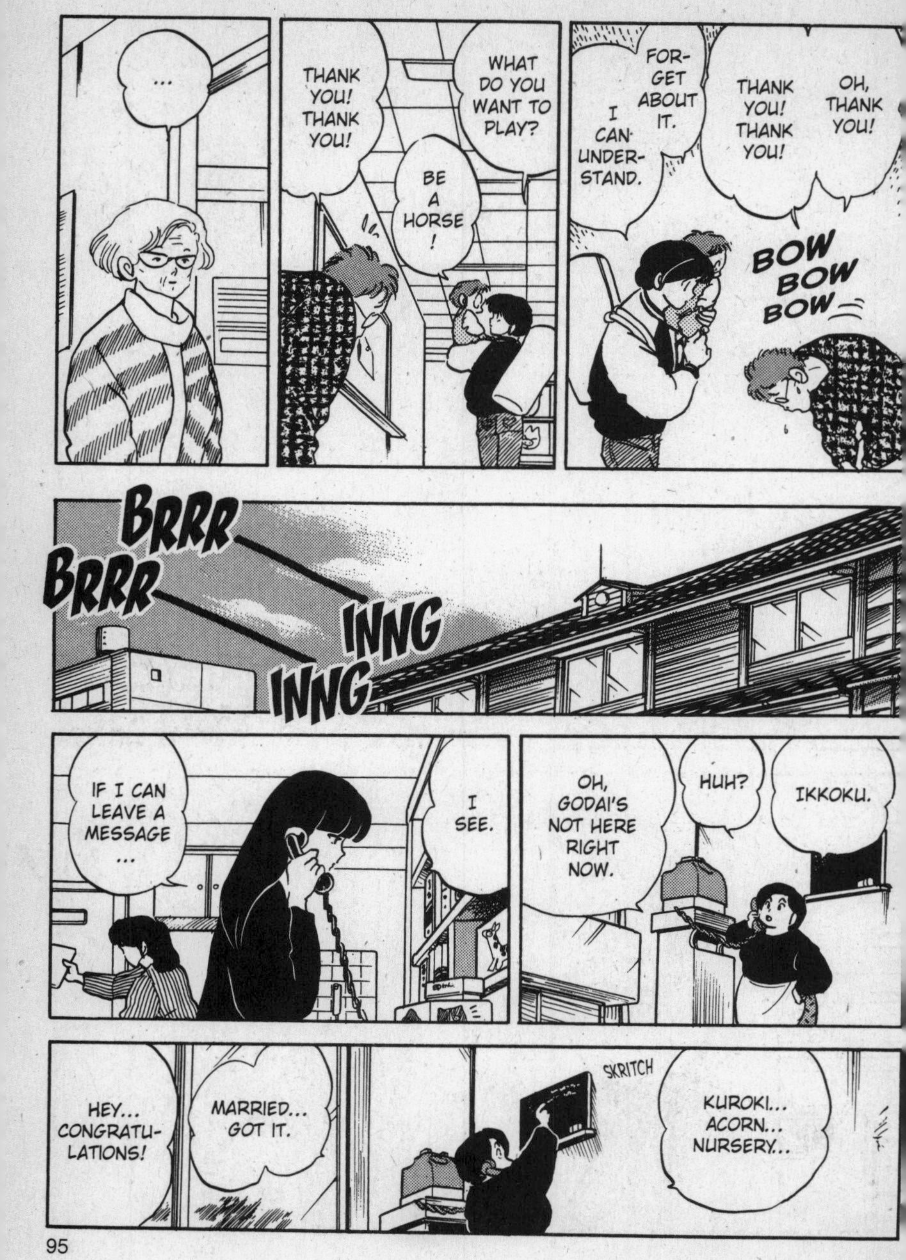
OH, THANK YOU!
THANK YOU! THANK YOU!
FOR-GET ABOUT IT.
I CAN UNDER-STAND.
BOW BOW BOW
WHAT DO YOU WANT TO PLAY?
THANK YOU! THANK YOU!
BE A HORSE!
...
BRRR BRRR
INNG INNG
IKKOKU.
HUH?
OH, GODAI'S NOT HERE RIGHT NOW.
I SEE.
IF I CAN LEAVE A MESSAGE ...
KUROKI... ACORN... NURSERY...
SKRITCH
MARRIED... GOT IT.
HEY... CONGRATULATIONS!

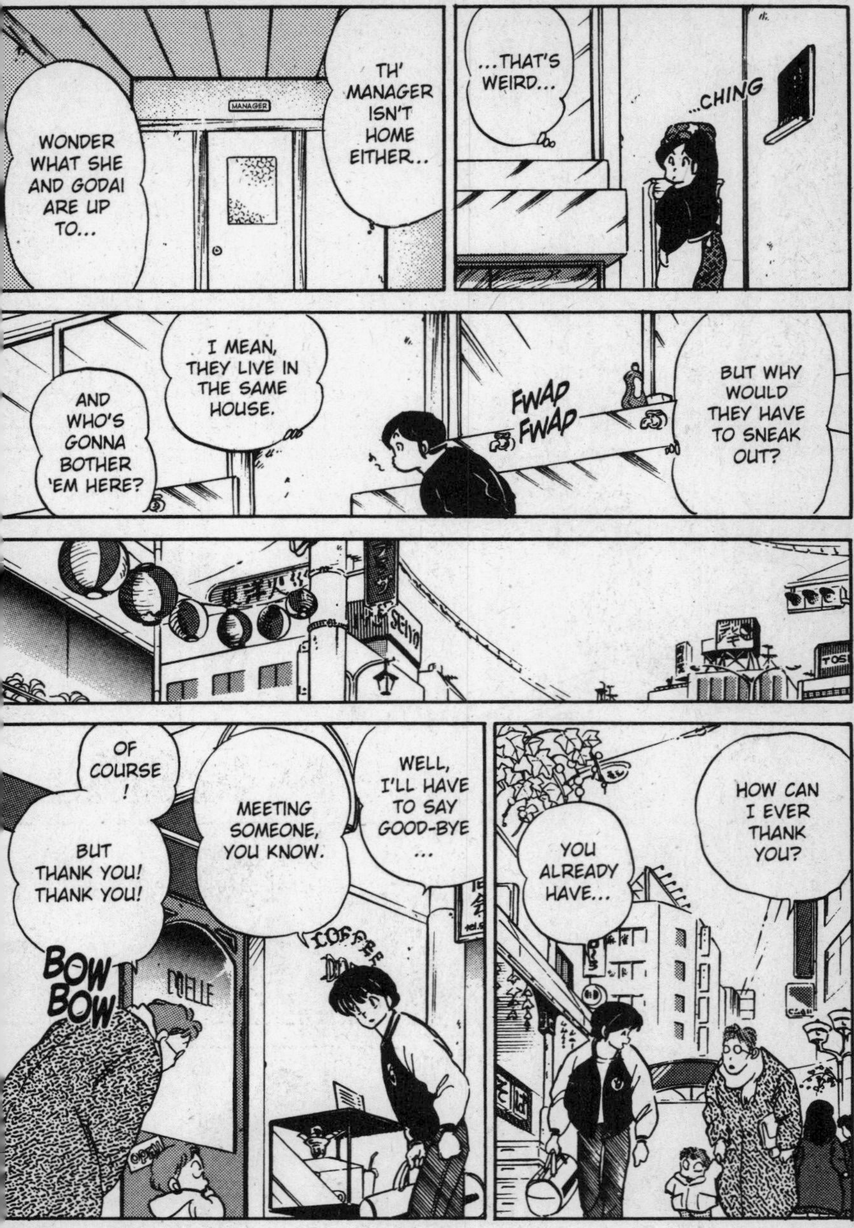
...CHING
...THAT'S WEIRD...
TH' MANAGER ISN'T HOME EITHER...
WONDER WHAT SHE AND GODAI ARE UP TO...
FWAP FWAP
BUT WHY WOULD THEY HAVE TO SNEAK OUT?
I MEAN, THEY LIVE IN THE SAME HOUSE.
AND WHO'S GONNA BOTHER 'EM HERE?
HOW CAN I EVER THANK YOU?
YOU ALREADY HAVE...
WELL, I'LL HAVE TO SAY GOOD-BYE ...
MEETING SOMEONE, YOU KNOW.
OF COURSE!
BUT THANK YOU! THANK YOU!
BOW BOW

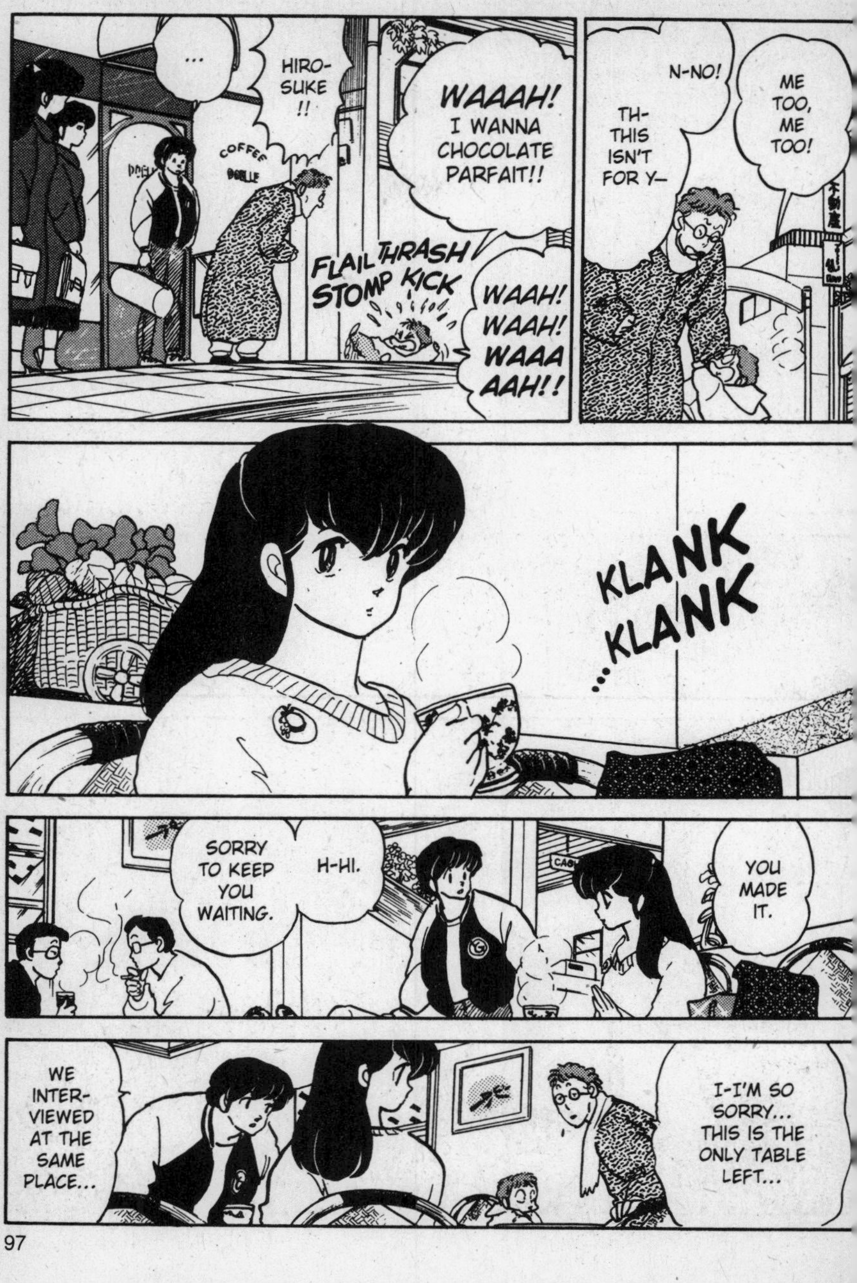
...
HIRO-
SUKE
!!
COFFEE
WAAAH!
I WANNA
CHOCOLATE
PARFAIT!!
FLAIL THRASH
STOMP KICK
WAAH!
WAAH!
WAAA
AAH!!
N-NO!
TH-
THIS
ISN'T
FOR Y—
ME
TOO,
ME
TOO!
KLANK
KLANK
...
SORRY
TO KEEP
YOU
WAITING.
H-HI.
YOU
MADE
IT.
WE
INTER-
VIEWED
AT THE
SAME
PLACE...
I-I'M SO
SORRY...
THIS IS THE
ONLY TABLE
LEFT...

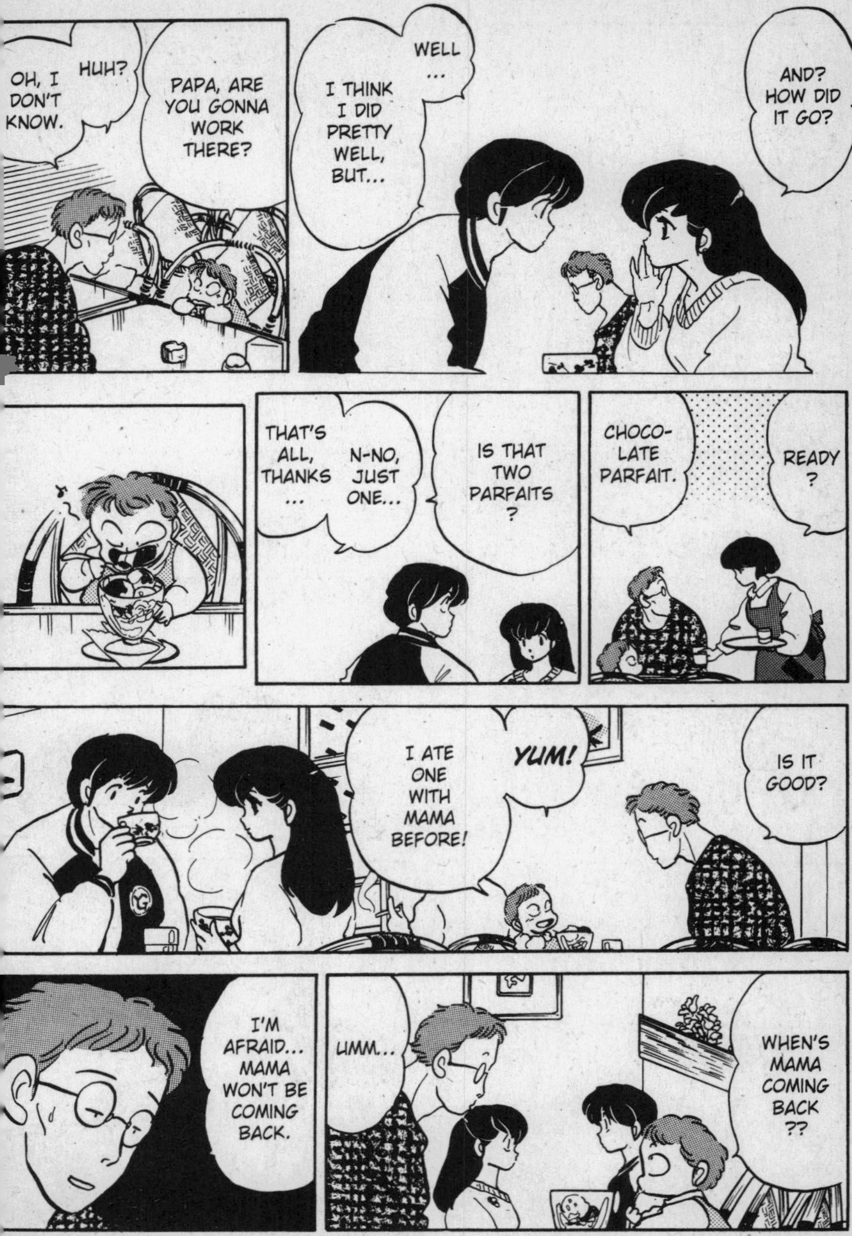
AND? HOW DID IT GO?
WELL ...
I THINK I DID PRETTY WELL, BUT...
PAPA, ARE YOU GONNA WORK THERE?
HUH?
OH, I DON'T KNOW.
READY?
CHOCO-LATE PARFAIT.
IS THAT TWO PARFAITS?
N-NO, JUST ONE...
THAT'S ALL, THANKS ...
IS IT GOOD?
YUM!
I ATE ONE WITH MAMA BEFORE!
WHEN'S MAMA COMING BACK??
UMM...
I'M AFRAID... MAMA WON'T BE COMING BACK.

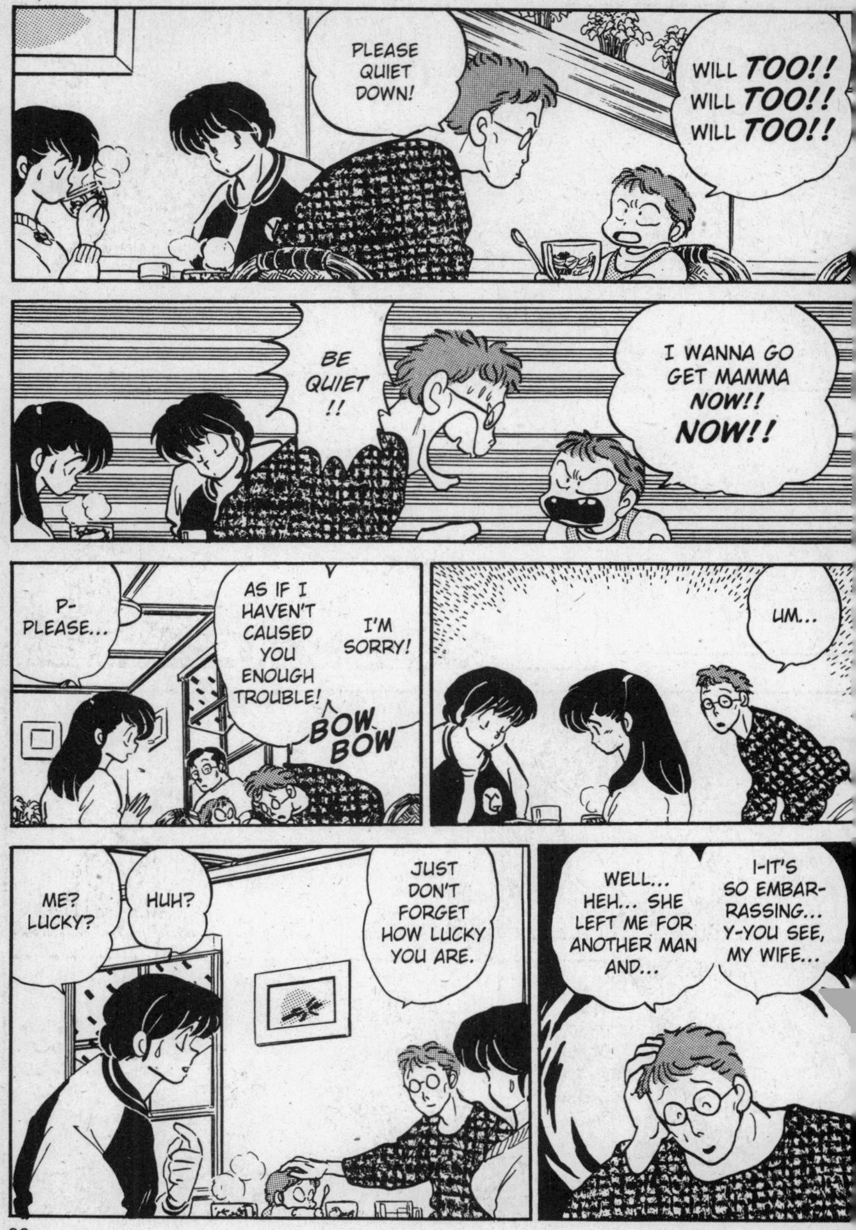
WILL TOO!! WILL TOO!! WILL TOO!!
PLEASE QUIET DOWN!
I WANNA GO GET MAMMA NOW!! NOW!!
BE QUIET !!
UM...
I'M SORRY!
AS IF I HAVEN'T CAUSED YOU ENOUGH TROUBLE!
BOW BOW
P-PLEASE...
I-IT'S SO EMBARRASSING... Y-YOU SEE, MY WIFE...
WELL... HEH... SHE LEFT ME FOR ANOTHER MAN AND...
JUST DON'T FORGET HOW LUCKY YOU ARE.
HUH?
ME? LUCKY?

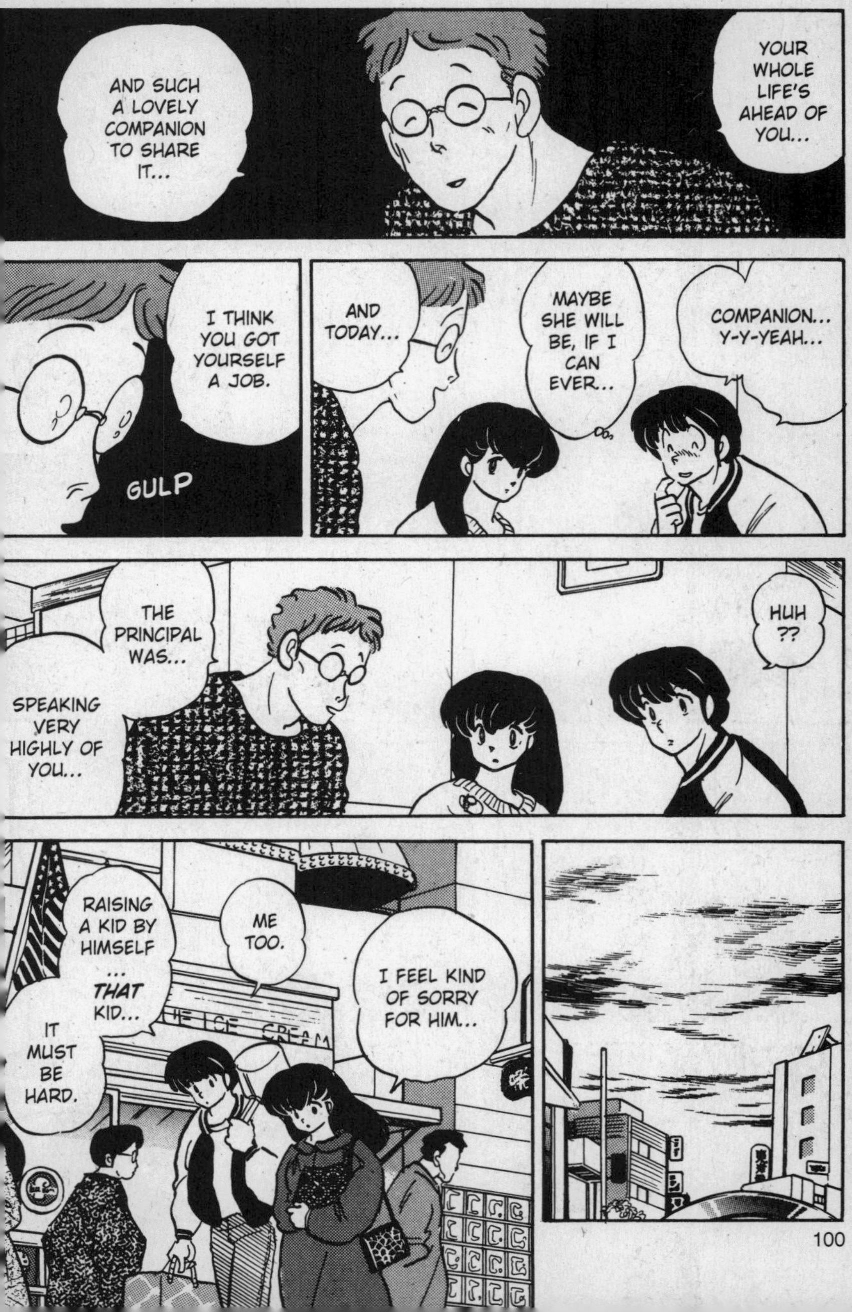
YOUR WHOLE LIFE'S AHEAD OF YOU...
AND SUCH A LOVELY COMPANION TO SHARE IT...
COMPANION... Y-Y-YEAH...
MAYBE SHE WILL BE, IF I CAN EVER...
AND TODAY...
I THINK YOU GOT YOURSELF A JOB.
GULP
HUH ??
THE PRINCIPAL WAS...
SPEAKING VERY HIGHLY OF YOU...
I FEEL KIND OF SORRY FOR HIM...
ME TOO.
RAISING A KID BY HIMSELF ... *THAT* KID...
IT MUST BE HARD.

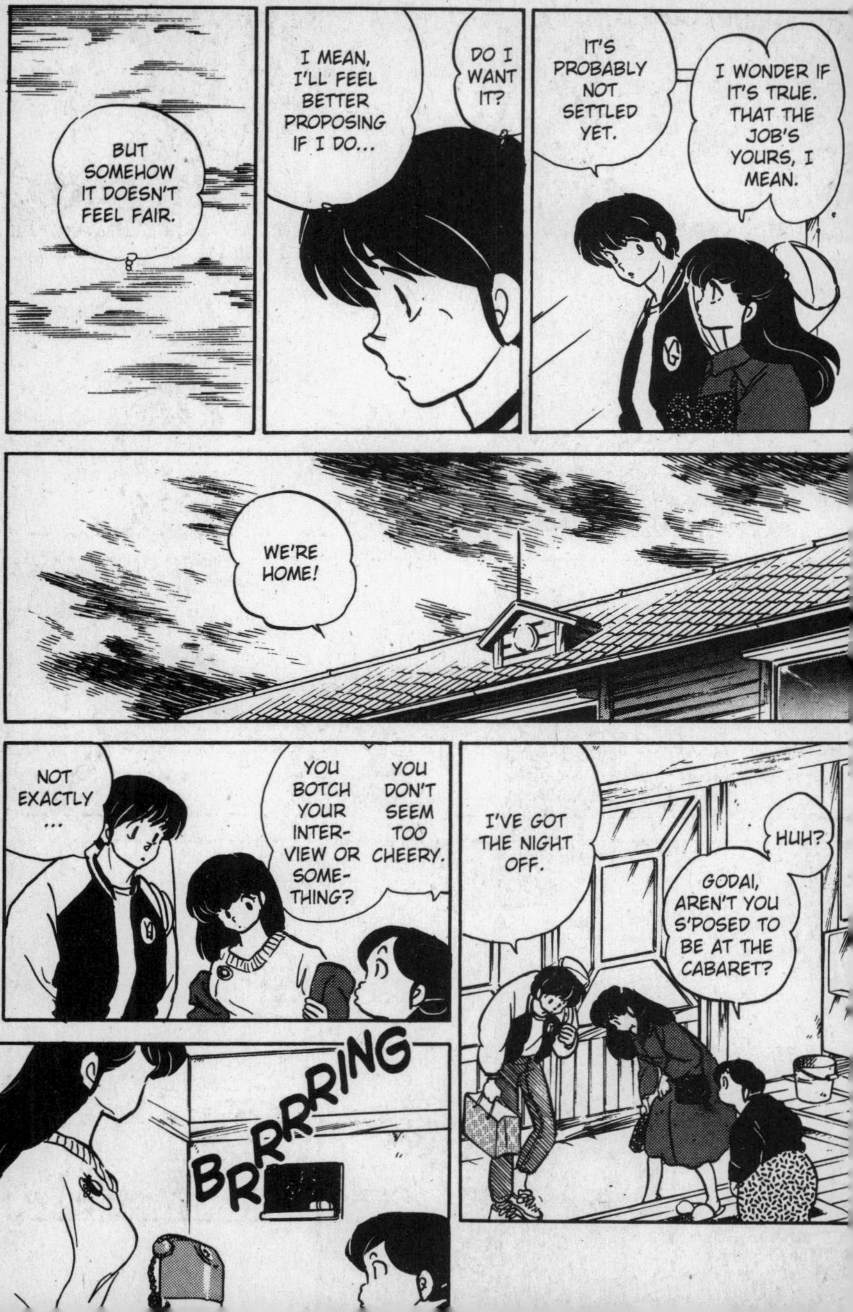
I WONDER IF IT'S TRUE. THAT THE JOB'S YOURS, I MEAN.
IT'S PROBABLY NOT SETTLED YET.
DO I WANT IT?
I MEAN, I'LL FEEL BETTER PROPOSING IF I DO...
BUT SOMEHOW IT DOESN'T FEEL FAIR.
WE'RE HOME!
HUH?
GODAI, AREN'T YOU S'POSED TO BE AT THE CABARET?
I'VE GOT THE NIGHT OFF.
YOU DON'T SEEM TOO CHEERY.
YOU BOTCH YOUR INTER-VIEW OR SOME-THING?
NOT EXACTLY ...
BRRRRING

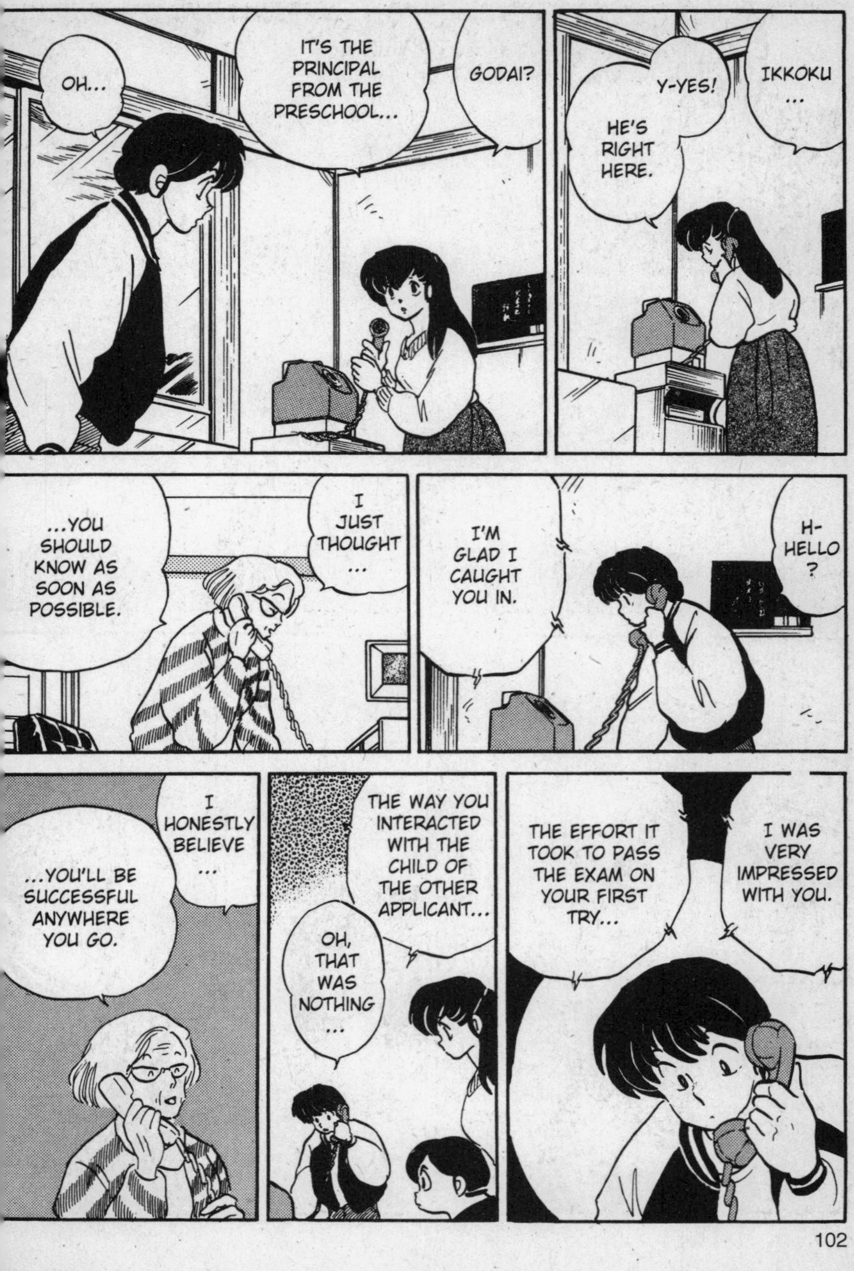
IKKOKU ...
Y-YES!
HE'S RIGHT HERE.
GODAI?
IT'S THE PRINCIPAL FROM THE PRESCHOOL...
OH...
H-HELLO?
I'M GLAD I CAUGHT YOU IN.
I JUST THOUGHT ...
...YOU SHOULD KNOW AS SOON AS POSSIBLE.
I WAS VERY IMPRESSED WITH YOU.
THE EFFORT IT TOOK TO PASS THE EXAM ON YOUR FIRST TRY...
THE WAY YOU INTERACTED WITH THE CHILD OF THE OTHER APPLICANT...
OH, THAT WAS NOTHING ...
I HONESTLY BELIEVE ...
...YOU'LL BE SUCCESSFUL ANYWHERE YOU GO.

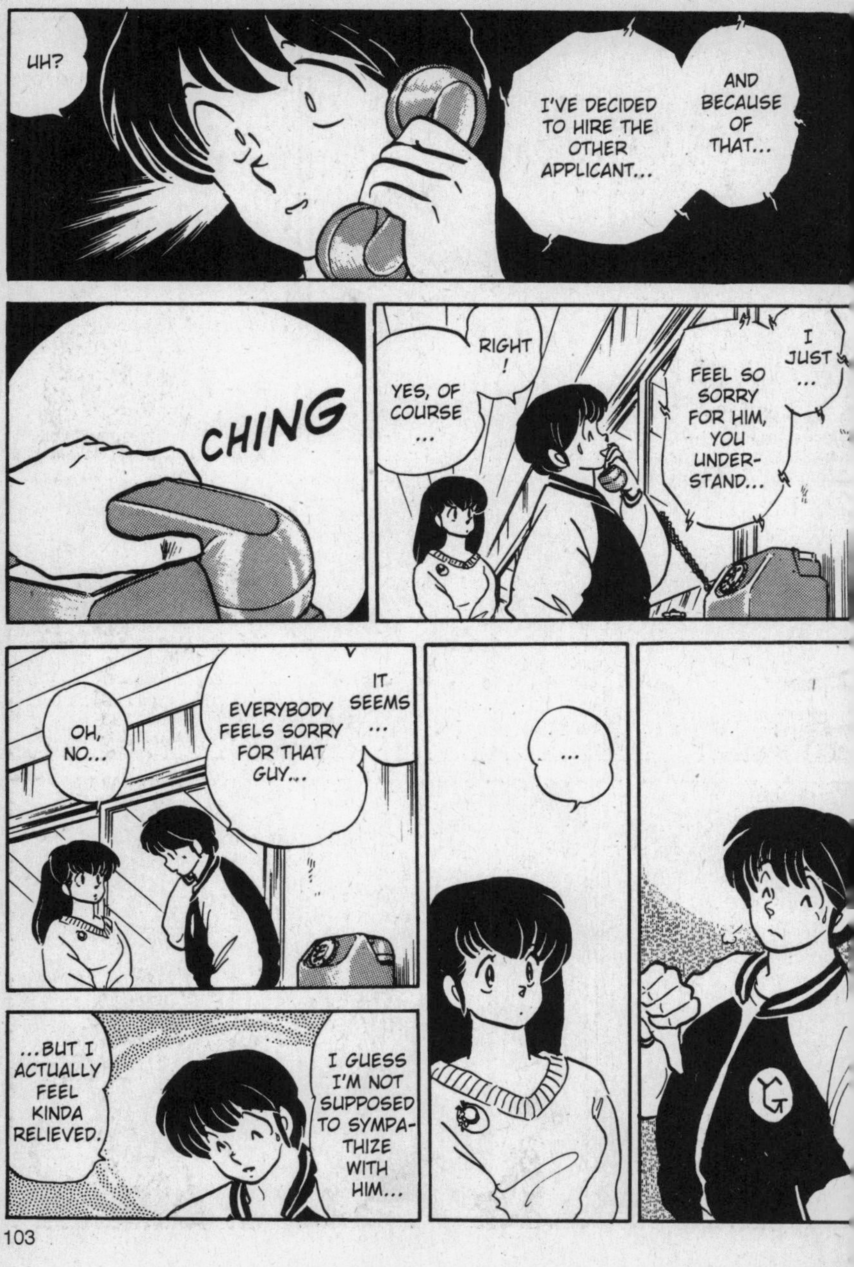
AND BECAUSE OF THAT...
I'VE DECIDED TO HIRE THE OTHER APPLICANT...
UH?
I JUST...
FEEL SO SORRY FOR HIM, YOU UNDER-STAND...
RIGHT!
YES, OF COURSE...
CHING
...
IT SEEMS...
EVERYBODY FEELS SORRY FOR THAT GUY...
OH, NO...
I GUESS I'M NOT SUPPOSED TO SYMPA-THIZE WITH HIM...
...BUT I ACTUALLY FEEL KINDA RELIEVED.

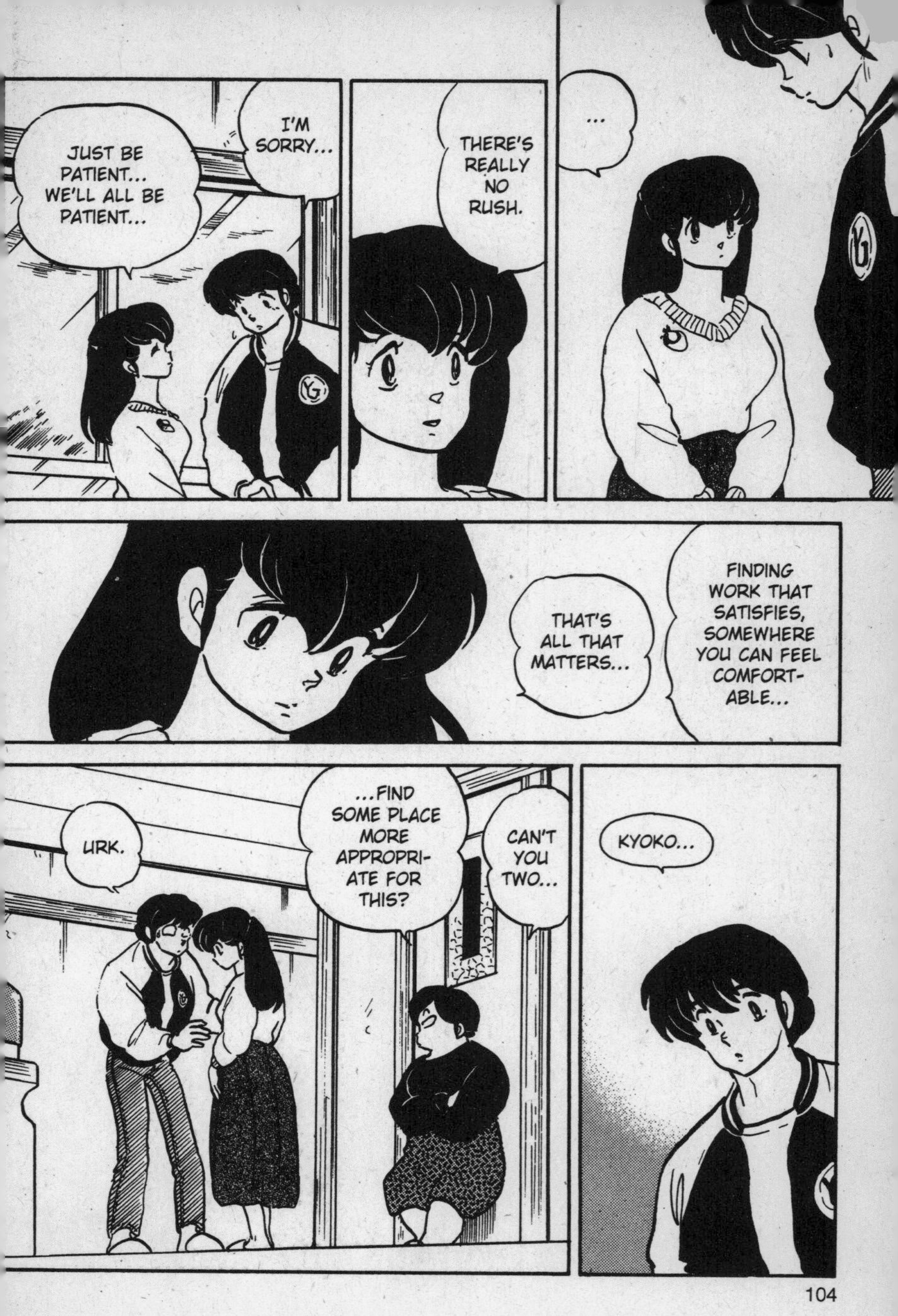
...
THERE'S REALLY NO RUSH.
I'M SORRY...
JUST BE PATIENT... WE'LL ALL BE PATIENT...
FINDING WORK THAT SATISFIES, SOMEWHERE YOU CAN FEEL COMFORT-ABLE...
THAT'S ALL THAT MATTERS...
KYOKO...
CAN'T YOU TWO...
...FIND SOME PLACE MORE APPROPRI-ATE FOR THIS?
URK.

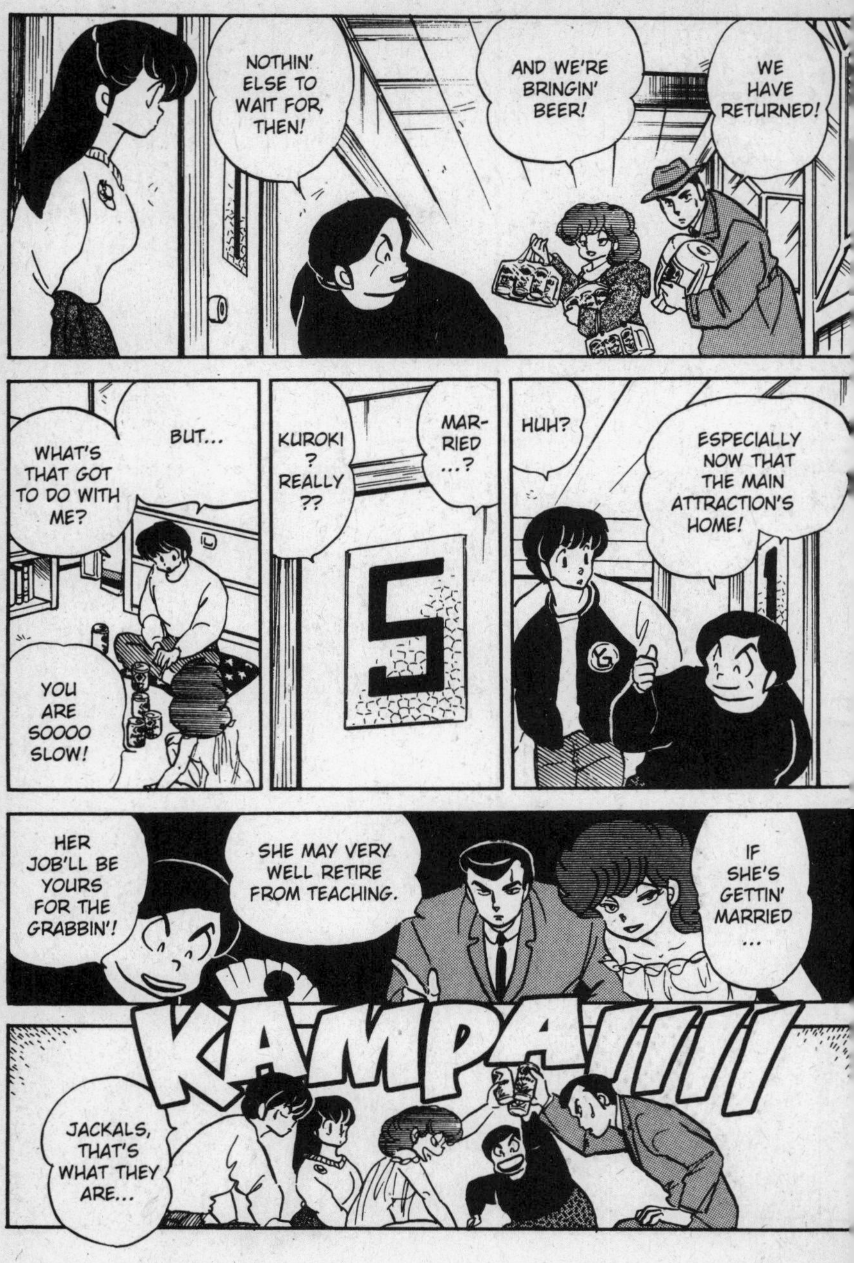
WE HAVE RETURNED!
AND WE'RE BRINGIN' BEER!
NOTHIN' ELSE TO WAIT FOR, THEN!
ESPECIALLY NOW THAT THE MAIN ATTRACTION'S HOME!
HUH?
MAR-RIED ...?
KUROKI ? REALLY ??
BUT...
WHAT'S THAT GOT TO DO WITH ME?
YOU ARE SOOOO SLOW!
IF SHE'S GETTIN' MARRIED ...
SHE MAY VERY WELL RETIRE FROM TEACHING.
HER JOB'LL BE YOURS FOR THE GRABBIN'!
KAMPAI!!!!
JACKALS, THAT'S WHAT THEY ARE...

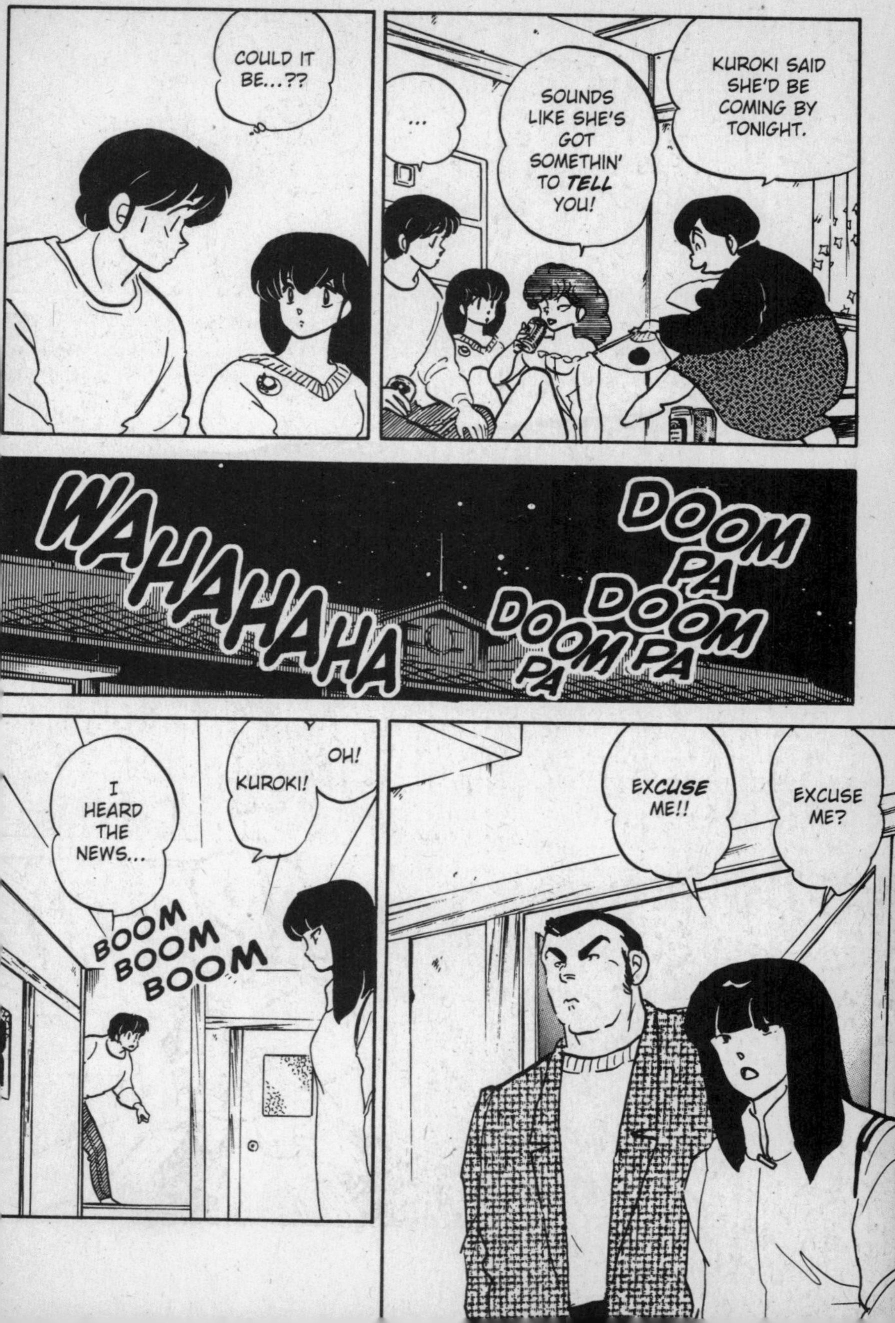
KUROKI SAID SHE'D BE COMING BY TONIGHT.
SOUNDS LIKE SHE'S GOT SOMETHIN' TO TELL YOU!
...
COULD IT BE...??
DOOM PA DOOM PA DOOM PA
WAHAHAHAHA
EXCUSE ME?
EXCUSE ME!!
OH!
KUROKI!
I HEARD THE NEWS...
BOOM BOOM BOOM

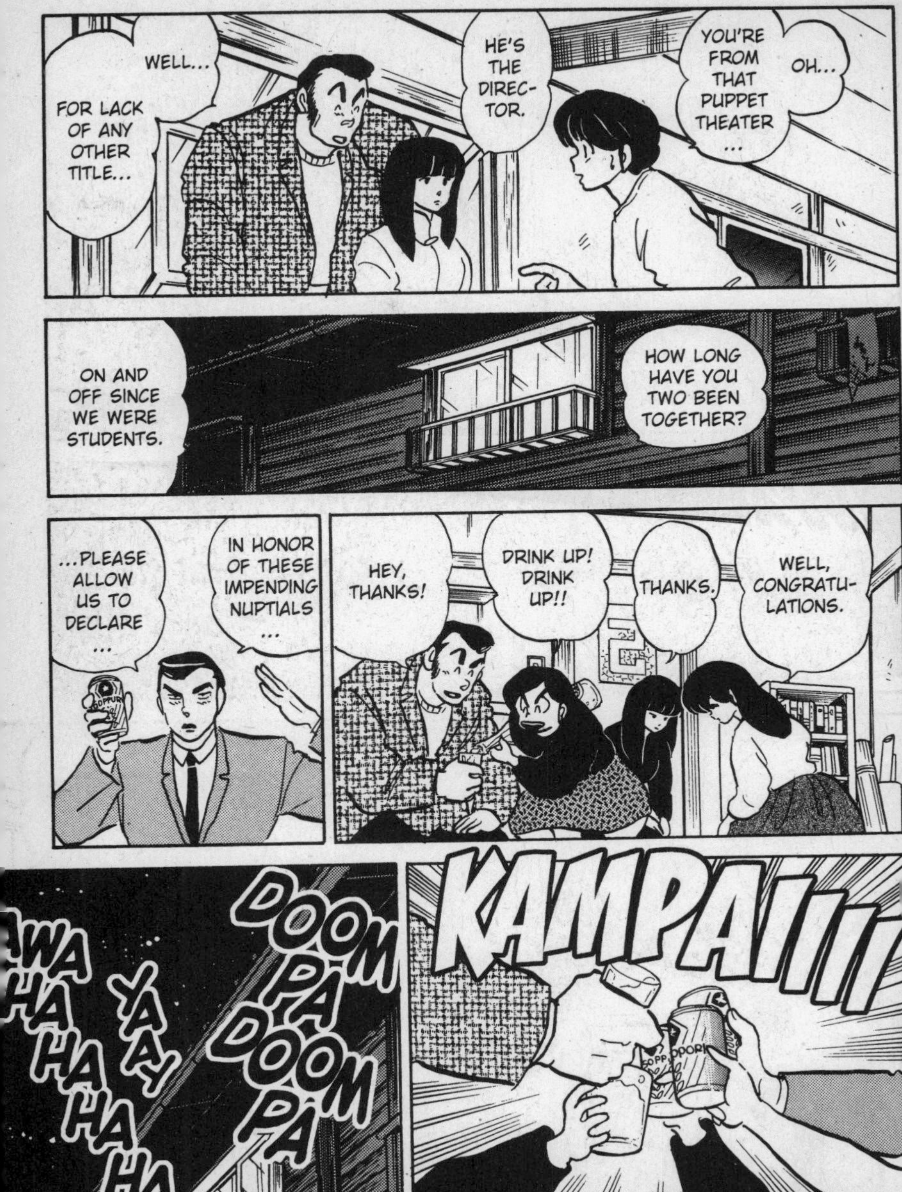
OH...
YOU'RE FROM THAT PUPPET THEATER ...
HE'S THE DIRECTOR.
WELL...
FOR LACK OF ANY OTHER TITLE...
HOW LONG HAVE YOU TWO BEEN TOGETHER?
ON AND OFF SINCE WE WERE STUDENTS.
WELL, CONGRATULATIONS.
THANKS.
DRINK UP! DRINK UP!!
HEY, THANKS!
IN HONOR OF THESE IMPENDING NUPTIALS ...
...PLEASE ALLOW US TO DECLARE ...
KAMPAIIII
DOOM PA DOOM PA
YAAAI
WAHAHAHAHAHA

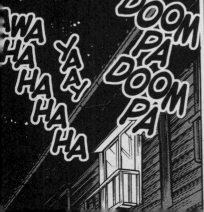

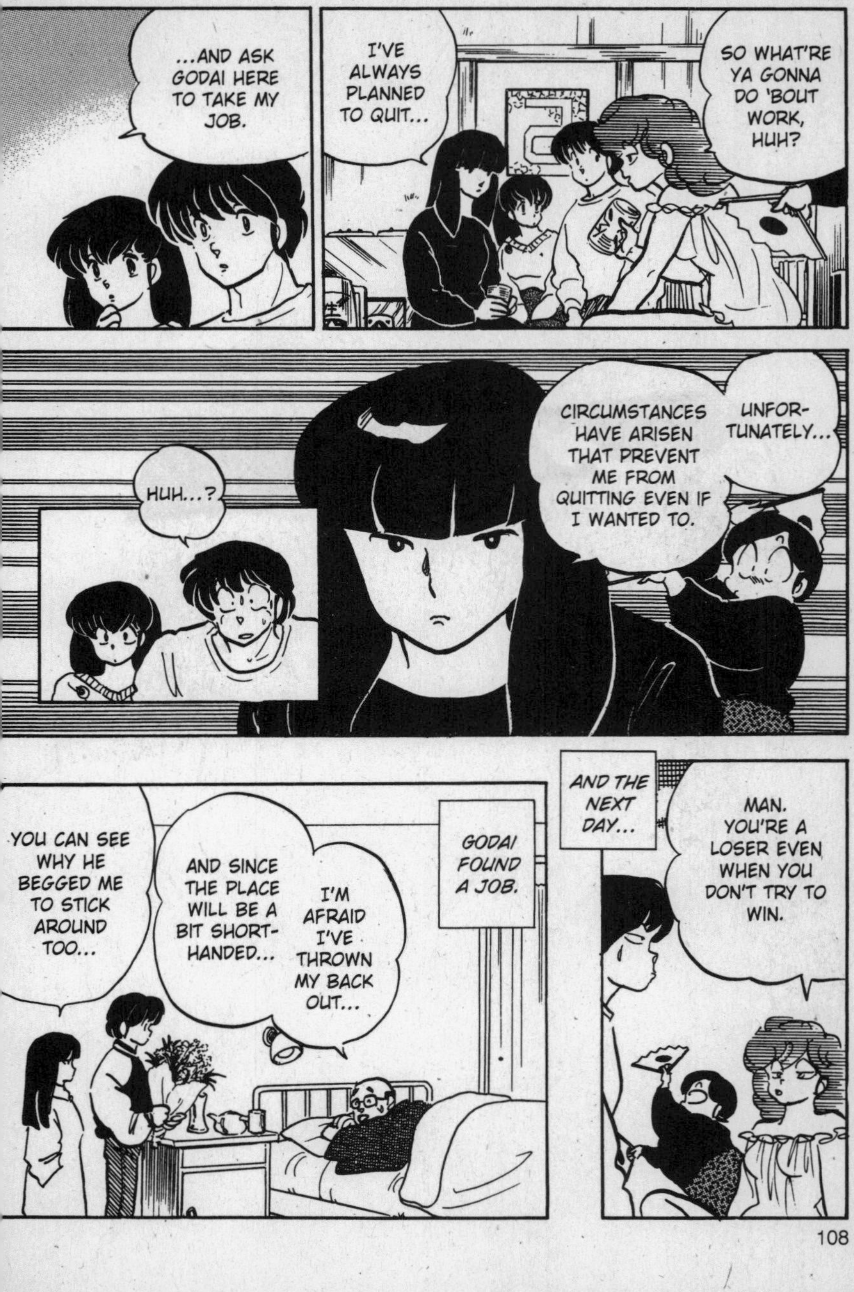
SO WHAT'RE YA GONNA DO 'BOUT WORK, HUH?
I'VE ALWAYS PLANNED TO QUIT...
...AND ASK GODAI HERE TO TAKE MY JOB.
UNFORTUNATELY...
CIRCUMSTANCES HAVE ARISEN THAT PREVENT ME FROM QUITTING EVEN IF I WANTED TO.
HUH...?
AND THE NEXT DAY...
MAN. YOU'RE A LOSER EVEN WHEN YOU DON'T TRY TO WIN.
GODAI FOUND A JOB.
I'M AFRAID I'VE THROWN MY BACK OUT...
AND SINCE THE PLACE WILL BE A BIT SHORT-HANDED...
YOU CAN SEE WHY HE BEGGED ME TO STICK AROUND TOO...

PART SIX
...IF IT EVER HAPPENS

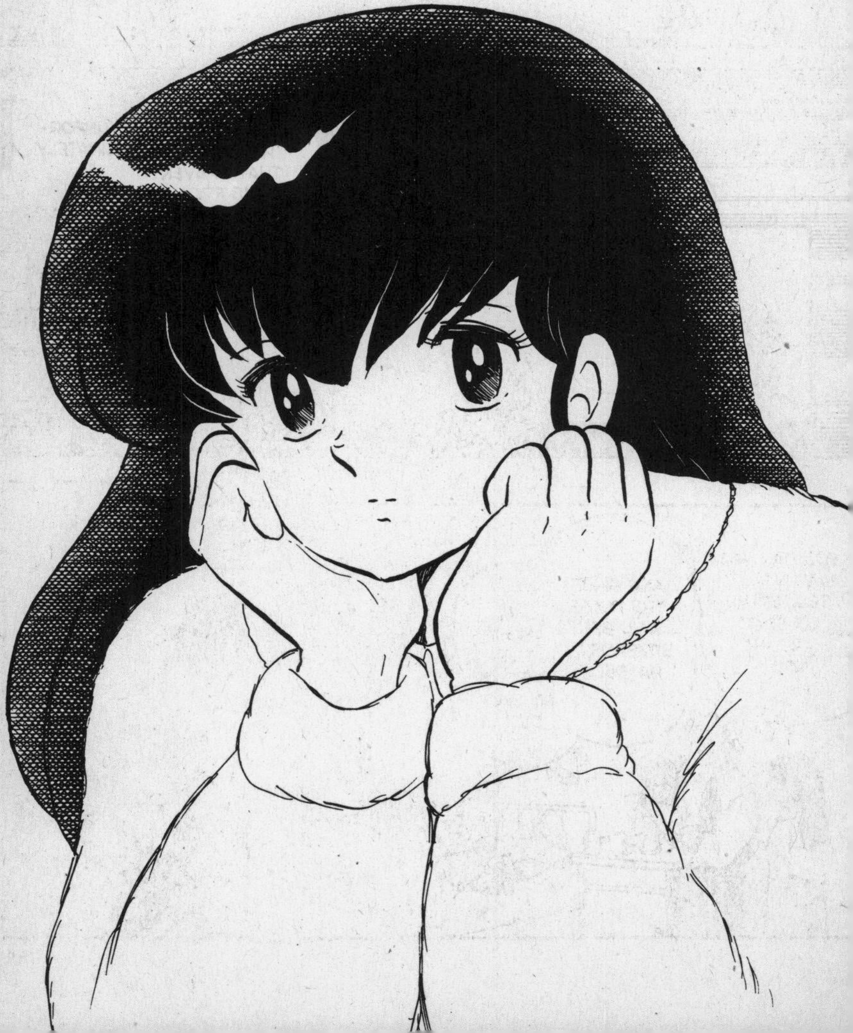

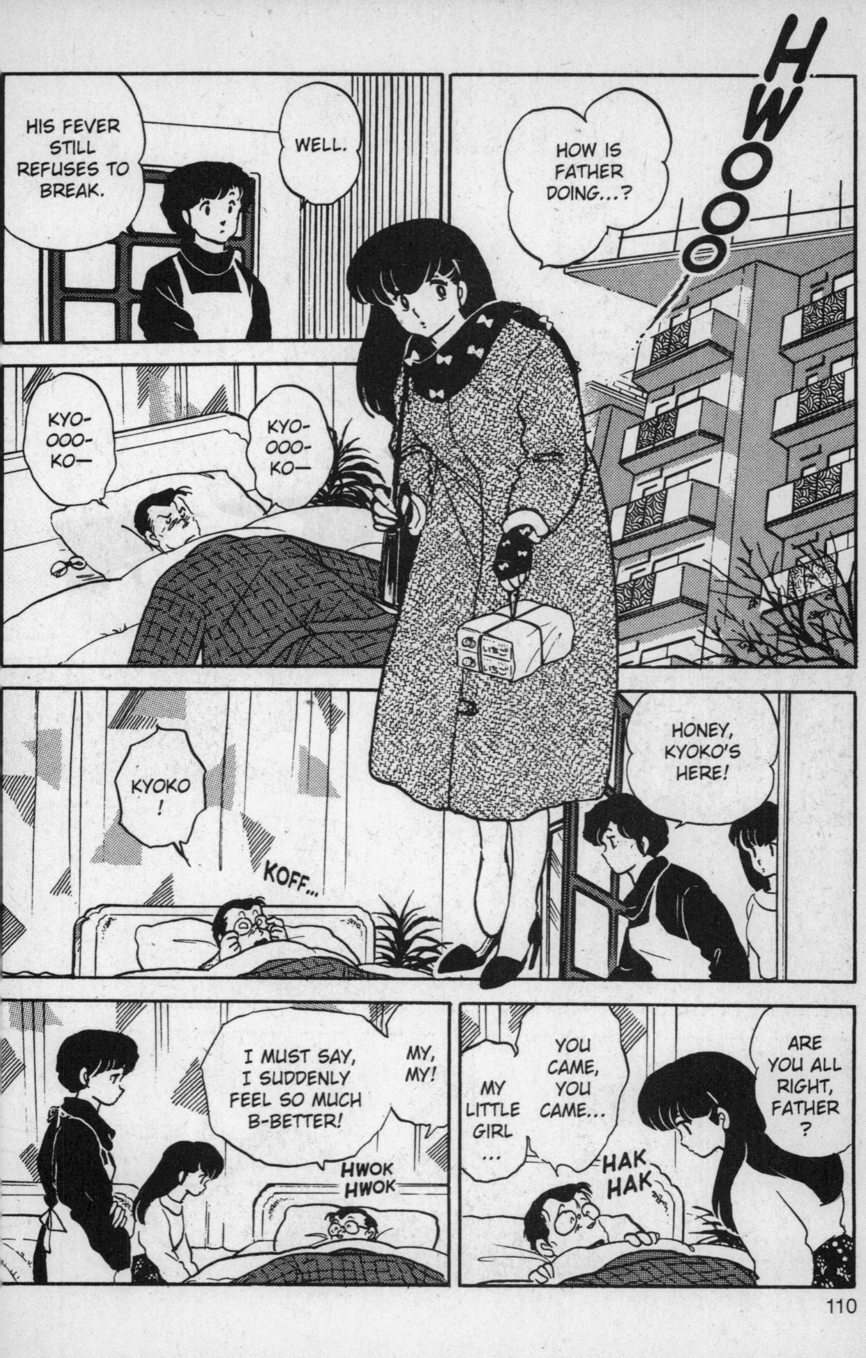
HWOOOO
HOW IS FATHER DOING...?
WELL.
HIS FEVER STILL REFUSES TO BREAK.
KYO-OOO-KO—
KYO-OOO-KO—
HONEY, KYOKO'S HERE!
KYOKO!
KOFF...
ARE YOU ALL RIGHT, FATHER?
YOU CAME, YOU CAME...
MY LITTLE GIRL...
HAK HAK
MY, MY!
I MUST SAY, I SUDDENLY FEEL SO MUCH B-BETTER!
HWOK HWOK

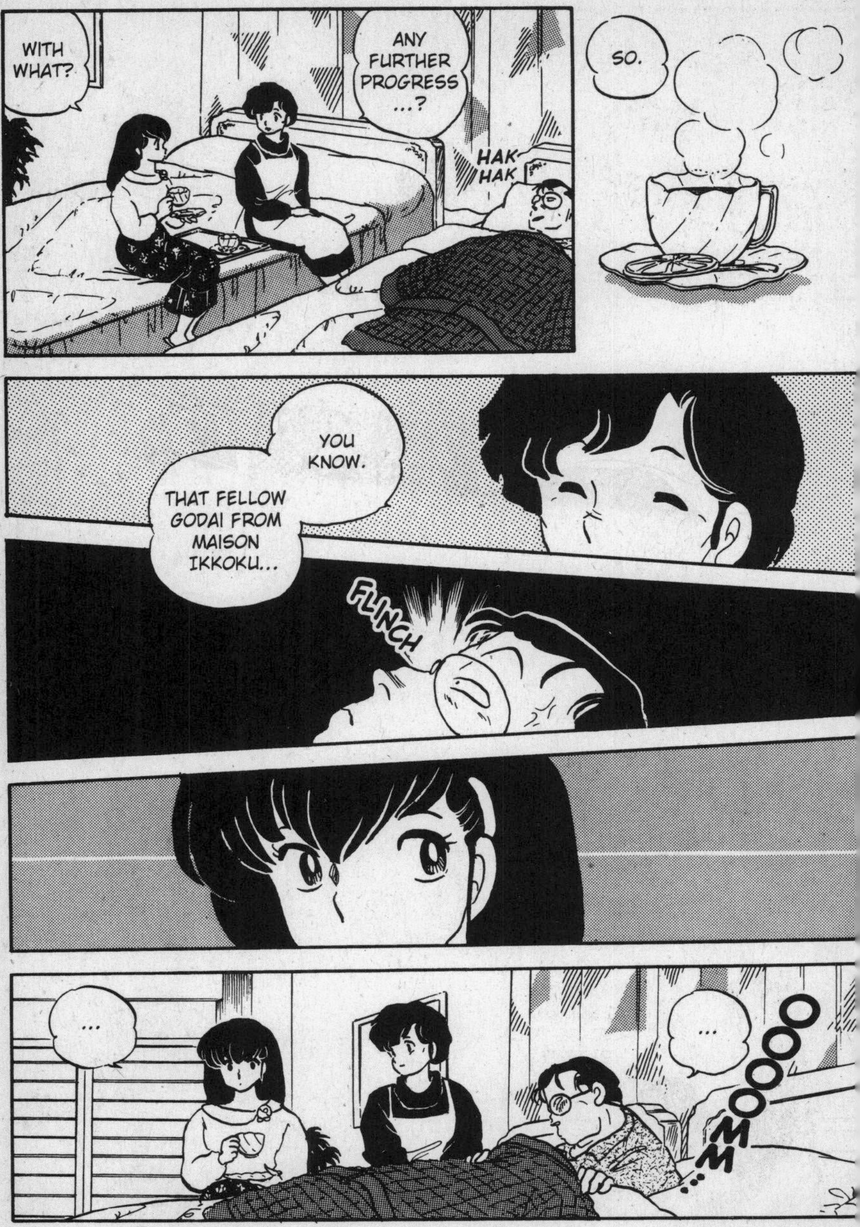
SO.
ANY FURTHER PROGRESS ...?
HAK HAK
WITH WHAT?
YOU KNOW.
THAT FELLOW GODAI FROM MAISON IKKOKU...
FLINCH
...
OOOOOOMM...
...

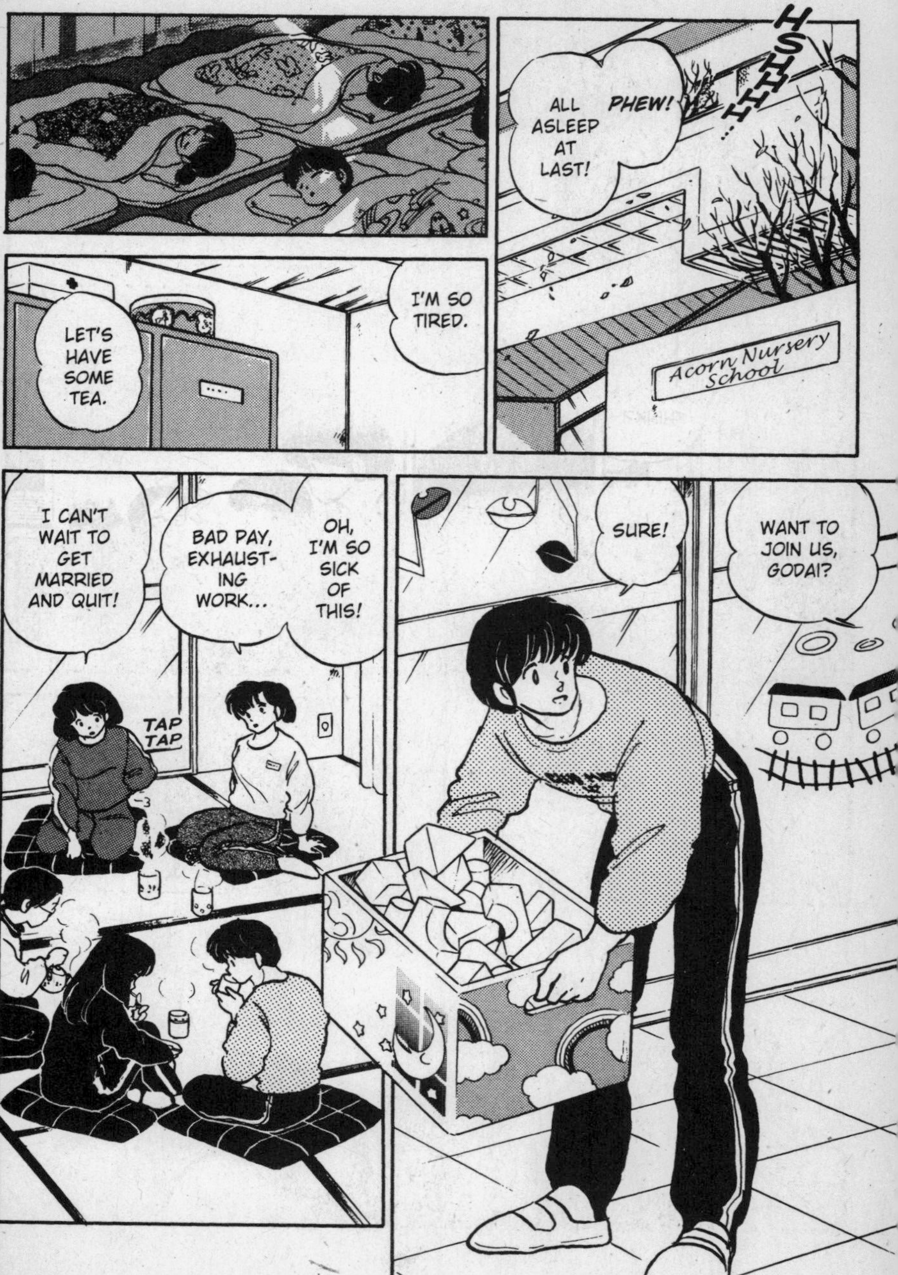
HSHHHH...
PHEW!
ALL ASLEEP AT LAST!
Acorn Nursery School
I'M SO TIRED.
LET'S HAVE SOME TEA.
WANT TO JOIN US, GODAI?
SURE!
OH, I'M SO SICK OF THIS!
BAD PAY, EXHAUST-ING WORK...
I CAN'T WAIT TO GET MARRIED AND QUIT!
TAP TAP

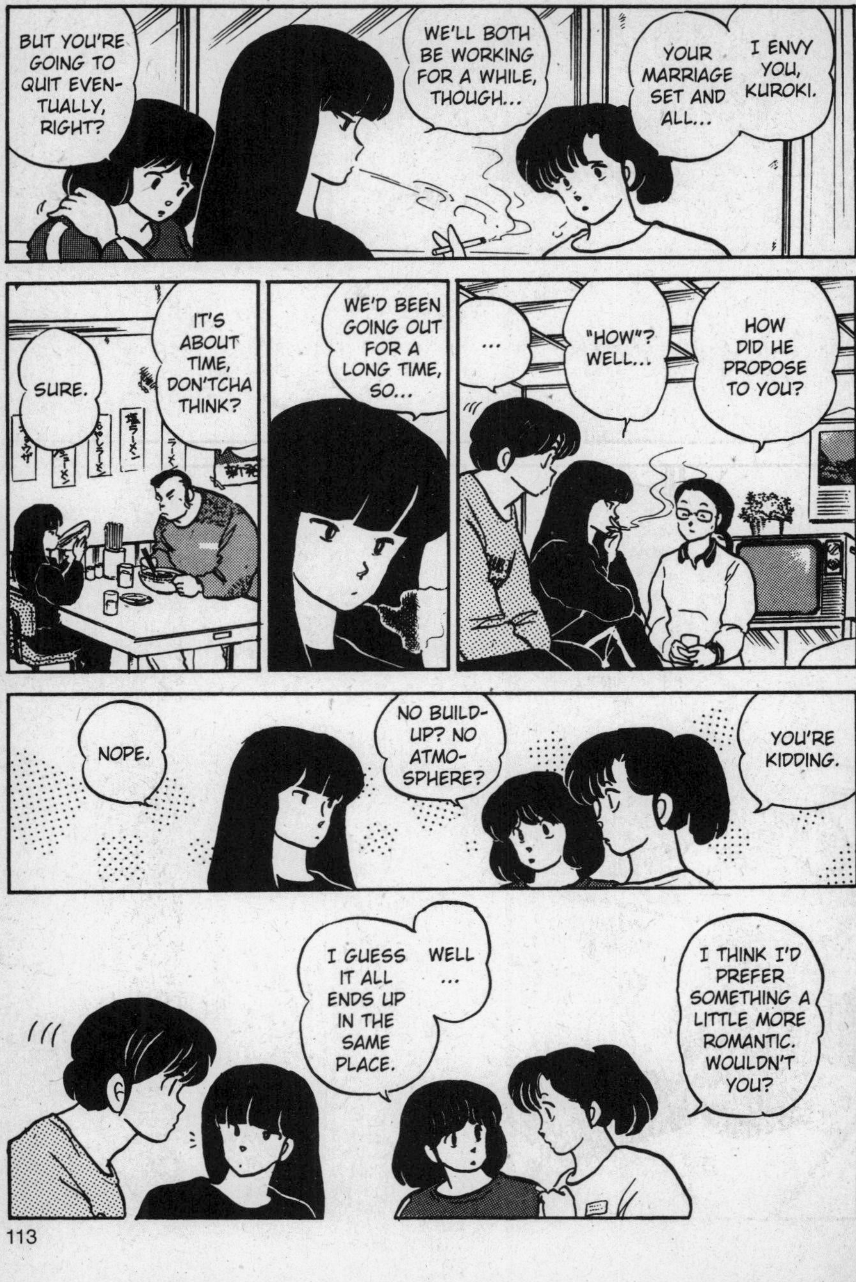
I ENVY YOU, KUROKI.
YOUR MARRIAGE SET AND ALL...
WE'LL BOTH BE WORKING FOR A WHILE, THOUGH...
BUT YOU'RE GOING TO QUIT EVEN-TUALLY, RIGHT?
HOW DID HE PROPOSE TO YOU?
"HOW"? WELL...
...
WE'D BEEN GOING OUT FOR A LONG TIME, SO...
IT'S ABOUT TIME, DON'TCHA THINK?
SURE.
YOU'RE KIDDING.
NO BUILD-UP? NO ATMO-SPHERE?
NOPE.
I THINK I'D PREFER SOMETHING A LITTLE MORE ROMANTIC. WOULDN'T YOU?
WELL ...
I GUESS IT ALL ENDS UP IN THE SAME PLACE.

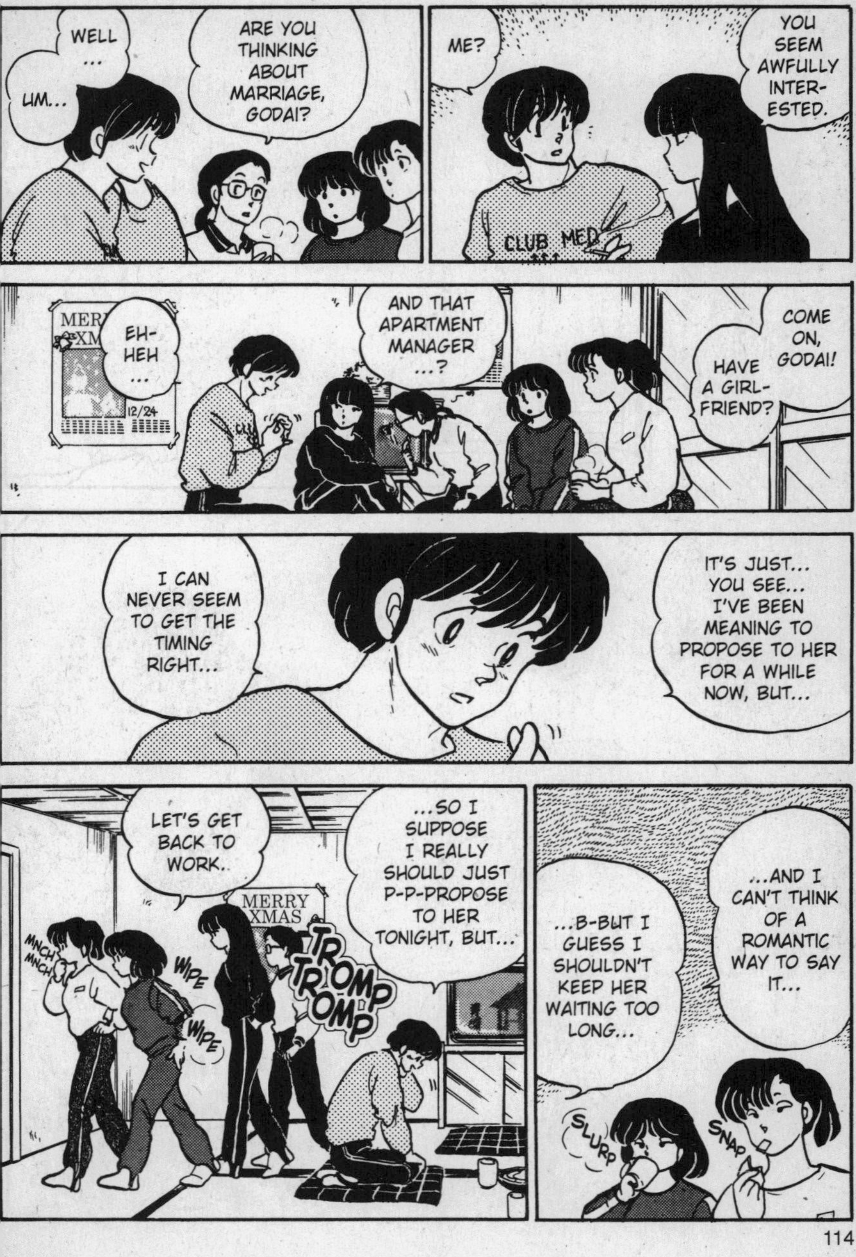
YOU SEEM AWFULLY INTER-ESTED.
ME?
ARE YOU THINKING ABOUT MARRIAGE, GODAI?
WELL ... UM...
COME ON, GODAI!
HAVE A GIRL-FRIEND?
AND THAT APARTMENT MANAGER ...?
EH-HEH ...
12/24
IT'S JUST... YOU SEE... I'VE BEEN MEANING TO PROPOSE TO HER FOR A WHILE NOW, BUT...
I CAN NEVER SEEM TO GET THE TIMING RIGHT...
...AND I CAN'T THINK OF A ROMANTIC WAY TO SAY IT...
...B-BUT I GUESS I SHOULDN'T KEEP HER WAITING TOO LONG...
SNAP
SLURP
...SO I SUPPOSE I REALLY SHOULD JUST P-P-PROPOSE TO HER TONIGHT, BUT...
LET'S GET BACK TO WORK.
TROMP TROMP
MERRY XMAS
WIPE WIPE
MNCH MNCH

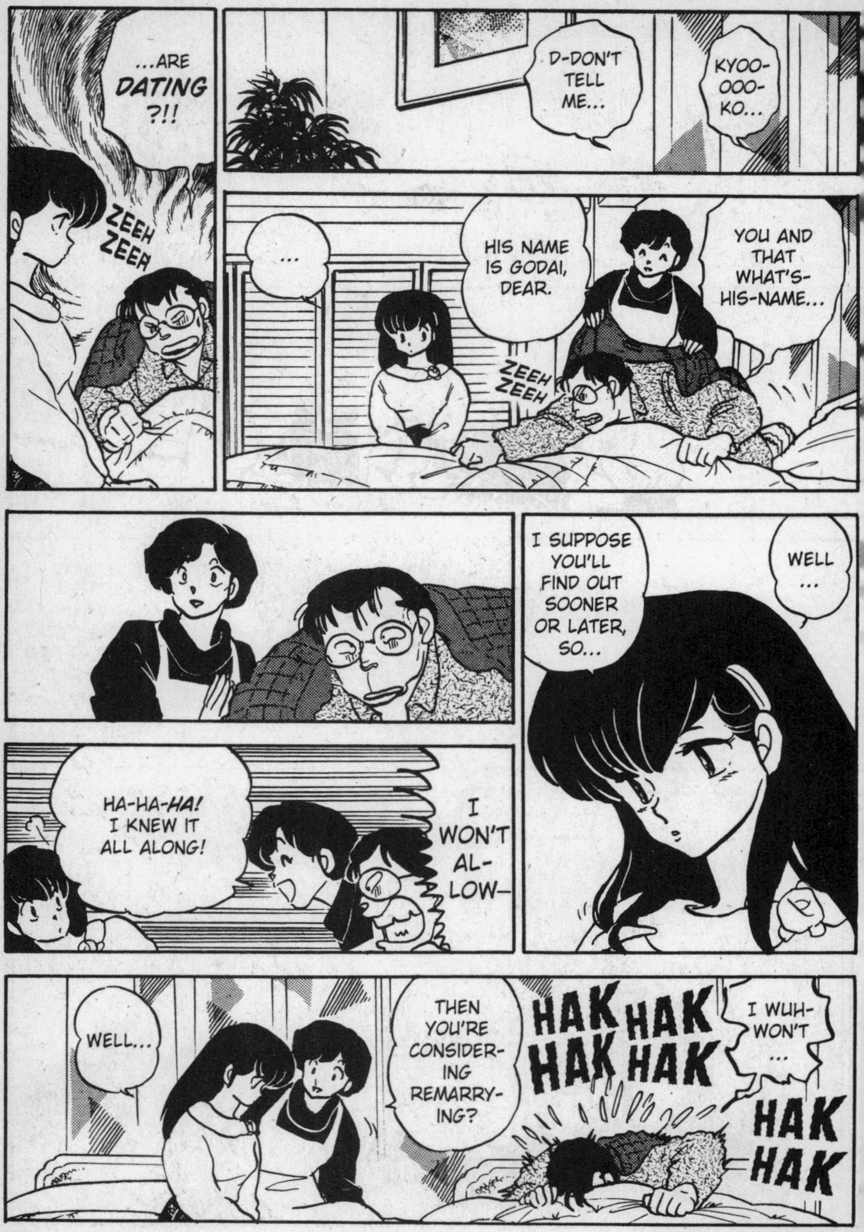
KYOO-OOO-KO...
D-DON'T TELL ME...
YOU AND THAT WHAT'S-HIS-NAME...
HIS NAME IS GODAI, DEAR.
ZEEH ZEEH
...
...ARE DATING?!!
ZEEH ZEEH
WELL...
I SUPPOSE YOU'LL FIND OUT SOONER OR LATER, SO...
I WON'T AL-LOW—
HA-HA-HA! I KNEW IT ALL ALONG!
I WUH-WON'T ...
HAK HAK HAK HAK
HAK HAK
THEN YOU'RE CONSIDER-ING REMARRY-ING?
WELL...

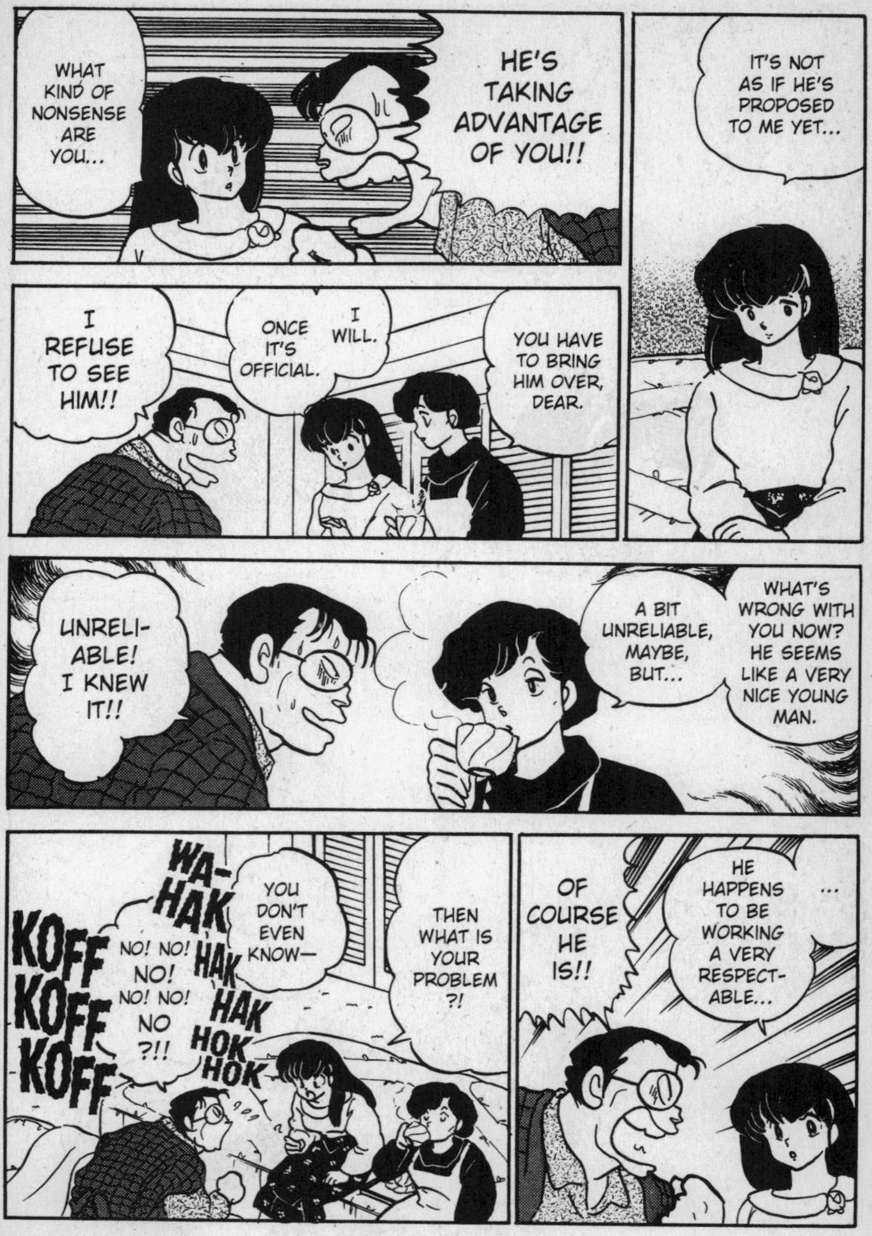
IT'S NOT AS IF HE'S PROPOSED TO ME YET...
HE'S TAKING ADVANTAGE OF YOU!!
WHAT KIND OF NONSENSE ARE YOU...
YOU HAVE TO BRING HIM OVER, DEAR.
I WILL.
ONCE IT'S OFFICIAL.
I REFUSE TO SEE HIM!!
WHAT'S WRONG WITH YOU NOW? HE SEEMS LIKE A VERY NICE YOUNG MAN.
A BIT UNRELIABLE, MAYBE, BUT...
UNRELI-ABLE! I KNEW IT!!
...
HE HAPPENS TO BE WORKING A VERY RESPECT-ABLE...
OF COURSE HE IS!!
THEN WHAT IS YOUR PROBLEM ?!
YOU DON'T EVEN KNOW—
WA-HAK HAK HAK HOK HOK
NO! NO! NO! NO! NO! NO ?!!
KOFF KOFF KOFF KOFF

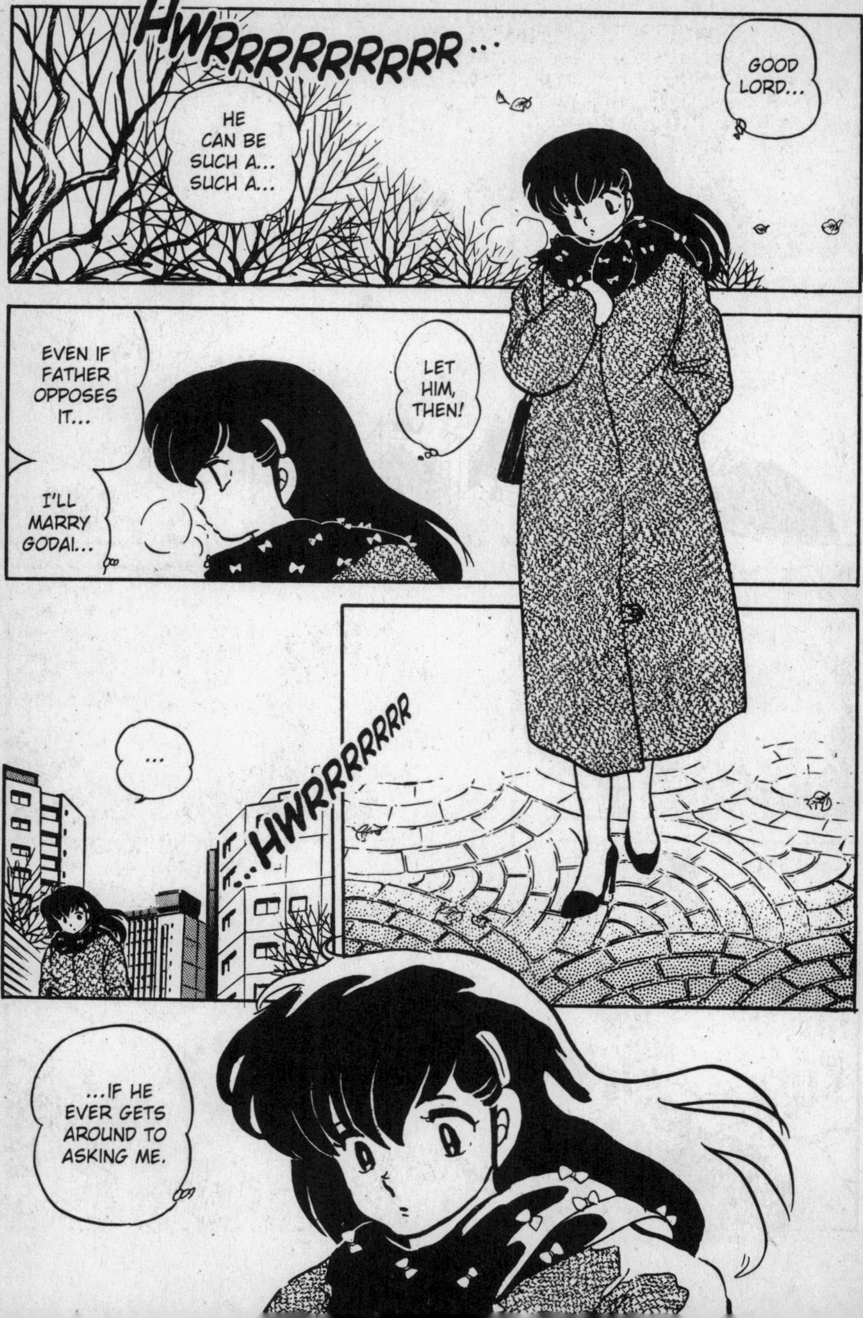
GOOD LORD...
HWRRRRRRRRR...
HE CAN BE SUCH A... SUCH A...
LET HIM, THEN!
EVEN IF FATHER OPPOSES IT...
I'LL MARRY GODAI...
...HWRRRRRRR
...
...IF HE EVER GETS AROUND TO ASKING ME.

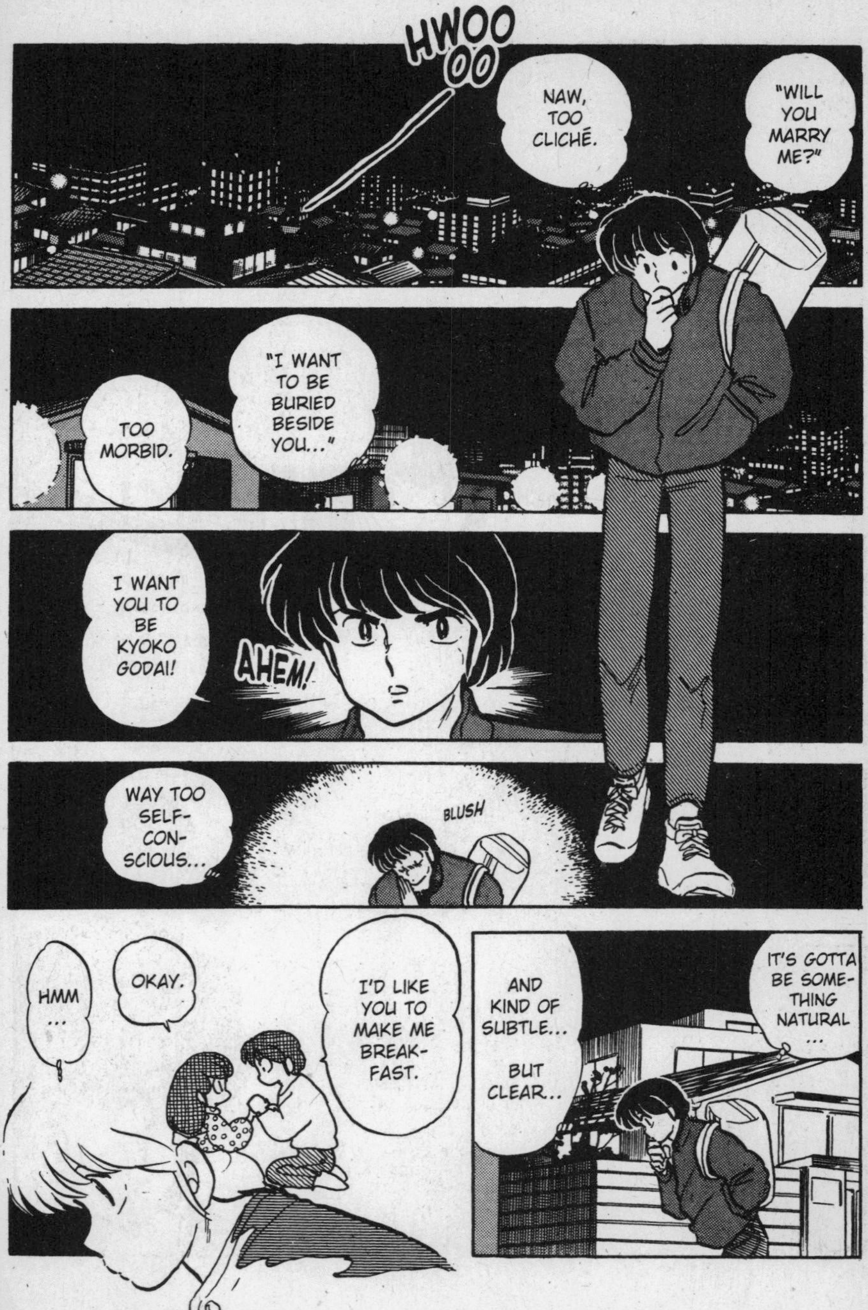
HWOOOO
"WILL YOU MARRY ME?"
NAW, TOO CLICHÉ.
"I WANT TO BE BURIED BESIDE YOU..."
TOO MORBID.
AHEM!
I WANT YOU TO BE KYOKO GODAI!
BLUSH
WAY TOO SELF-CONSCIOUS...
IT'S GOTTA BE SOMETHING NATURAL...
AND KIND OF SUBTLE...
BUT CLEAR...
I'D LIKE YOU TO MAKE ME BREAKFAST.
OKAY.
HMM...

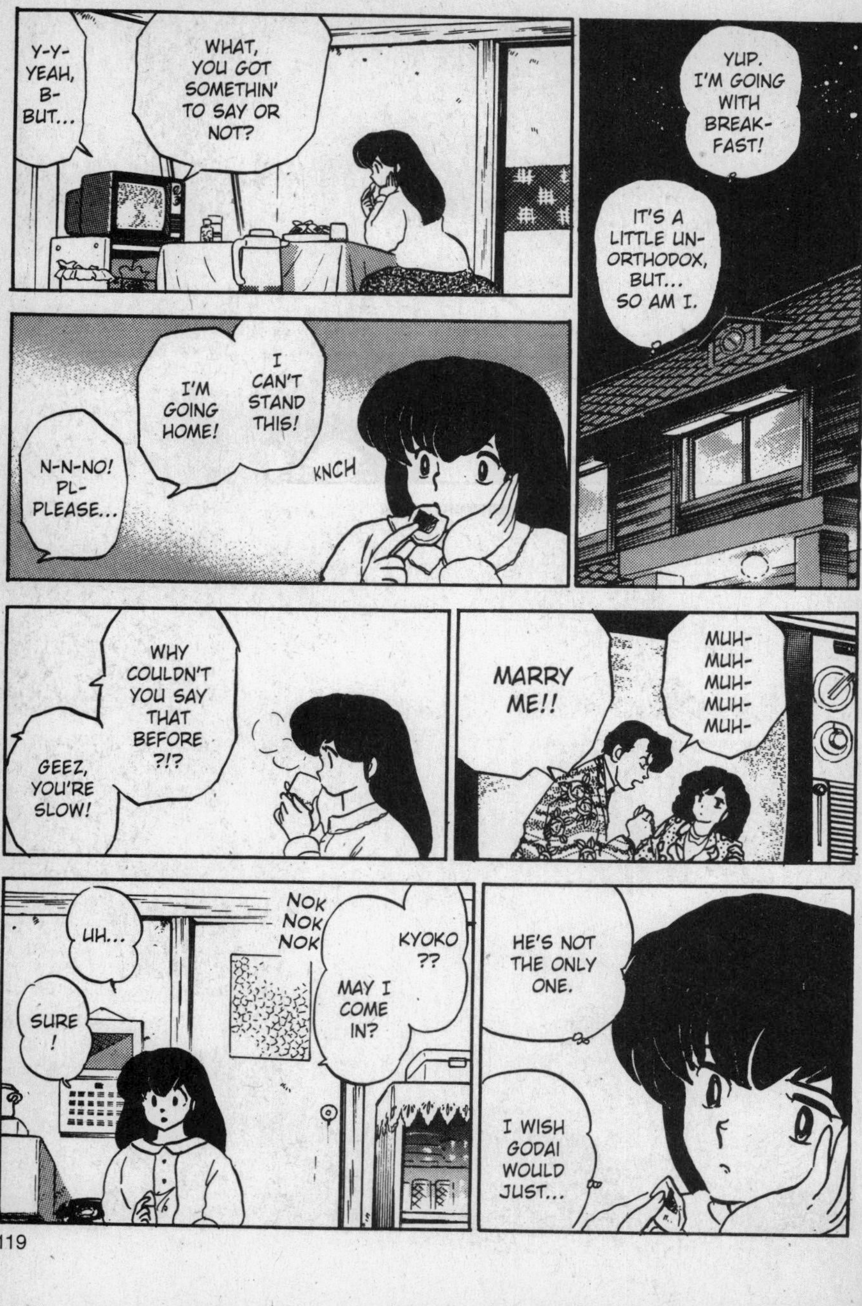
YUP. I'M GOING WITH BREAK-FAST!
IT'S A LITTLE UN-ORTHODOX, BUT... SO AM I.
WHAT, YOU GOT SOMETHIN' TO SAY OR NOT?
Y-Y-YEAH, B-BUT...
I CAN'T STAND THIS!
I'M GOING HOME!
KNCH
N-N-NO! PL-PLEASE...
MUH-MUH-MUH-MUH-MUH-
MARRY ME!!
WHY COULDN'T YOU SAY THAT BEFORE ?!?
GEEZ, YOU'RE SLOW!
HE'S NOT THE ONLY ONE.
I WISH GODAI WOULD JUST...
KYOKO ??
MAY I COME IN?
NOK NOK NOK
UH...
SURE !

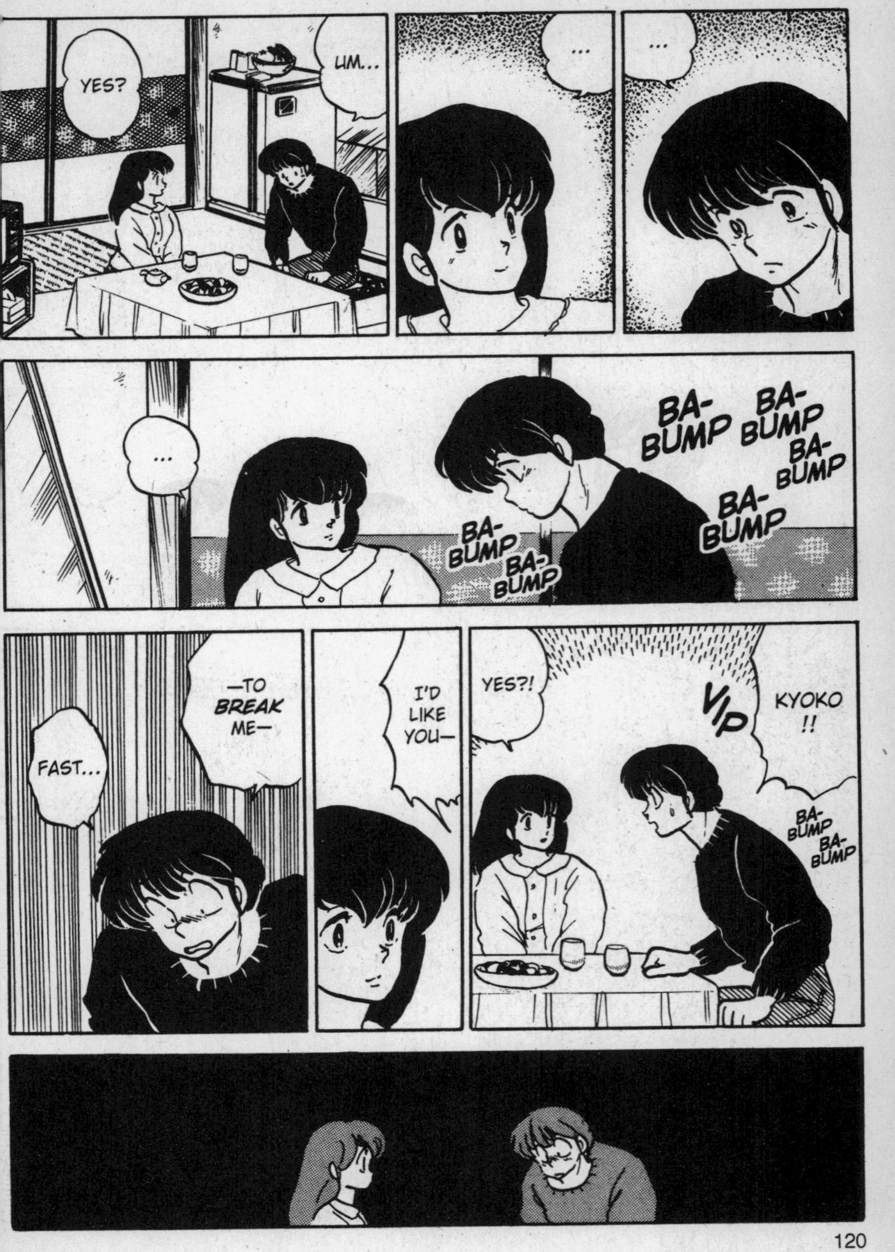
...
...
UM...
YES?
BA-BUMP
BA-BUMP
BA-BUMP
BA-BUMP
BA-BUMP
BA-BUMP
...
KYOKO !!
VIP
YES?!
BA-BUMP
BA-BUMP
I'D LIKE YOU—
—TO BREAK ME—
FAST...

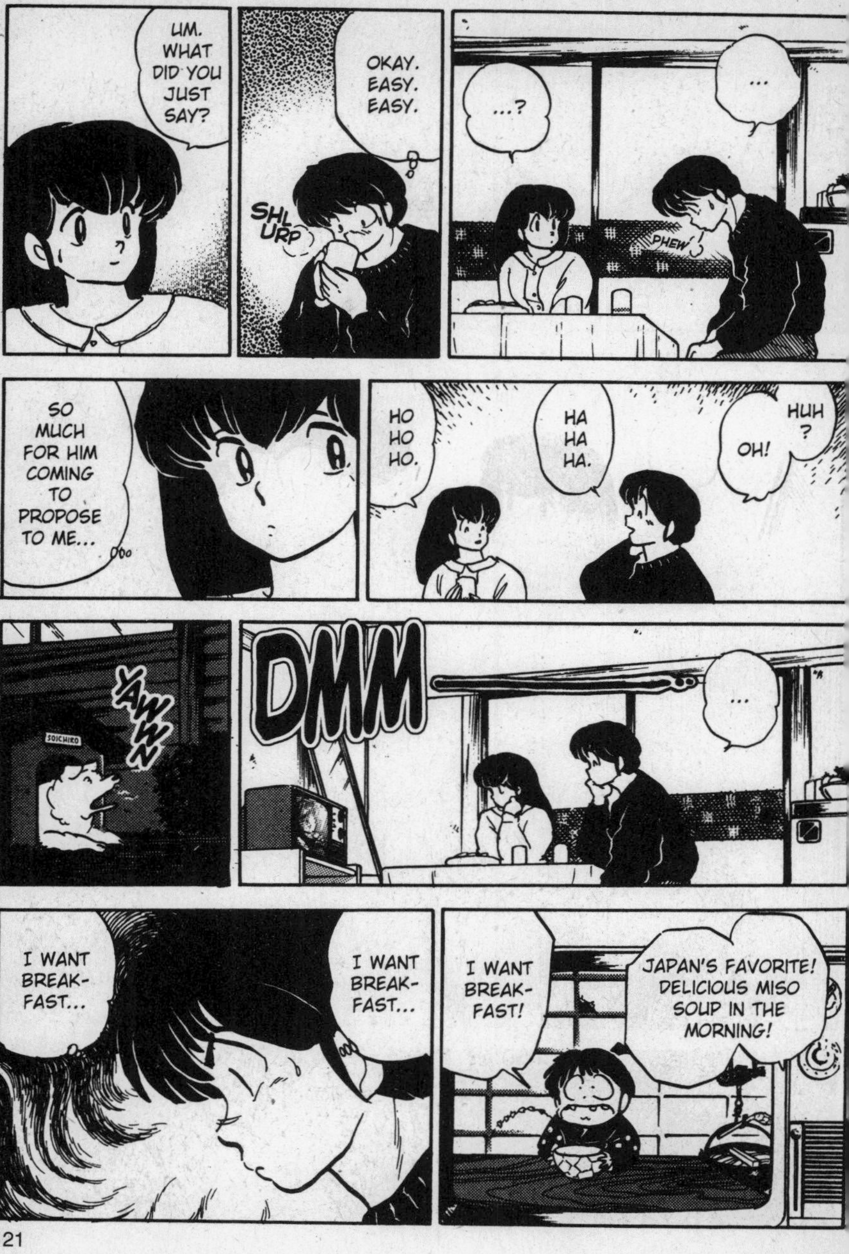
...
...?
PHEW
OKAY. EASY. EASY.
SHLURP
UM. WHAT DID YOU JUST SAY?
HUH?
OH!
HA HA HA.
HO HO HO.
SO MUCH FOR HIM COMING TO PROPOSE TO ME...
DMM
...
SOICHIRO
YAWWN
JAPAN'S FAVORITE! DELICIOUS MISO SOUP IN THE MORNING!
I WANT BREAK-FAST!
I WANT BREAK-FAST...
I WANT BREAK-FAST...

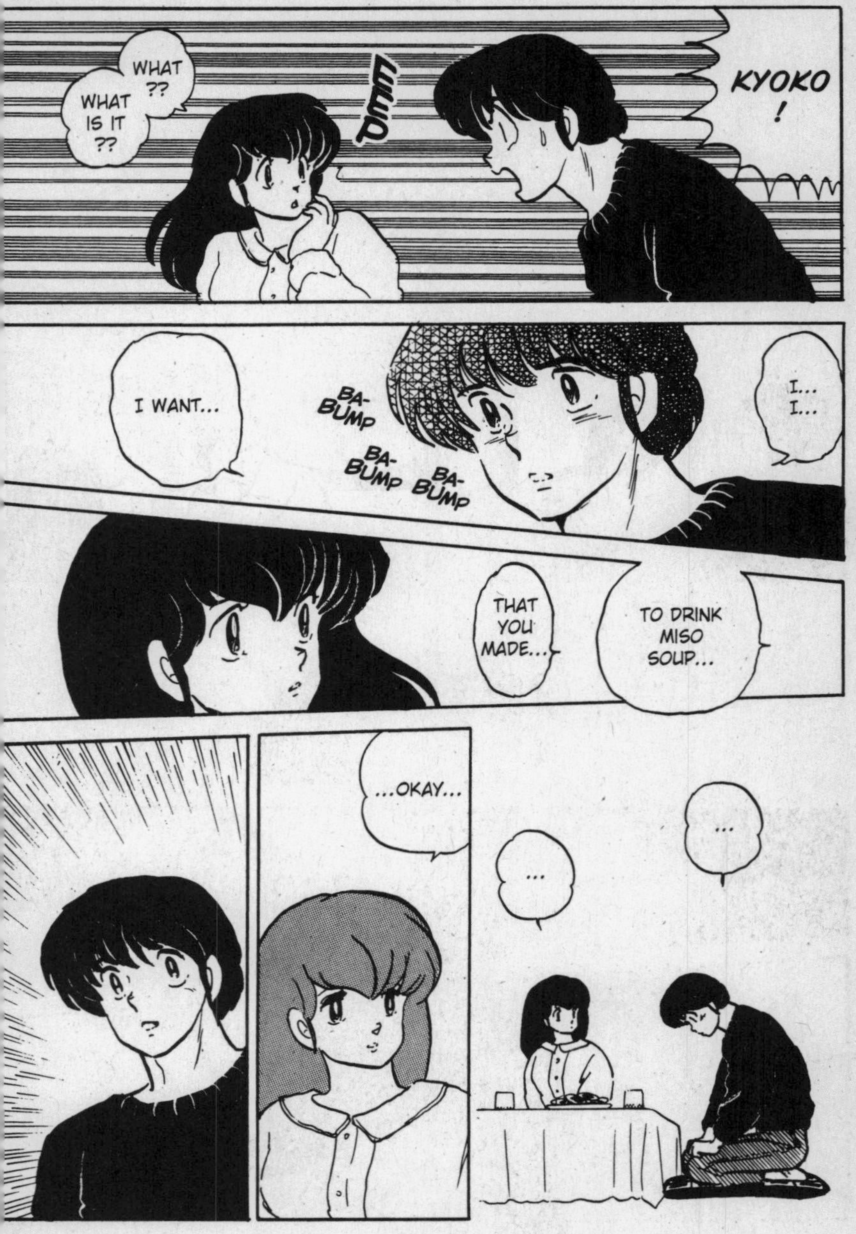
KYOKO !
EEP
WHAT ??
WHAT IS IT ??
I... I...
BA-BUMP
BA-BUMP
BA-BUMP
I WANT...
TO DRINK MISO SOUP...
THAT YOU MADE...
...
...
...OKAY...

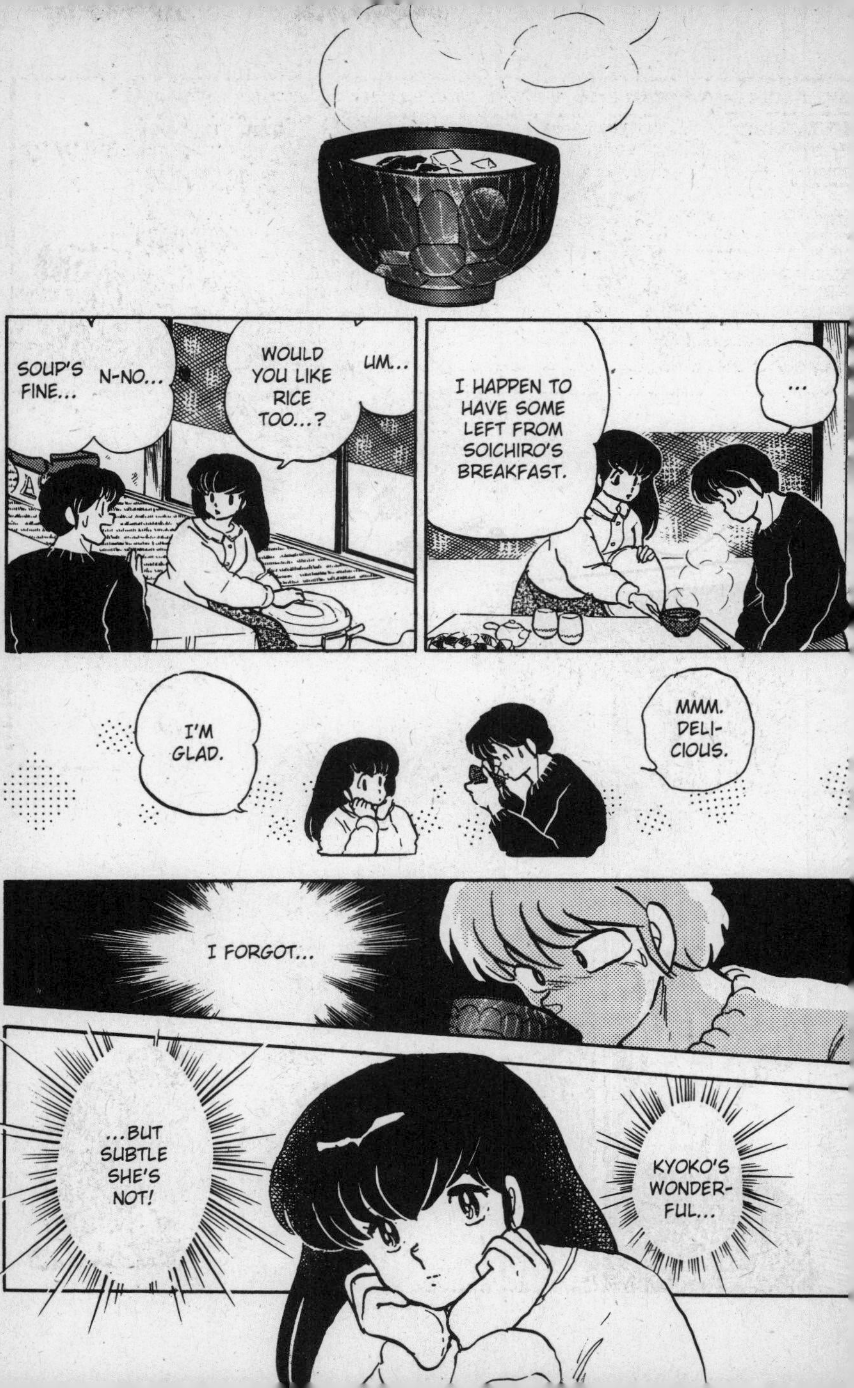
...
I HAPPEN TO HAVE SOME LEFT FROM SOICHIRO'S BREAKFAST.
UM...
WOULD YOU LIKE RICE TOO...?
N-NO...
SOUP'S FINE...
MMM. DELICIOUS.
I'M GLAD.
I FORGOT...
KYOKO'S WONDERFUL...
...BUT SUBTLE SHE'S NOT!

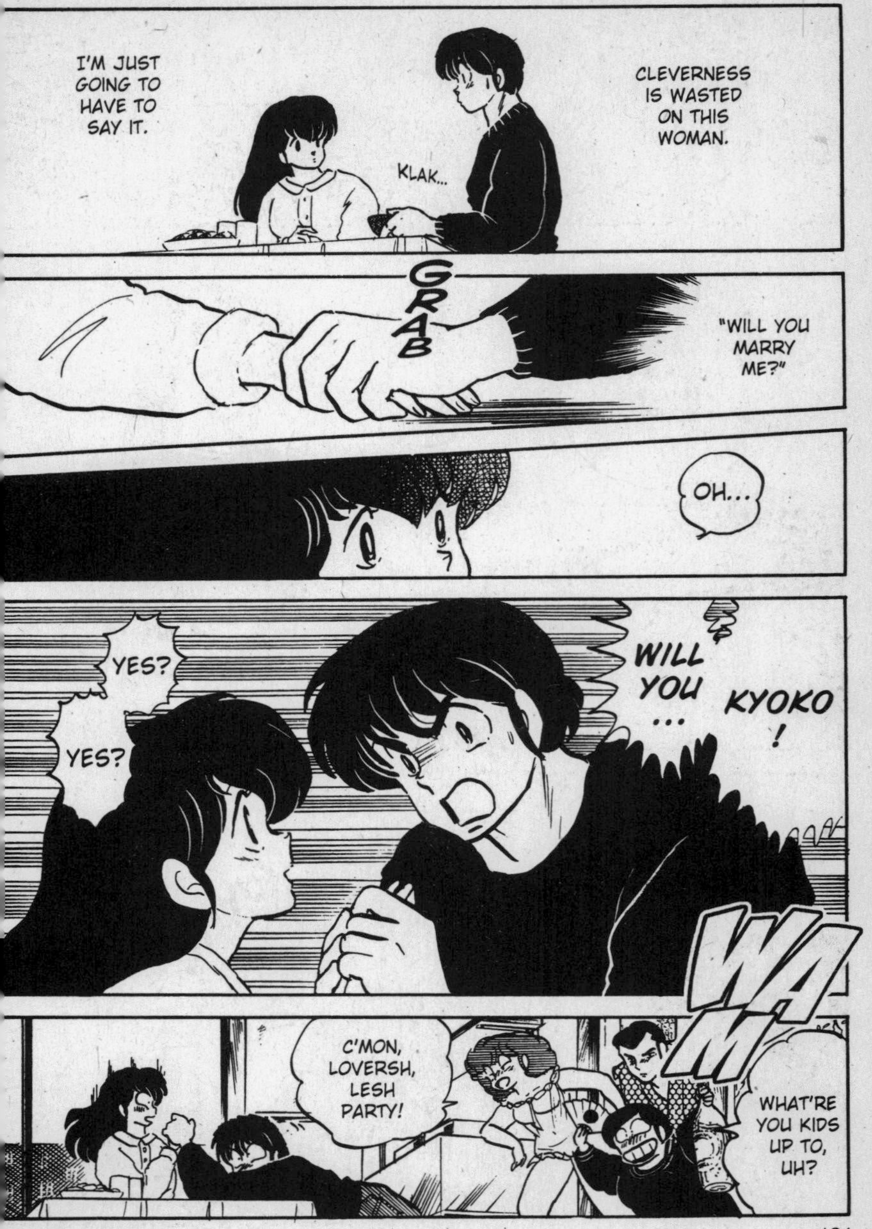

CLEVERNESS IS WASTED ON THIS WOMAN.
KLAK...
I'M JUST GOING TO HAVE TO SAY IT.
"WILL YOU MARRY ME?"
GRAB
OH...
KYOKO!
WILL YOU...
YES?
YES?
WAM
WHAT'RE YOU KIDS UP TO, UH?
C'MON, LOVERSH, LESH PARTY!

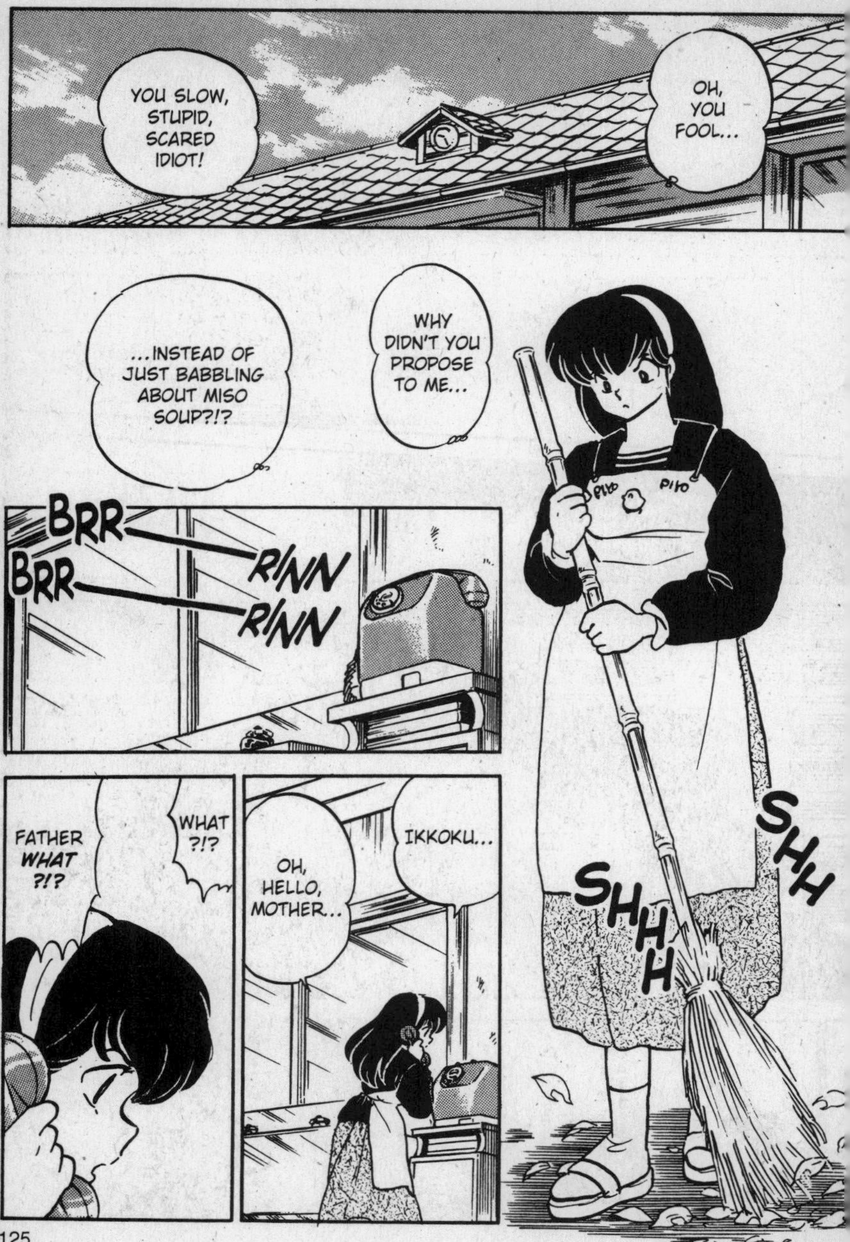

OH, YOU FOOL...
YOU SLOW, STUPID, SCARED IDIOT!
WHY DIDN'T YOU PROPOSE TO ME...
...INSTEAD OF JUST BABBLING ABOUT MISO SOUP?!?
PIYO PIYO
SHH
SHHHH
BRR RINN
BRR RINN
IKKOKU...
OH, HELLO, MOTHER...
WHAT ?!?
FATHER *WHAT* ?!?

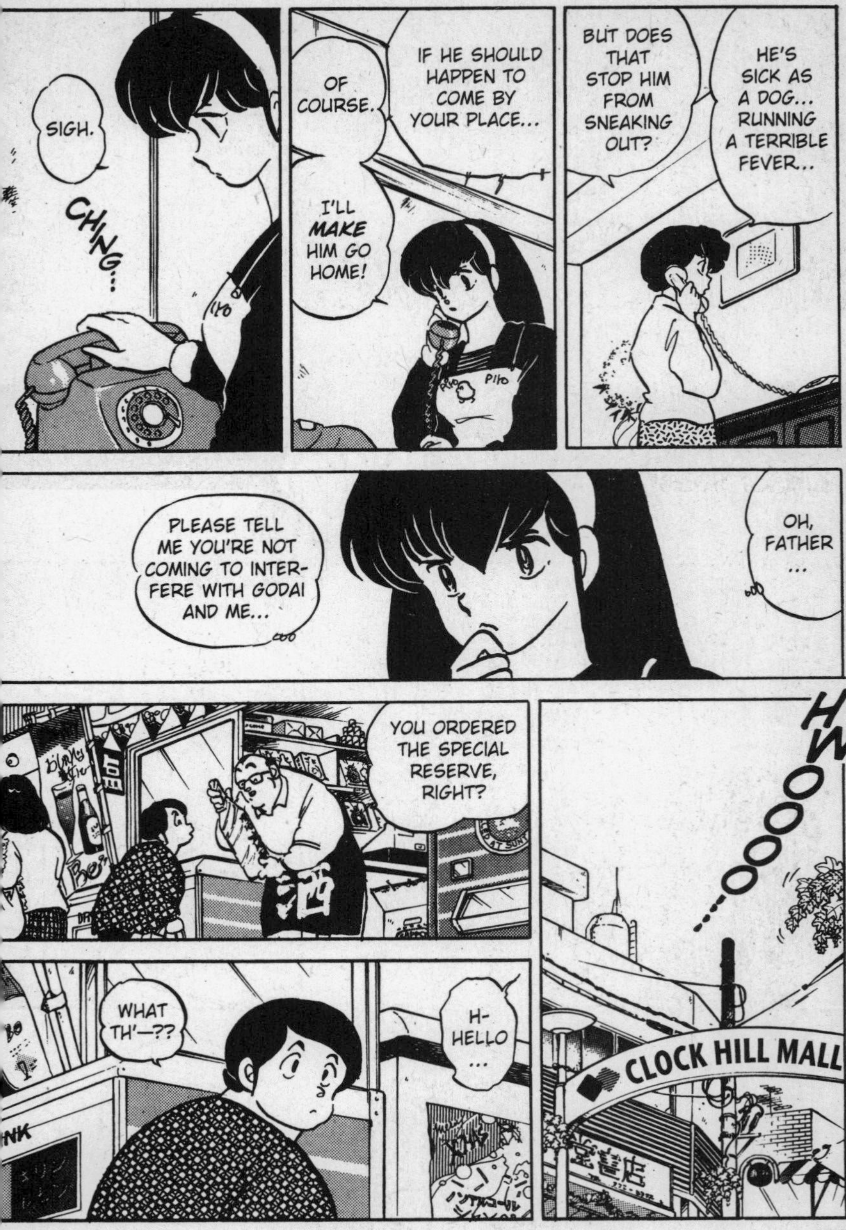
HE'S SICK AS A DOG... RUNNING A TERRIBLE FEVER...
BUT DOES THAT STOP HIM FROM SNEAKING OUT?
IF HE SHOULD HAPPEN TO COME BY YOUR PLACE...
OF COURSE.
I'LL *MAKE* HIM GO HOME!
SIGH.
CHING...
OH, FATHER...
PLEASE TELL ME YOU'RE NOT COMING TO INTERFERE WITH GODAI AND ME...
HWOOOOOO...
CLOCK HILL MALL
YOU ORDERED THE SPECIAL RESERVE, RIGHT?
H- HELLO...
WHAT TH'—??

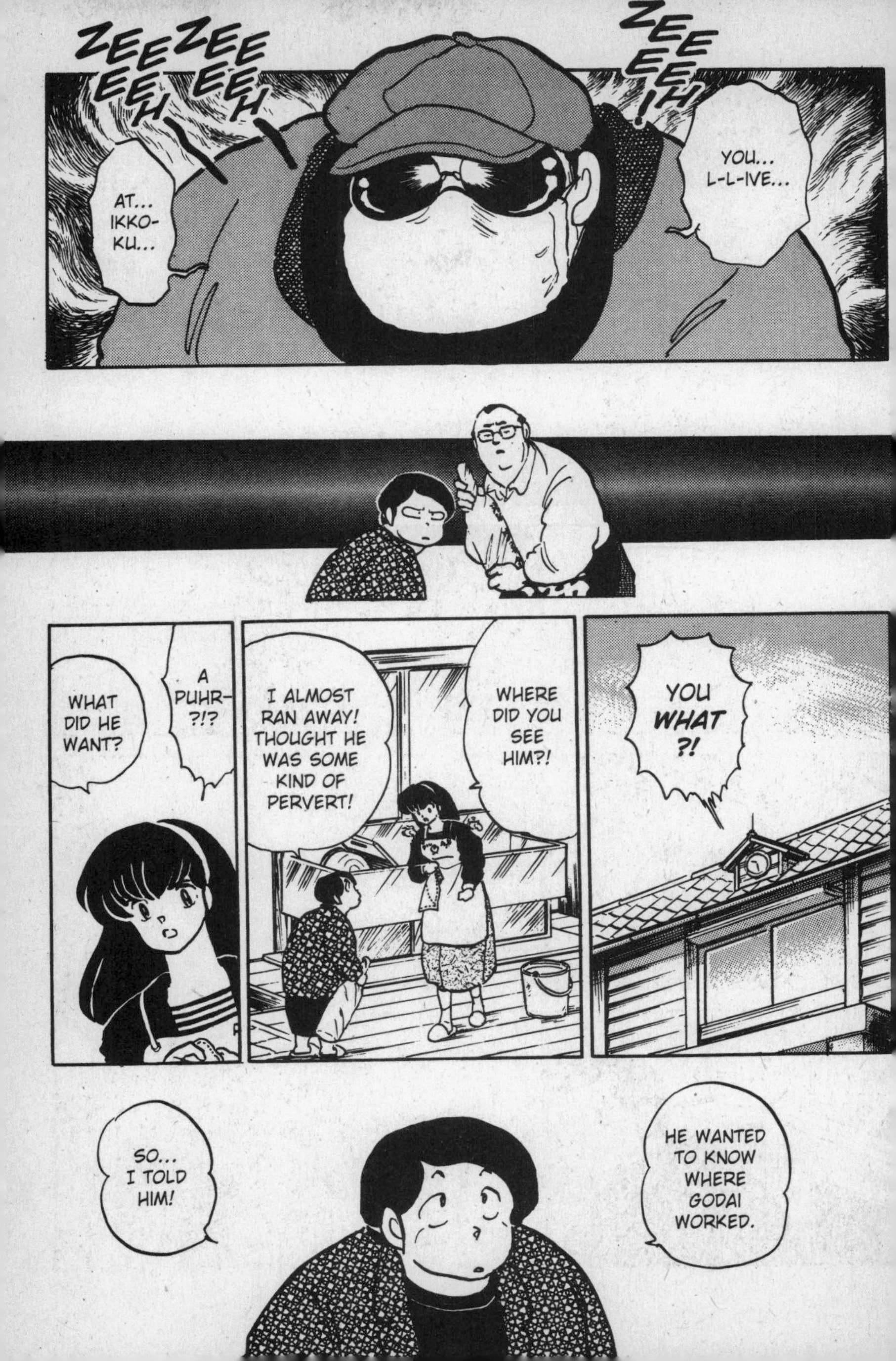
ZEEEEH!
ZEEEEH ZEEEEH
YOU... L-L-IVE...
AT... IKKO-KU...
YOU WHAT?!
WHERE DID YOU SEE HIM?!
I ALMOST RAN AWAY! THOUGHT HE WAS SOME KIND OF PERVERT!
A PUHR-?!?
WHAT DID HE WANT?
HE WANTED TO KNOW WHERE GODAI WORKED.
SO... I TOLD HIM!

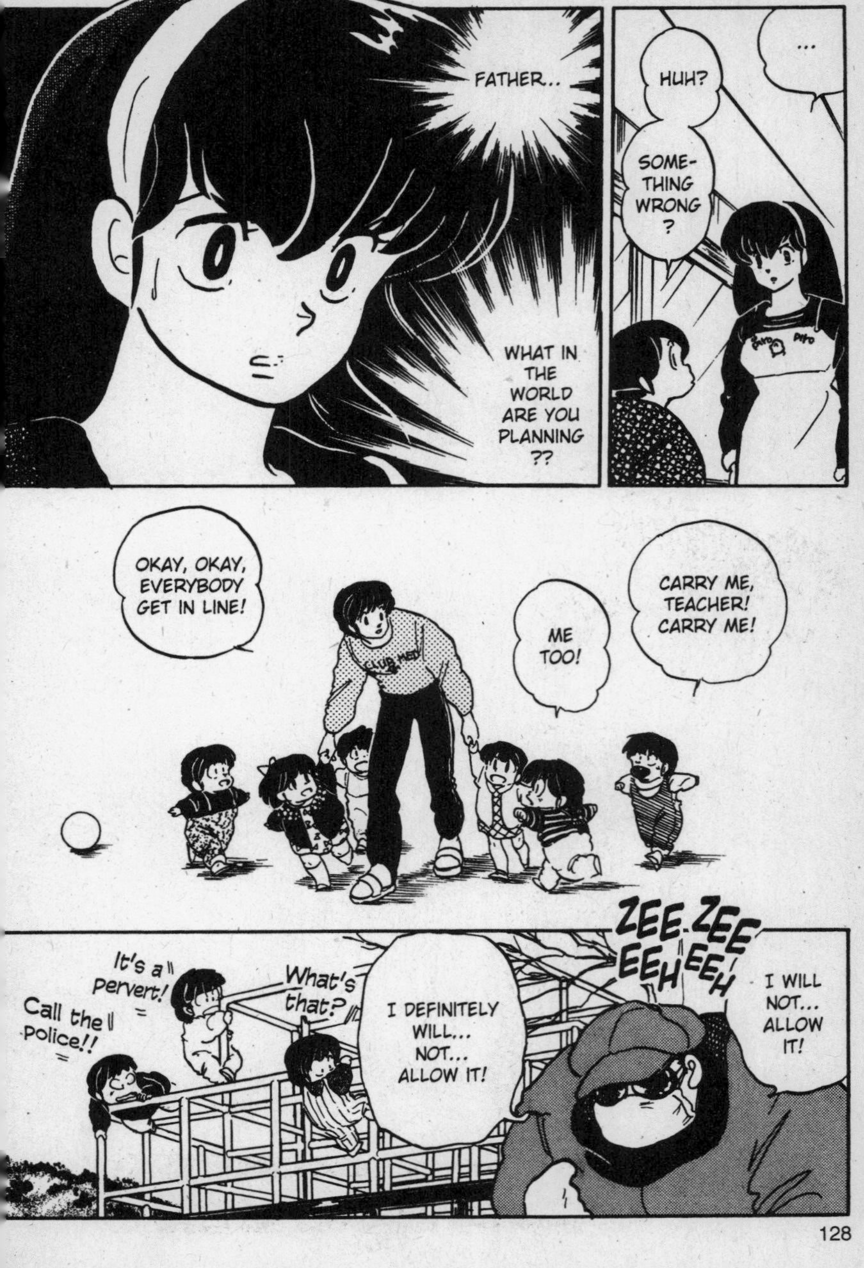
...
HUH?
SOMETHING WRONG?
FATHER...
WHAT IN THE WORLD ARE YOU PLANNING??
CARRY ME, TEACHER! CARRY ME!
ME TOO!
OKAY, OKAY, EVERYBODY GET IN LINE!
ZEE-ZEE EEEH EEEH
I WILL NOT... ALLOW IT!
I DEFINITELY WILL... NOT... ALLOW IT!
What's that?
It's a pervert!
Call the police!!

PART SEVEN
PROMISES

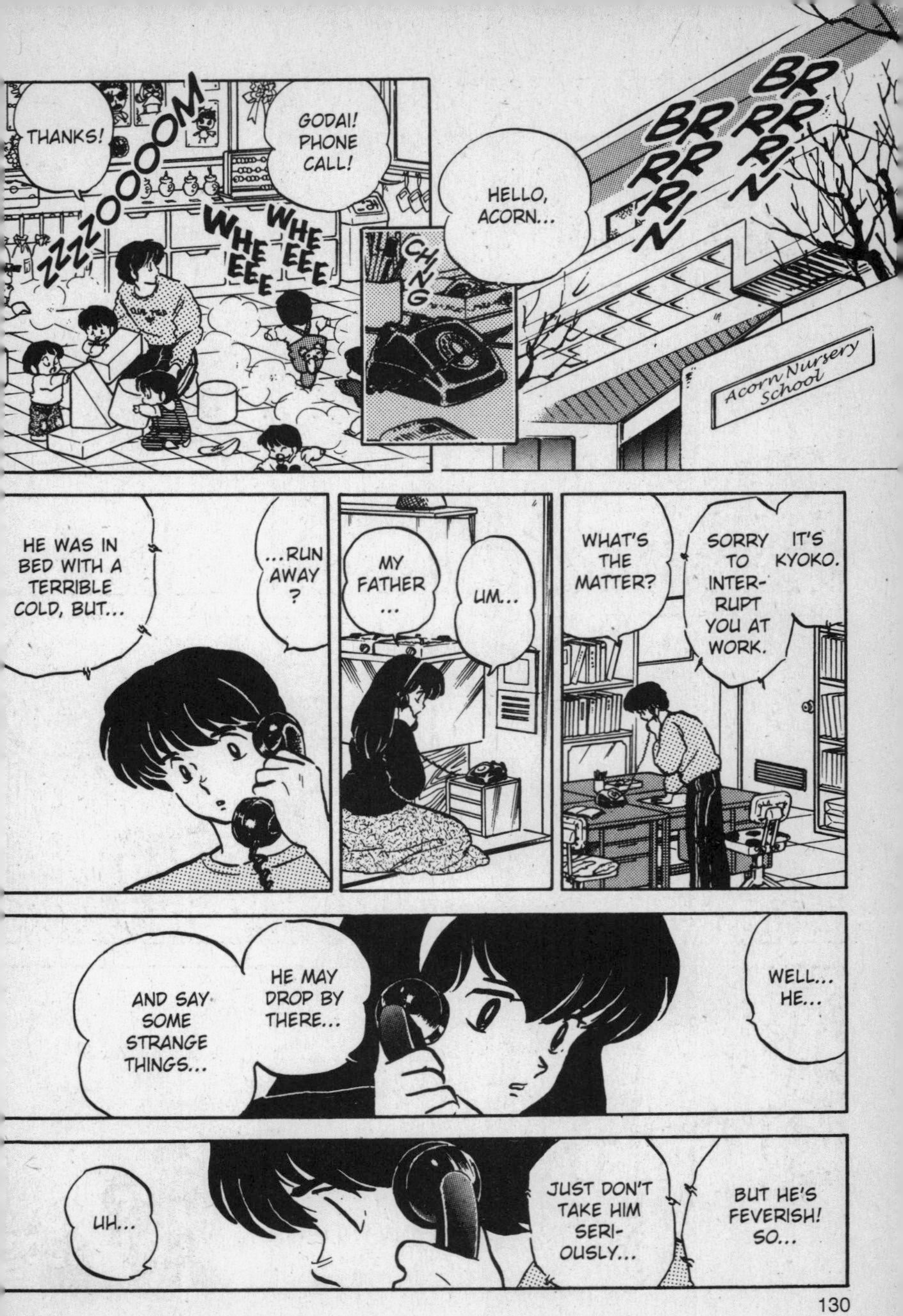
BRRRRIN
BRRRRIN
Acorn Nursery School
CHING
HELLO, ACORN...
GODAI! PHONE CALL!
THANKS!
ZZZZOOOOOM
WHEEEE
WHEEEE
IT'S KYOKO.
SORRY TO INTERRUPT YOU AT WORK.
WHAT'S THE MATTER?
UM...
MY FATHER...
...RUN AWAY?
HE WAS IN BED WITH A TERRIBLE COLD, BUT...
WELL... HE...
HE MAY DROP BY THERE...
AND SAY SOME STRANGE THINGS...
BUT HE'S FEVERISH! SO...
JUST DON'T TAKE HIM SERI-OUSLY...
UH...

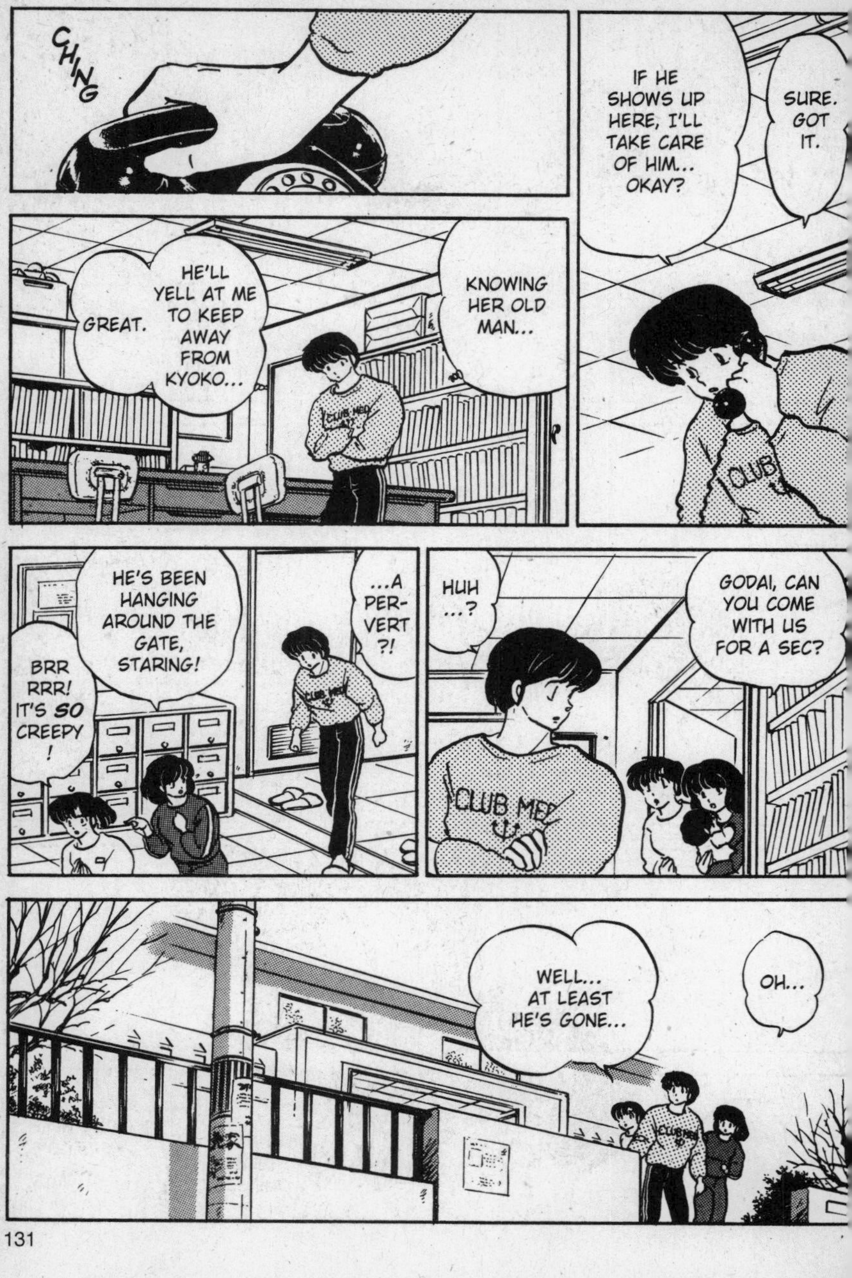
IF HE SHOWS UP HERE, I'LL TAKE CARE OF HIM... OKAY?
SURE. GOT IT.
CHING
KNOWING HER OLD MAN...
HE'LL YELL AT ME TO KEEP AWAY FROM KYOKO...
GREAT.
GODAI, CAN YOU COME WITH US FOR A SEC?
HUH ...?
...A PER-VERT?!
HE'S BEEN HANGING AROUND THE GATE, STARING!
BRR RRR! IT'S *SO* CREEPY!
OH...
WELL... AT LEAST HE'S GONE...

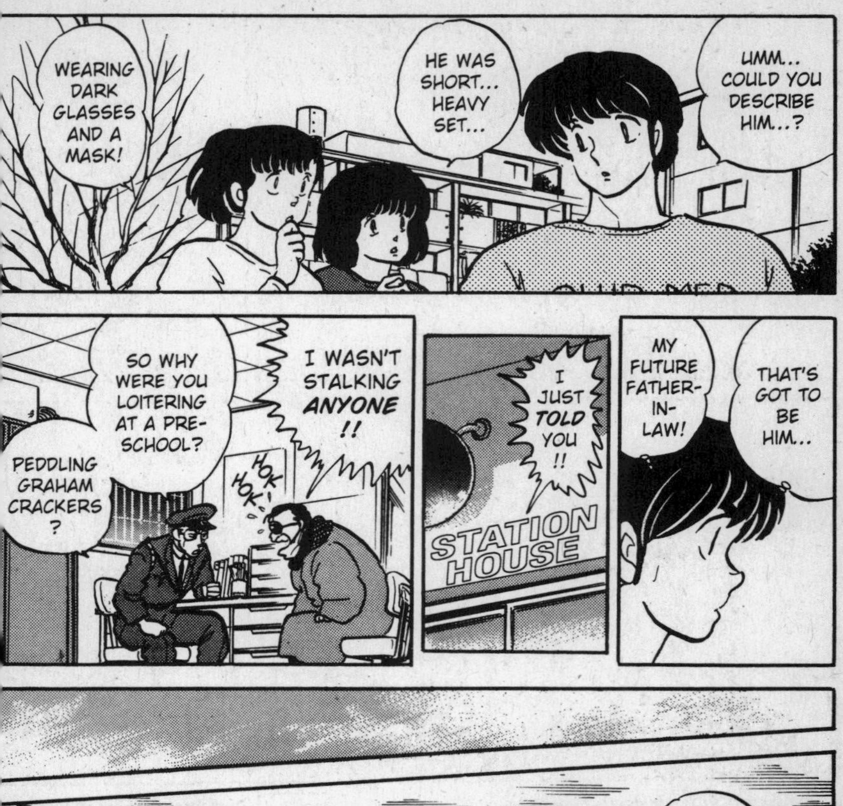
UMM... COULD YOU DESCRIBE HIM...?
HE WAS SHORT... HEAVY SET...
WEARING DARK GLASSES AND A MASK!
THAT'S GOT TO BE HIM...
MY FUTURE FATHER-IN-LAW!
STATION HOUSE
I JUST TOLD YOU!!
I WASN'T STALKING ANYONE!!
SO WHY WERE YOU LOITERING AT A PRE-SCHOOL?
HOK HOK
PEDDLING GRAHAM CRACKERS?
THE NERVE OF HIM!
DOESN'T HE KNOW I PAY HIS SALARY?

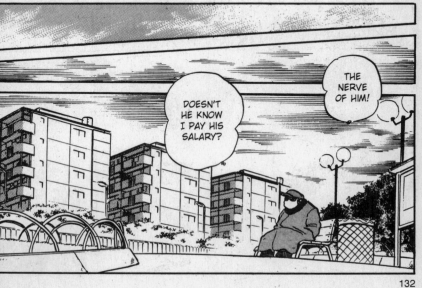

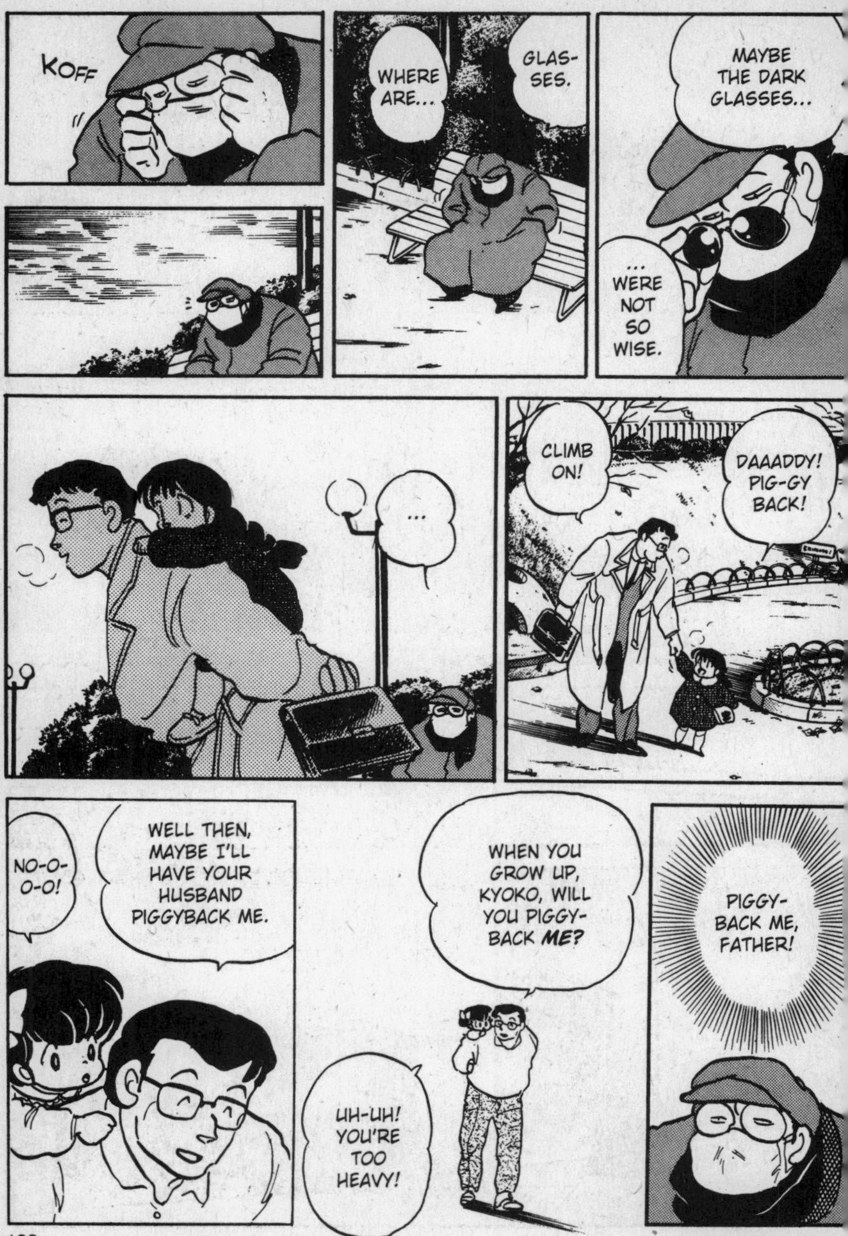
MAYBE THE DARK GLASSES...
...WERE NOT SO WISE.
GLAS-SES.
WHERE ARE...
KOFF
DAAADDY! PIG-GY BACK!
CLIMB ON!
...
PIGGY-BACK ME, FATHER!
WHEN YOU GROW UP, KYOKO, WILL YOU PIGGY-BACK **ME?**
UH-UH! YOU'RE TOO HEAVY!
WELL THEN, MAYBE I'LL HAVE YOUR HUSBAND PIGGYBACK ME.
NO-O-O-O!

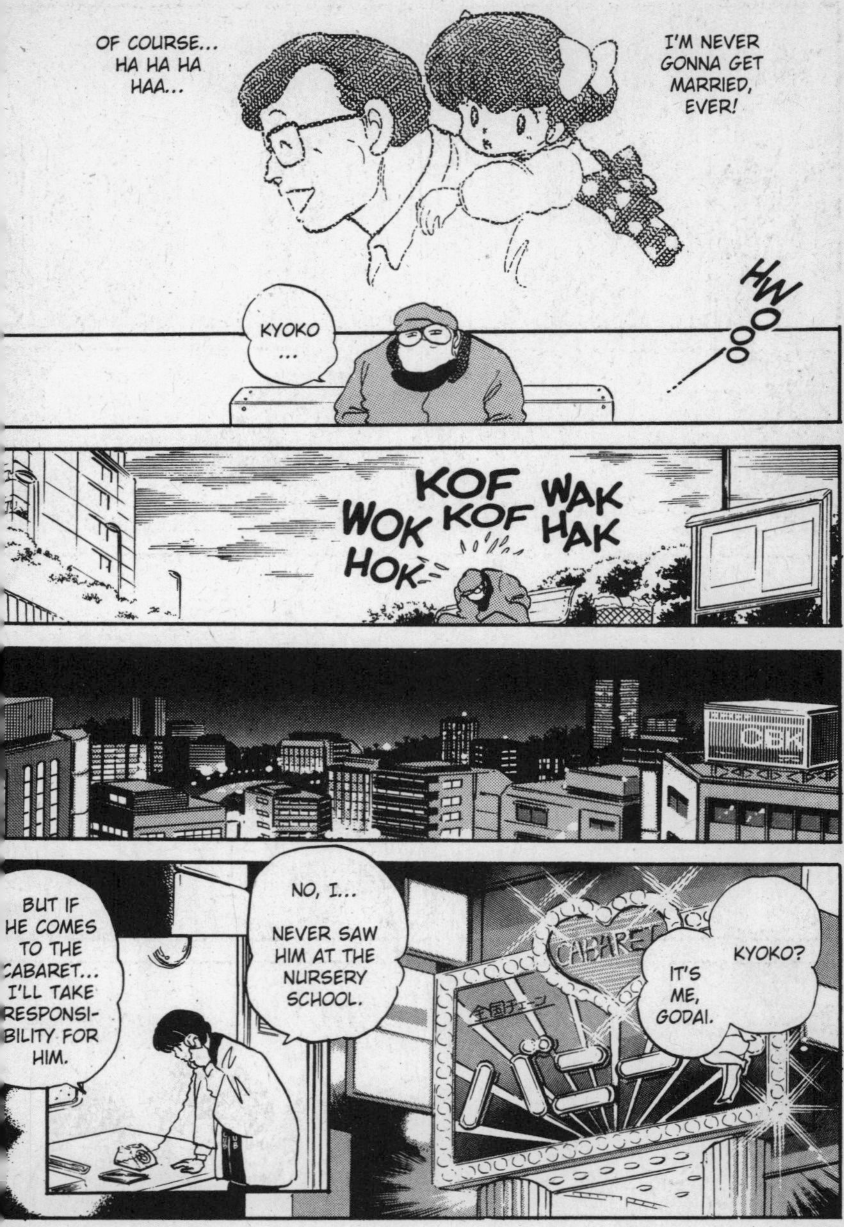
I'M NEVER GONNA GET MARRIED, EVER!
OF COURSE... HA HA HA HAA...
HWOOOO
KYOKO ...
WAK HAK
KOF KOF
WOK HOK
CBK
KYOKO?
IT'S ME, GODAI.
CABARET
全国チェーン
NO, I...
NEVER SAW HIM AT THE NURSERY SCHOOL.
BUT IF HE COMES TO THE CABARET... I'LL TAKE RESPONSI-BILITY FOR HIM.

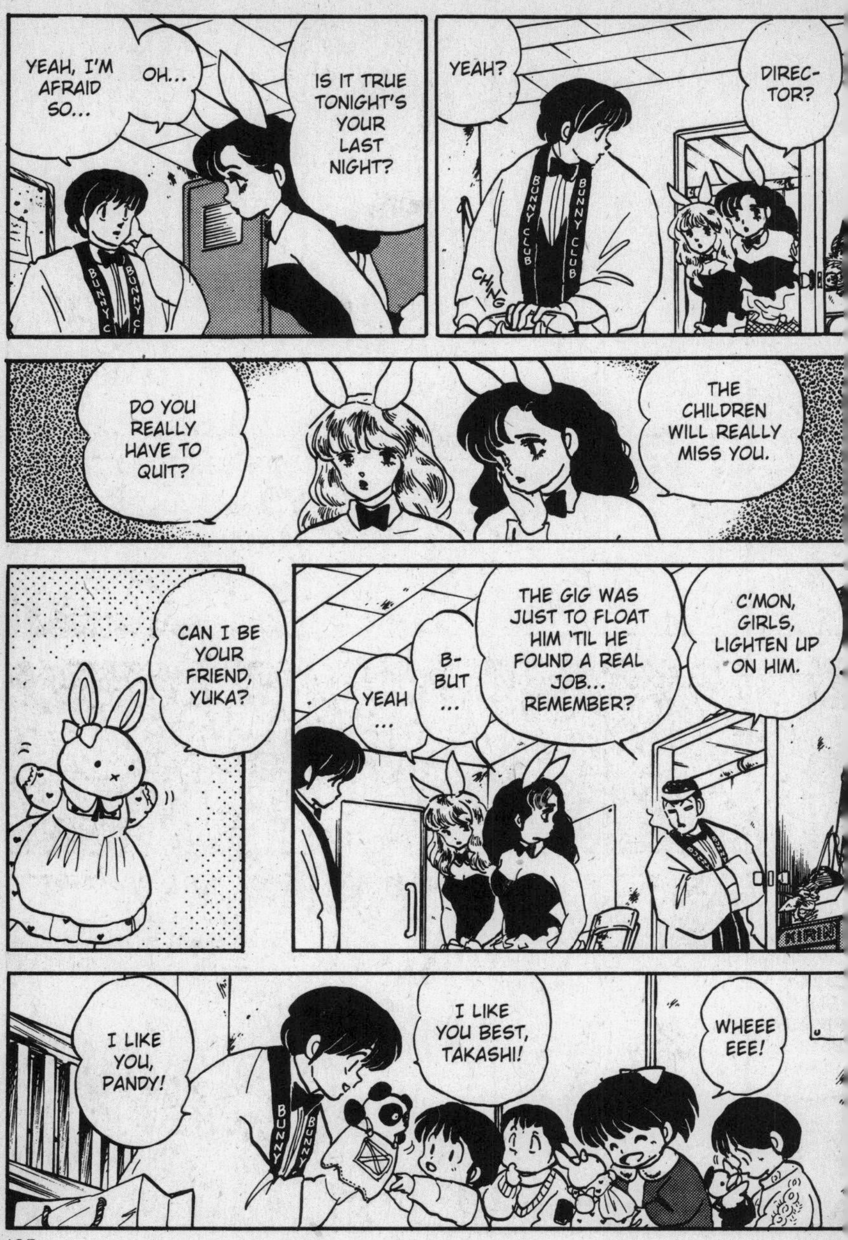
DIREC-TOR?
YEAH?
CHING
IS IT TRUE TONIGHT'S YOUR LAST NIGHT?
OH...
YEAH, I'M AFRAID SO...
THE CHILDREN WILL REALLY MISS YOU.
DO YOU REALLY HAVE TO QUIT?
C'MON, GIRLS, LIGHTEN UP ON HIM.
THE GIG WAS JUST TO FLOAT HIM 'TIL HE FOUND A REAL JOB... REMEMBER?
B-BUT ...
YEAH ...
CAN I BE YOUR FRIEND, YUKA?
WHEEE EEE!
I LIKE YOU BEST, TAKASHI!
I LIKE YOU, PANDY!

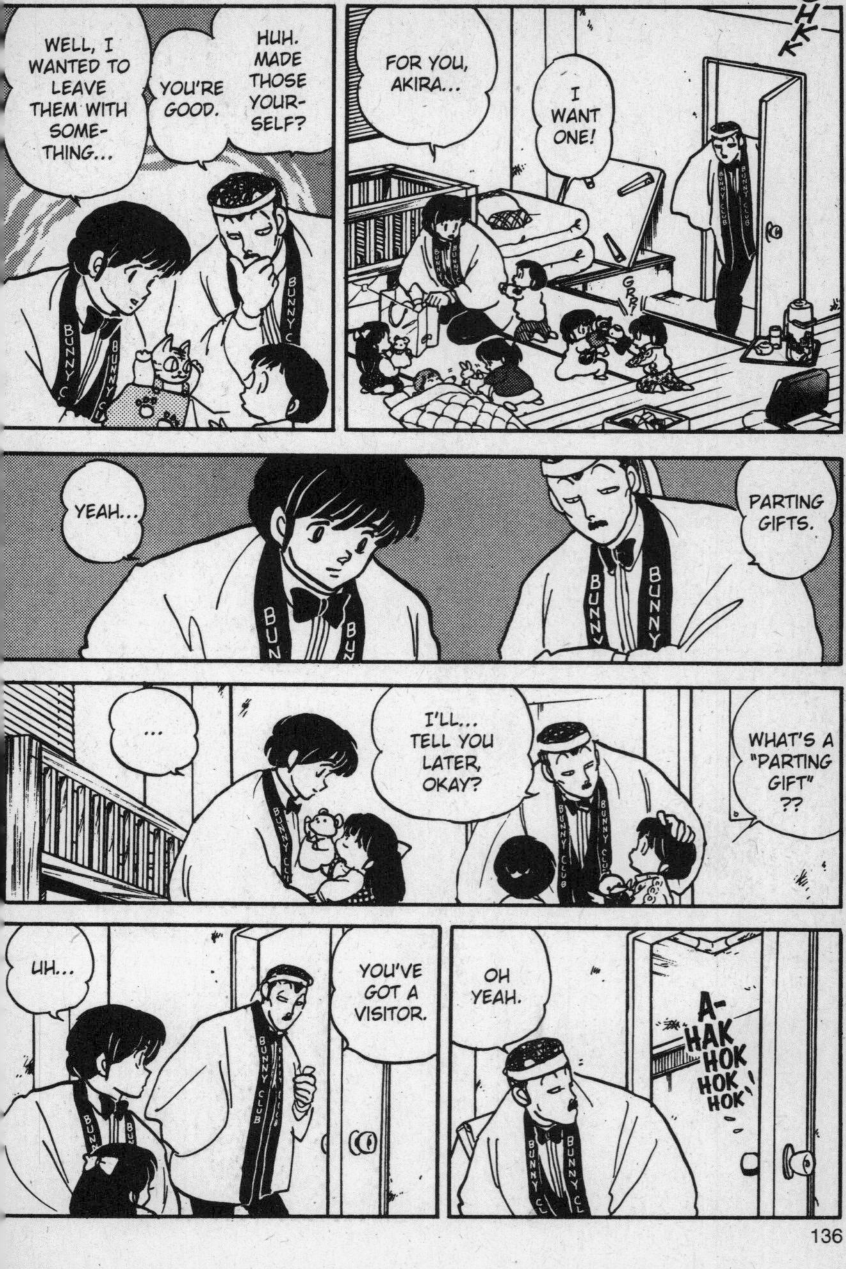

CHKK
FOR YOU, AKIRA...
I WANT ONE!
GRR!
HUH. MADE THOSE YOURSELF?
YOU'RE GOOD.
WELL, I WANTED TO LEAVE THEM WITH SOMETHING...
PARTING GIFTS.
YEAH...
WHAT'S A "PARTING GIFT"??
I'LL... TELL YOU LATER, OKAY?
...
A-HAK HOK HOK HOK
OH YEAH.
YOU'VE GOT A VISITOR.
UH...

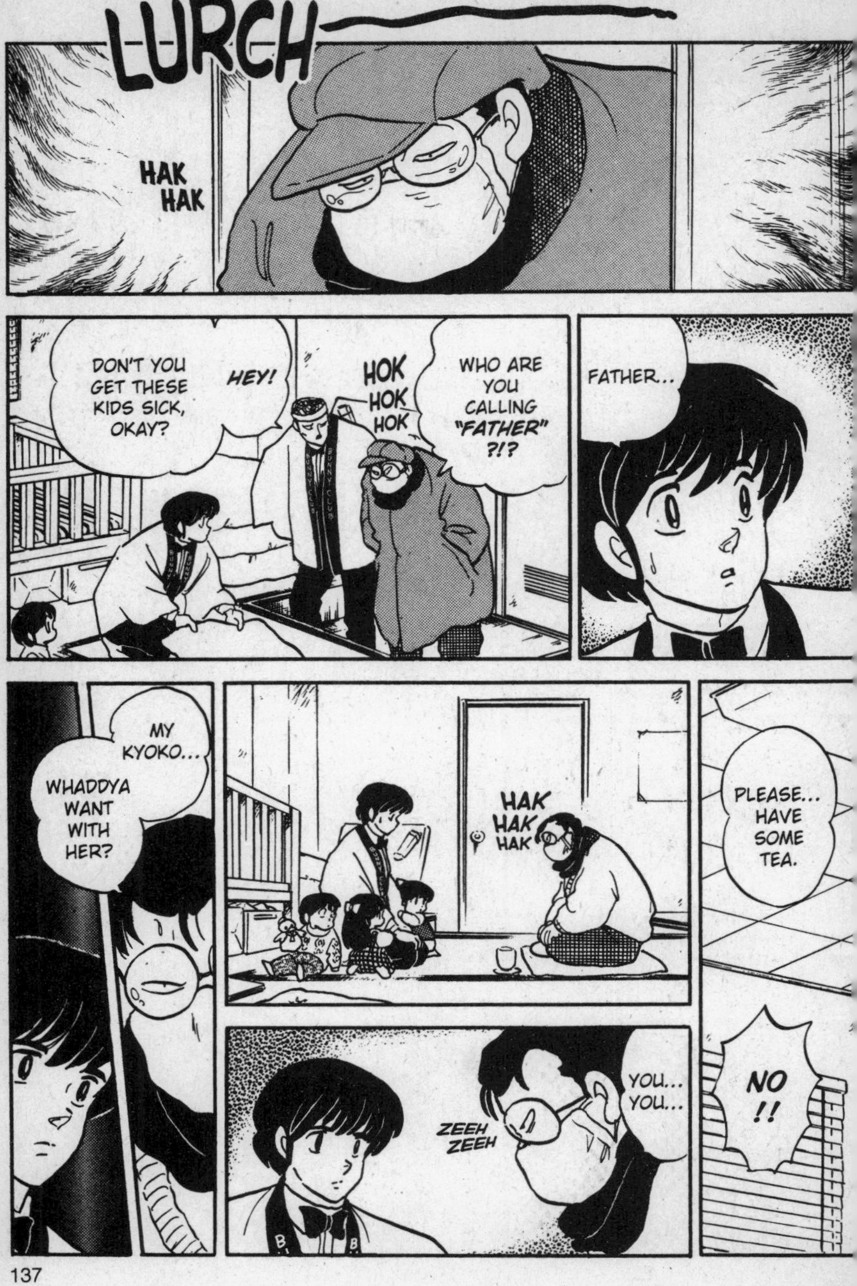
LURCH
HAK HAK
FATHER...
WHO ARE YOU CALLING "FATHER" ?!?
HOK HOK HOK
HEY!
DON'T YOU GET THESE KIDS SICK, OKAY?
PLEASE... HAVE SOME TEA.
NO !!
HAK HAK HAK
YOU... YOU...
ZEEH ZEEH
MY KYOKO...
WHADDYA WANT WITH HER?

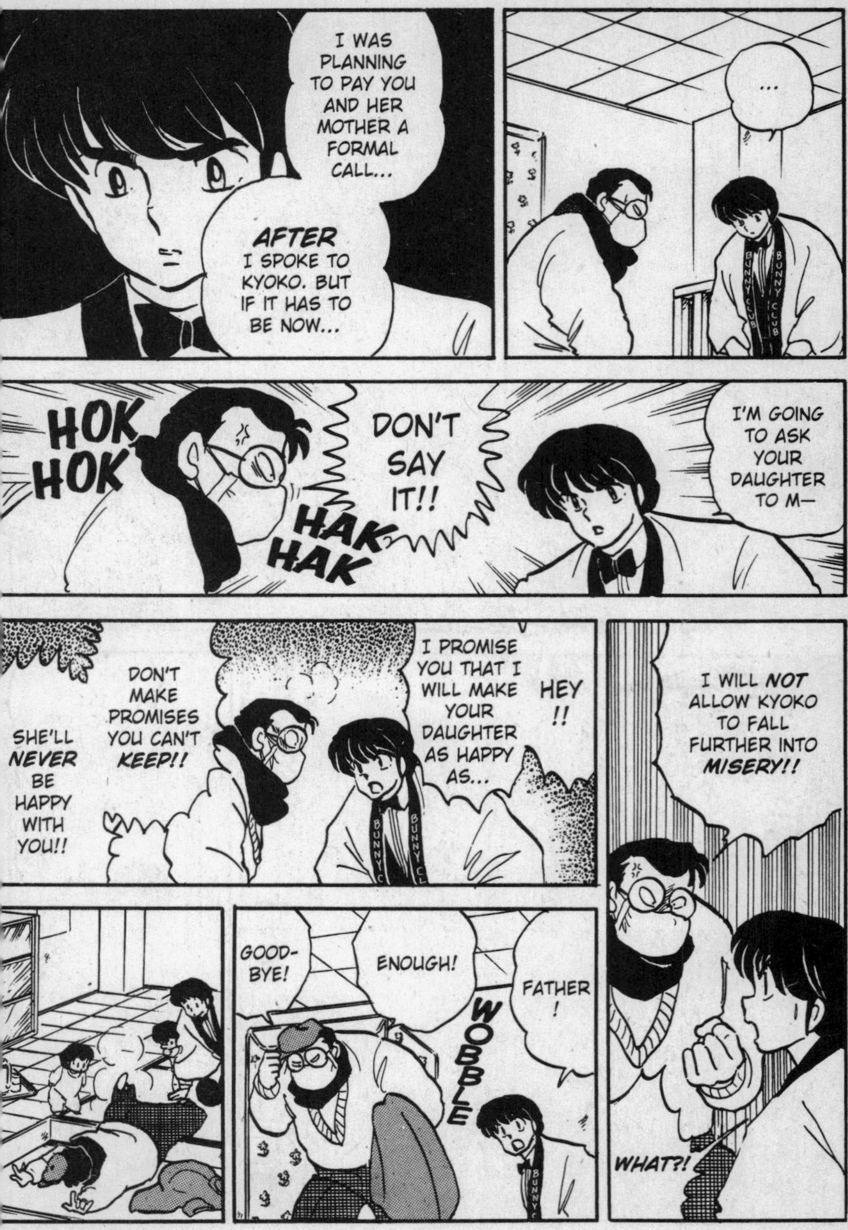
...
I WAS PLANNING TO PAY YOU AND HER MOTHER A FORMAL CALL...
AFTER I SPOKE TO KYOKO. BUT IF IT HAS TO BE NOW...
I'M GOING TO ASK YOUR DAUGHTER TO M—
DON'T SAY IT!!
HAK HAK
HOK HOK
I WILL NOT ALLOW KYOKO TO FALL FURTHER INTO MISERY!!
WHAT?!
HEY !!
I PROMISE YOU THAT I WILL MAKE YOUR DAUGHTER AS HAPPY AS...
DON'T MAKE PROMISES YOU CAN'T KEEP!!
SHE'LL NEVER BE HAPPY WITH YOU!!
FATHER !
WOBBLE
ENOUGH!
GOOD-BYE!

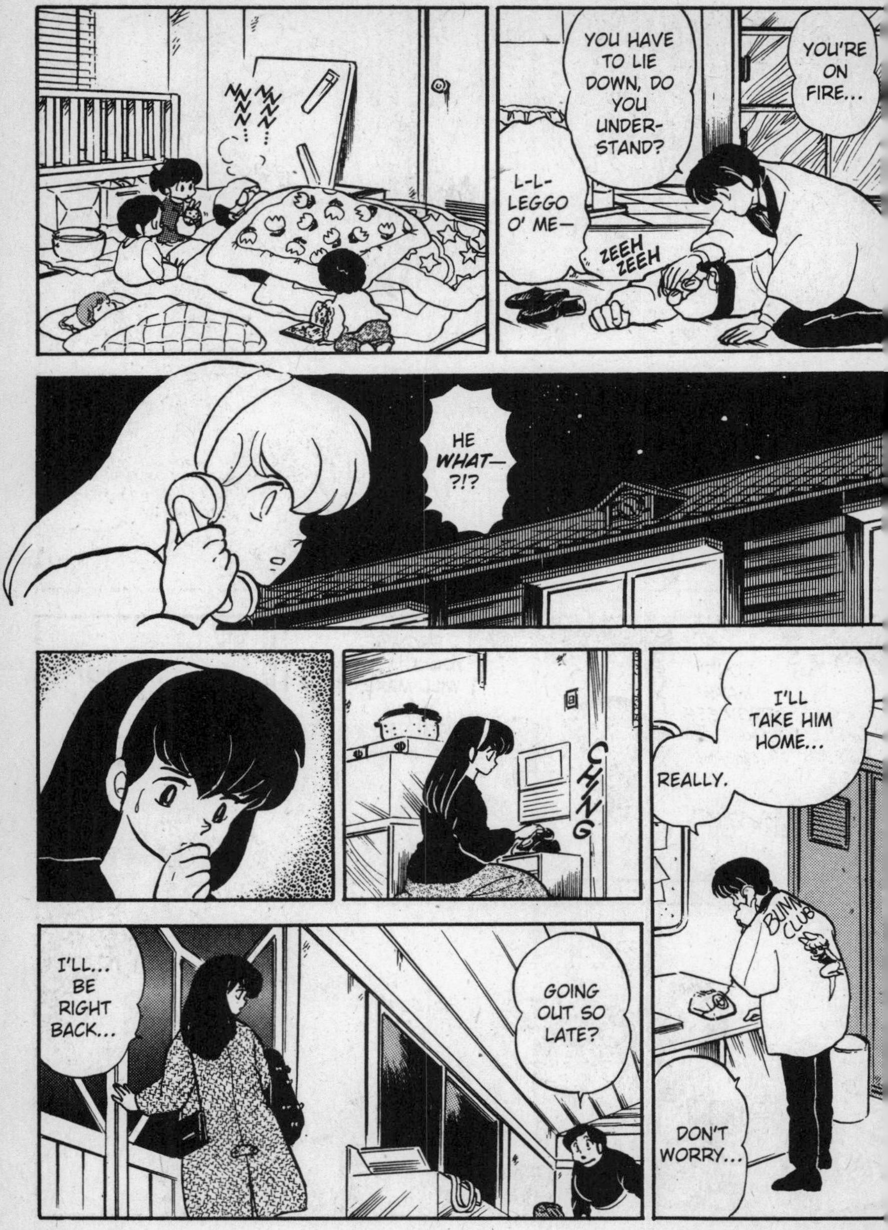
YOU'RE ON FIRE...
YOU HAVE TO LIE DOWN, DO YOU UNDERSTAND?
L-L-LEGGO O' ME—
ZEEH ZEEH
HE *WHAT*— ?!?
I'LL TAKE HIM HOME...
REALLY.
DON'T WORRY...
CHING
GOING OUT SO LATE?
I'LL... BE RIGHT BACK...

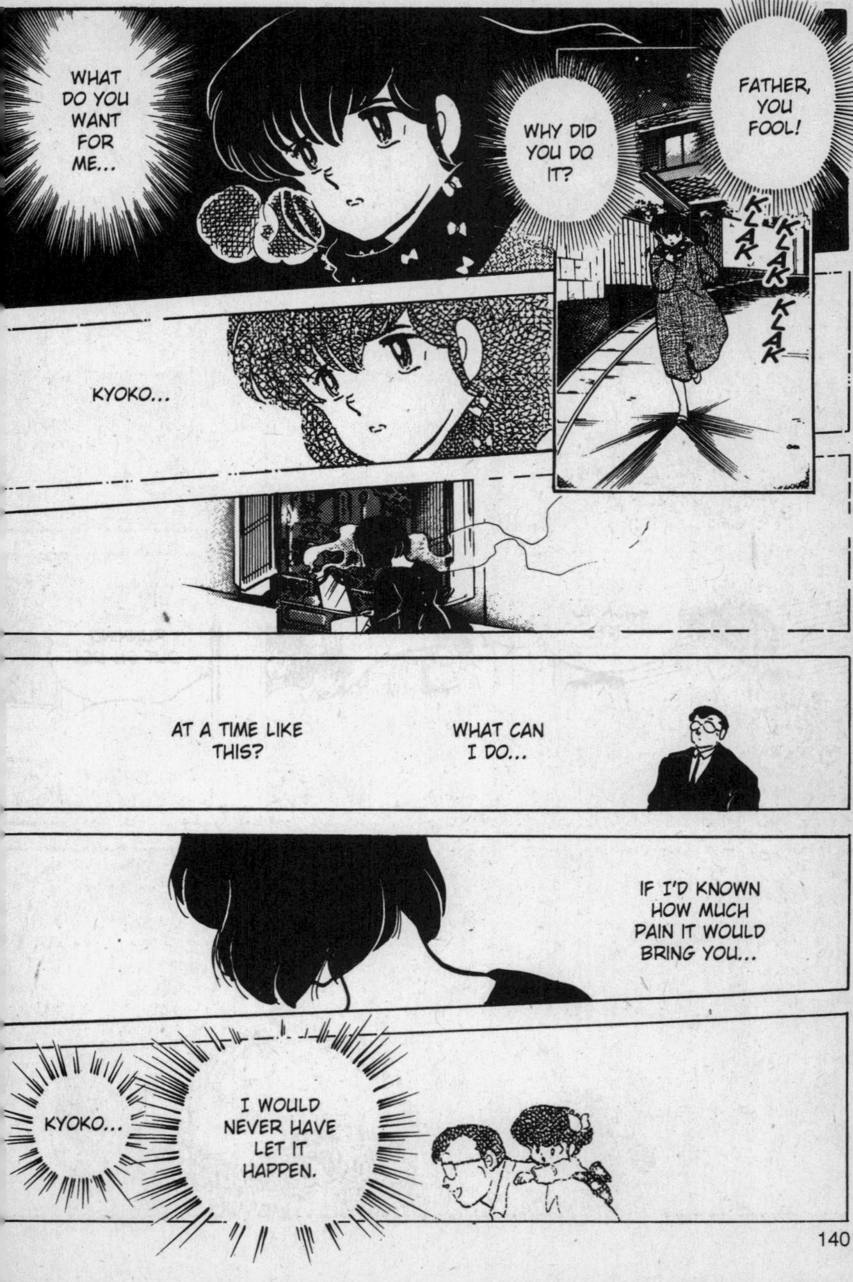
FATHER, YOU FOOL!
WHY DID YOU DO IT?
WHAT DO YOU WANT FOR ME...
KLAK KLAK KLAK KLAK
KYOKO...
WHAT CAN I DO...
AT A TIME LIKE THIS?
IF I'D KNOWN HOW MUCH PAIN IT WOULD BRING YOU...
I WOULD NEVER HAVE LET IT HAPPEN.
KYOKO...

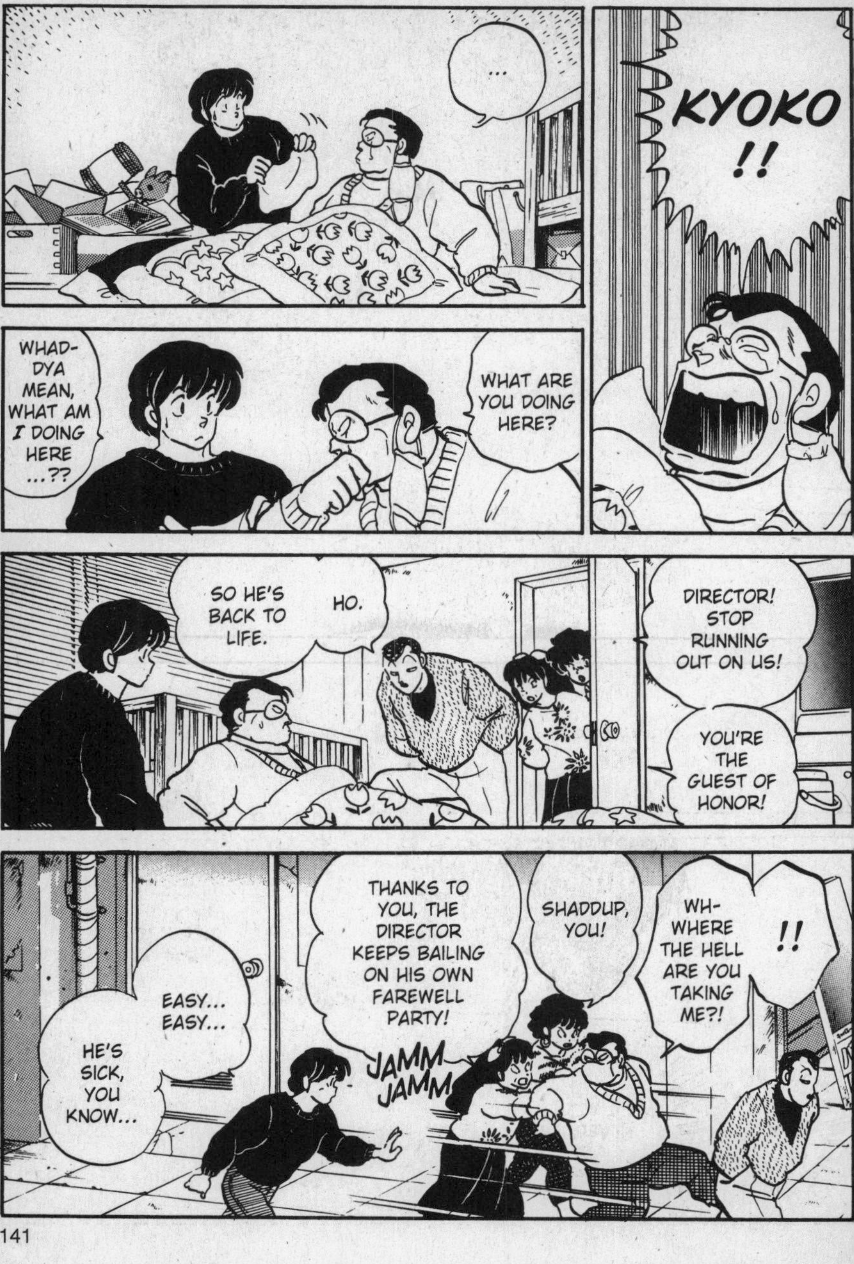
KYOKO !!
...
WHAT ARE YOU DOING HERE?
WHADDYA MEAN, WHAT AM I DOING HERE ...??
DIRECTOR! STOP RUNNING OUT ON US!
YOU'RE THE GUEST OF HONOR!
HO.
SO HE'S BACK TO LIFE.
!!
WH- WHERE THE HELL ARE YOU TAKING ME?!
SHADDUP, YOU!
THANKS TO YOU, THE DIRECTOR KEEPS BAILING ON HIS OWN FAREWELL PARTY!
JAMM JAMM
EASY... EASY...
HE'S SICK, YOU KNOW...

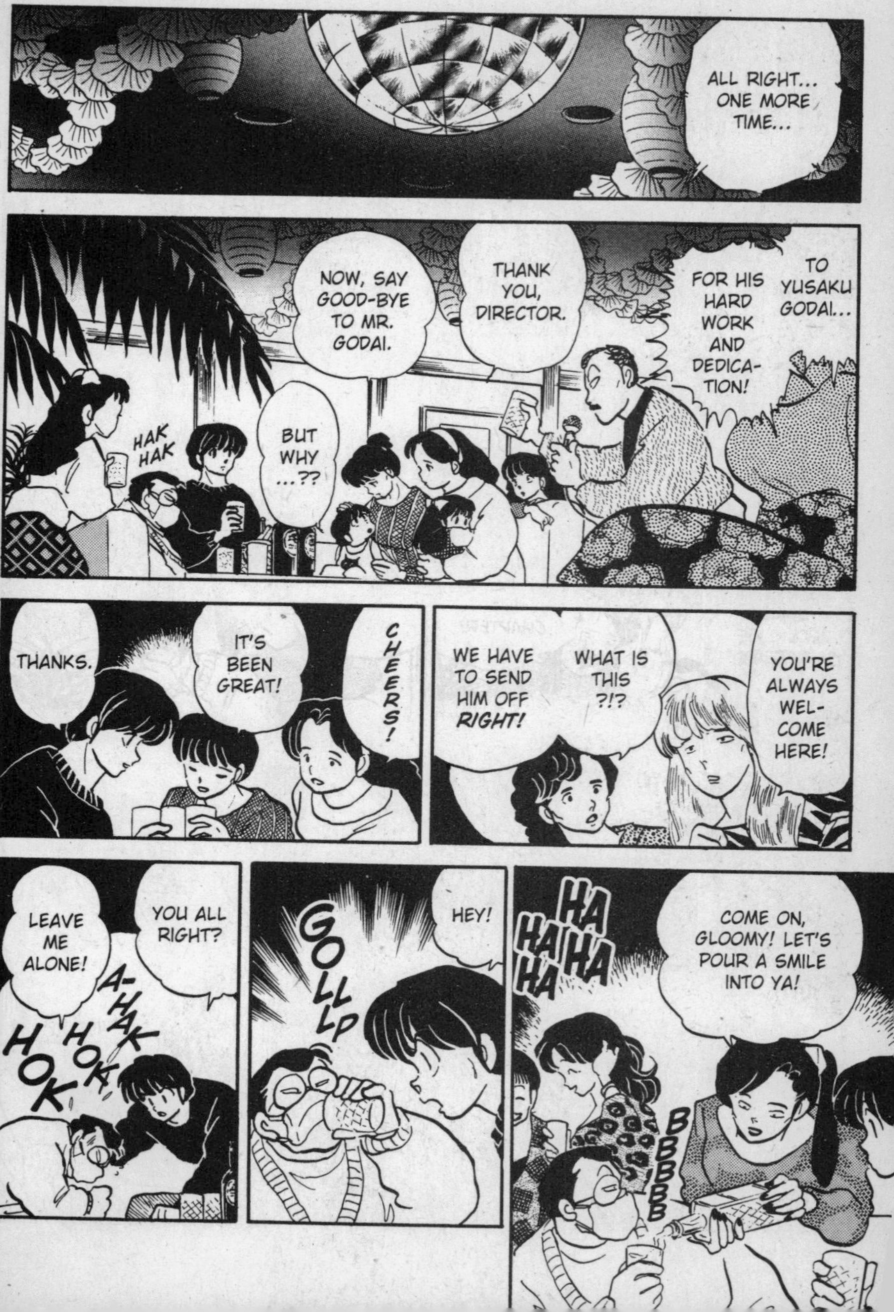
ALL RIGHT... ONE MORE TIME...
TO YUSAKU GODAI...
FOR HIS HARD WORK AND DEDICA-TION!
THANK YOU, DIRECTOR.
NOW, SAY GOOD-BYE TO MR. GODAI.
BUT WHY ...??
HAK HAK
YOU'RE ALWAYS WEL-COME HERE!
WHAT IS THIS ?!?
WE HAVE TO SEND HIM OFF *RIGHT!*
CHEERS!
IT'S BEEN GREAT!
THANKS.
COME ON, GLOOMY! LET'S POUR A SMILE INTO YA!
HA HA HA HA HA
BBBBBB
HEY!
GOLLLP
YOU ALL RIGHT?
LEAVE ME ALONE!
A-HAK HOK HOK

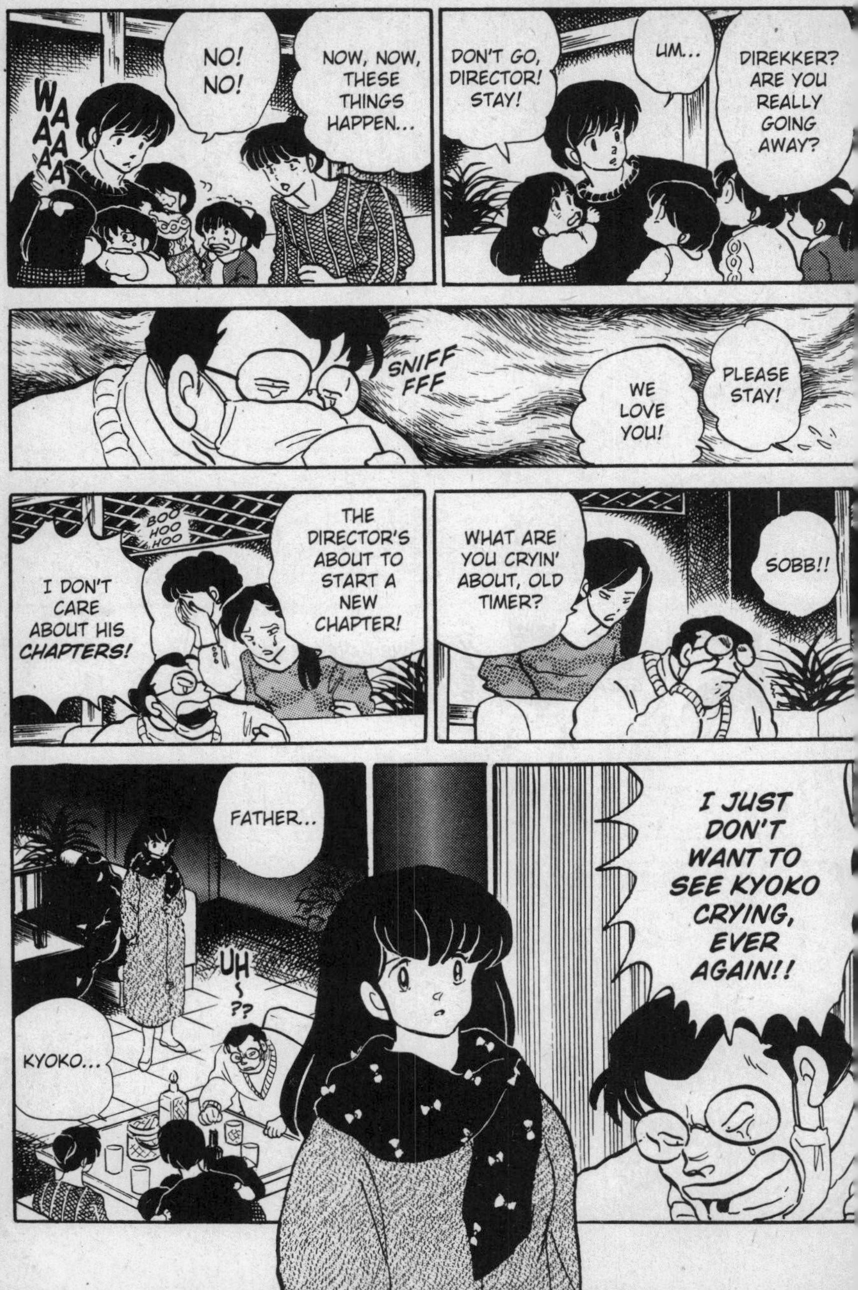
DIREKKER? ARE YOU REALLY GOING AWAY?
UM...
DON'T GO, DIRECTOR! STAY!
NOW, NOW, THESE THINGS HAPPEN...
NO! NO!
WAAAAA
PLEASE STAY!
WE LOVE YOU!
SNIFF FFF
SOBB!!
WHAT ARE YOU CRYIN' ABOUT, OLD TIMER?
THE DIRECTOR'S ABOUT TO START A NEW CHAPTER!
BOO HOO HOO
I DON'T CARE ABOUT HIS *CHAPTERS!*
I JUST DON'T WANT TO SEE KYOKO CRYING, EVER AGAIN!!
FATHER...
UH~ ??
KYOKO...

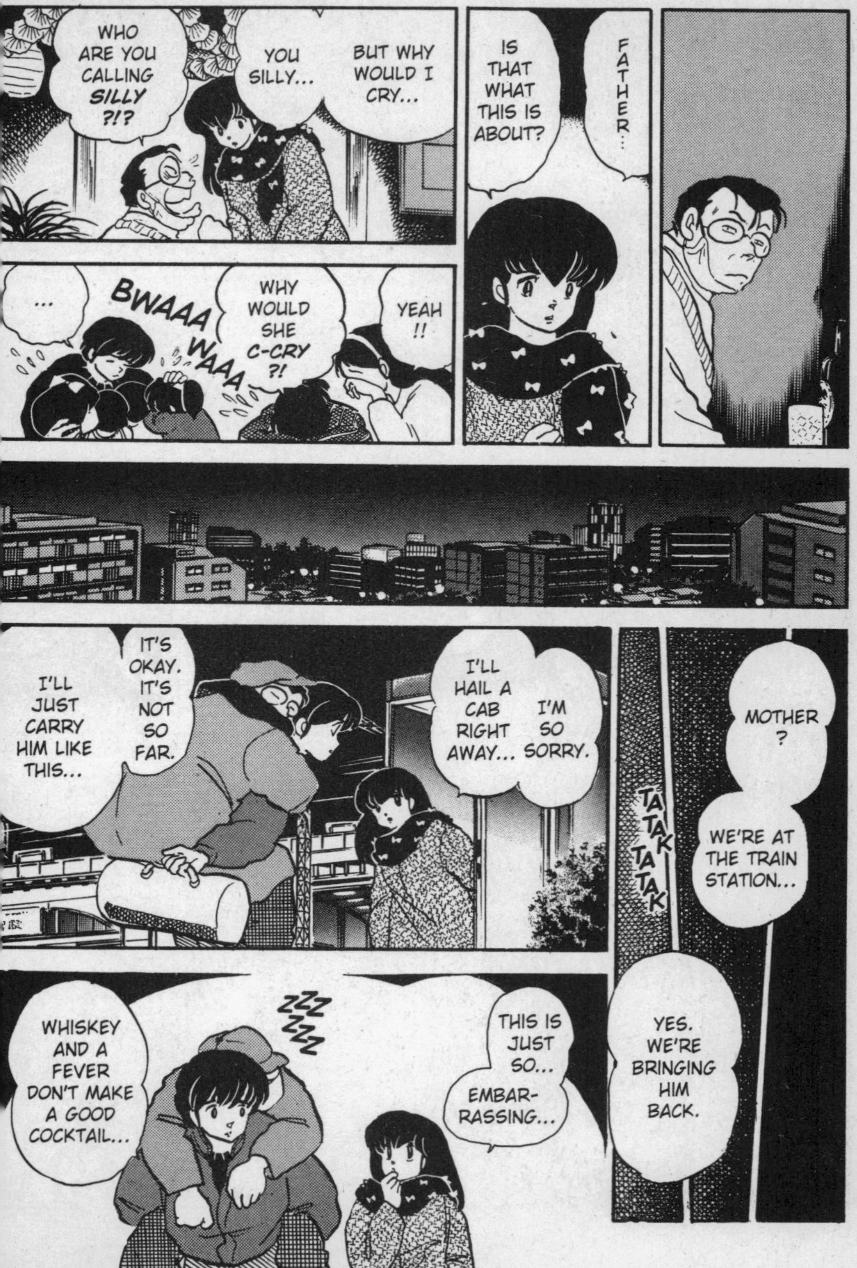
FATHER...
IS THAT WHAT THIS IS ABOUT?
BUT WHY WOULD I CRY...
YOU SILLY...
WHO ARE YOU CALLING SILLY ?!?
YEAH !!
WHY WOULD SHE C-CRY ?!
BWAAA WAAA
...
MOTHER ?
TATAK TATAK
WE'RE AT THE TRAIN STATION...
I'M SO SORRY.
I'LL HAIL A CAB RIGHT AWAY...
IT'S OKAY. IT'S NOT SO FAR.
I'LL JUST CARRY HIM LIKE THIS...
YES. WE'RE BRINGING HIM BACK.
THIS IS JUST SO...
EMBARRASSING...
ZZZ ZZZ
WHISKEY AND A FEVER DON'T MAKE A GOOD COCKTAIL...

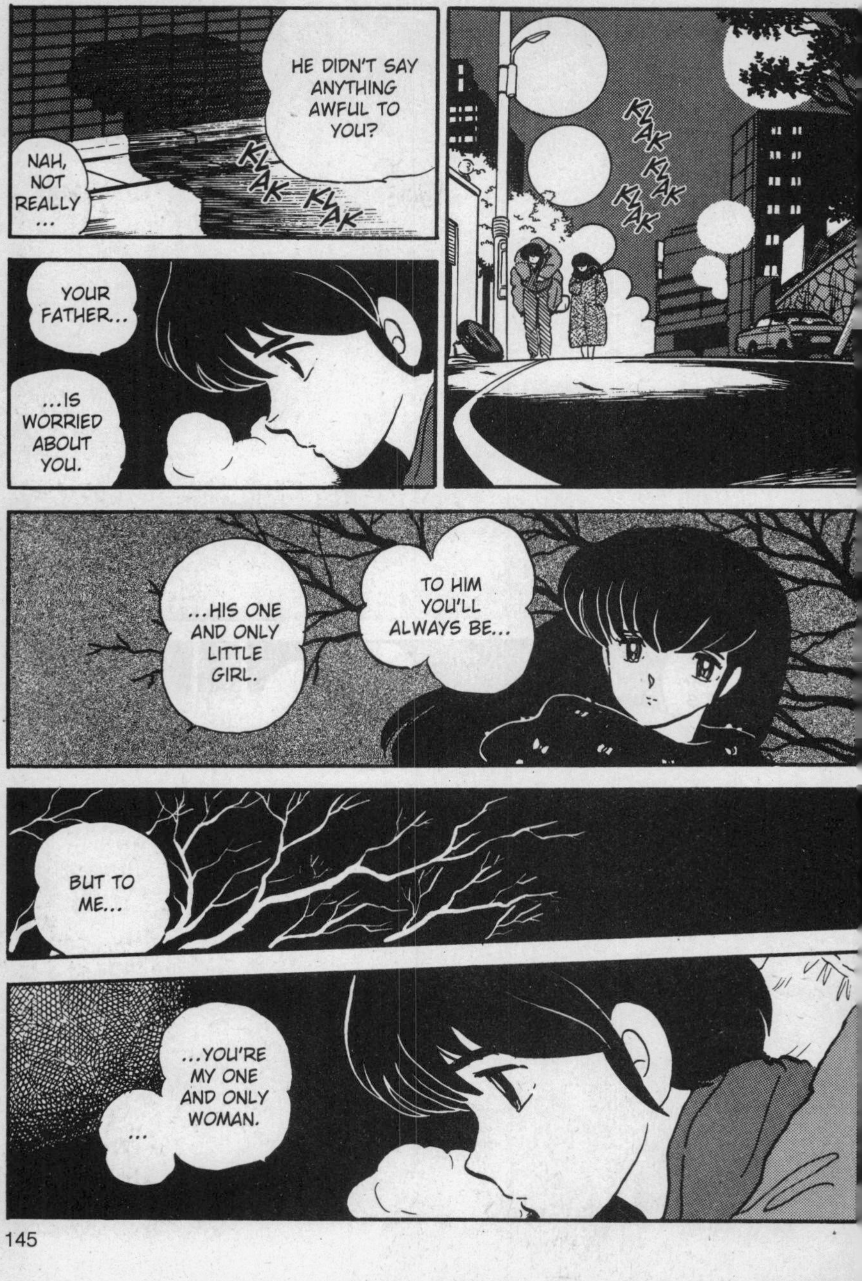
KLAK
KLAK
KLAK
HE DIDN'T SAY ANYTHING AWFUL TO YOU?
NAH, NOT REALLY ...
KLAK
KLAK
YOUR FATHER...
...IS WORRIED ABOUT YOU.
TO HIM YOU'LL ALWAYS BE...
...HIS ONE AND ONLY LITTLE GIRL.
BUT TO ME...
...YOU'RE MY ONE AND ONLY WOMAN.
...

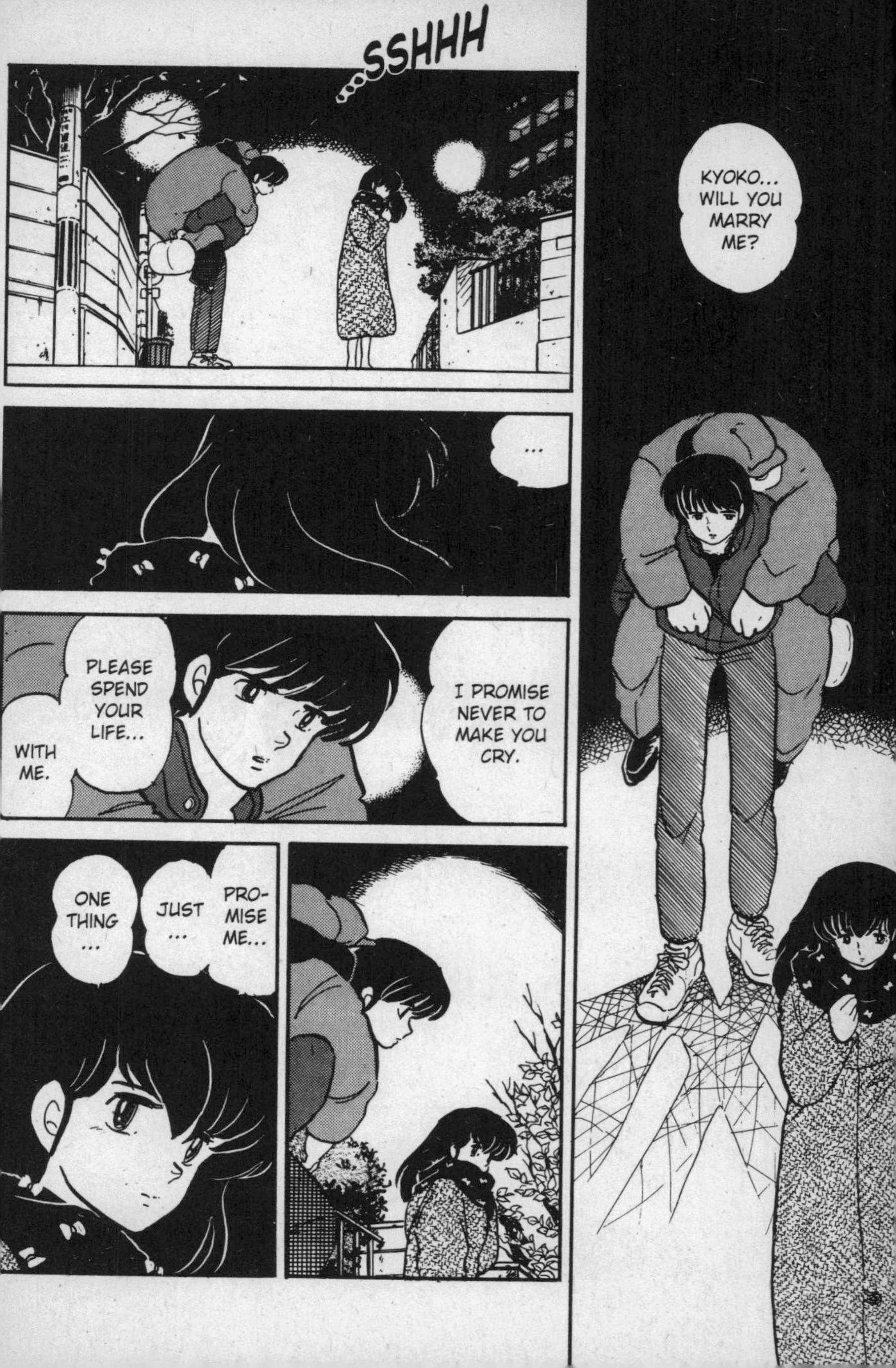
KYOKO... WILL YOU MARRY ME?
SSHHH
...
I PROMISE NEVER TO MAKE YOU CRY.
PLEASE SPEND YOUR LIFE...
WITH ME.
PRO-MISE ME...
JUST...
ONE THING...

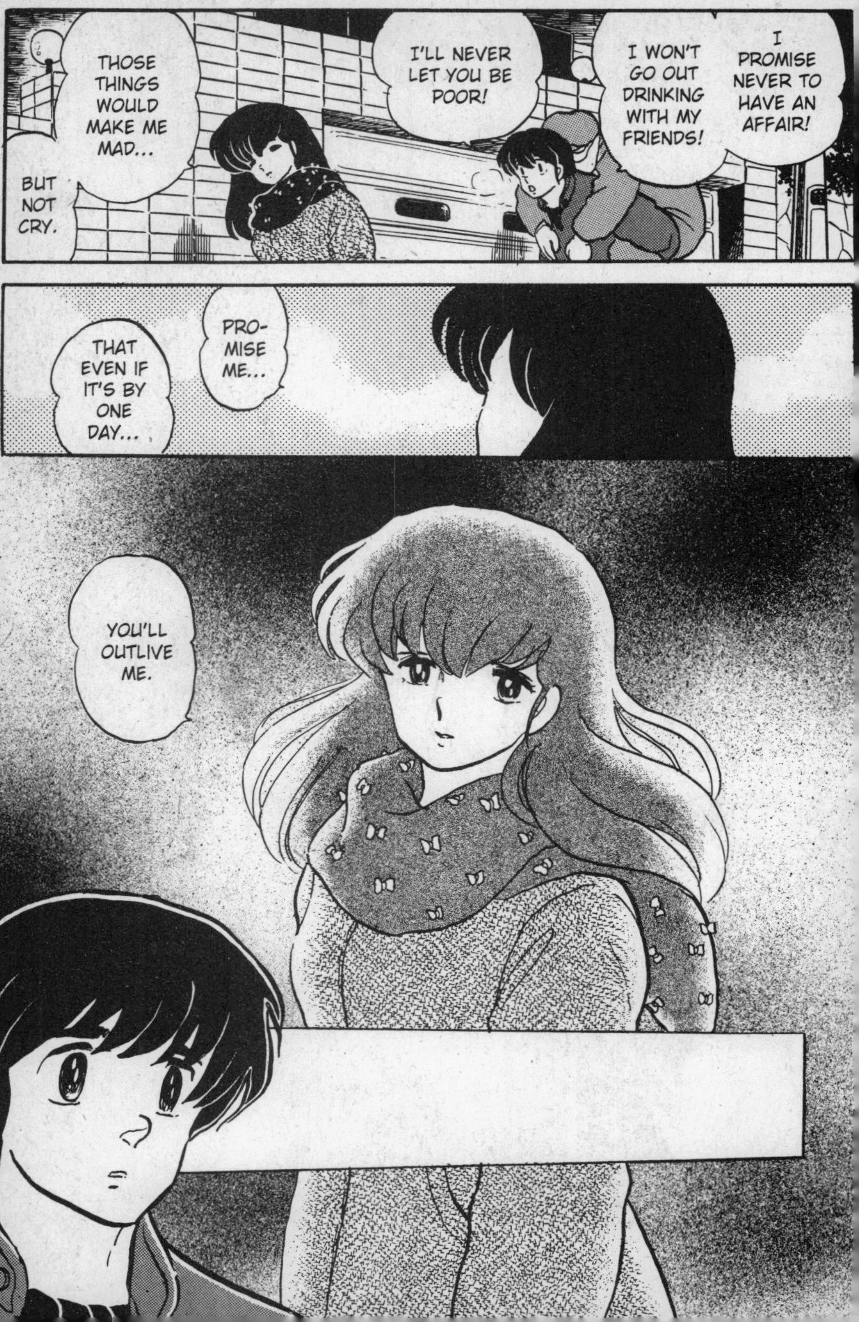
I PROMISE NEVER TO HAVE AN AFFAIR!
I WON'T GO OUT DRINKING WITH MY FRIENDS!
I'LL NEVER LET YOU BE POOR!
THOSE THINGS WOULD MAKE ME MAD...
BUT NOT CRY.
PRO-MISE ME...
THAT EVEN IF IT'S BY ONE DAY...
YOU'LL OUTLIVE ME.

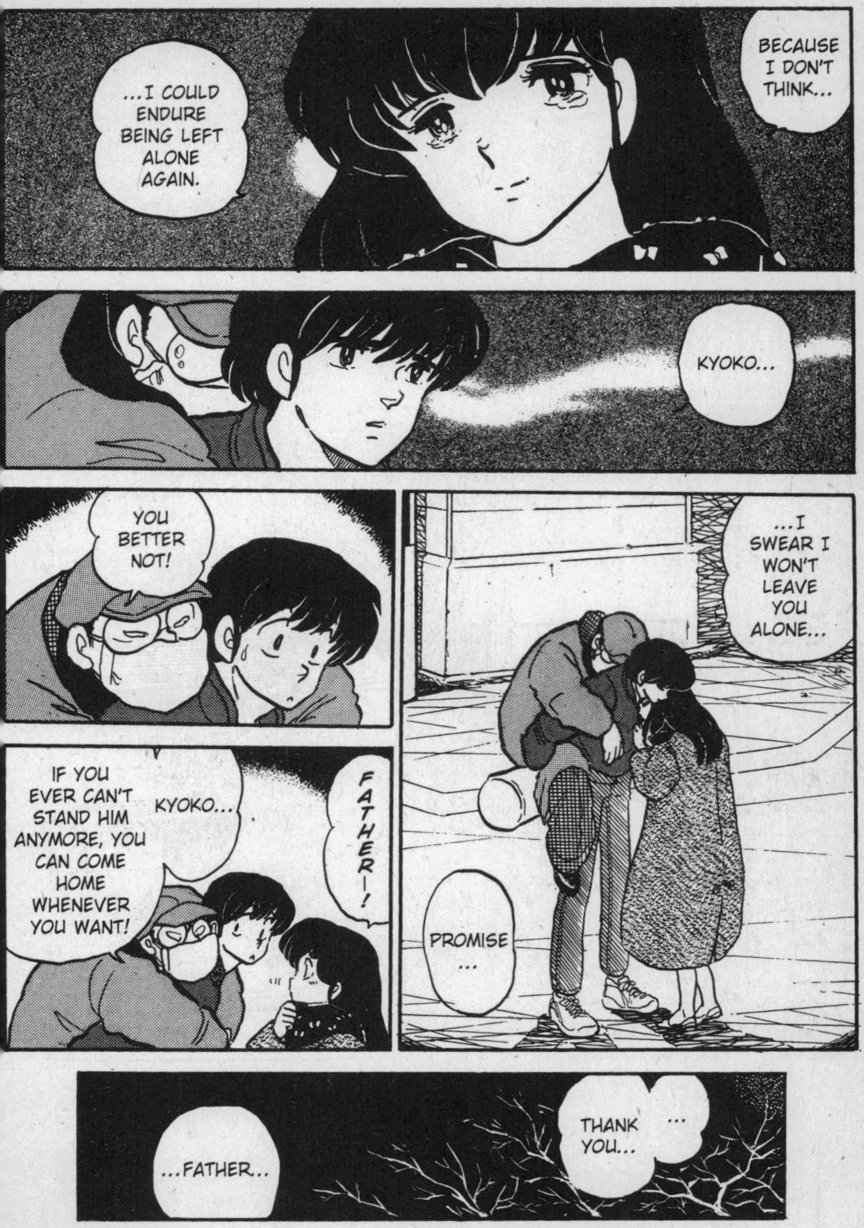
BECAUSE I DON'T THINK...
...I COULD ENDURE BEING LEFT ALONE AGAIN.
KYOKO...
...I SWEAR I WON'T LEAVE YOU ALONE...
PROMISE...
YOU BETTER NOT!
FATHER—!
KYOKO...
IF YOU EVER CAN'T STAND HIM ANYMORE, YOU CAN COME HOME WHENEVER YOU WANT!
THANK YOU... ...
...FATHER...

PART EIGHT

HEIRLOOMS

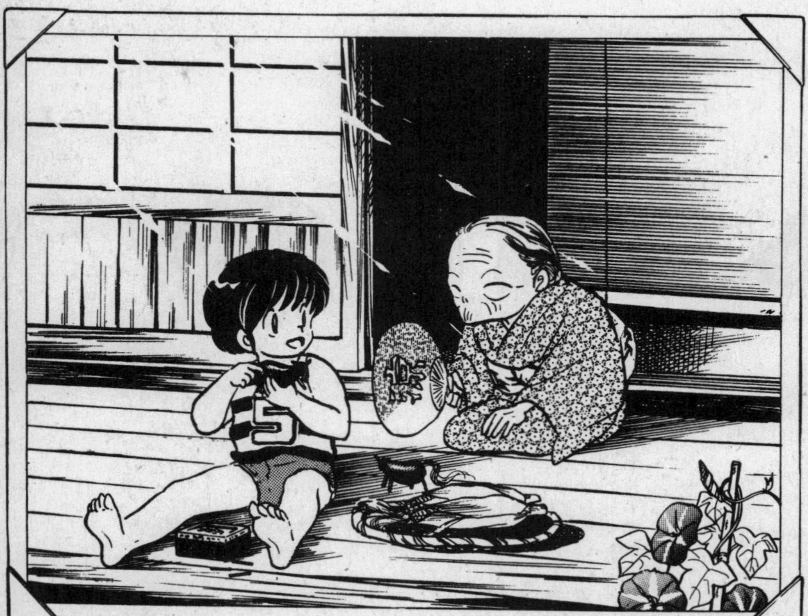

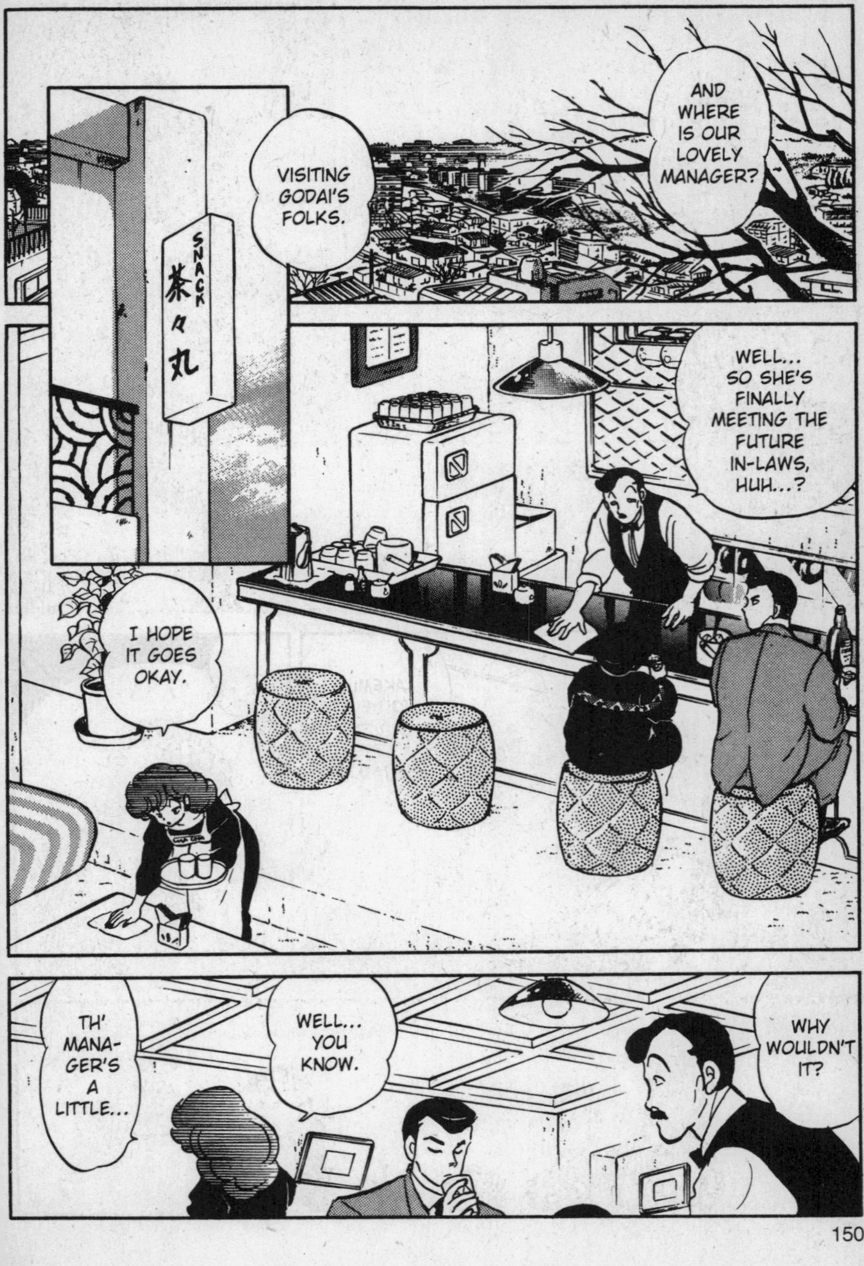
AND WHERE IS OUR LOVELY MANAGER?
VISITING GODAI'S FOLKS.
SNACK
茶々丸
WELL... SO SHE'S FINALLY MEETING THE FUTURE IN-LAWS, HUH...?
I HOPE IT GOES OKAY.
WHY WOULDN'T IT?
WELL... YOU KNOW.
TH' MANA-GER'S A LITTLE...

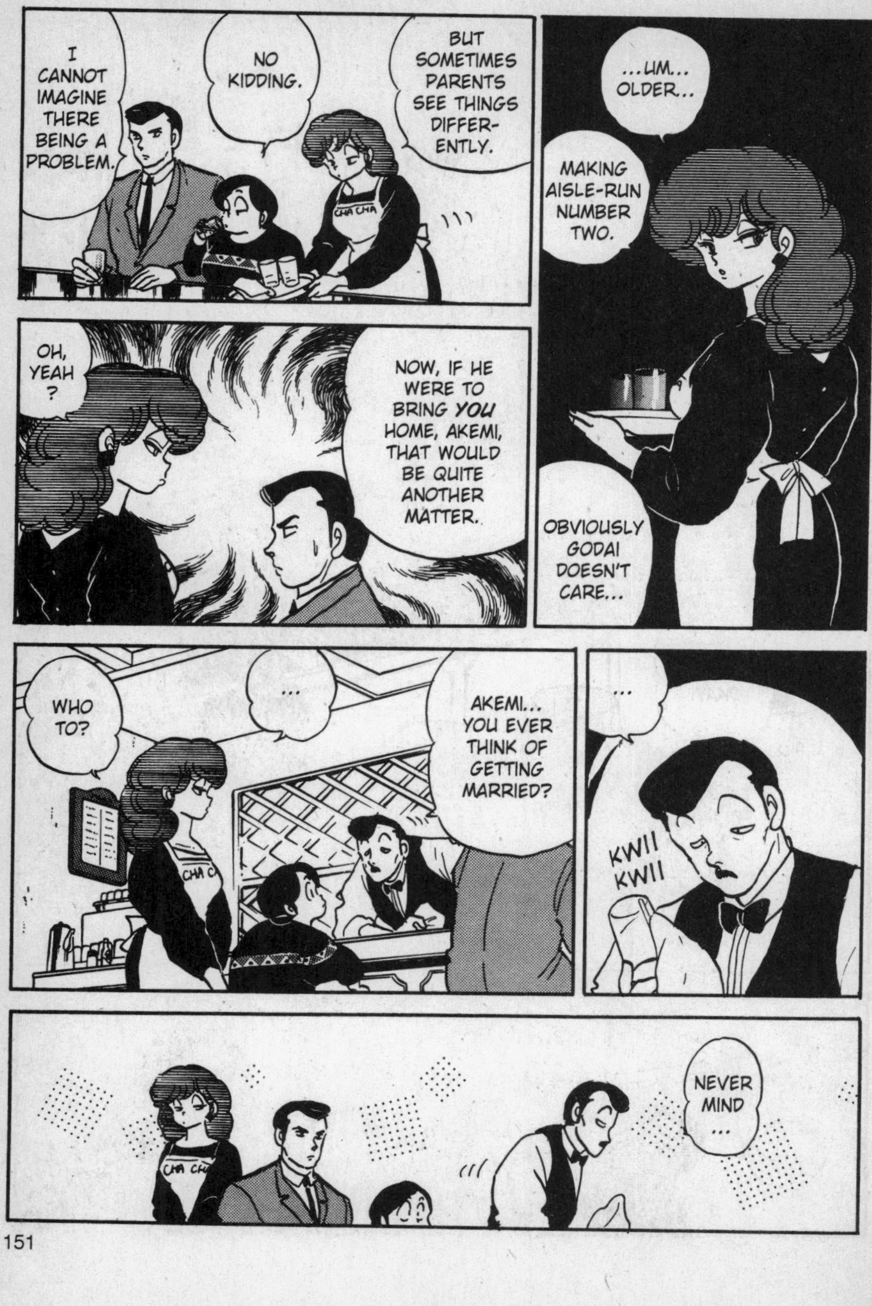
...UM... OLDER...
MAKING AISLE-RUN NUMBER TWO.
OBVIOUSLY GODAI DOESN'T CARE...
BUT SOMETIMES PARENTS SEE THINGS DIFFER-ENTLY.
NO KIDDING.
I CANNOT IMAGINE THERE BEING A PROBLEM.
NOW, IF HE WERE TO BRING *YOU* HOME, AKEMI, THAT WOULD BE QUITE ANOTHER MATTER.
OH, YEAH ?
...
KWII KWII
AKEMI... YOU EVER THINK OF GETTING MARRIED?
...
WHO TO?
NEVER MIND ...

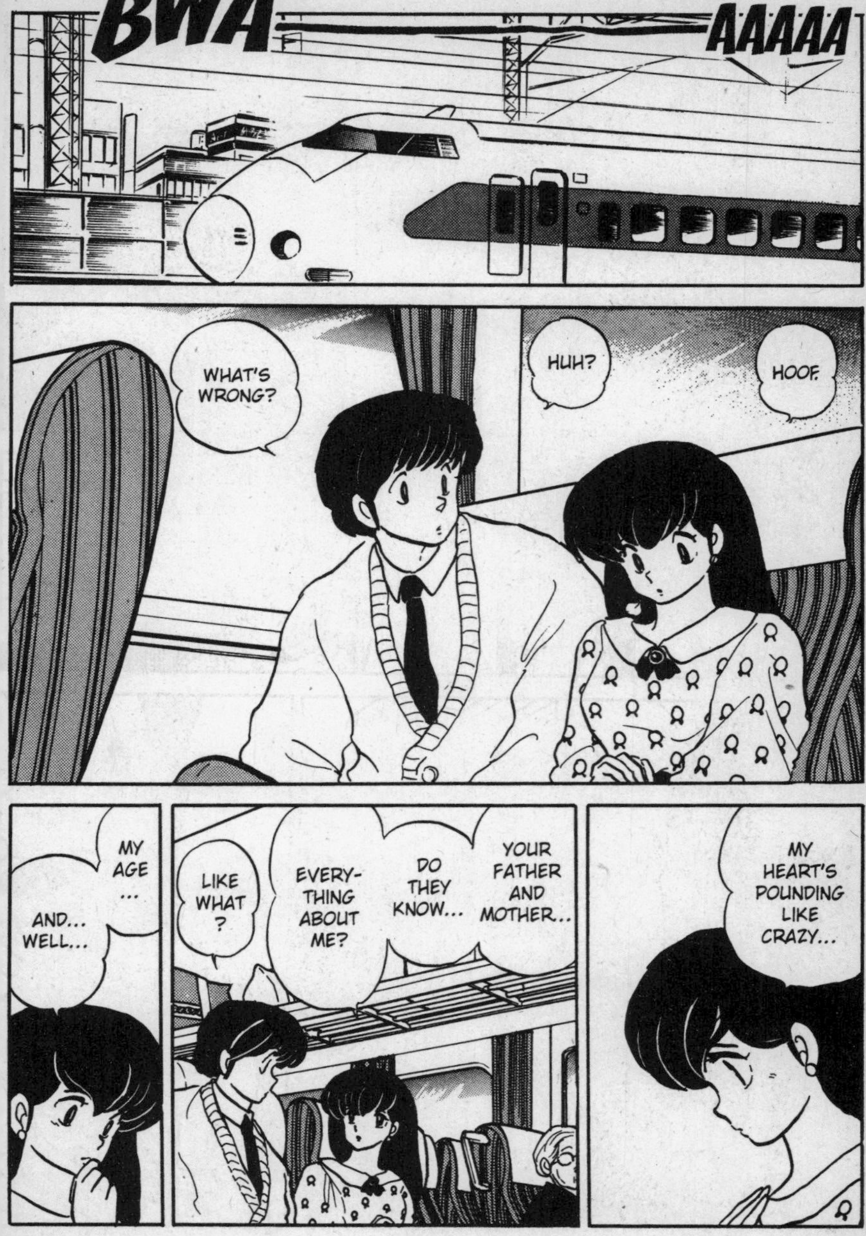
BWA AAAAA
HOOF.
HUH?
WHAT'S WRONG?
MY HEART'S POUNDING LIKE CRAZY...
YOUR FATHER AND MOTHER...
DO THEY KNOW...
EVERY-THING ABOUT ME?
LIKE WHAT?
MY AGE...
AND... WELL...

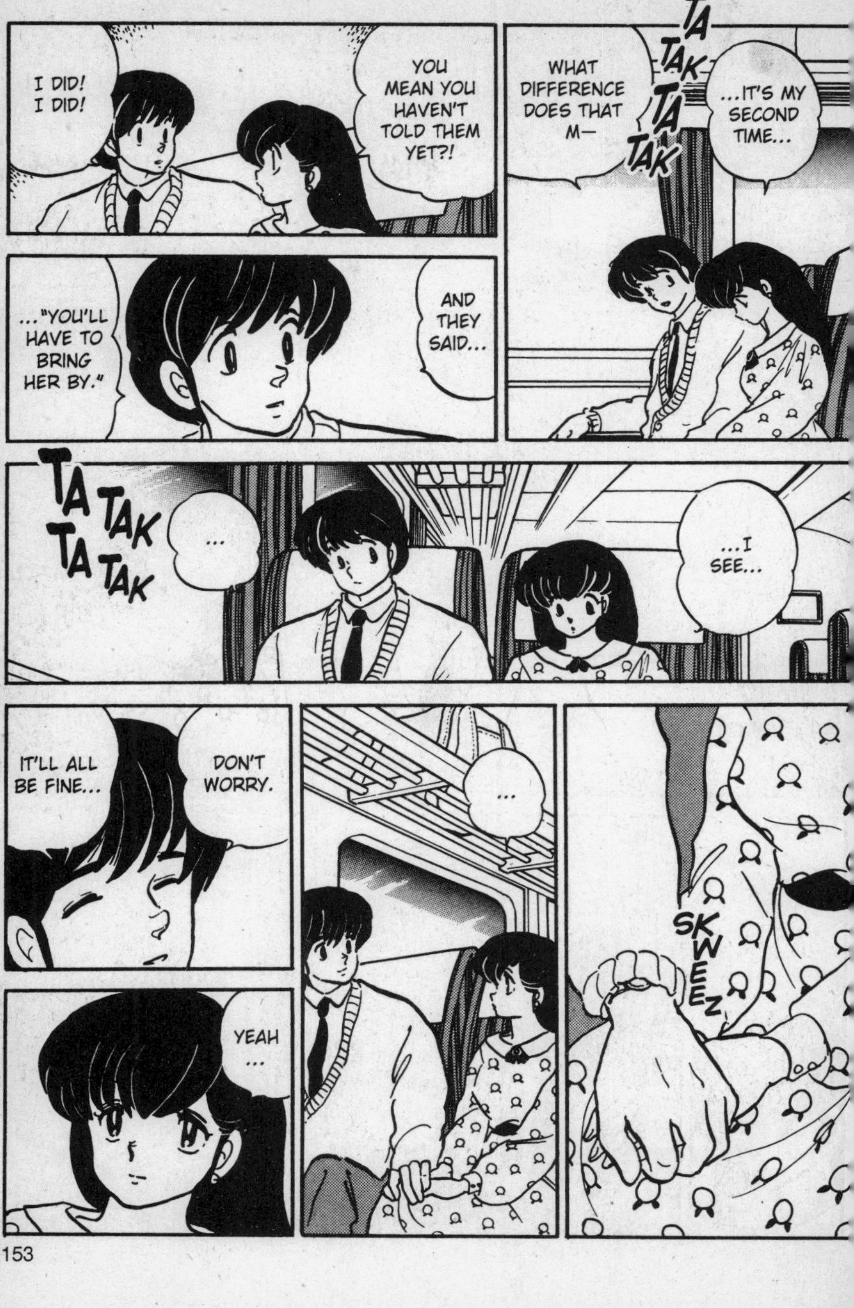
...IT'S MY SECOND TIME...
TA TAK TA TAK
WHAT DIFFERENCE DOES THAT M—
YOU MEAN YOU HAVEN'T TOLD THEM YET?!
I DID! I DID!
AND THEY SAID...
..."YOU'LL HAVE TO BRING HER BY."
...I SEE...
...
TA TAK TA TAK
SKWEEZ
...
DON'T WORRY.
IT'LL ALL BE FINE...
YEAH ...

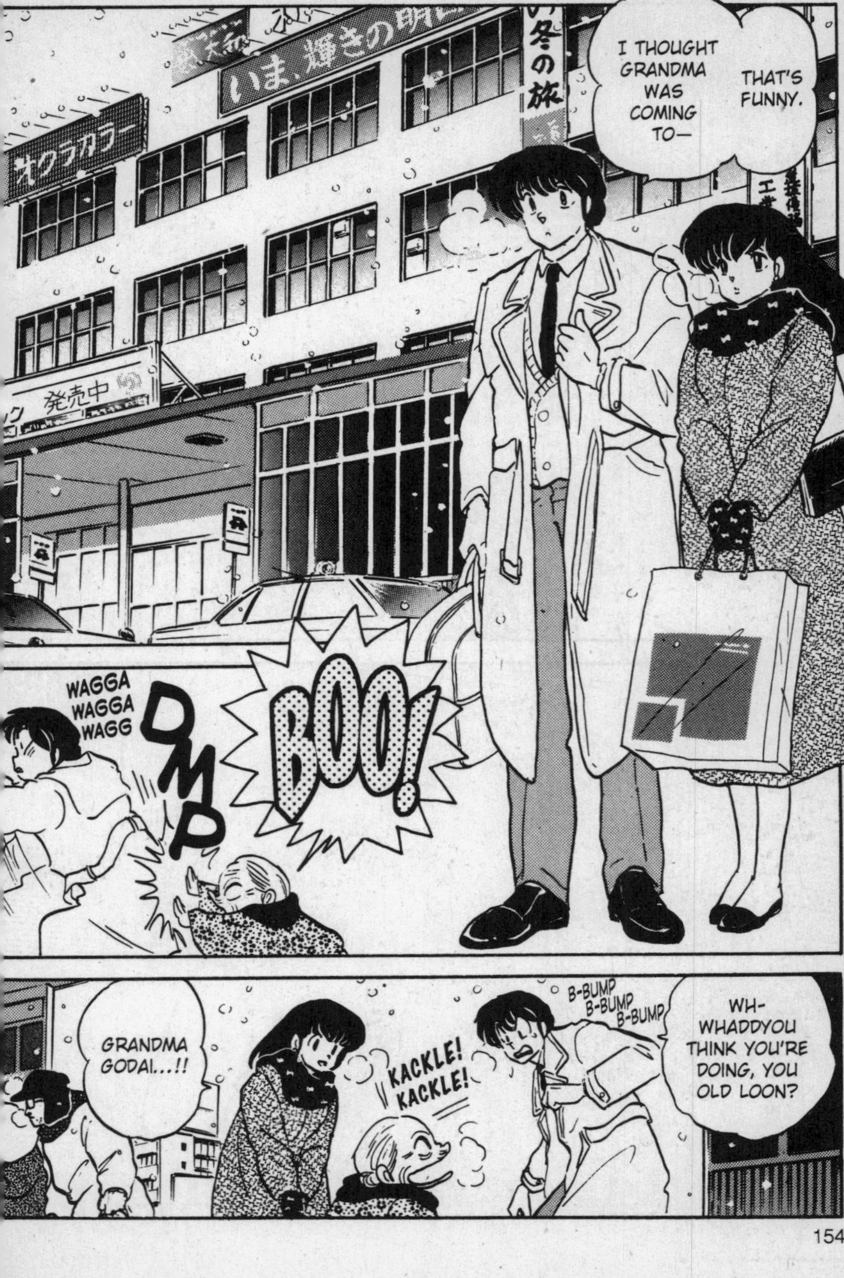
THAT'S FUNNY.
I THOUGHT GRANDMA WAS COMING TO—
冬の旅
オクラカラー
発売中
BOO!
DMP
WAGGA WAGGA WAGG
WH- WHADDYOU THINK YOU'RE DOING, YOU OLD LOON?
B-BUMP B-BUMP B-BUMP
KACKLE! KACKLE!
GRANDMA GODAI...!!

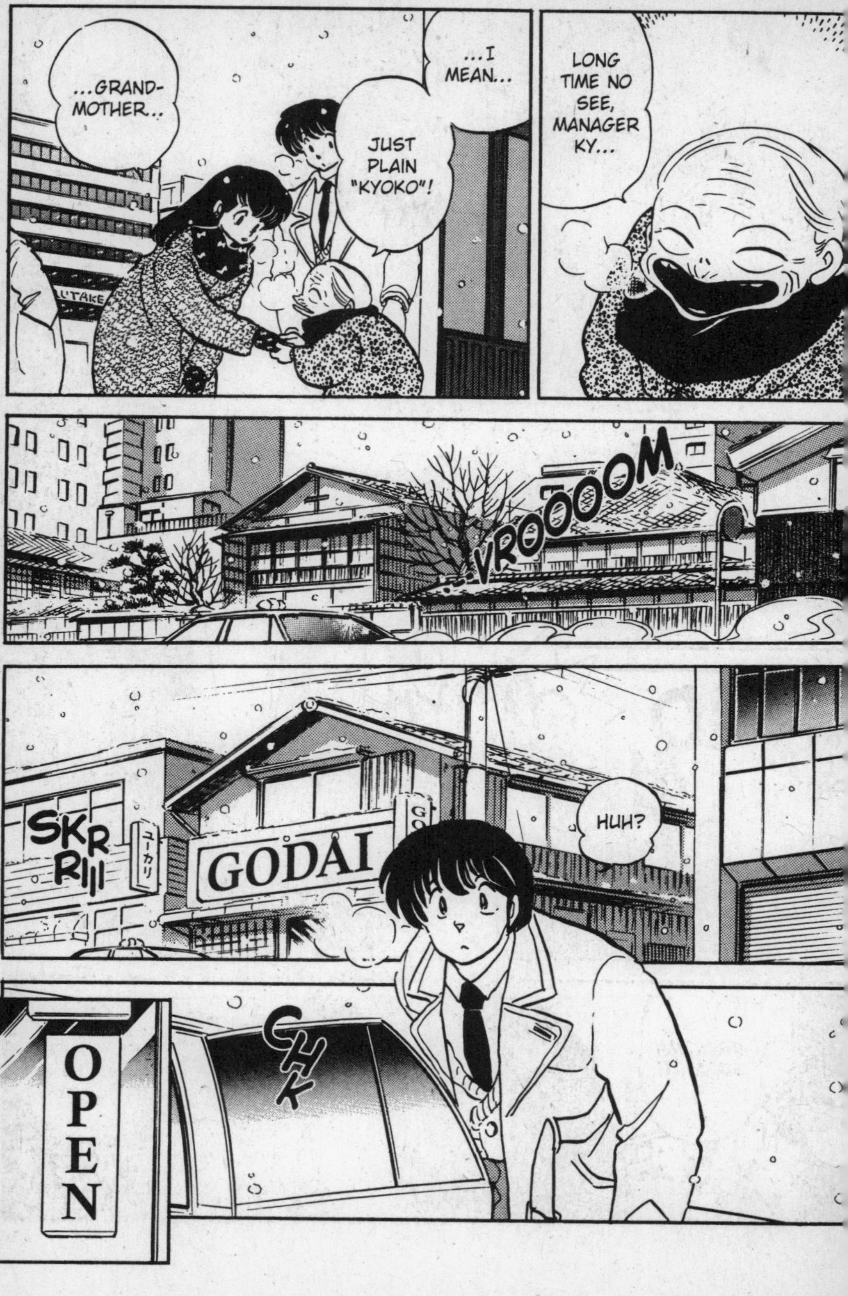
LONG TIME NO SEE, MANAGER KY...
...I MEAN...
JUST PLAIN "KYOKO"!
...GRAND-MOTHER...
VROOOOM
HUH?
GODAI
ユーカリ
SKRRIII
CHK
OPEN

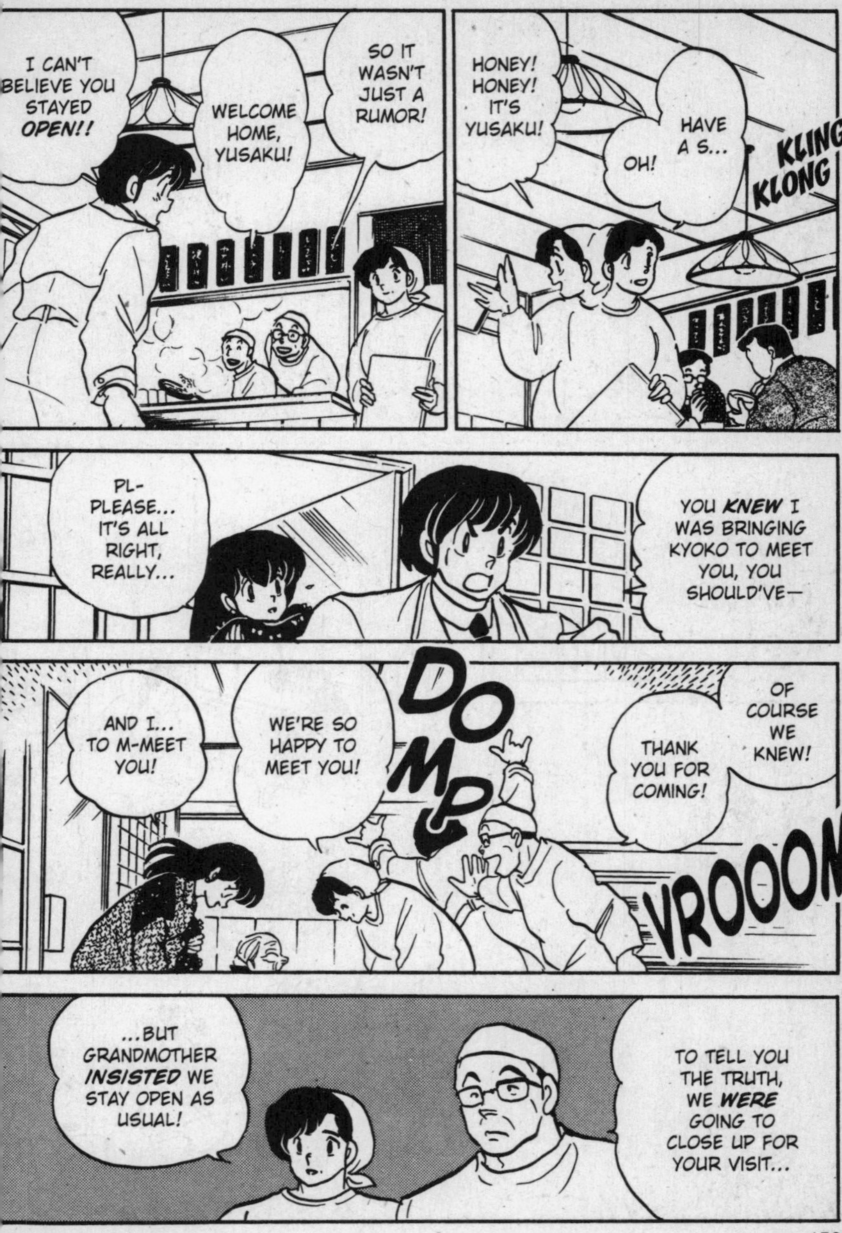
KLING KLONG
HAVE A S...
OH!
HONEY! HONEY! IT'S YUSAKU!
SO IT WASN'T JUST A RUMOR!
WELCOME HOME, YUSAKU!
I CAN'T BELIEVE YOU STAYED *OPEN!!*
YOU *KNEW* I WAS BRINGING KYOKO TO MEET YOU, YOU SHOULD'VE—
PL- PLEASE... IT'S ALL RIGHT, REALLY...
OF COURSE WE KNEW!
THANK YOU FOR COMING!
VROOOM
DOMP
WE'RE SO HAPPY TO MEET YOU!
AND I... TO M-MEET YOU!
TO TELL YOU THE TRUTH, WE *WERE* GOING TO CLOSE UP FOR YOUR VISIT...
...BUT GRANDMOTHER *INSISTED* WE STAY OPEN AS USUAL!

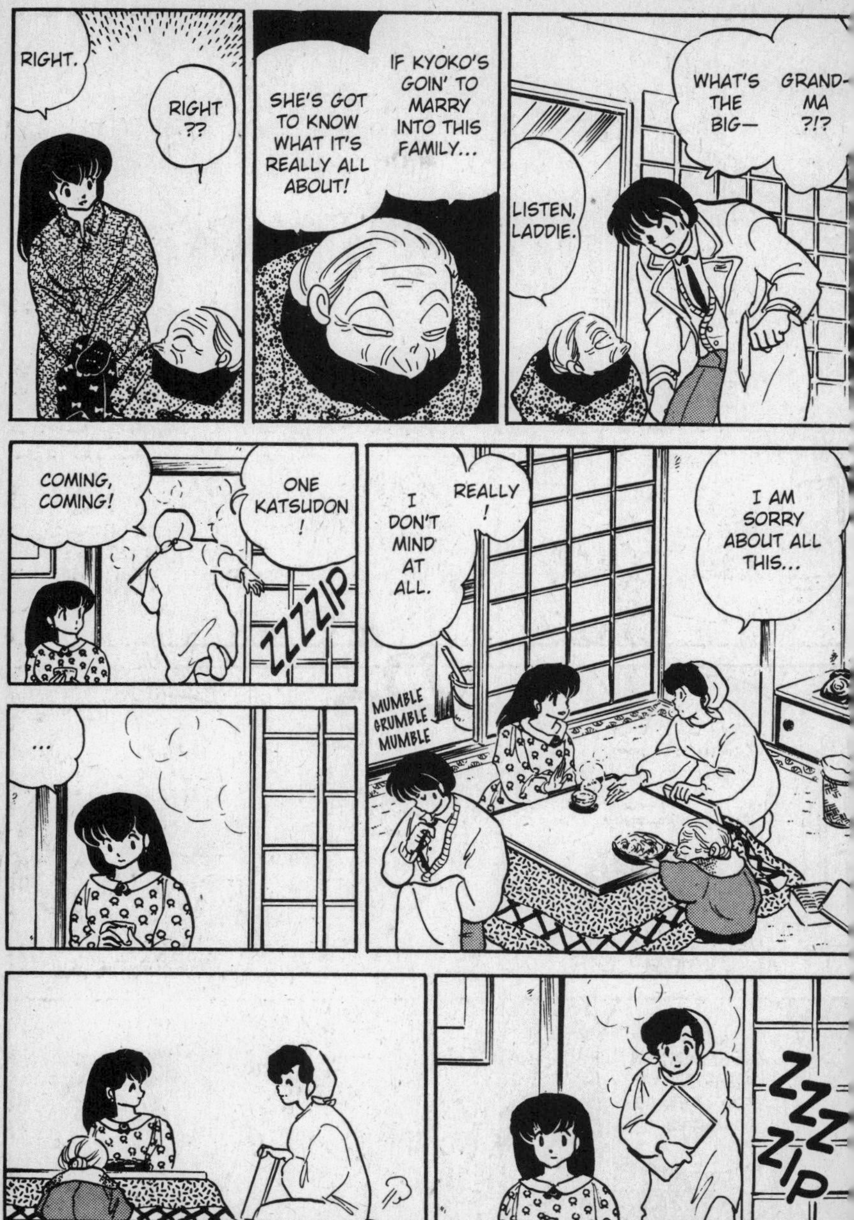
GRAND-MA ?!?
WHAT'S THE BIG—
LISTEN, LADDIE.
IF KYOKO'S GOIN' TO MARRY INTO THIS FAMILY...
SHE'S GOT TO KNOW WHAT IT'S REALLY ALL ABOUT!
RIGHT.
RIGHT ??
I AM SORRY ABOUT ALL THIS...
REALLY!
I DON'T MIND AT ALL.
MUMBLE GRUMBLE MUMBLE
ONE KATSUDON!
COMING, COMING!
ZZZZIP
...
ZZZZIP

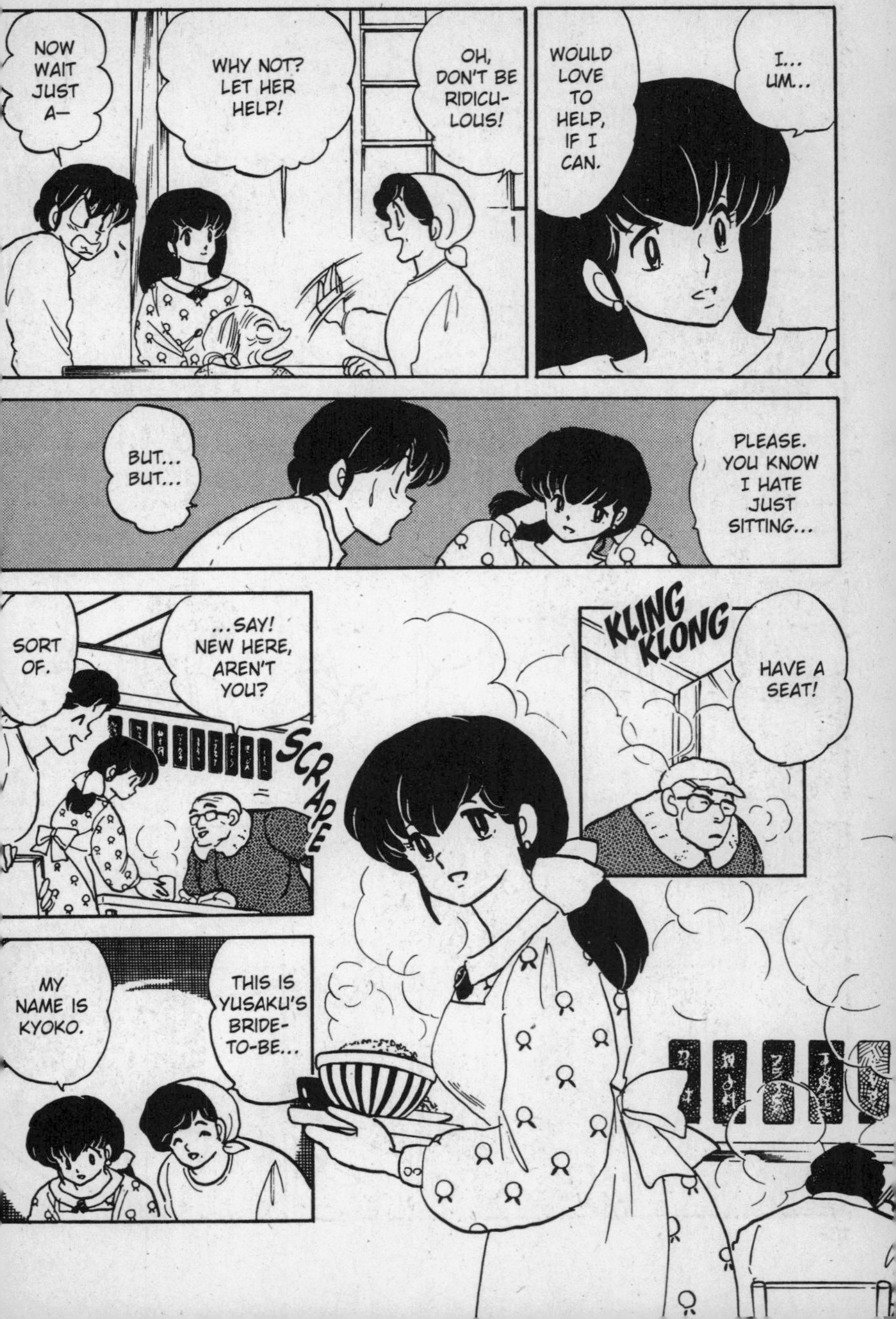

I... UM...
WOULD LOVE TO HELP, IF I CAN.
OH, DON'T BE RIDICU-LOUS!
WHY NOT? LET HER HELP!
NOW WAIT JUST A—
PLEASE. YOU KNOW I HATE JUST SITTING...
BUT... BUT...
KLING KLONG
HAVE A SEAT!
...SAY! NEW HERE, AREN'T YOU?
SCRAPE
SORT OF.
THIS IS YUSAKU'S BRIDE-TO-BE...
MY NAME IS KYOKO.

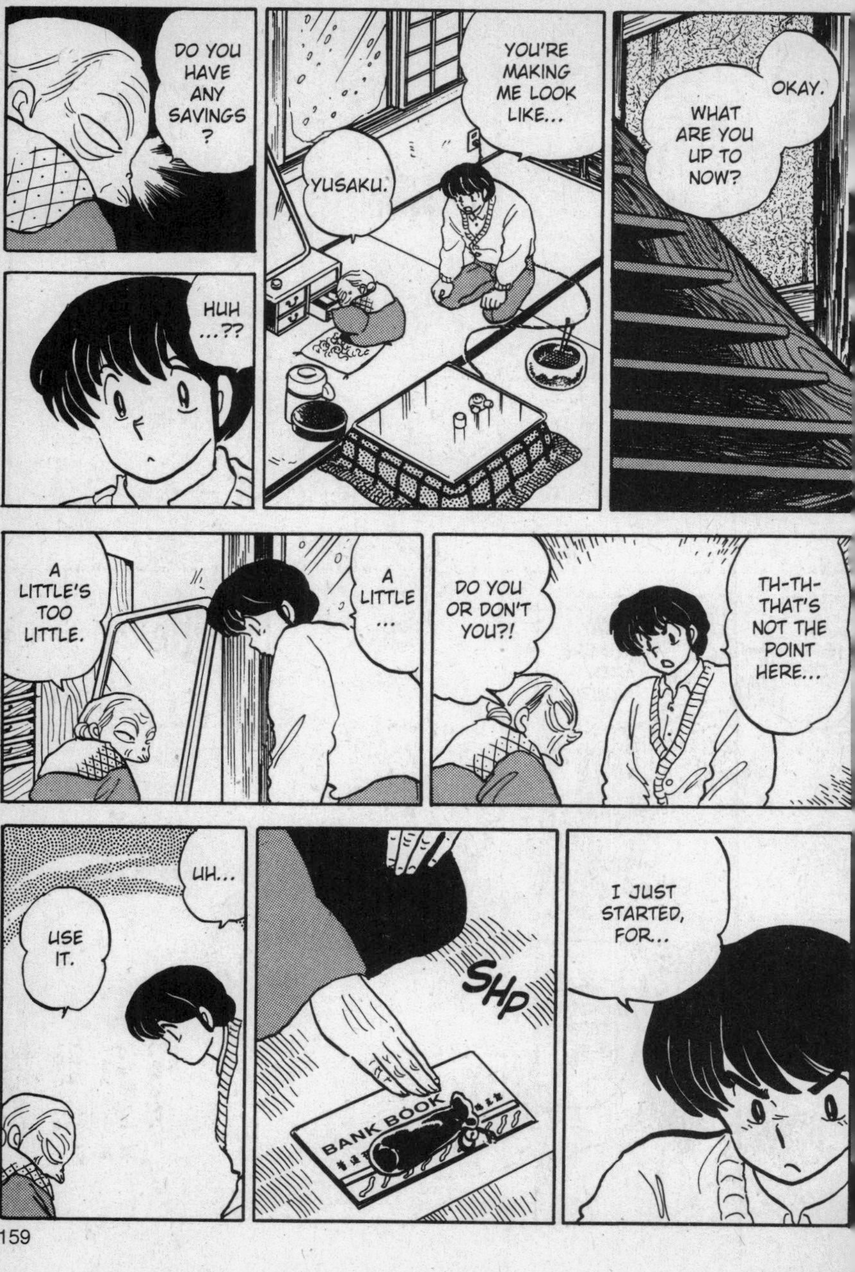
OKAY.
WHAT ARE YOU UP TO NOW?
YOU'RE MAKING ME LOOK LIKE...
YUSAKU.
DO YOU HAVE ANY SAVINGS?
HUH...??
TH-TH-THAT'S NOT THE POINT HERE...
DO YOU OR DON'T YOU?!
A LITTLE...
A LITTLE'S TOO LITTLE.
I JUST STARTED, FOR...
SHP
BANK BOOK
UH...
USE IT.

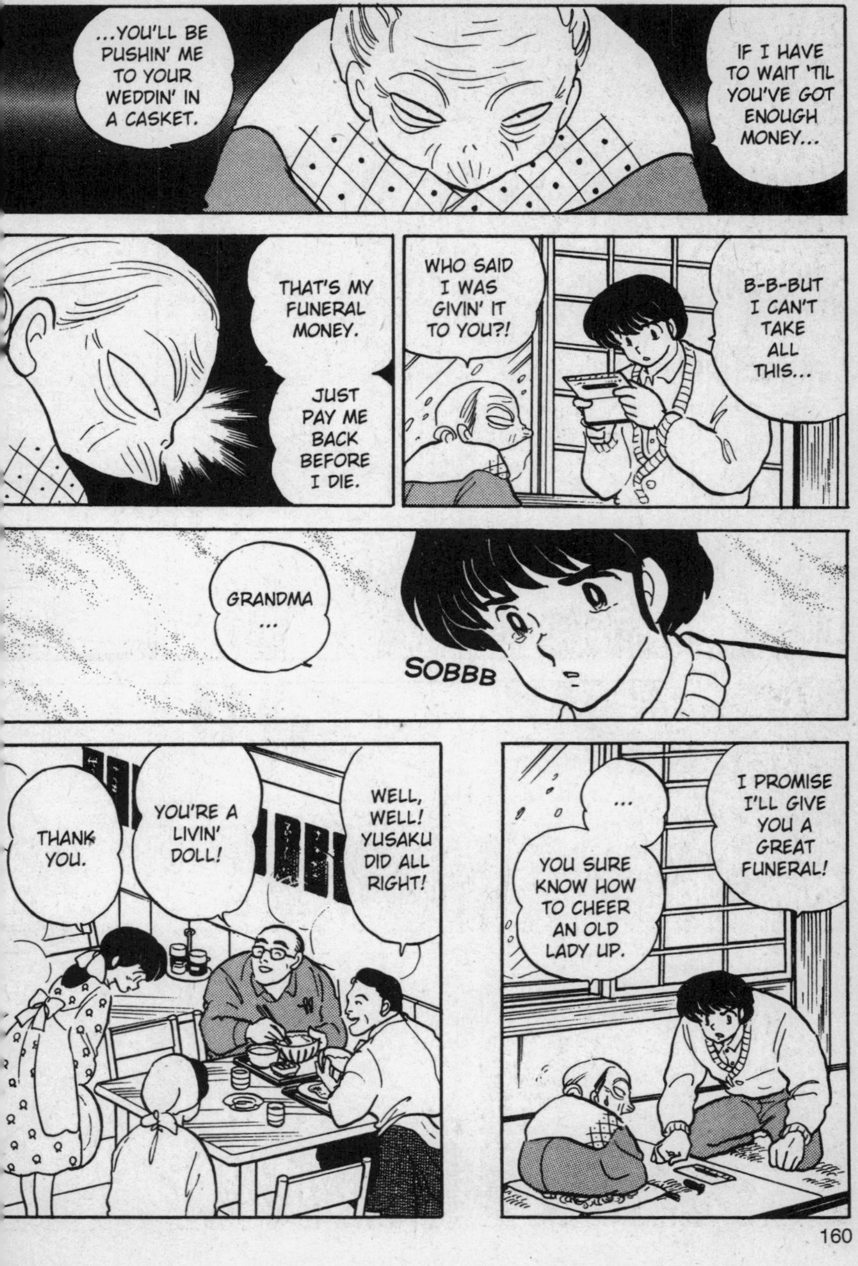
IF I HAVE TO WAIT 'TIL YOU'VE GOT ENOUGH MONEY...
...YOU'LL BE PUSHIN' ME TO YOUR WEDDIN' IN A CASKET.
B-B-BUT I CAN'T TAKE ALL THIS...
WHO SAID I WAS GIVIN' IT TO YOU?!
THAT'S MY FUNERAL MONEY.
JUST PAY ME BACK BEFORE I DIE.
GRANDMA ...
SOBBB
I PROMISE I'LL GIVE YOU A GREAT FUNERAL!
...
YOU SURE KNOW HOW TO CHEER AN OLD LADY UP.
WELL, WELL! YUSAKU DID ALL RIGHT!
YOU'RE A LIVIN' DOLL!
THANK YOU.

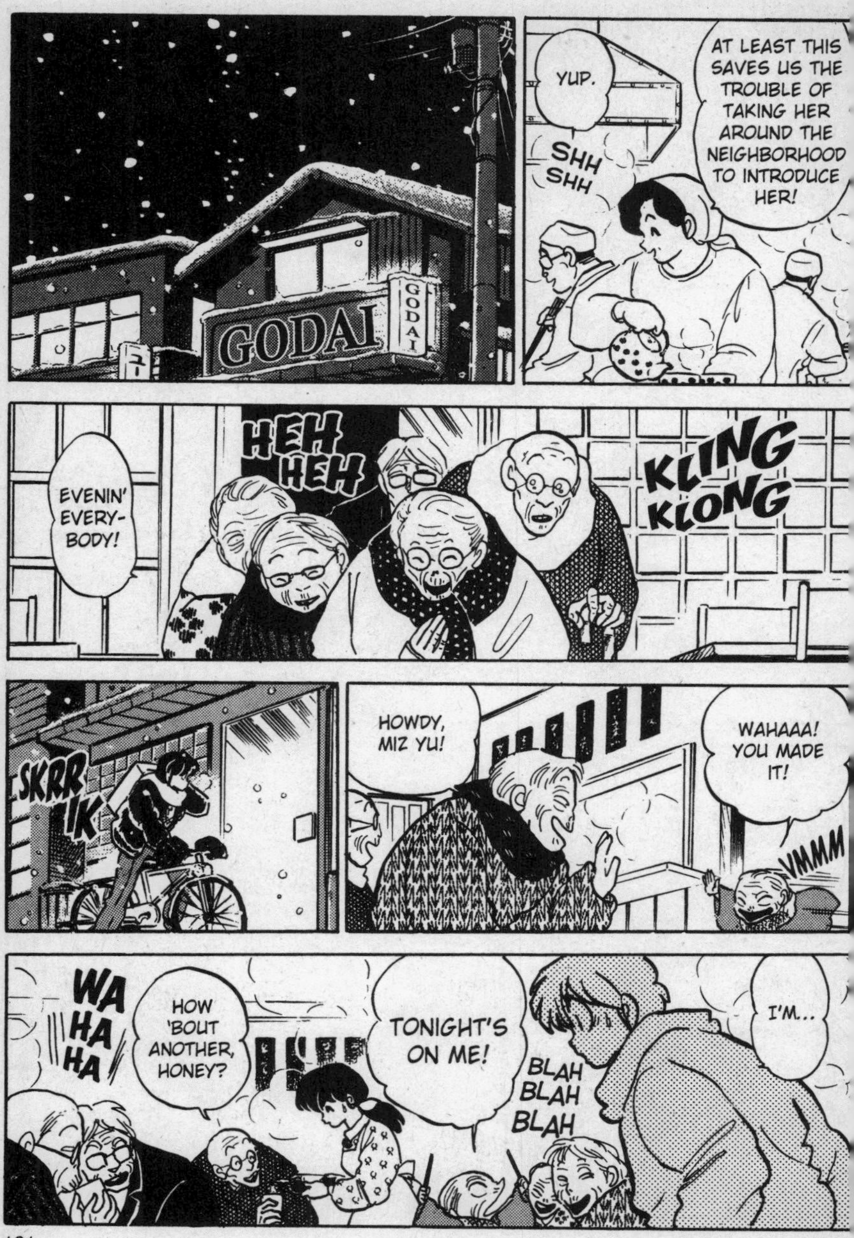
AT LEAST THIS SAVES US THE TROUBLE OF TAKING HER AROUND THE NEIGHBORHOOD TO INTRODUCE HER!
YUP.
SHH SHH
GODAI
KLING KLONG
HEH HEH
EVENIN' EVERY-BODY!
WAHAAA! YOU MADE IT!
VMMM
HOWDY, MIZ YU!
SKRRIK
I'M...
BLAH BLAH BLAH
TONIGHT'S ON ME!
HOW 'BOUT ANOTHER, HONEY?
WA HA HA

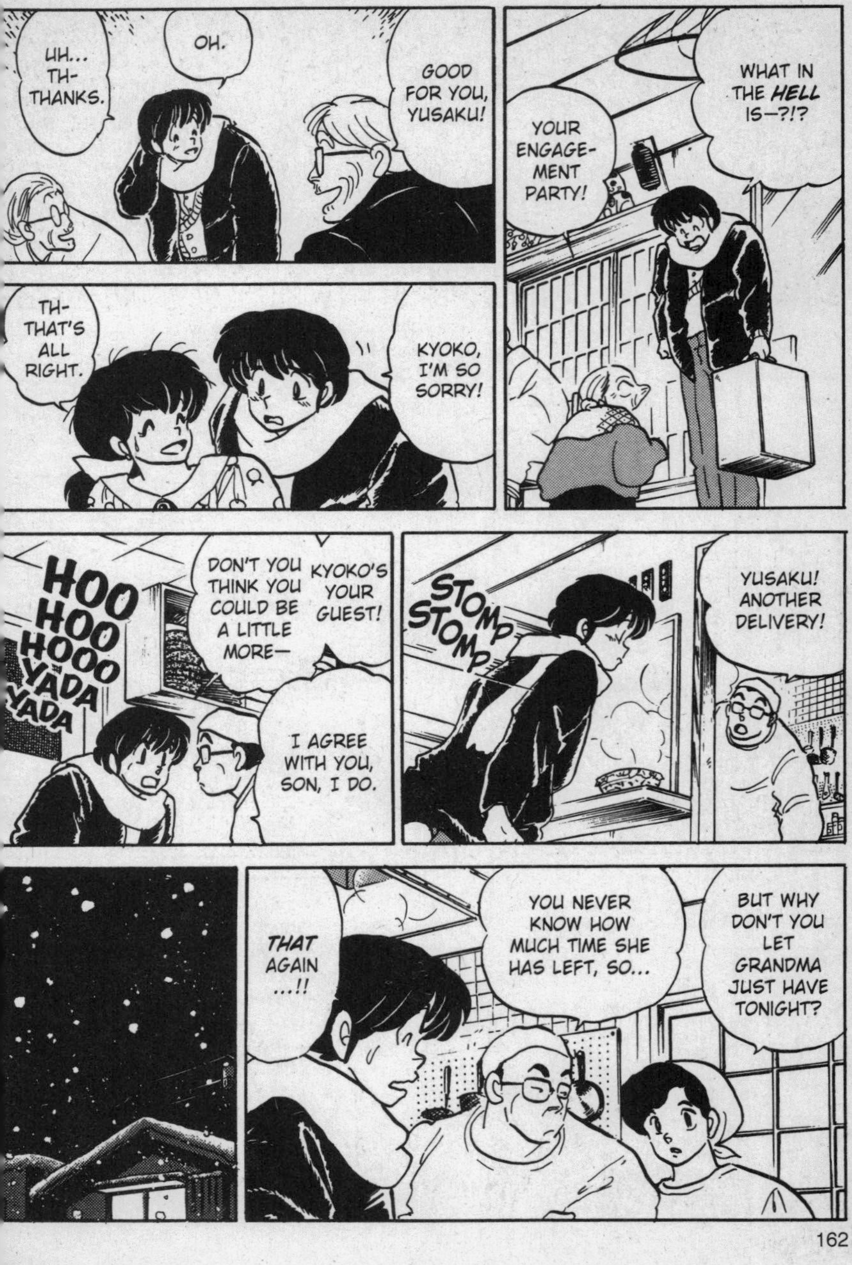
WHAT IN THE *HELL* IS—?!?
YOUR ENGAGEMENT PARTY!
GOOD FOR YOU, YUSAKU!
OH.
UH... TH- THANKS.
KYOKO, I'M SO SORRY!
TH- THAT'S ALL RIGHT.
YUSAKU! ANOTHER DELIVERY!
STOMP STOMP
KYOKO'S YOUR GUEST!
DON'T YOU THINK YOU COULD BE A LITTLE MORE—
I AGREE WITH YOU, SON, I DO.
HOO HOO HOOO YADA YADA
BUT WHY DON'T YOU LET GRANDMA JUST HAVE TONIGHT?
YOU NEVER KNOW HOW MUCH TIME SHE HAS LEFT, SO...
THAT AGAIN ...!!

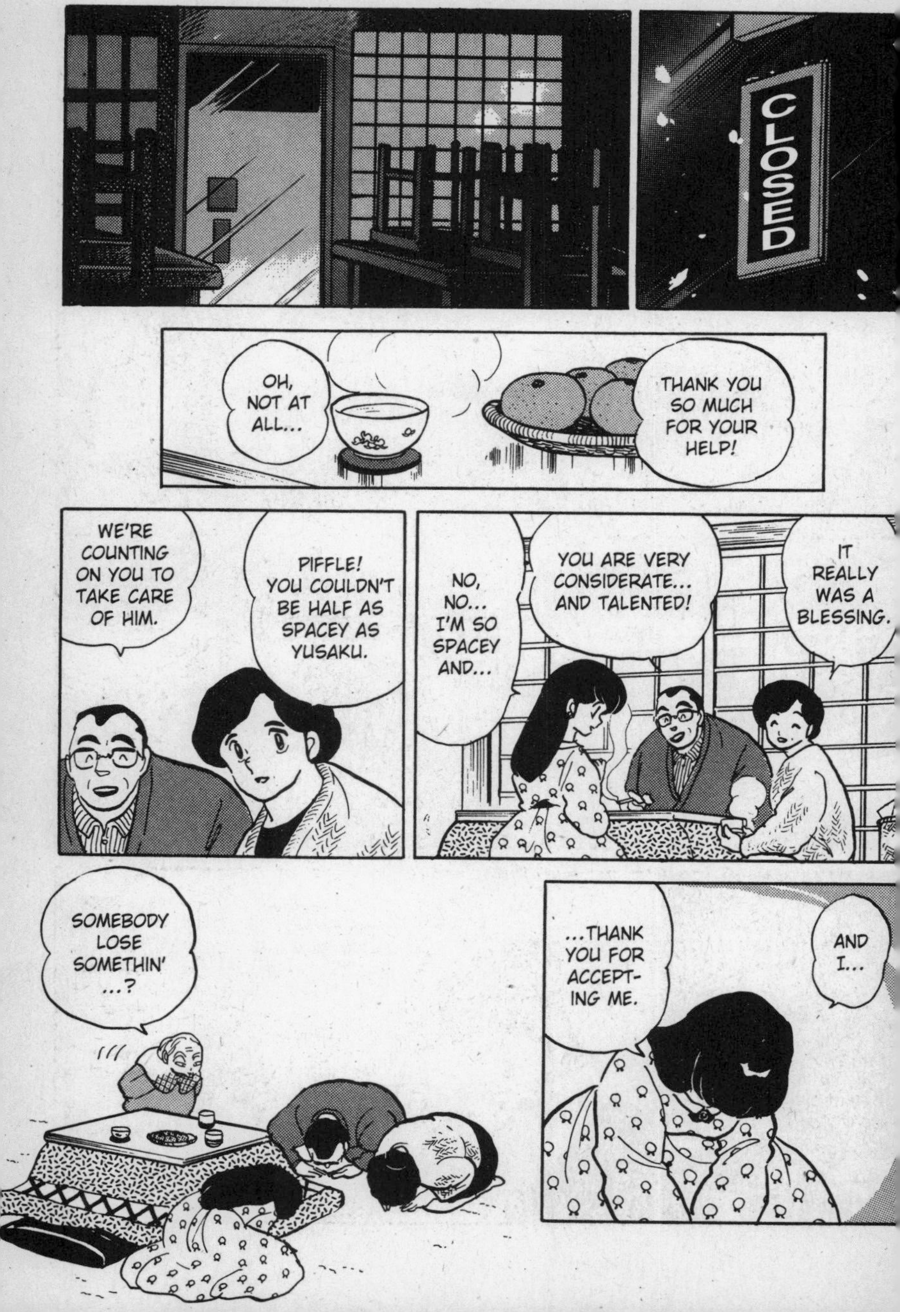
CLOSED
THANK YOU SO MUCH FOR YOUR HELP!
OH, NOT AT ALL...
IT REALLY WAS A BLESSING.
YOU ARE VERY CONSIDERATE... AND TALENTED!
NO, NO... I'M SO SPACEY AND...
PIFFLE! YOU COULDN'T BE HALF AS SPACEY AS YUSAKU.
WE'RE COUNTING ON YOU TO TAKE CARE OF HIM.
AND I...
...THANK YOU FOR ACCEPT-ING ME.
SOMEBODY LOSE SOMETHIN' ...?

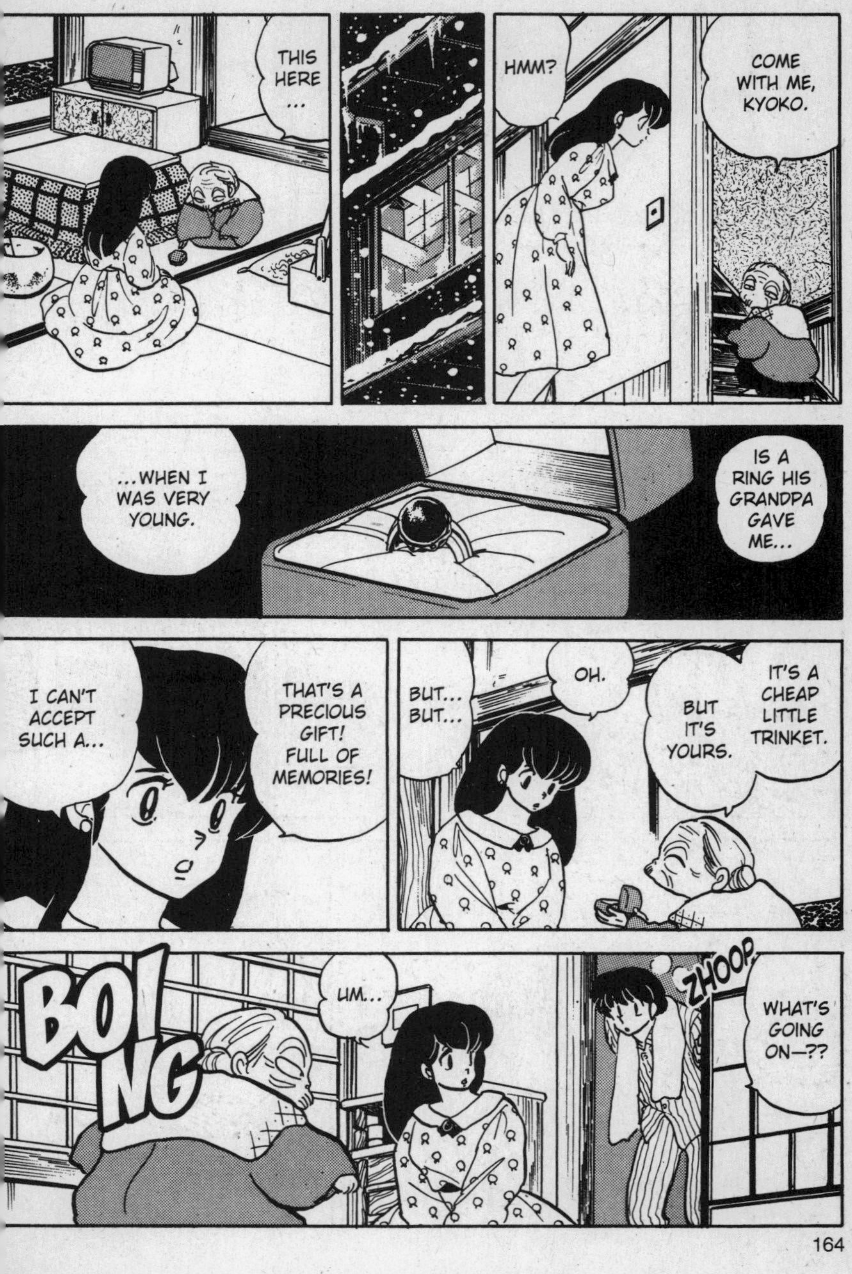
COME WITH ME, KYOKO.
HMM?
THIS HERE ...
IS A RING HIS GRANDPA GAVE ME...
...WHEN I WAS VERY YOUNG.
IT'S A CHEAP LITTLE TRINKET.
BUT IT'S YOURS.
OH.
BUT... BUT...
THAT'S A PRECIOUS GIFT! FULL OF MEMORIES!
I CAN'T ACCEPT SUCH A...
WHAT'S GOING ON—??
ZHOOP
UM...
BOING

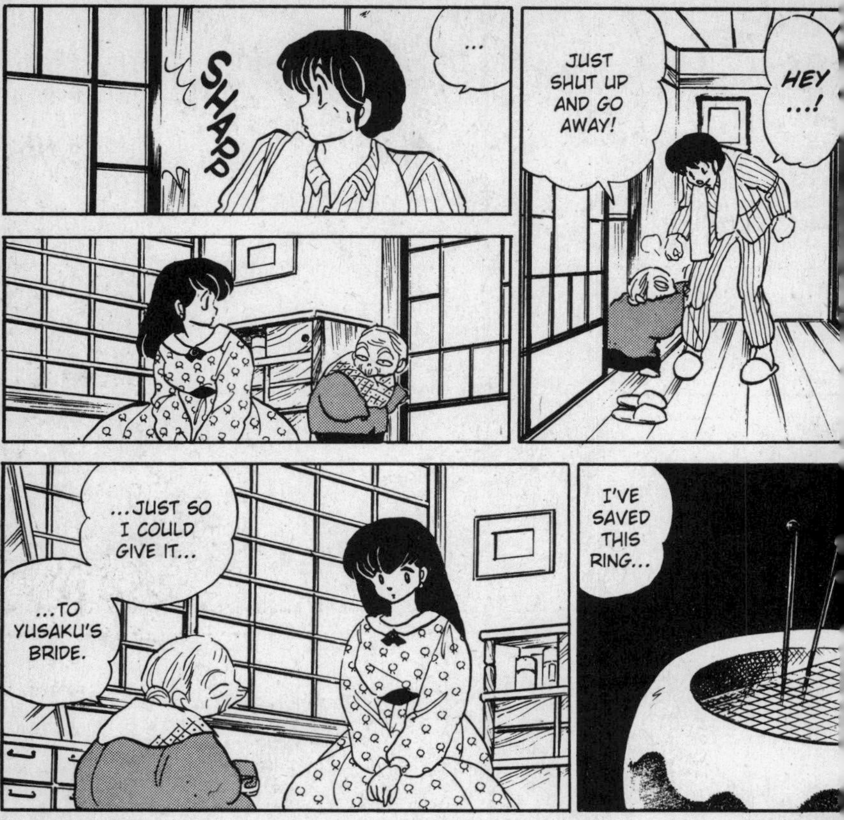
HEY ...!
JUST SHUT UP AND GO AWAY!
...
SHAPP
I'VE SAVED THIS RING...
...JUST SO I COULD GIVE IT...
...TO YUSAKU'S BRIDE.
CONSIDER IT AN HEIRLOOM.
YOUR HEIR-LOOM. PLEASE.
BUT REALLY...
...THE MARRIAGE HASN'T BEEN SET, AND...
I RAISED THAT BOY, YUSAKU.

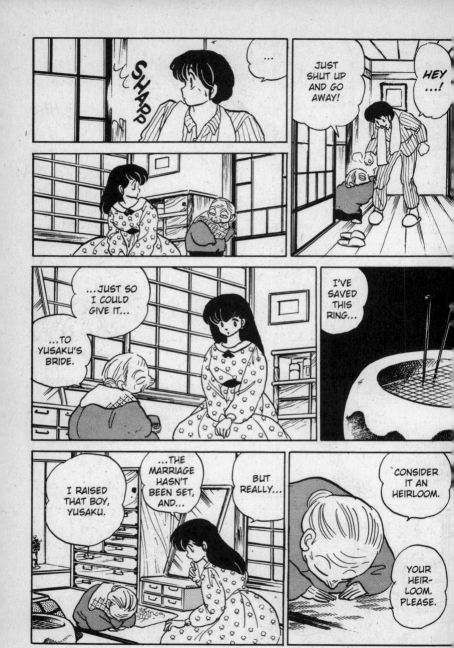

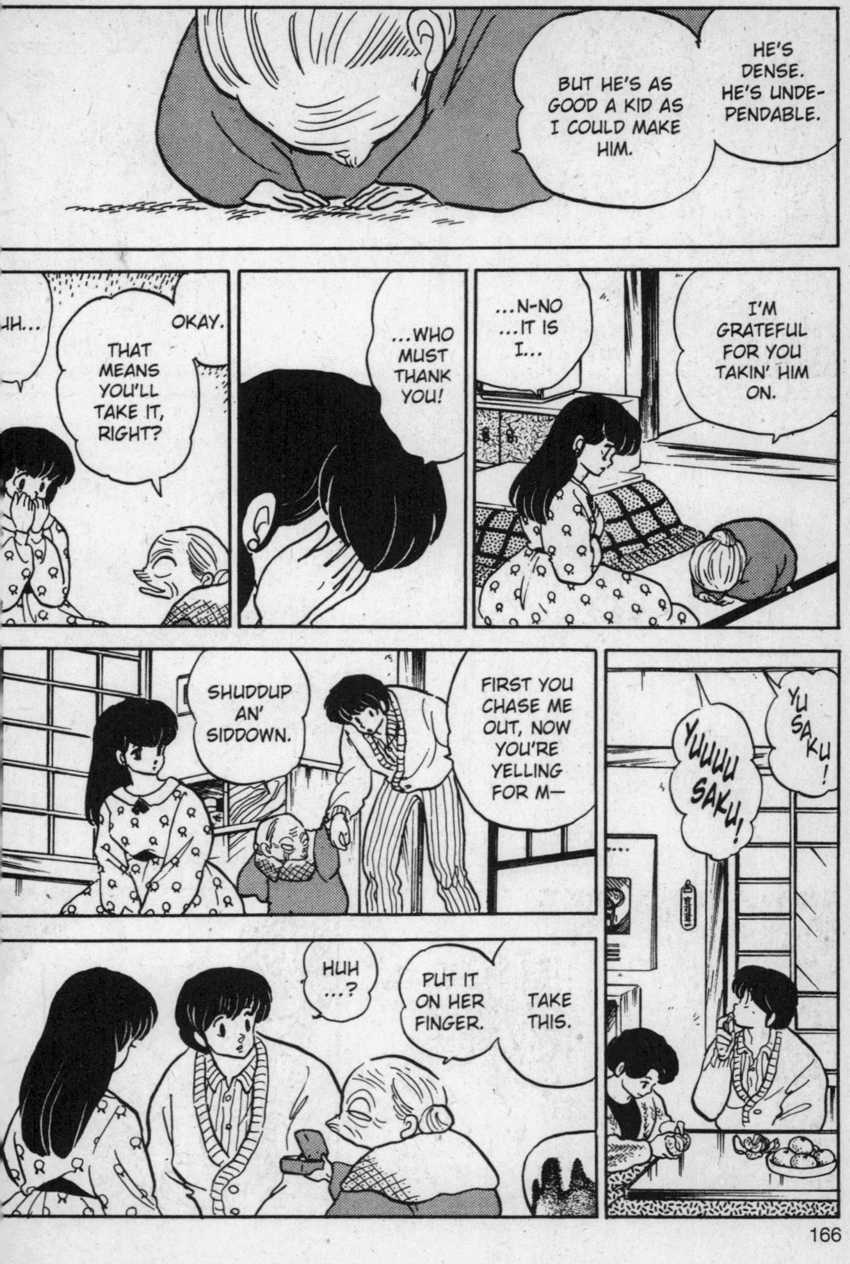
HE'S DENSE. HE'S UNDE-PENDABLE.
BUT HE'S AS GOOD A KID AS I COULD MAKE HIM.
I'M GRATEFUL FOR YOU TAKIN' HIM ON.
...N-NO ...IT IS I...
...WHO MUST THANK YOU!
OKAY.
THAT MEANS YOU'LL TAKE IT, RIGHT?
YUSAKU!
YUUUUSAKU!
FIRST YOU CHASE ME OUT, NOW YOU'RE YELLING FOR M—
SHUDDUP AN' SIDDOWN.
TAKE THIS.
PUT IT ON HER FINGER.
HUH ...?

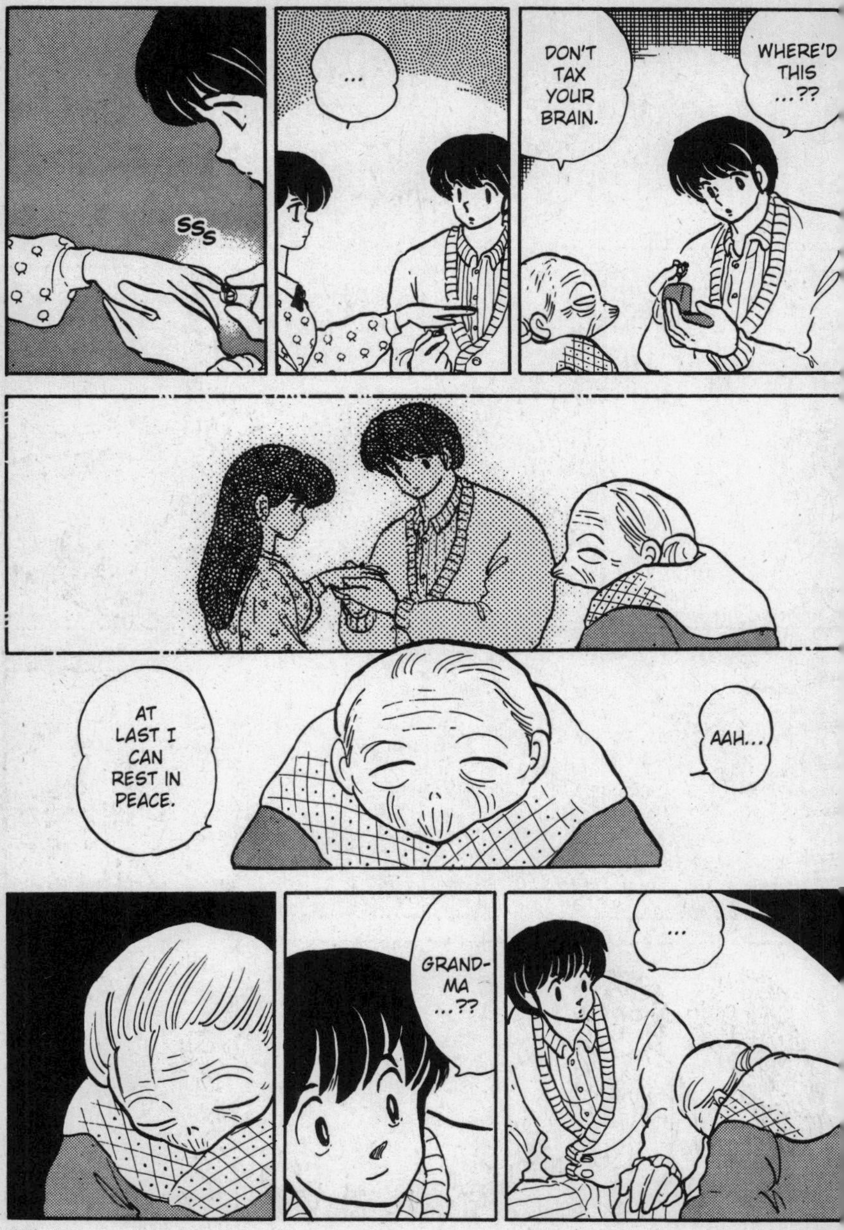
WHERE'D THIS ...??
DON'T TAX YOUR BRAIN.
...
SSS
AAH...
AT LAST I CAN REST IN PEACE.
...
GRAND-MA ...??

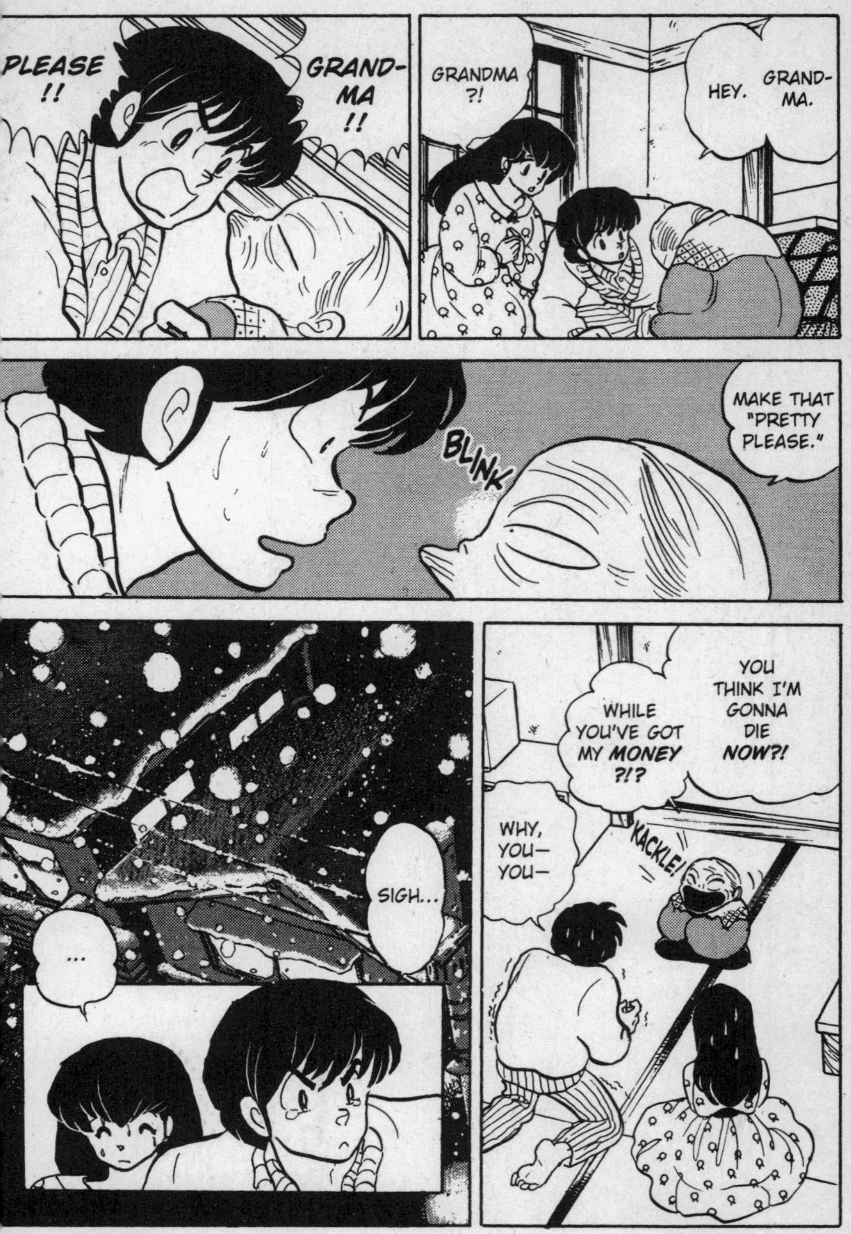
HEY. GRAND-MA.
GRANDMA ?!
GRAND-MA !!
PLEASE !!
MAKE THAT "PRETTY PLEASE."
BLINK
YOU THINK I'M GONNA DIE NOW?!
WHILE YOU'VE GOT MY MONEY ?!?
KACKLE!
WHY, YOU— YOU—
SIGH...
...

PART NINE
BENEATH THE CHERRY TREE

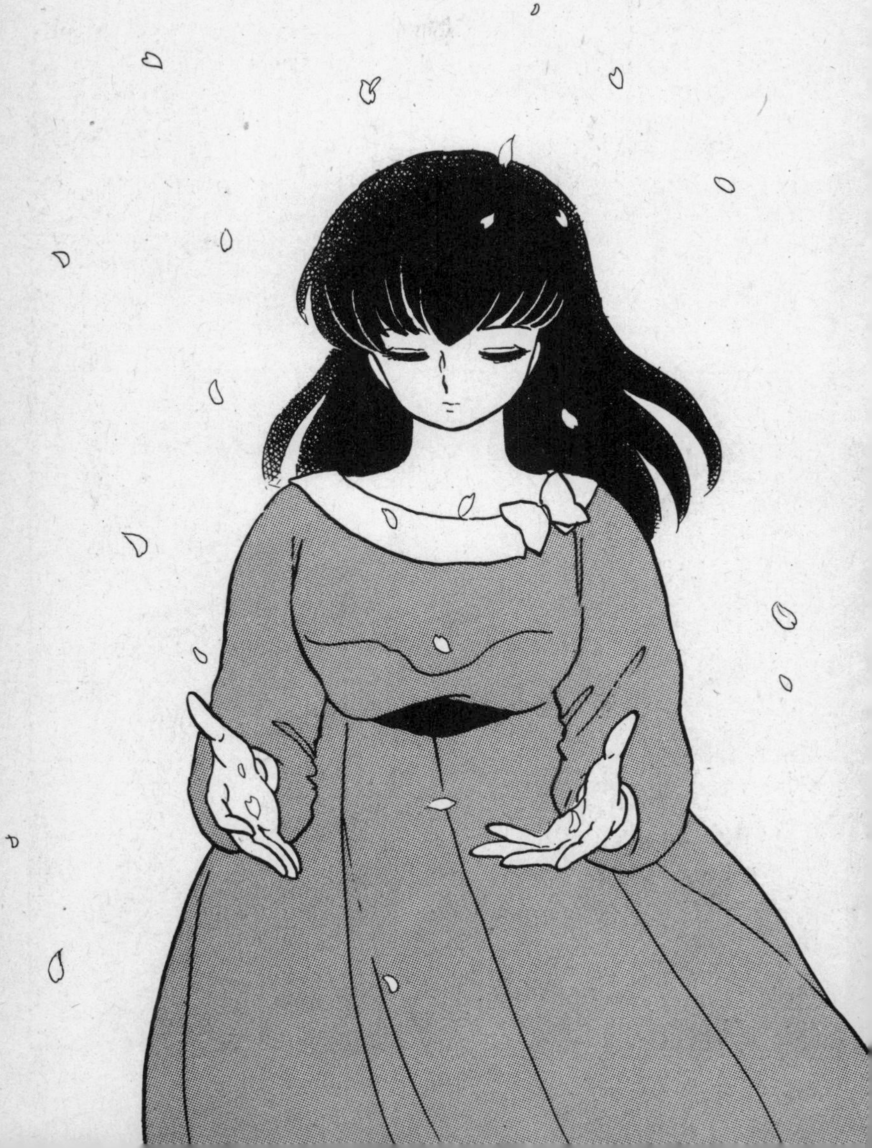

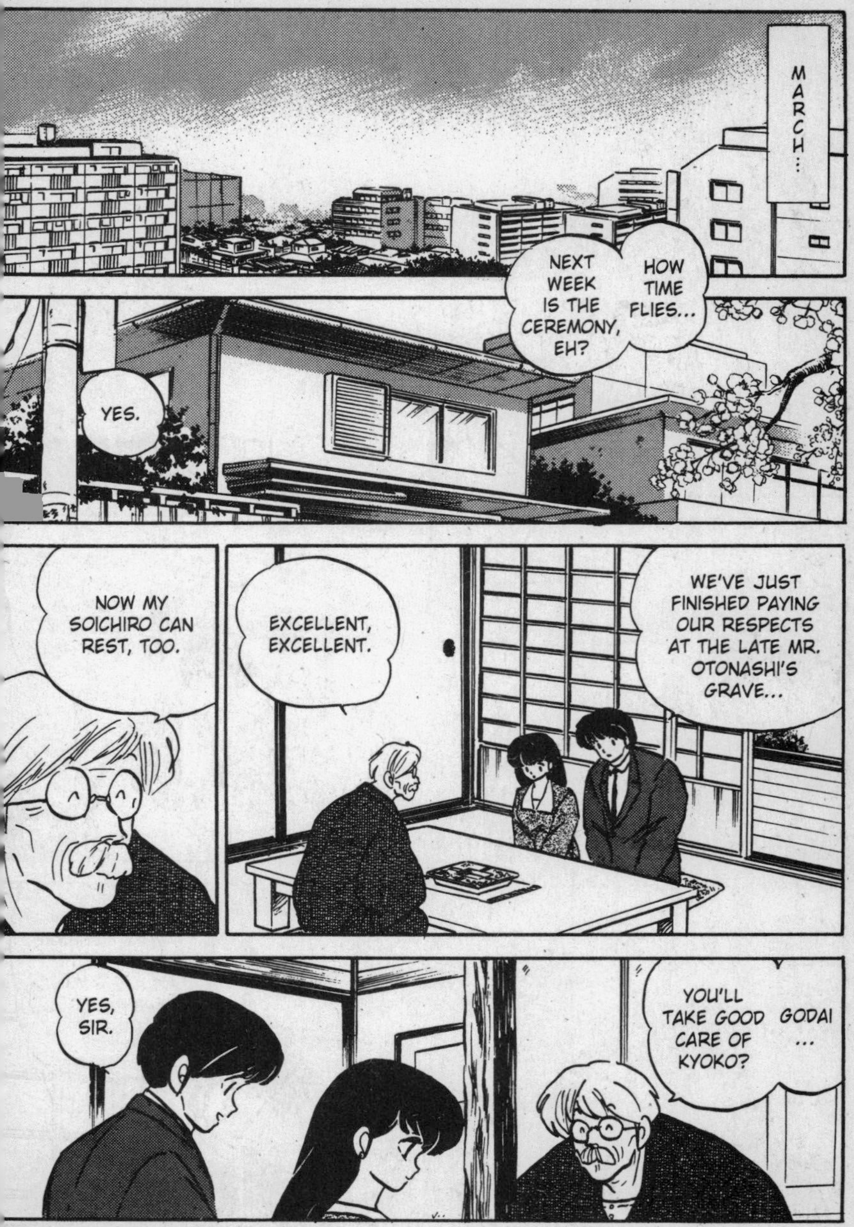

MARCH...
HOW TIME FLIES...
NEXT WEEK IS THE CEREMONY, EH?
YES.
WE'VE JUST FINISHED PAYING OUR RESPECTS AT THE LATE MR. OTONASHI'S GRAVE...
EXCELLENT, EXCELLENT.
NOW MY SOICHIRO CAN REST, TOO.
GODAI...
YOU'LL TAKE GOOD CARE OF KYOKO?
YES, SIR.

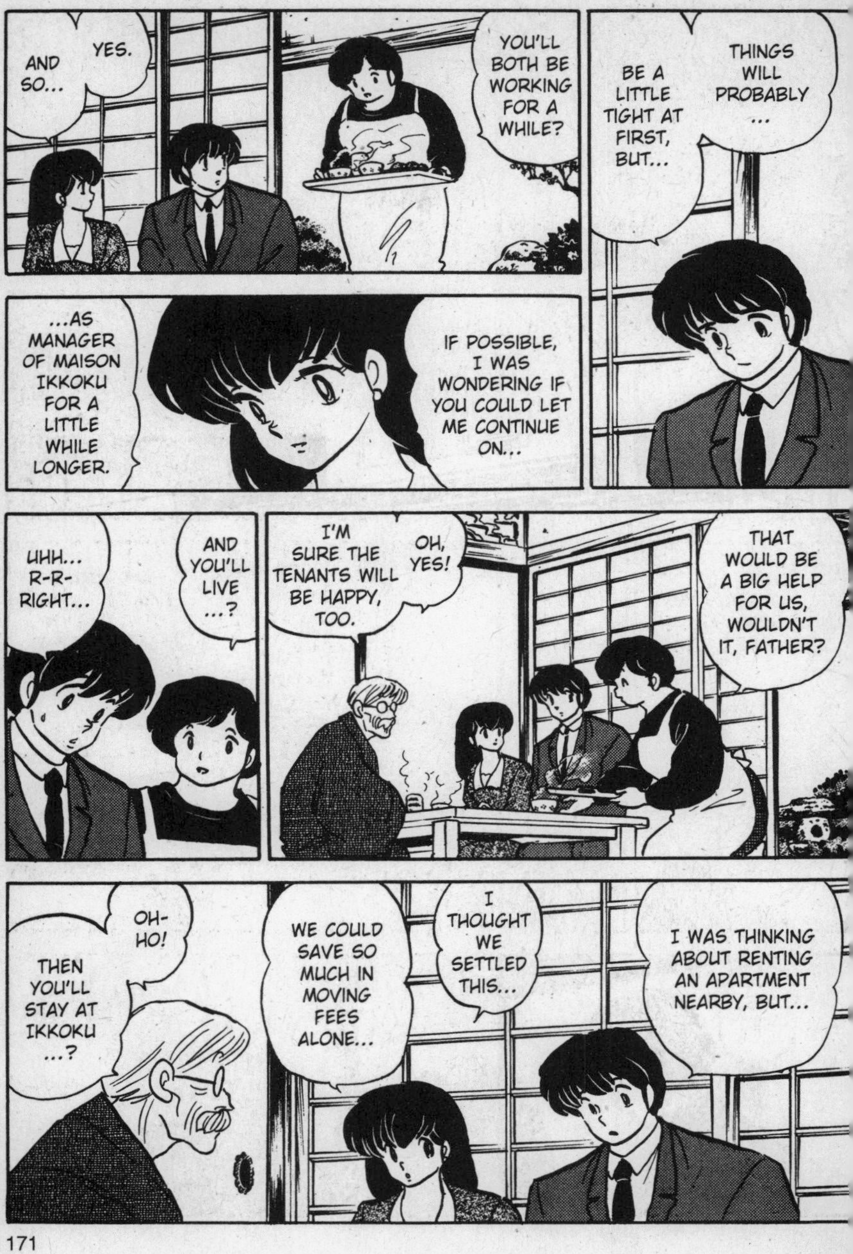
THINGS WILL PROBABLY ...
BE A LITTLE TIGHT AT FIRST, BUT...
YOU'LL BOTH BE WORKING FOR A WHILE?
YES.
AND SO...
IF POSSIBLE, I WAS WONDERING IF YOU COULD LET ME CONTINUE ON...
...AS MANAGER OF MAISON IKKOKU FOR A LITTLE WHILE LONGER.
THAT WOULD BE A BIG HELP FOR US, WOULDN'T IT, FATHER?
OH, YES!
I'M SURE THE TENANTS WILL BE HAPPY, TOO.
AND YOU'LL LIVE ...?
UHH... R-R-RIGHT...
I WAS THINKING ABOUT RENTING AN APARTMENT NEARBY, BUT...
I THOUGHT WE SETTLED THIS...
WE COULD SAVE SO MUCH IN MOVING FEES ALONE...
OH-HO!
THEN YOU'LL STAY AT IKKOKU ...?

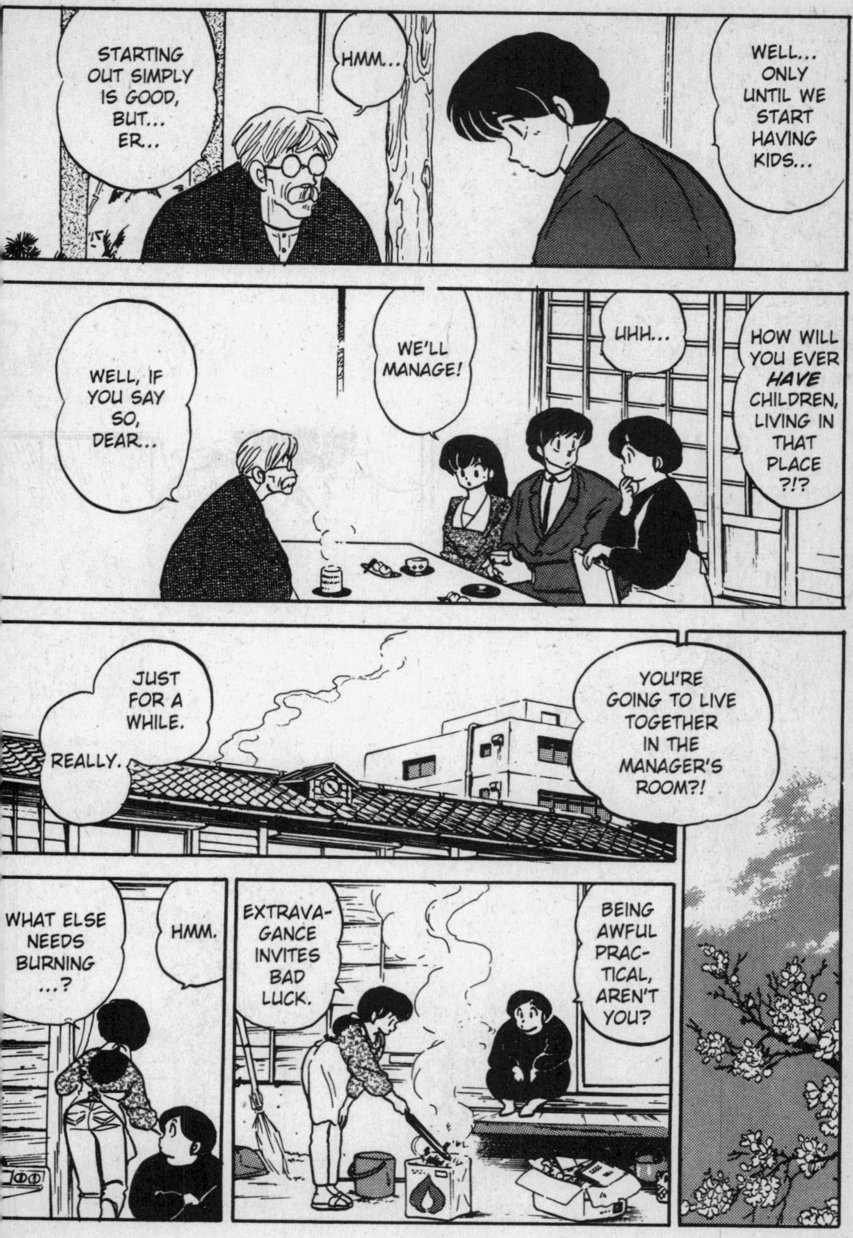
WELL... ONLY UNTIL WE START HAVING KIDS...
HMM...
STARTING OUT SIMPLY IS GOOD, BUT... ER...
HOW WILL YOU EVER *HAVE* CHILDREN, LIVING IN THAT PLACE ?!?
UHH...
WE'LL MANAGE!
WELL, IF YOU SAY SO, DEAR...
YOU'RE GOING TO LIVE TOGETHER IN THE MANAGER'S ROOM?!
JUST FOR A WHILE.
REALLY.
BEING AWFUL PRAC-TICAL, AREN'T YOU?
EXTRAVA-GANCE INVITES BAD LUCK.
HMM.
WHAT ELSE NEEDS BURNING ...?

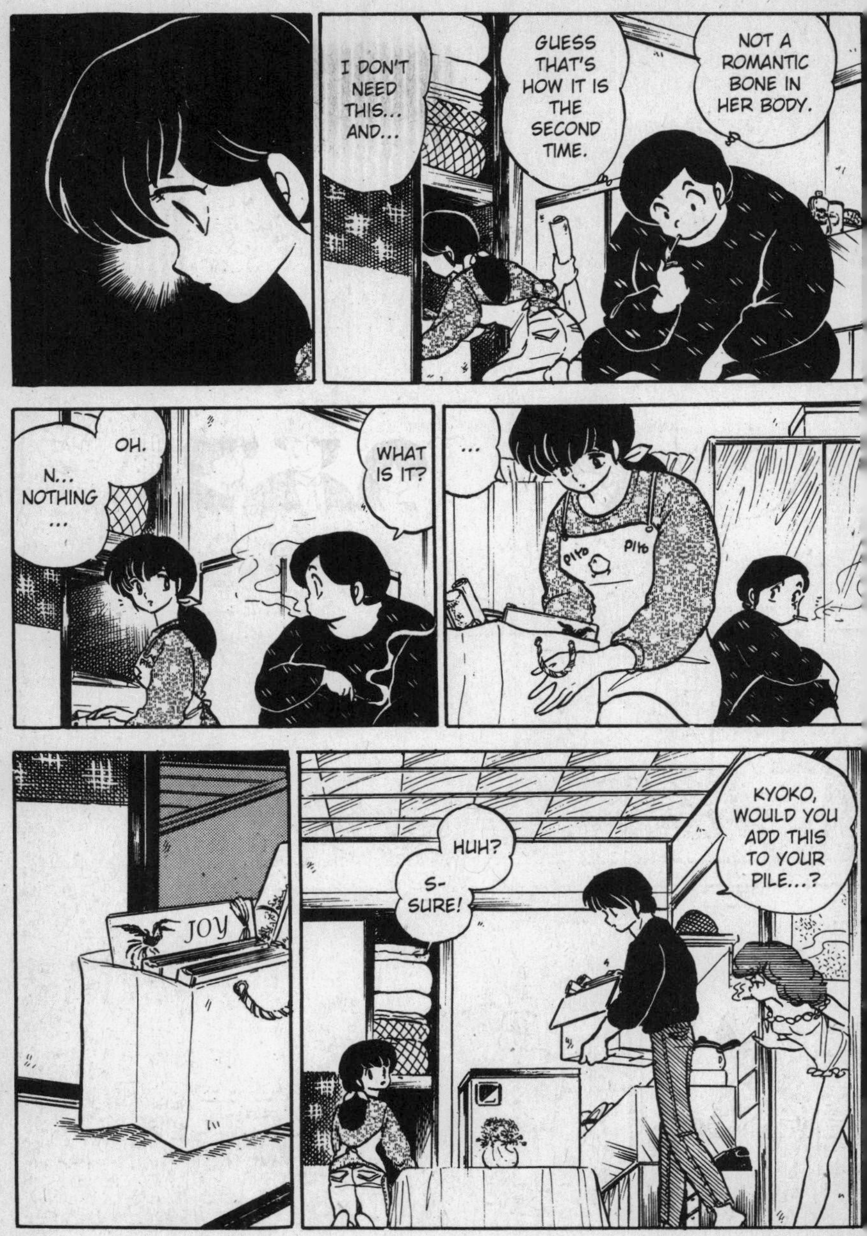
NOT A ROMANTIC BONE IN HER BODY.
GUESS THAT'S HOW IT IS THE SECOND TIME.
I DON'T NEED THIS... AND...
...
WHAT IS IT?
OH.
N... NOTHING ...
KYOKO, WOULD YOU ADD THIS TO YOUR PILE...?
HUH?
S- SURE!
JOY

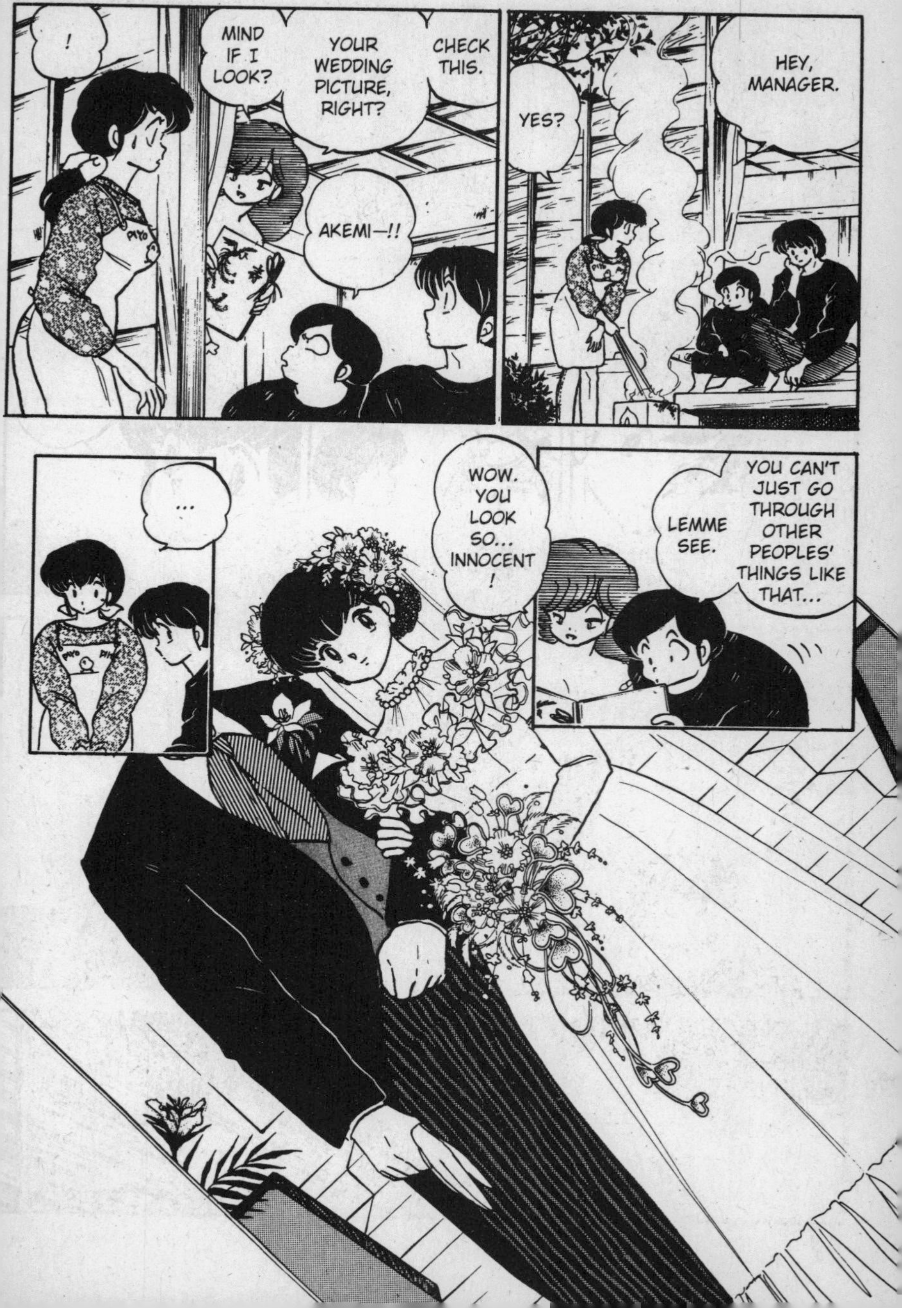
HEY, MANAGER.
YES?
CHECK THIS.
YOUR WEDDING PICTURE, RIGHT?
MIND IF I LOOK?
AKEMI—!!
!
YOU CAN'T JUST GO THROUGH OTHER PEOPLES' THINGS LIKE THAT...
LEMME SEE.
WOW. YOU LOOK SO... INNOCENT!
...

UM...

SHE LOOKS GREAT!

CHECK IT OUT, GODAI!

Y'KNOW, THIS IS THE FIRST TIME...

...I'VE EVER SEEN YOUR HUSBAND.

WOW.

BUT...

THEY'RE NOT FORCING ME...

THAT IS...

TH-THERE'S REALLY NO NEED TO FORCE HIM...

THERE'S NOTHING TO APOLO-GIZE FOR...

I'M SORRY.

YES... HE WAS.

HE LOOKS LIKE A VERY KIND MAN.

...

I SHOULDN'T KEEP YOUR THINGS HERE ANYMORE.

I'M SORRY, SOICHIRO.

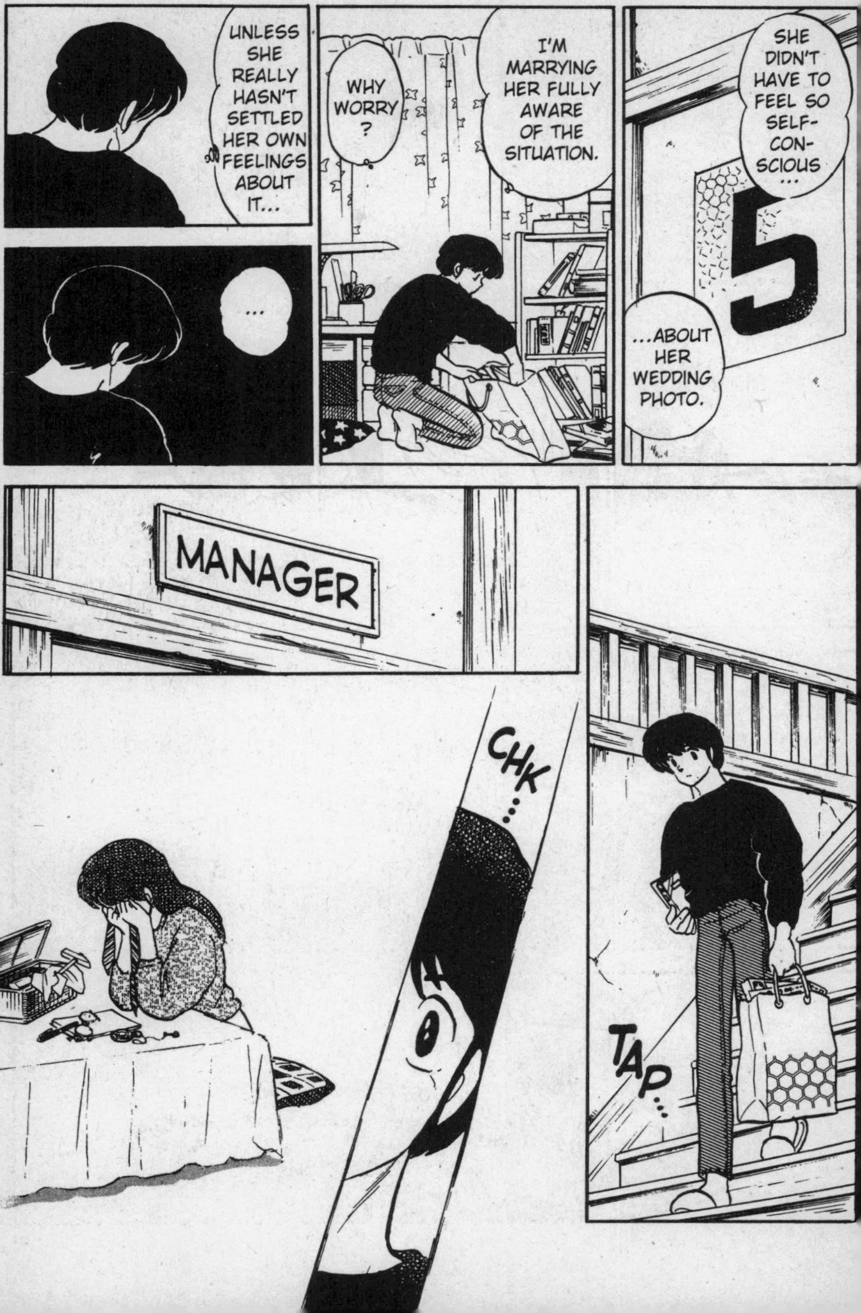
SHE DIDN'T HAVE TO FEEL SO SELF-CONSCIOUS...
5
...ABOUT HER WEDDING PHOTO.
I'M MARRYING HER FULLY AWARE OF THE SITUATION.
WHY WORRY?
UNLESS SHE REALLY HASN'T SETTLED HER OWN FEELINGS ABOUT IT...
...
TAP...
MANAGER
CHK...

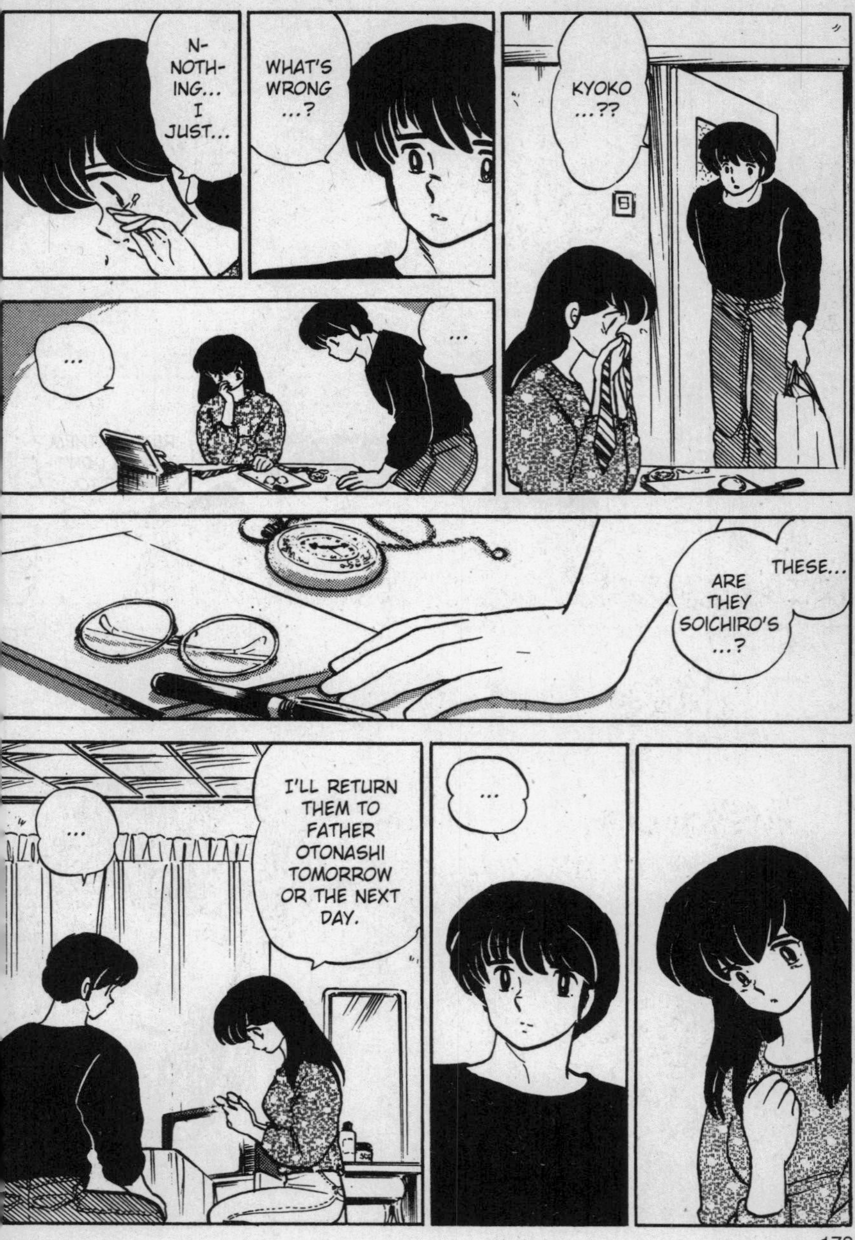
KYOKO ...??
WHAT'S WRONG ...?
N-NOTHING... I JUST...
...
...
THESE...
ARE THEY SOICHIRO'S ...?
...
I'LL RETURN THEM TO FATHER OTONASHI TOMORROW OR THE NEXT DAY.
...

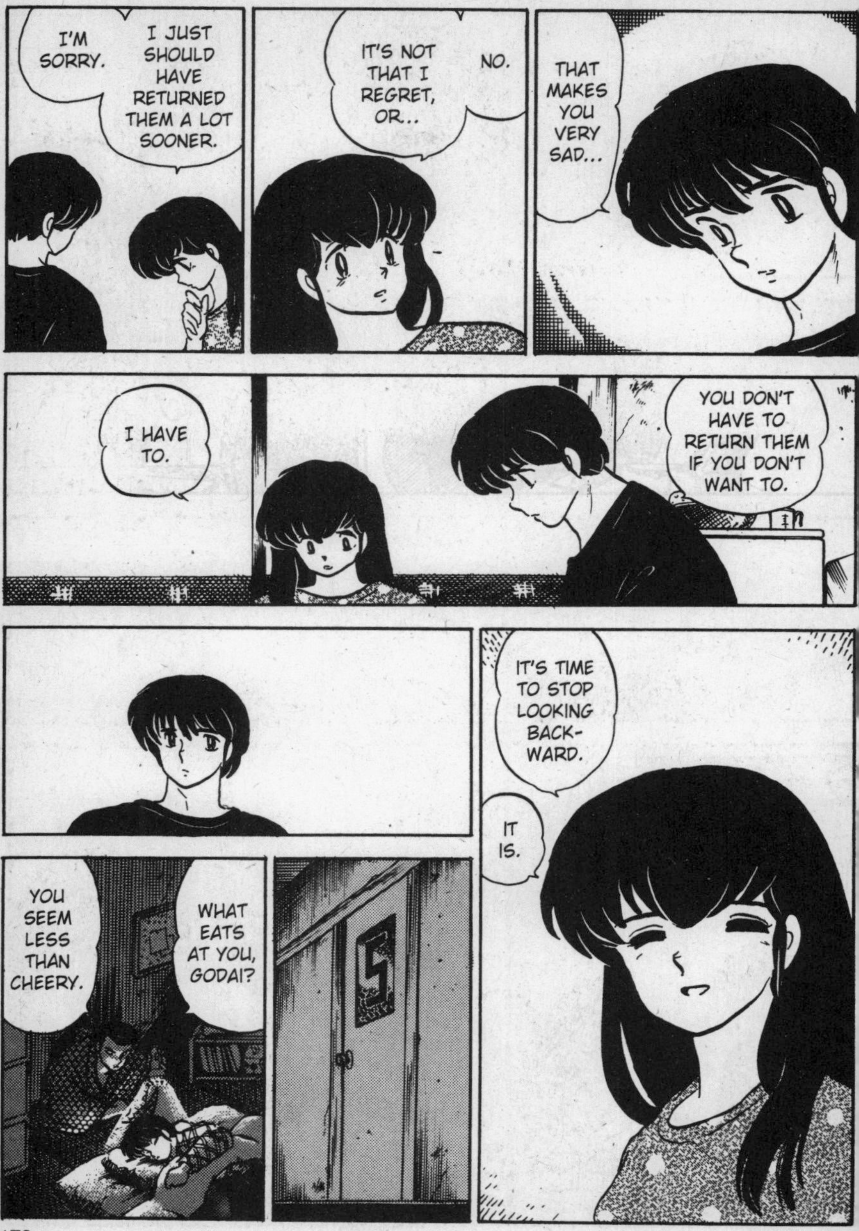
THAT MAKES YOU VERY SAD...
NO.
IT'S NOT THAT I REGRET, OR...
I'M SORRY.
I JUST SHOULD HAVE RETURNED THEM A LOT SOONER.
YOU DON'T HAVE TO RETURN THEM IF YOU DON'T WANT TO.
I HAVE TO.
IT'S TIME TO STOP LOOKING BACK-WARD.
IT IS.
WHAT EATS AT YOU, GODAI?
YOU SEEM LESS THAN CHEERY.

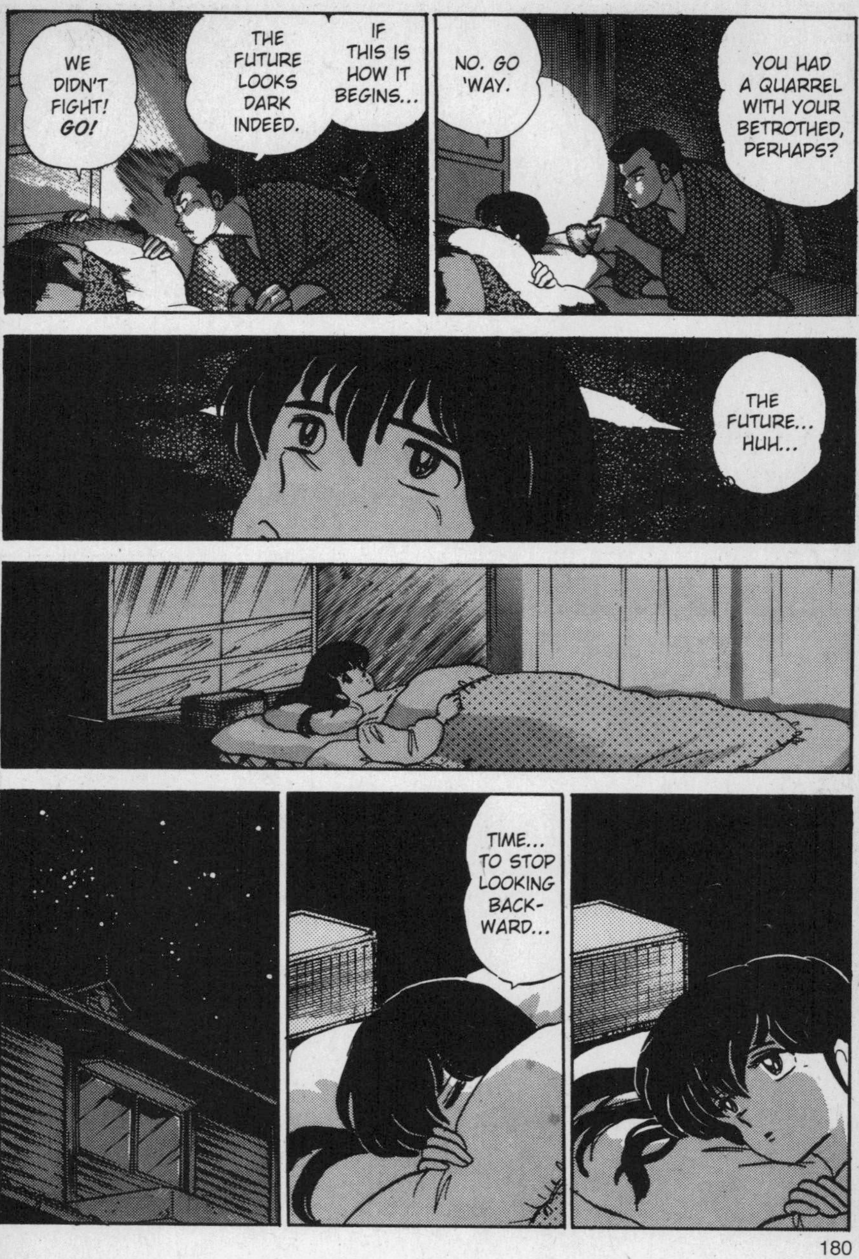
YOU HAD A QUARREL WITH YOUR BETROTHED, PERHAPS?
NO. GO 'WAY.
IF THIS IS HOW IT BEGINS...
THE FUTURE LOOKS DARK INDEED.
WE DIDN'T FIGHT! *GO!*
THE FUTURE... HUH...
TIME... TO STOP LOOKING BACK-WARD...

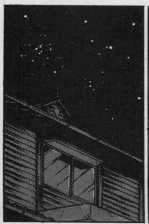

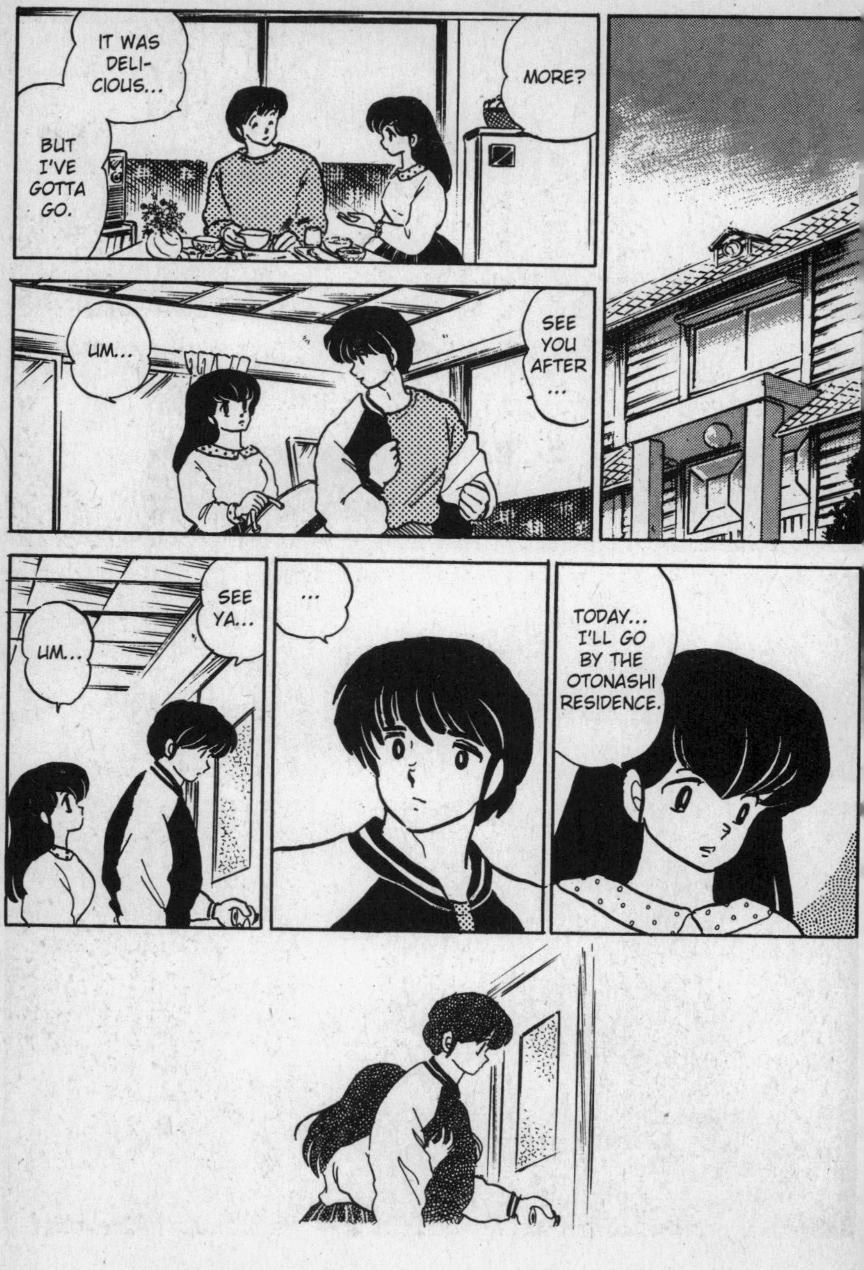
MORE?
IT WAS DELICIOUS...
BUT I'VE GOTTA GO.
SEE YOU AFTER...
UM...
TODAY... I'LL GO BY THE OTONASHI RESIDENCE.
...
SEE YA...
UM...

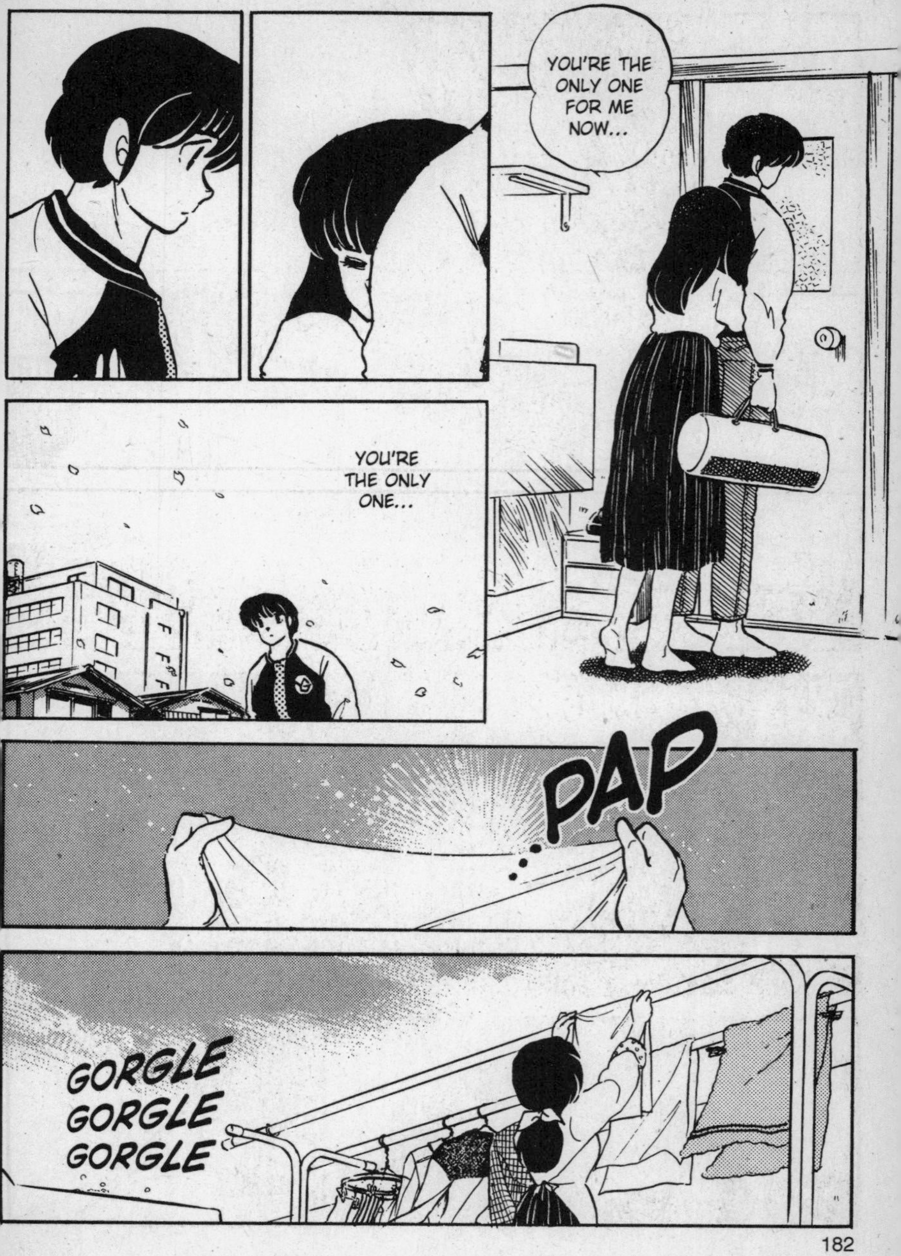
YOU'RE THE ONLY ONE FOR ME NOW...
YOU'RE THE ONLY ONE...
PAP
GORGLE GORGLE GORGLE

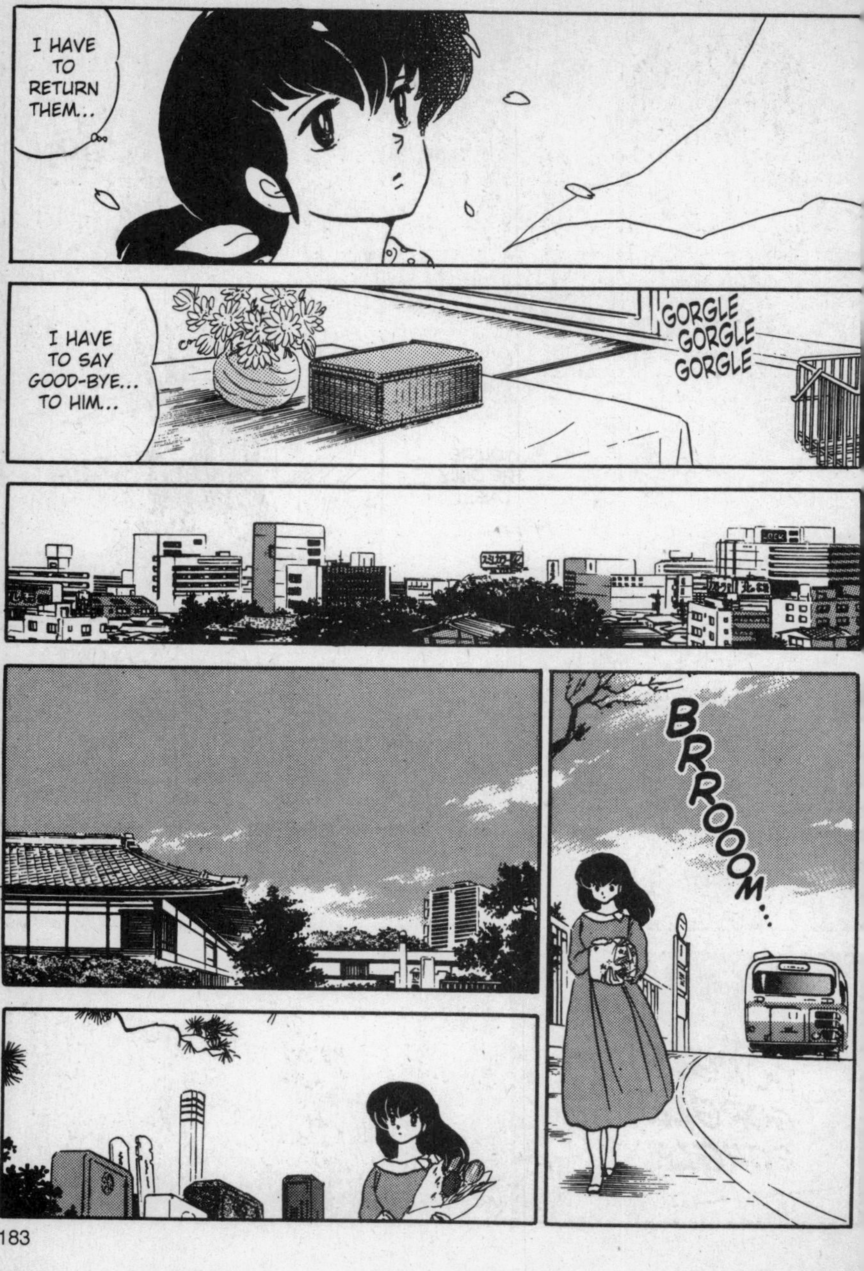
I HAVE TO RETURN THEM...
GORGLE GORGLE GORGLE
I HAVE TO SAY GOOD-BYE... TO HIM...
BRROOOM...

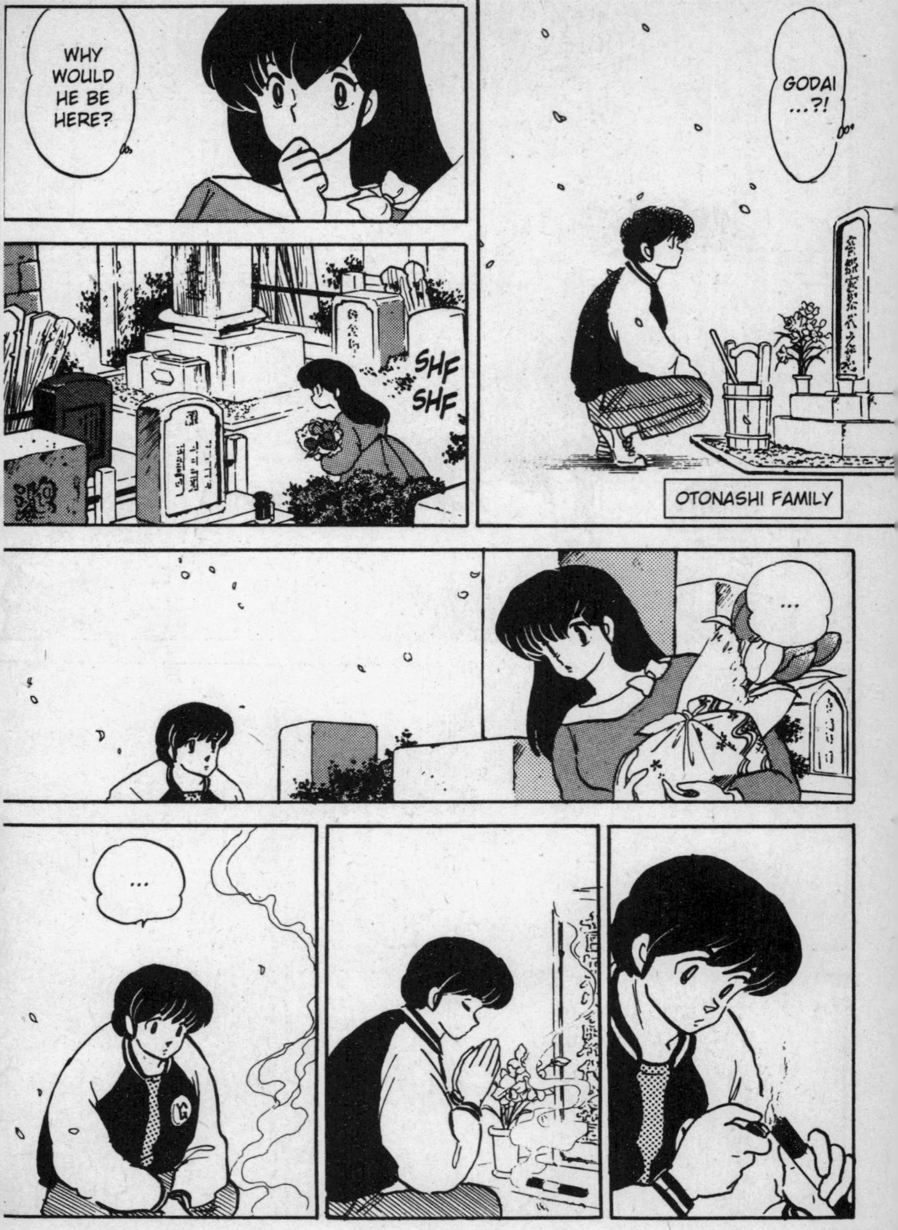

GODAI ...?!
OTONASHI FAMILY
WHY WOULD HE BE HERE?
SHF SHF
...
...

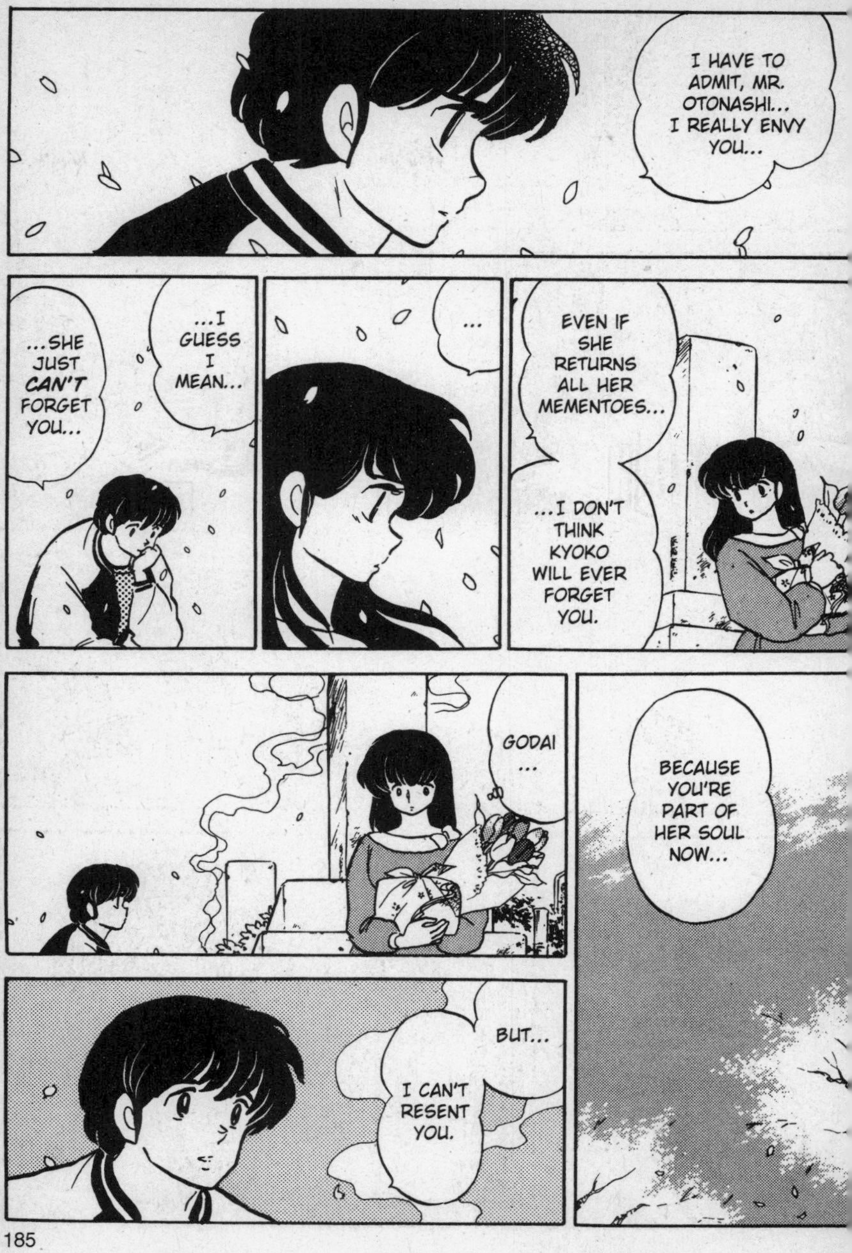
I HAVE TO ADMIT, MR. OTONASHI... I REALLY ENVY YOU...
EVEN IF SHE RETURNS ALL HER MEMENTOES...
...I DON'T THINK KYOKO WILL EVER FORGET YOU.
...
...I GUESS I MEAN...
...SHE JUST **CAN'T** FORGET YOU...
BECAUSE YOU'RE PART OF HER SOUL NOW...
GODAI ...
BUT...
I CAN'T RESENT YOU.

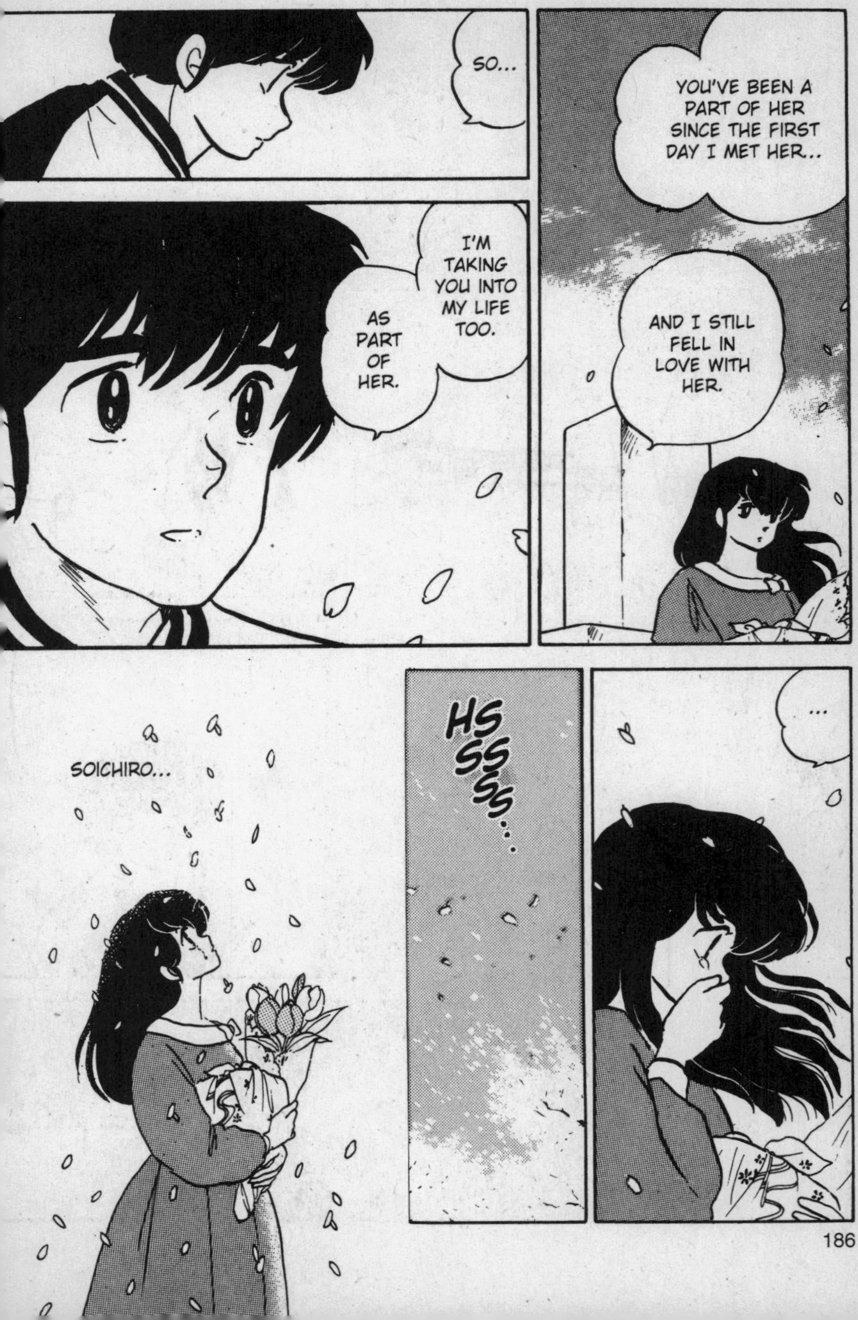
YOU'VE BEEN A PART OF HER SINCE THE FIRST DAY I MET HER...
AND I STILL FELL IN LOVE WITH HER.
SO...
I'M TAKING YOU INTO MY LIFE TOO.
AS PART OF HER.
...
HSSSS...
SOICHIRO...

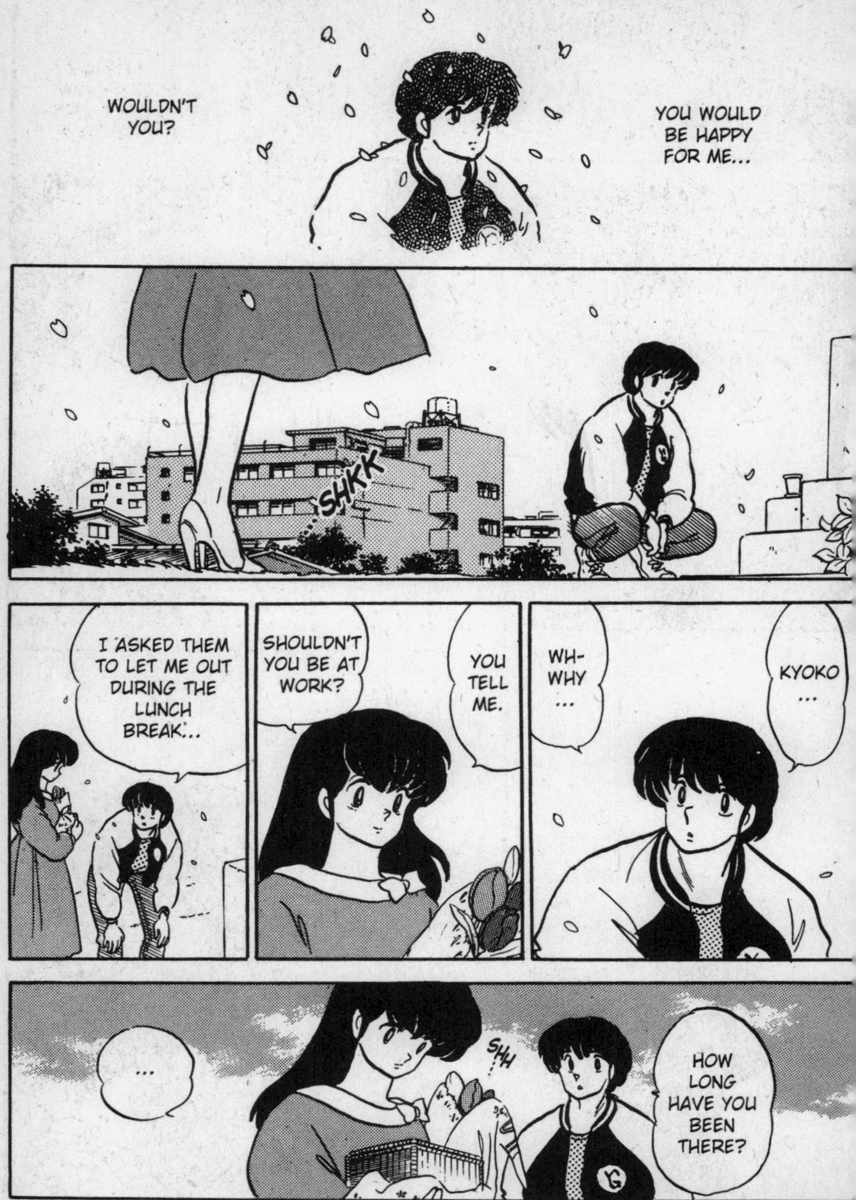
YOU WOULD BE HAPPY FOR ME...
WOULDN'T YOU?
SHKK
KYOKO ...
WH-WHY ...
YOU TELL ME.
SHOULDN'T YOU BE AT WORK?
I ASKED THEM TO LET ME OUT DURING THE LUNCH BREAK...
HOW LONG HAVE YOU BEEN THERE?
SHH
...

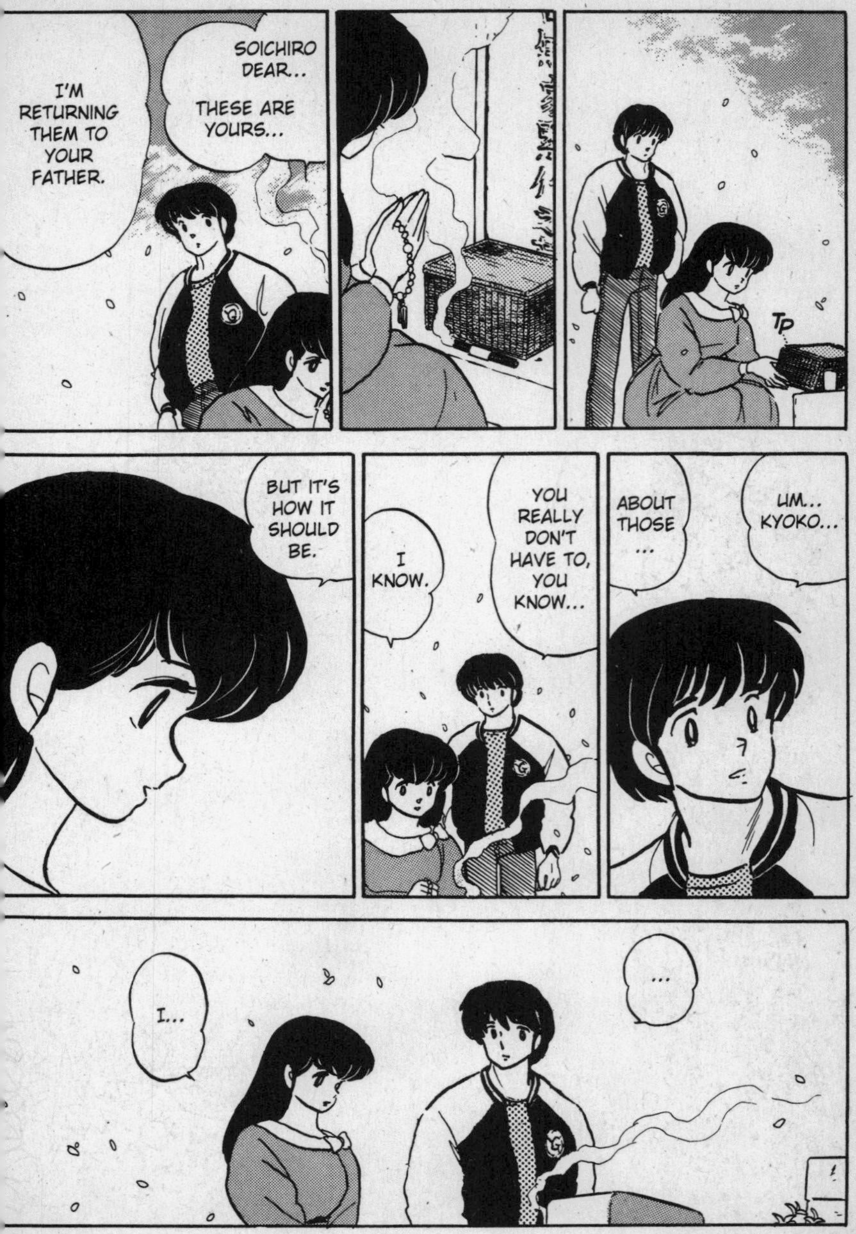

TP
SOICHIRO DEAR...
THESE ARE YOURS...
I'M RETURNING THEM TO YOUR FATHER.
UM... KYOKO...
ABOUT THOSE ...
YOU REALLY DON'T HAVE TO, YOU KNOW...
I KNOW.
BUT IT'S HOW IT SHOULD BE.
...
I...

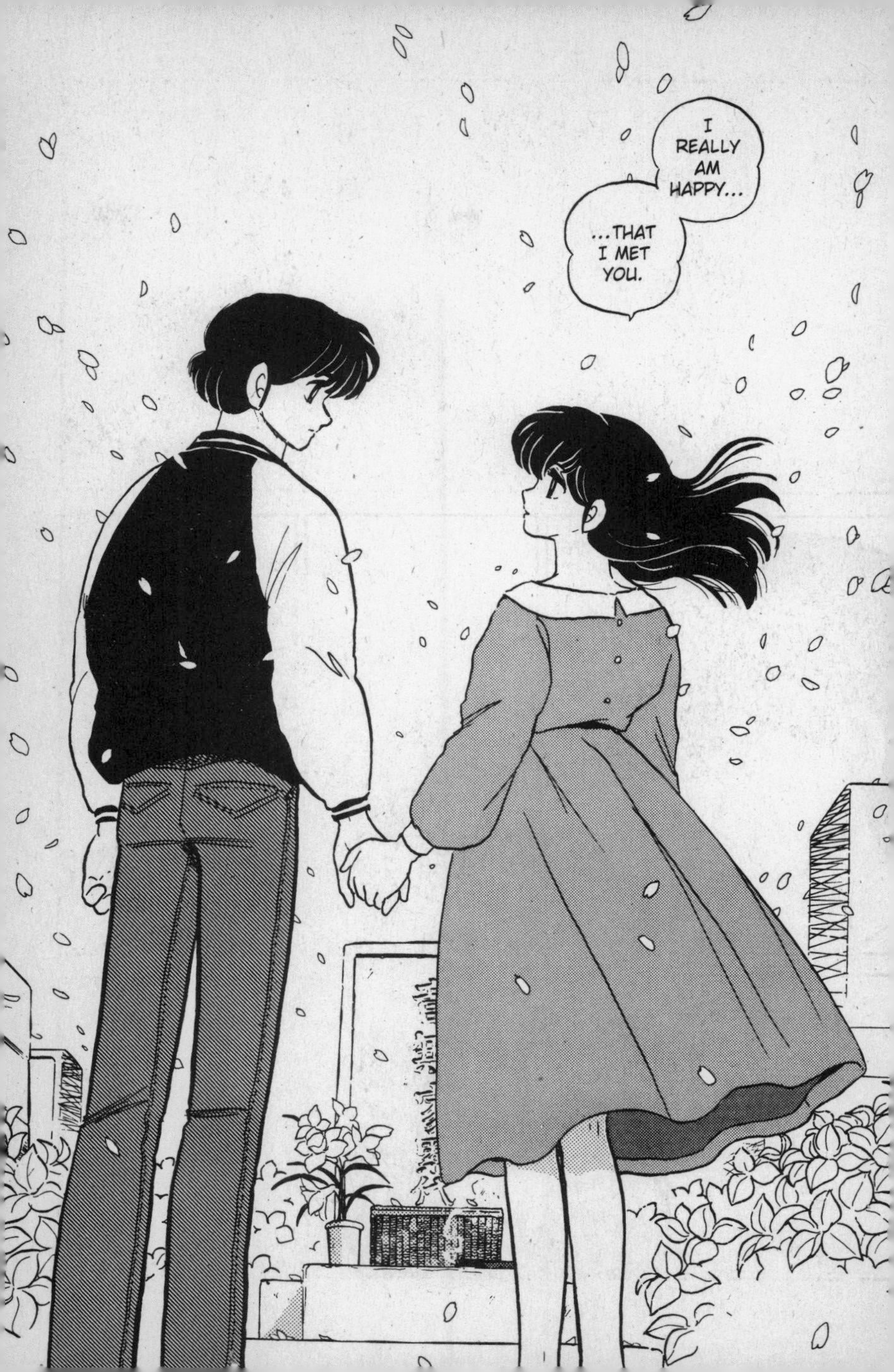
I REALLY AM HAPPY...
...THAT I MET YOU.

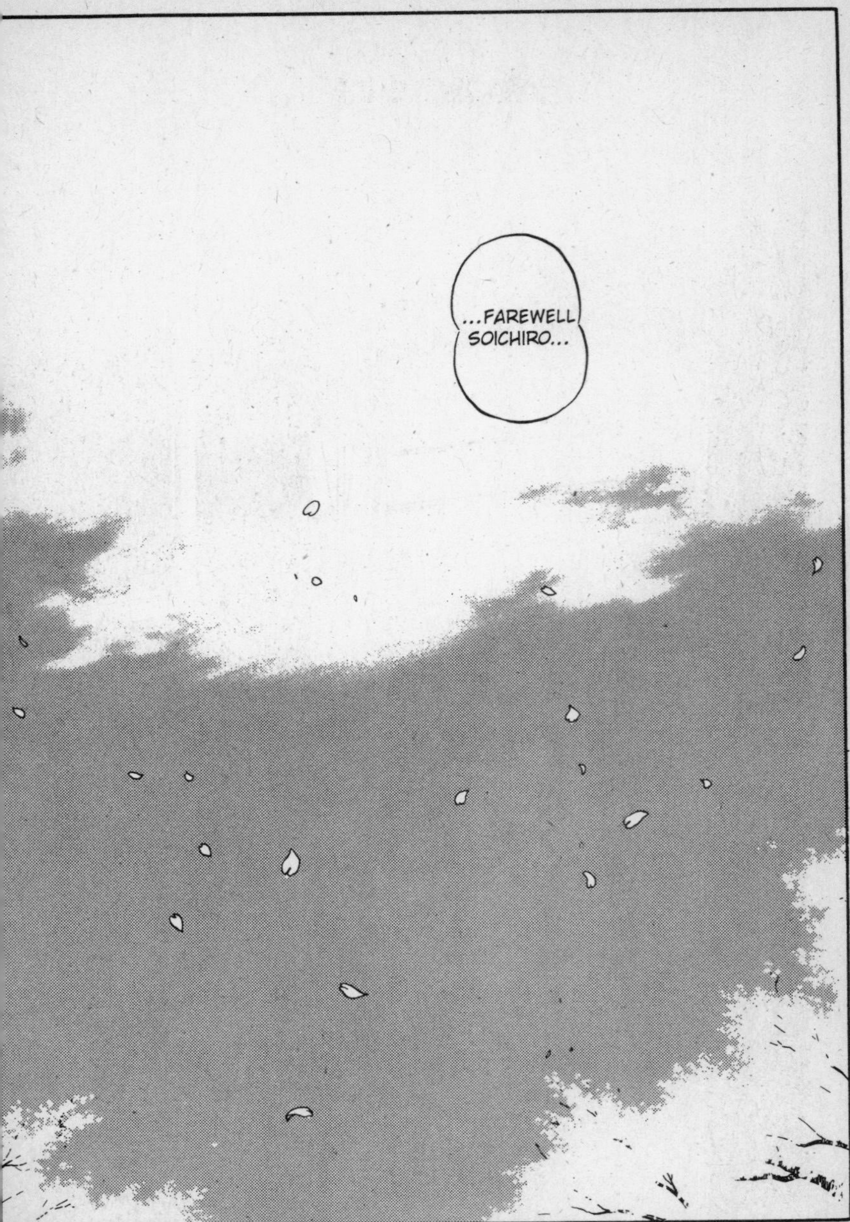
...FAREWELL SOICHIRO...

PART TEN

P. S. IKKOKU

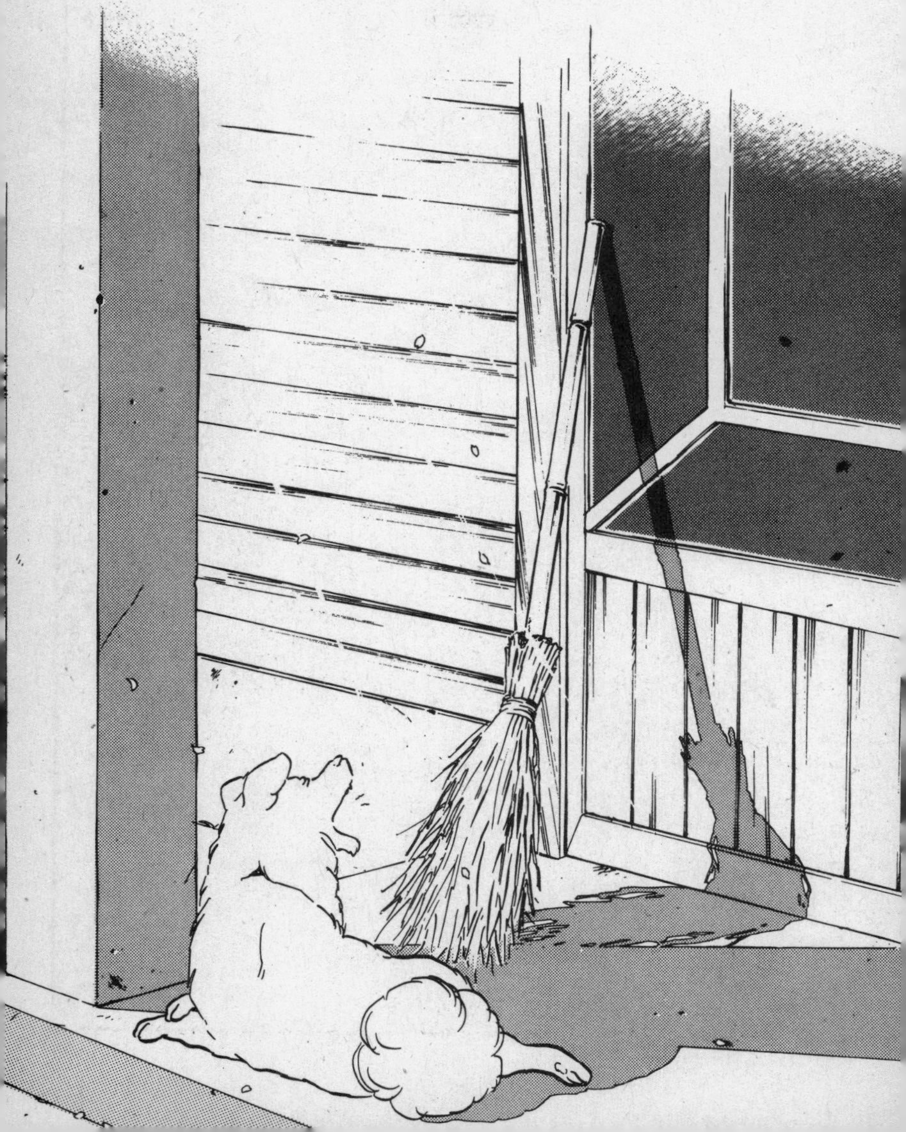

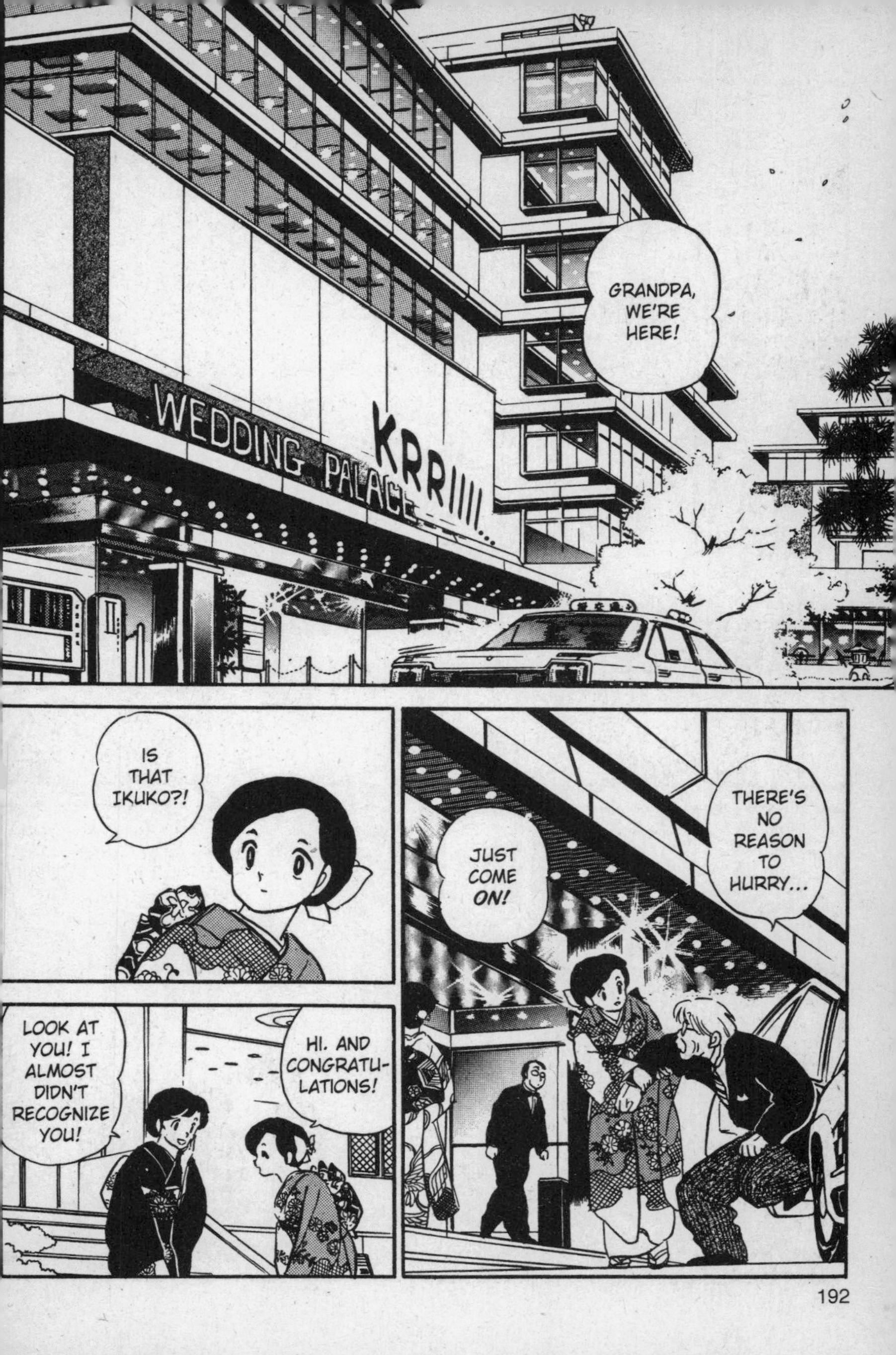
GRANDPA, WE'RE HERE!
KRR!!!!!...
WEDDING PALACE
THERE'S NO REASON TO HURRY...
JUST COME ON!
IS THAT IKUKO?!
HI. AND CONGRATULATIONS!
LOOK AT YOU! I ALMOST DIDN'T RECOGNIZE YOU!

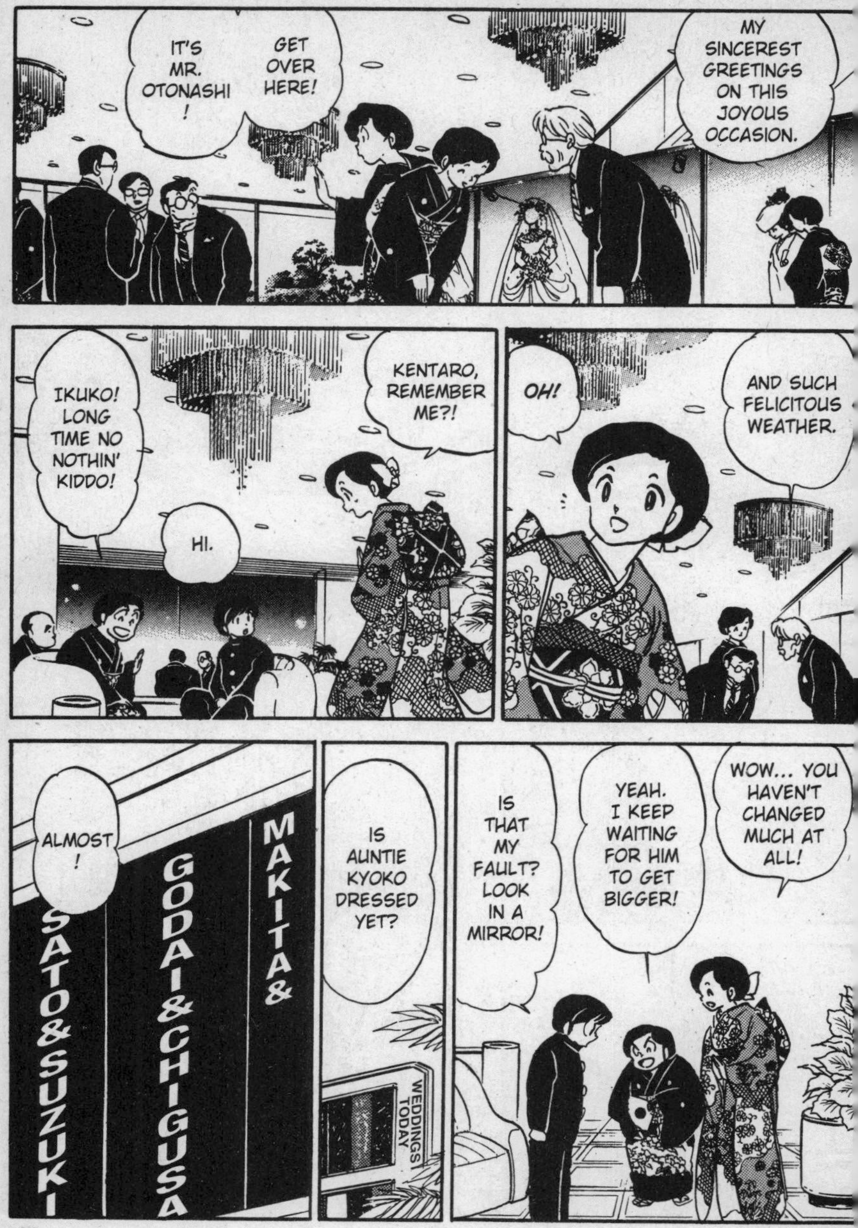
MY SINCEREST GREETINGS ON THIS JOYOUS OCCASION.
IT'S MR. OTONASHI! GET OVER HERE!
AND SUCH FELICITOUS WEATHER.
OH!
KENTARO, REMEMBER ME?!
IKUKO! LONG TIME NO NOTHIN' KIDDO!
HI.
WOW... YOU HAVEN'T CHANGED MUCH AT ALL!
YEAH. I KEEP WAITING FOR HIM TO GET BIGGER!
IS THAT MY FAULT? LOOK IN A MIRROR!
IS AUNTIE KYOKO DRESSED YET?
WEDDINGS TODAY
MAKITA&
GODAI&CHIGUSA
SATO&SUZUKI
ALMOST!

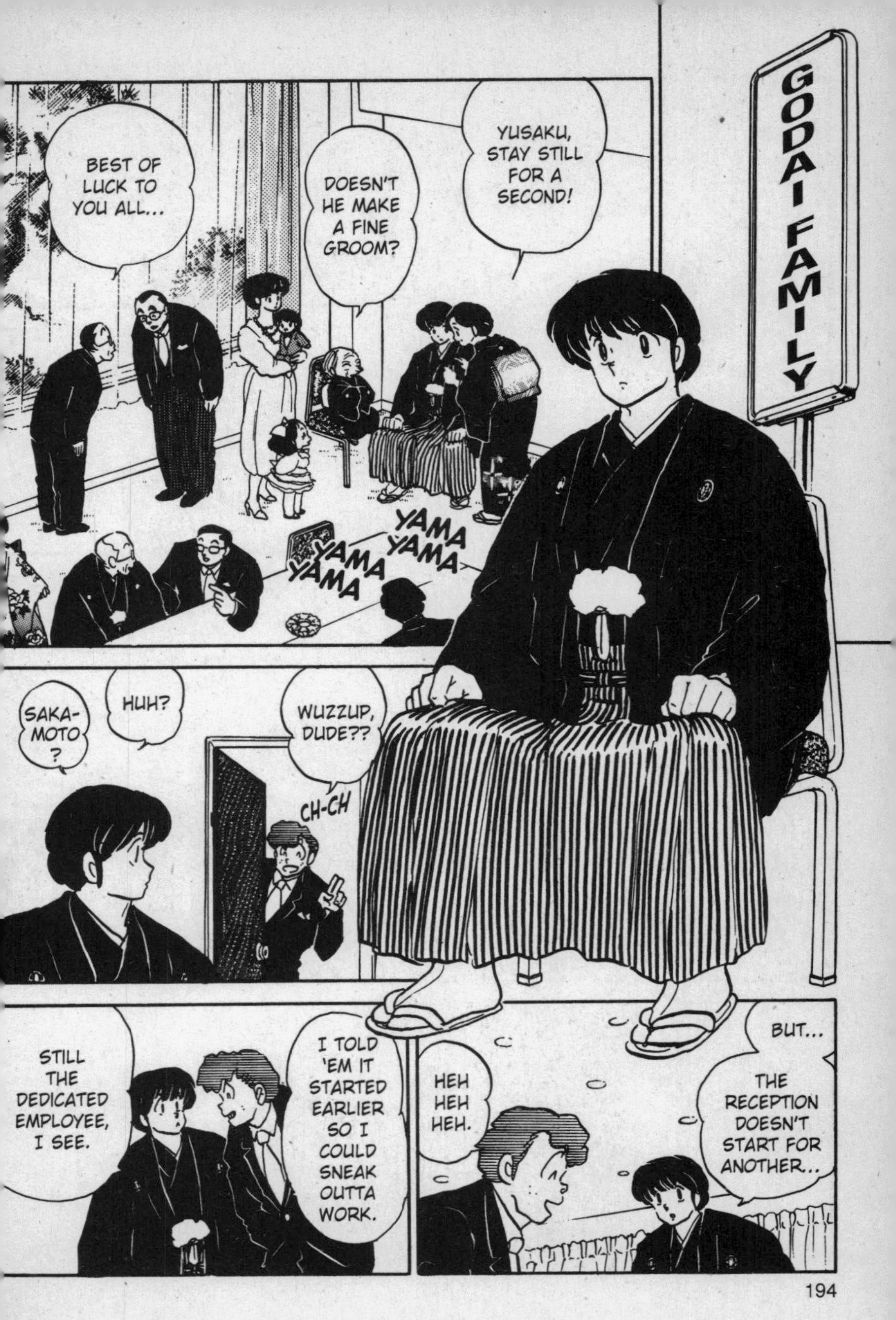
GODAI FAMILY
YUSAKU, STAY STILL FOR A SECOND!
DOESN'T HE MAKE A FINE GROOM?
BEST OF LUCK TO YOU ALL...
YAMA YAMA
YAMA YAMA
WUZZUP, DUDE??
CH-CH
HUH?
SAKA-MOTO?
BUT...
THE RECEPTION DOESN'T START FOR ANOTHER...
HEH HEH HEH.
I TOLD 'EM IT STARTED EARLIER SO I COULD SNEAK OUTTA WORK.
STILL THE DEDICATED EMPLOYEE, I SEE.

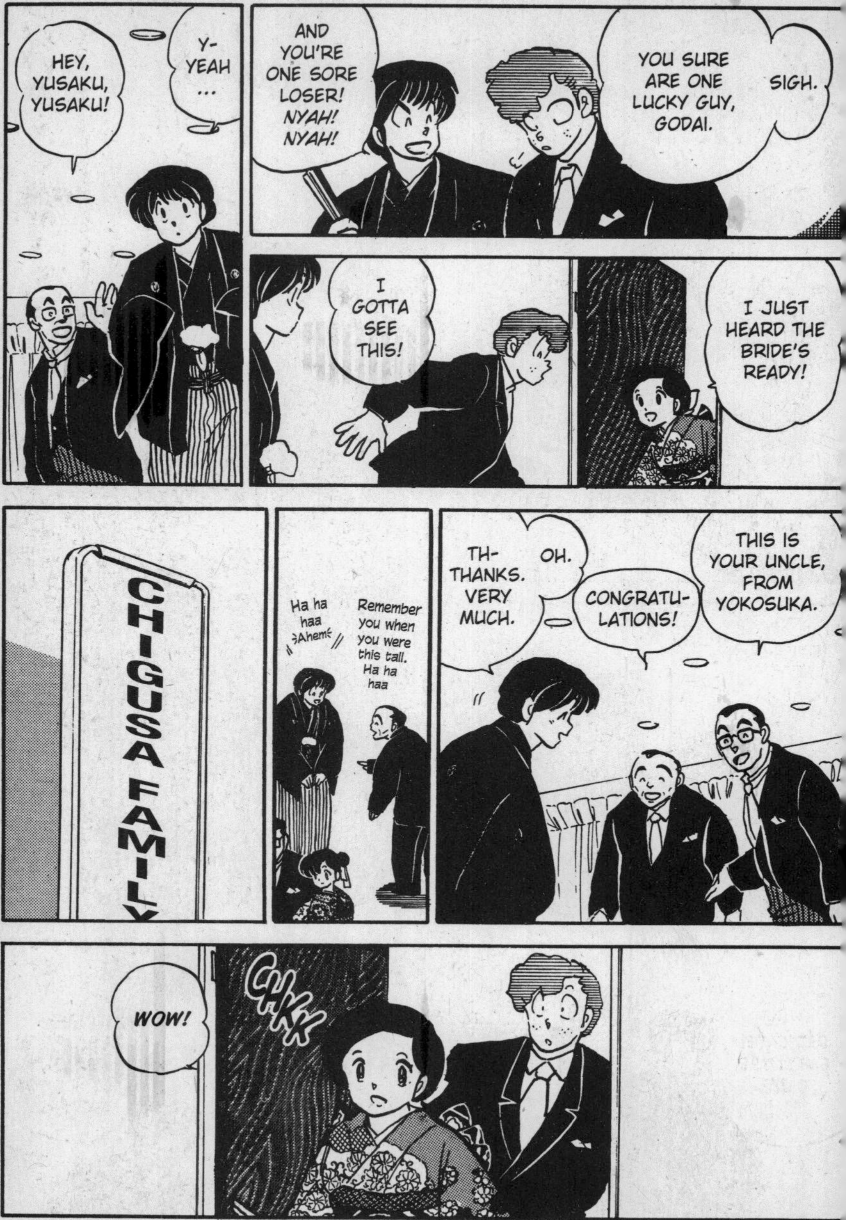
SIGH.
YOU SURE ARE ONE LUCKY GUY, GODAI.
AND YOU'RE ONE SORE LOSER! NYAH! NYAH!
I JUST HEARD THE BRIDE'S READY!
I GOTTA SEE THIS!
Y-YEAH ...
HEY, YUSAKU, YUSAKU!
THIS IS YOUR UNCLE, FROM YOKOSUKA.
CONGRATU-LATIONS!
OH.
TH-THANKS. VERY MUCH.
Remember you when you were this tall. Ha ha haa
Ha ha haa Ahem
CHIGUSA FAMILY
CHKK
WOW!

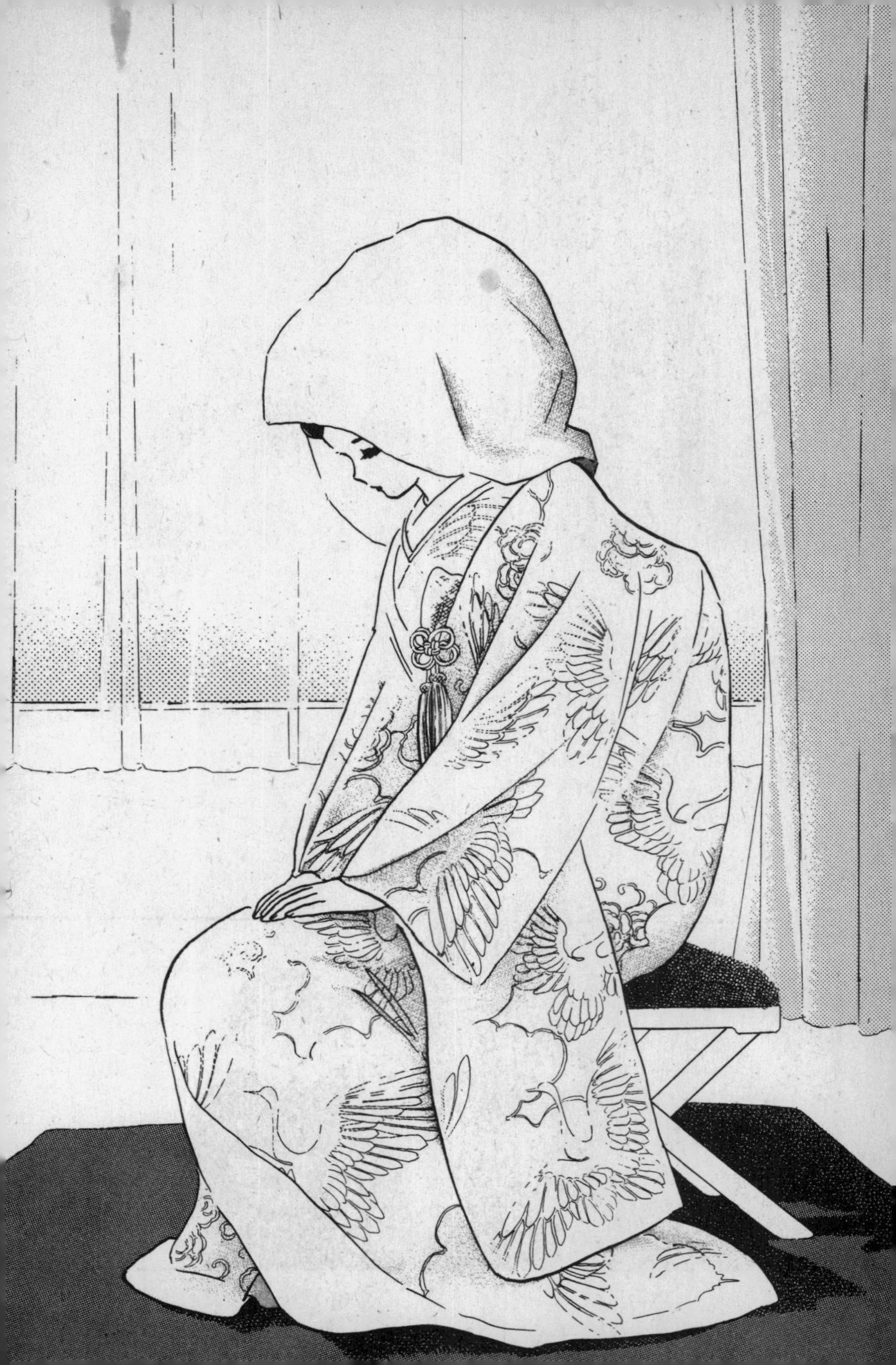

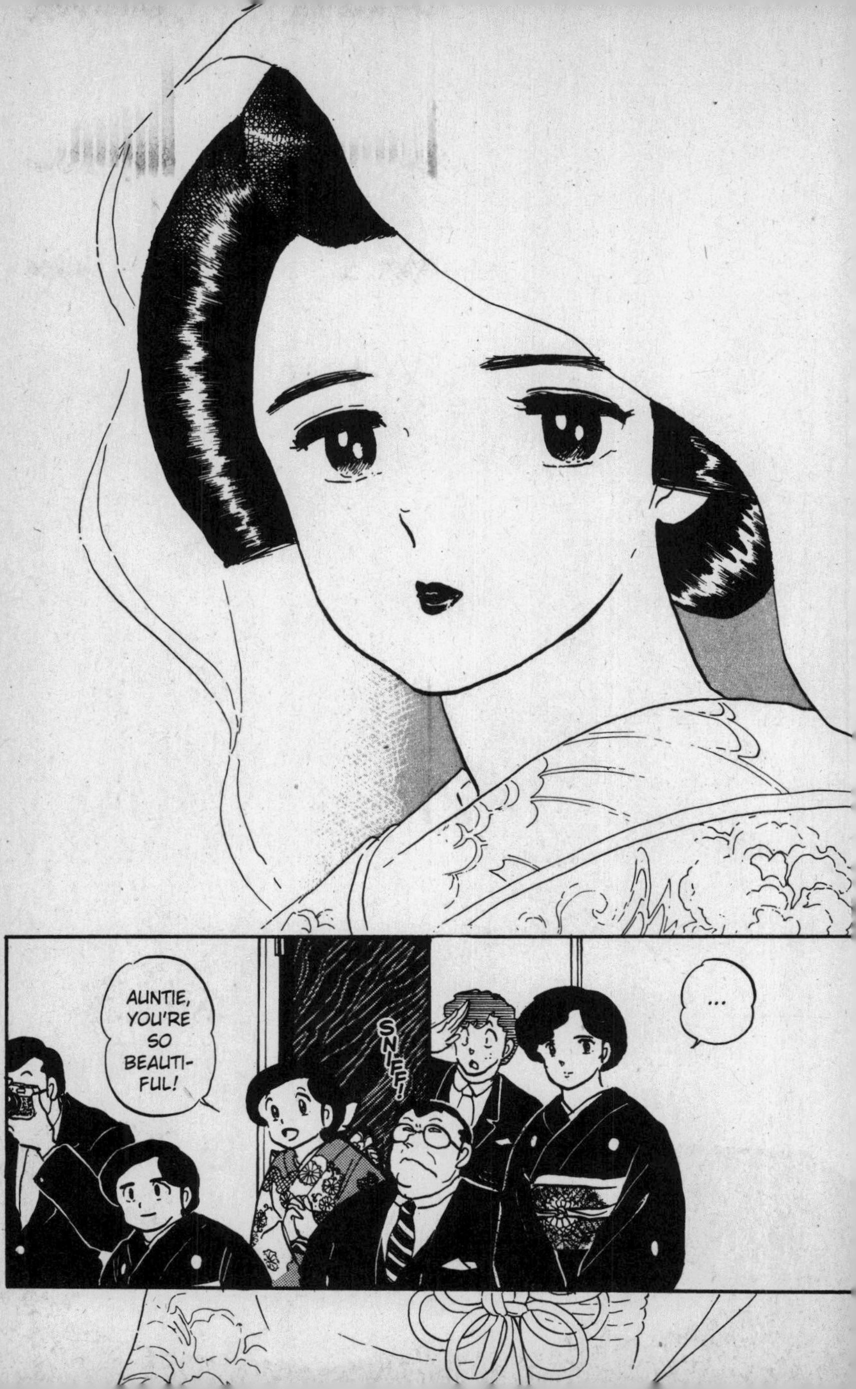
...
SNIFF!
AUNTIE, YOU'RE SO BEAUTIFUL!

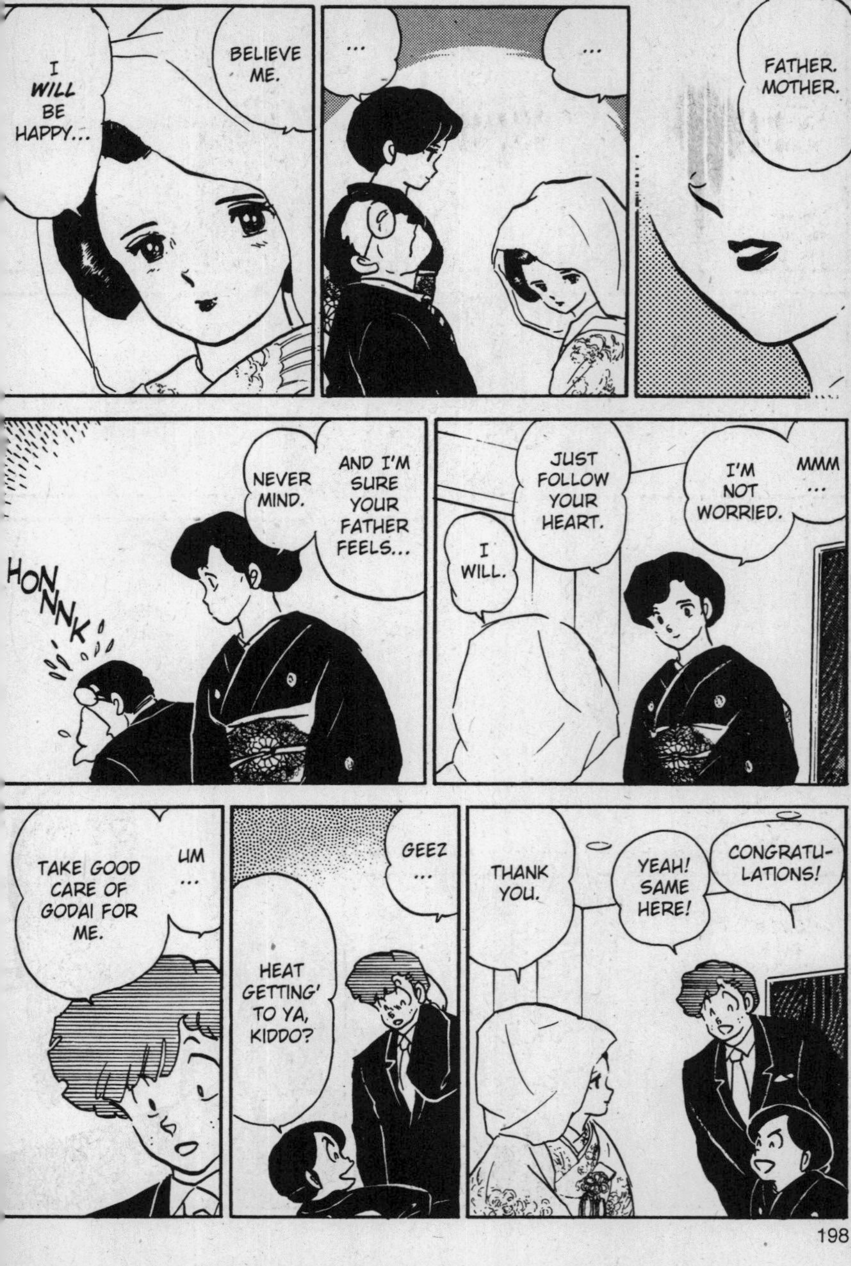
FATHER. MOTHER.
...
...
BELIEVE ME.
I *WILL* BE HAPPY...
MMM ...
I'M NOT WORRIED.
JUST FOLLOW YOUR HEART.
I WILL.
AND I'M SURE YOUR FATHER FEELS...
NEVER MIND.
HONNNK
CONGRATULATIONS!
YEAH! SAME HERE!
THANK YOU.
GEEZ ...
HEAT GETTING' TO YA, KIDDO?
UM ...
TAKE GOOD CARE OF GODAI FOR ME.

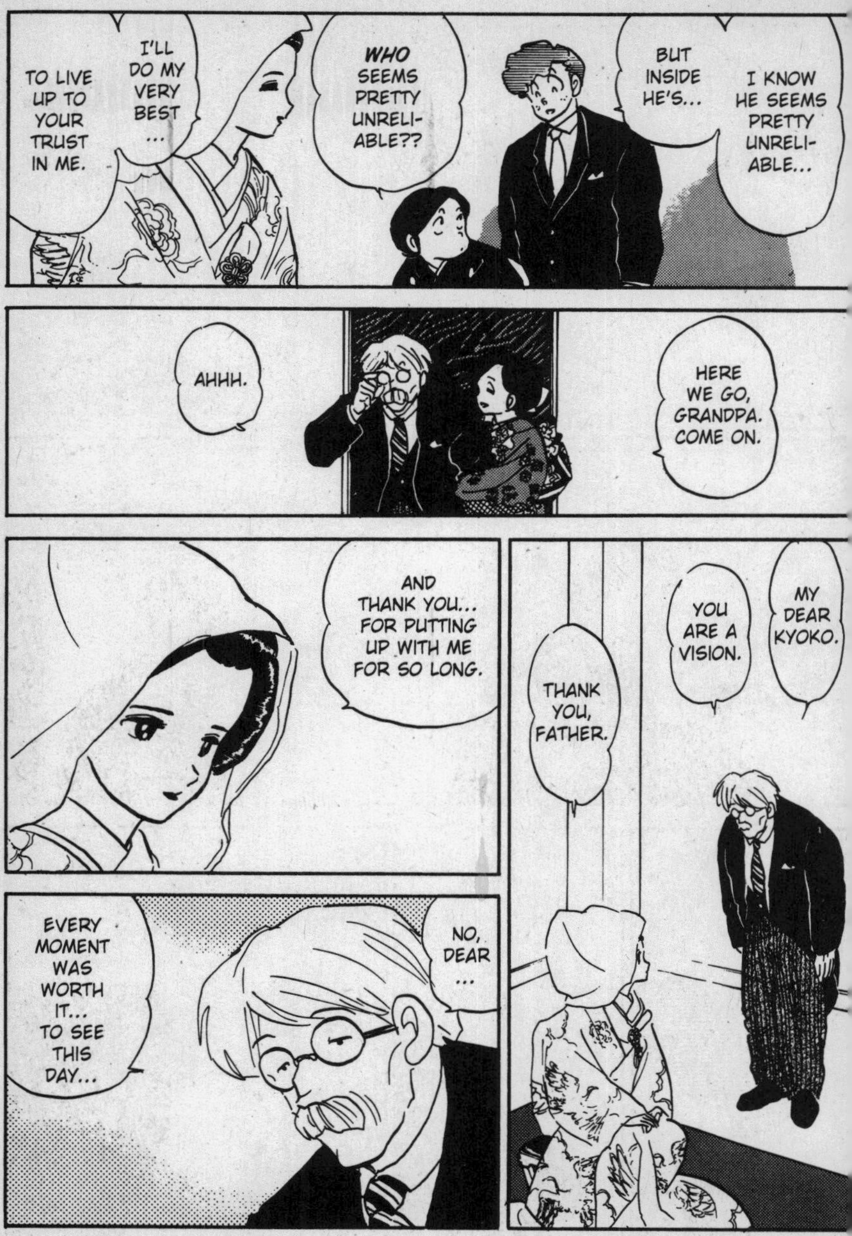
I KNOW HE SEEMS PRETTY UNRELIABLE...
BUT INSIDE HE'S...
WHO SEEMS PRETTY UNRELIABLE??
I'LL DO MY VERY BEST...
TO LIVE UP TO YOUR TRUST IN ME.
HERE WE GO, GRANDPA. COME ON.
AHHH.
MY DEAR KYOKO.
YOU ARE A VISION.
THANK YOU, FATHER.
AND THANK YOU... FOR PUTTING UP WITH ME FOR SO LONG.
NO, DEAR...
EVERY MOMENT WAS WORTH IT... TO SEE THIS DAY...

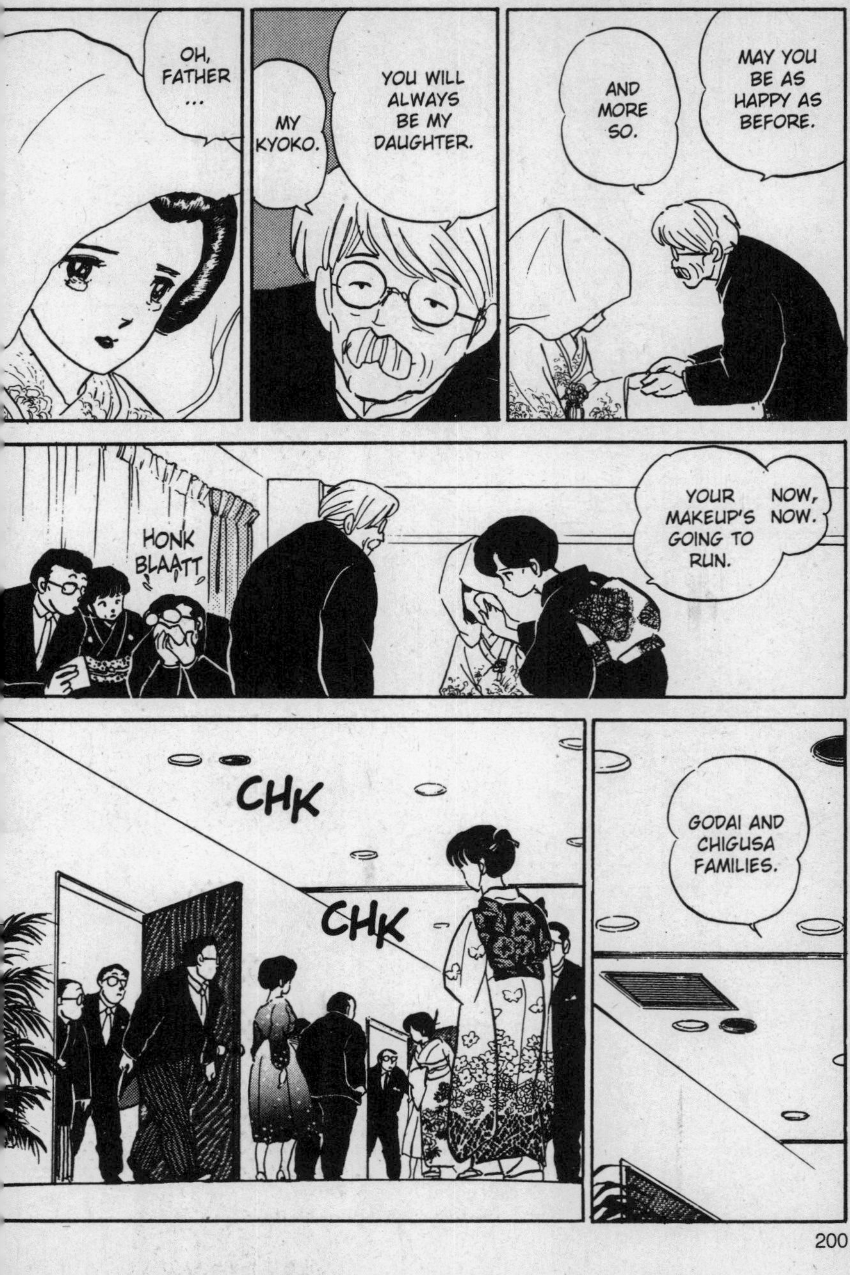
MAY YOU BE AS HAPPY AS BEFORE.
AND MORE SO.
YOU WILL ALWAYS BE MY DAUGHTER.
MY KYOKO.
OH, FATHER ...
NOW, NOW.
YOUR MAKEUP'S GOING TO RUN.
HONK BLAATT
GODAI AND CHIGUSA FAMILIES.
CHK
CHK

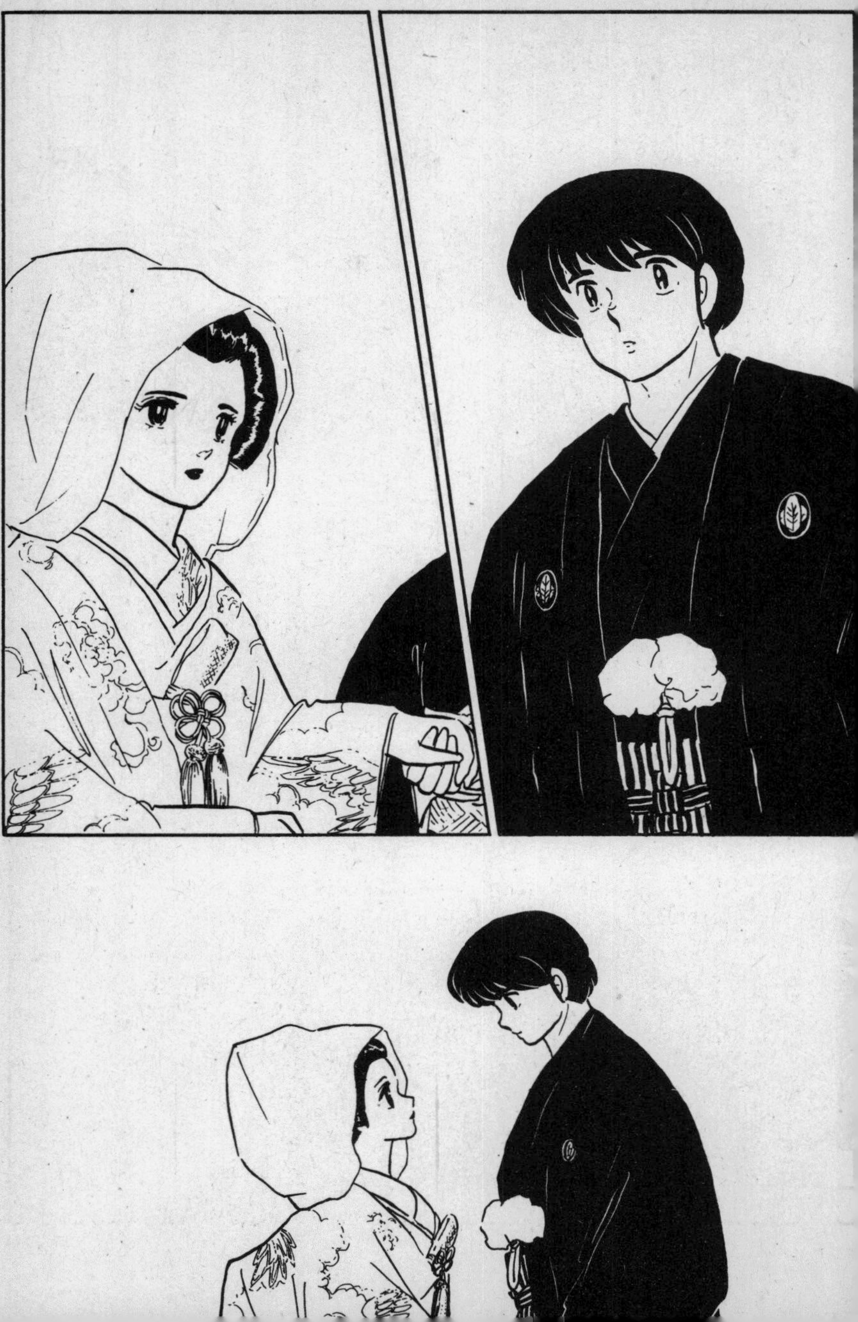

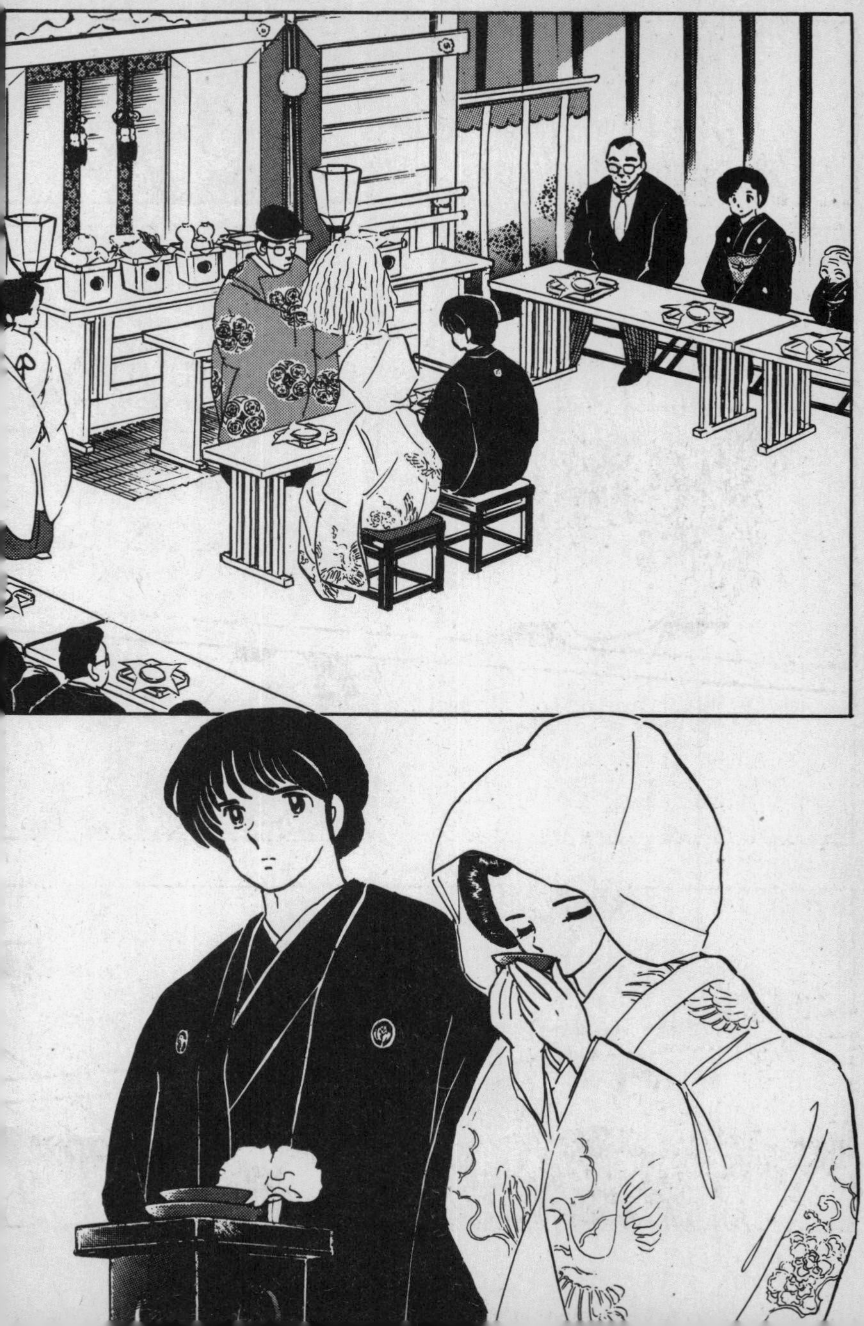

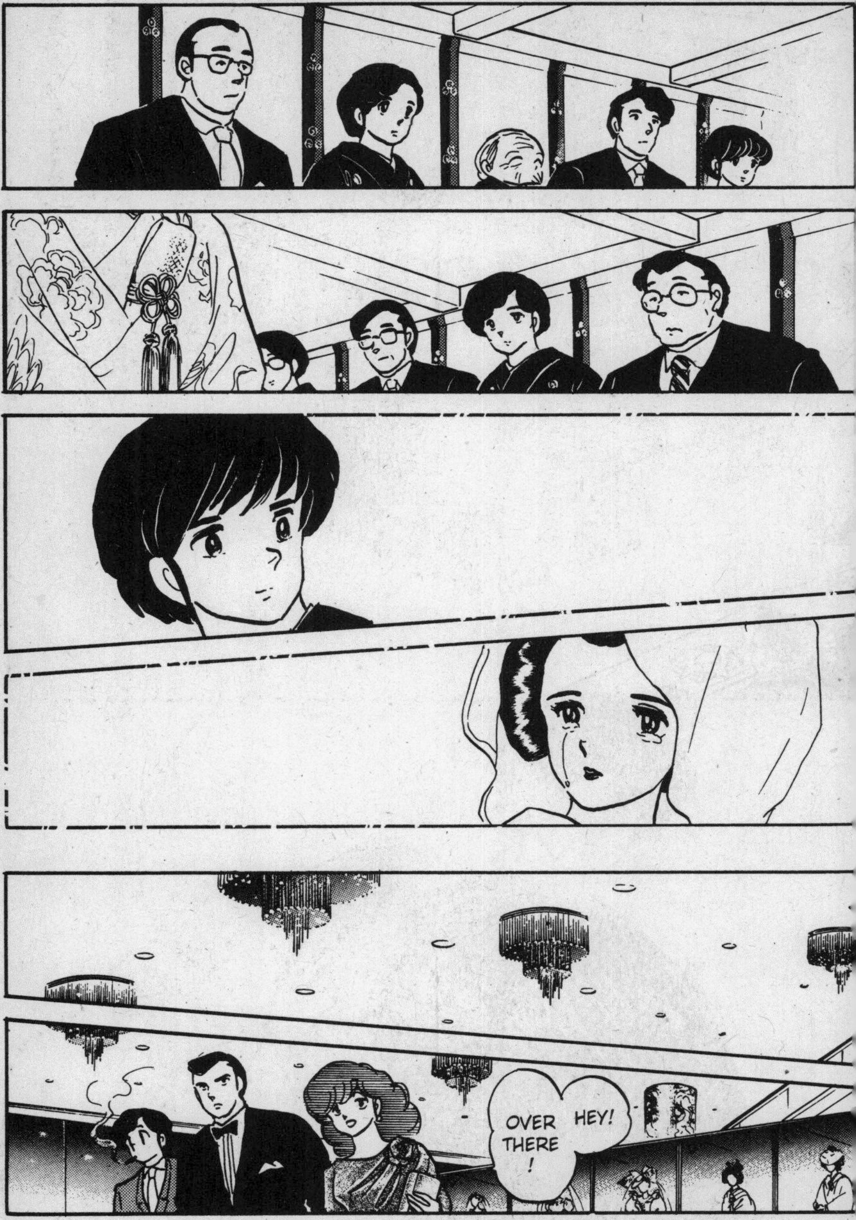
HEY! OVER THERE !

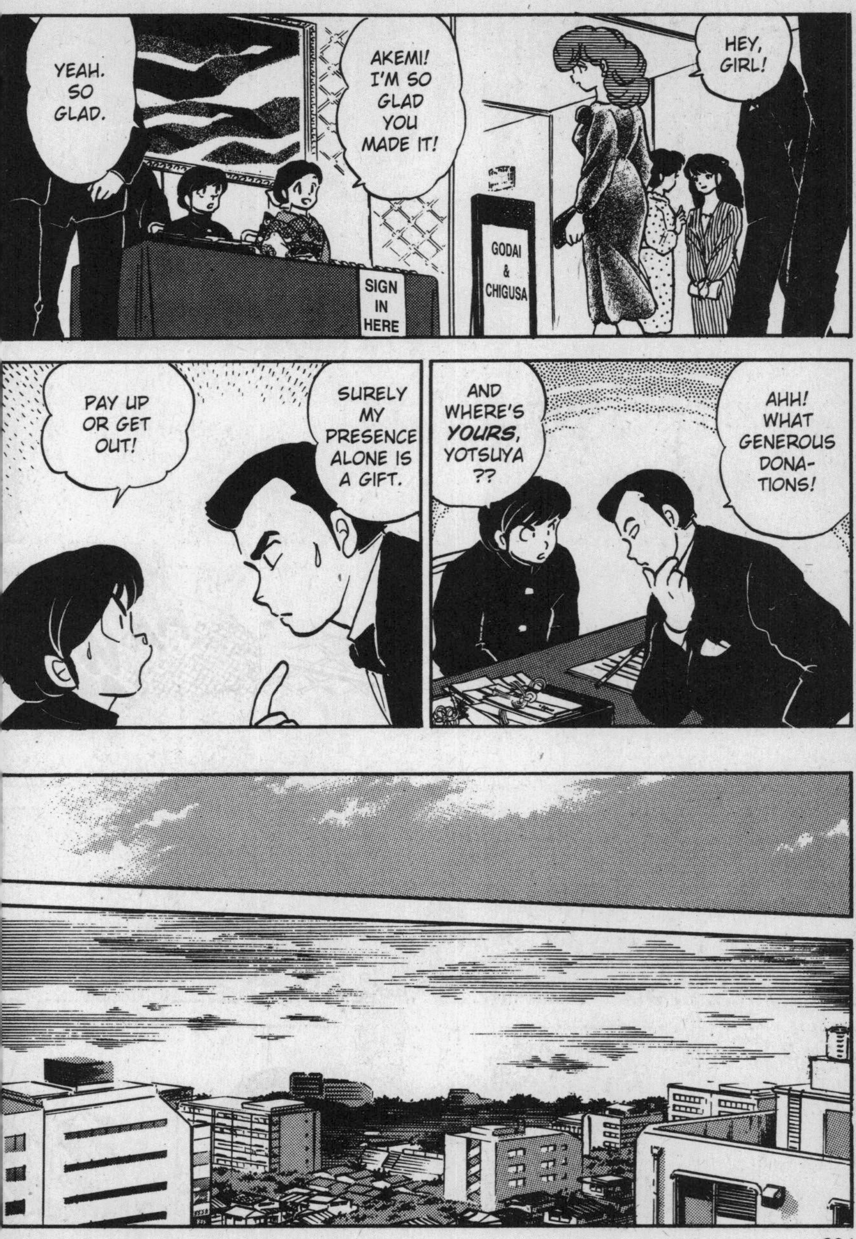
HEY, GIRL!
GODAI & CHIGUSA
AKEMI! I'M SO GLAD YOU MADE IT!
YEAH. SO GLAD.
SIGN IN HERE
AHH! WHAT GENEROUS DONA- TIONS!
AND WHERE'S ***YOURS***, YOTSUYA??
SURELY MY PRESENCE ALONE IS A GIFT.
PAY UP OR GET OUT!

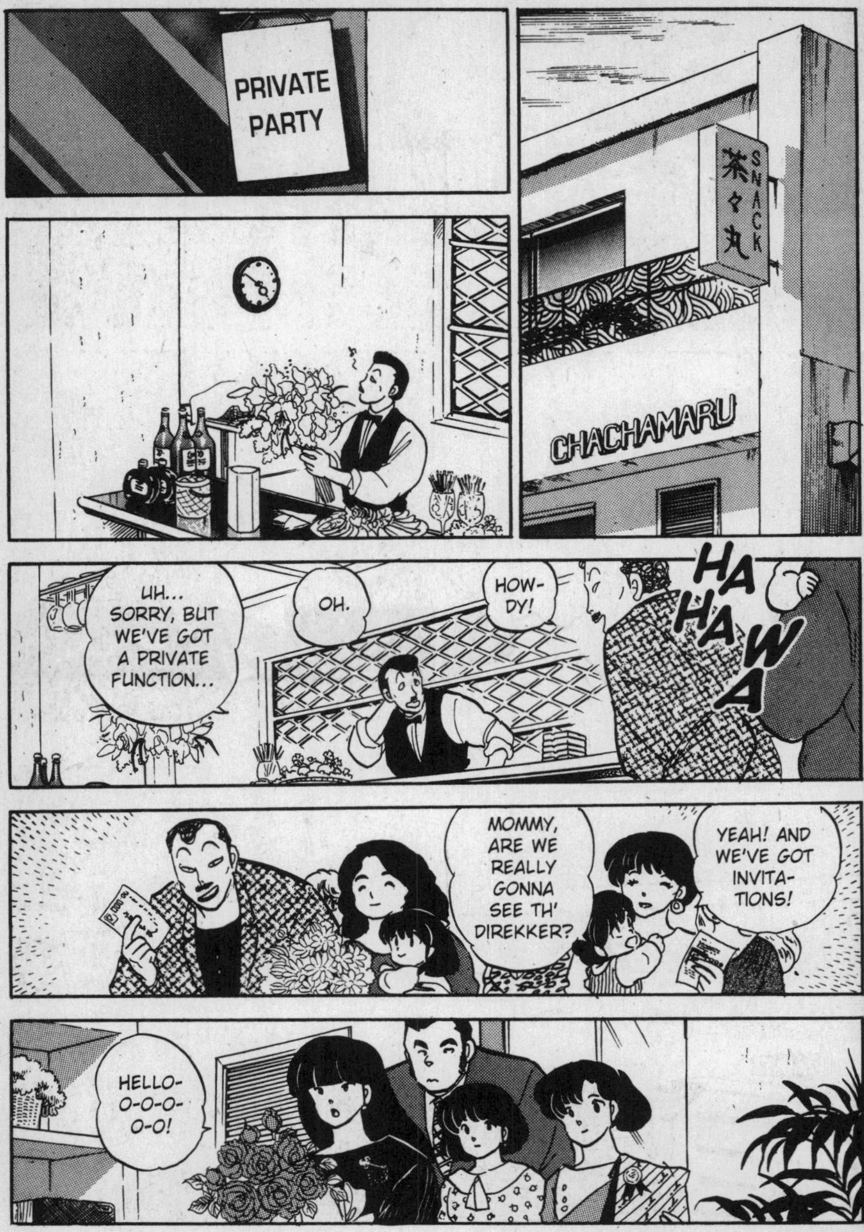
SNACK
茶々丸
CHACHAMARU
PRIVATE PARTY
HA HA HAW A
HOW-DY!
OH.
UH... SORRY, BUT WE'VE GOT A PRIVATE FUNCTION...
YEAH! AND WE'VE GOT INVITATIONS!
MOMMY, ARE WE REALLY GONNA SEE TH' DIREKKER?
HELLO-O-O-O-O-O!

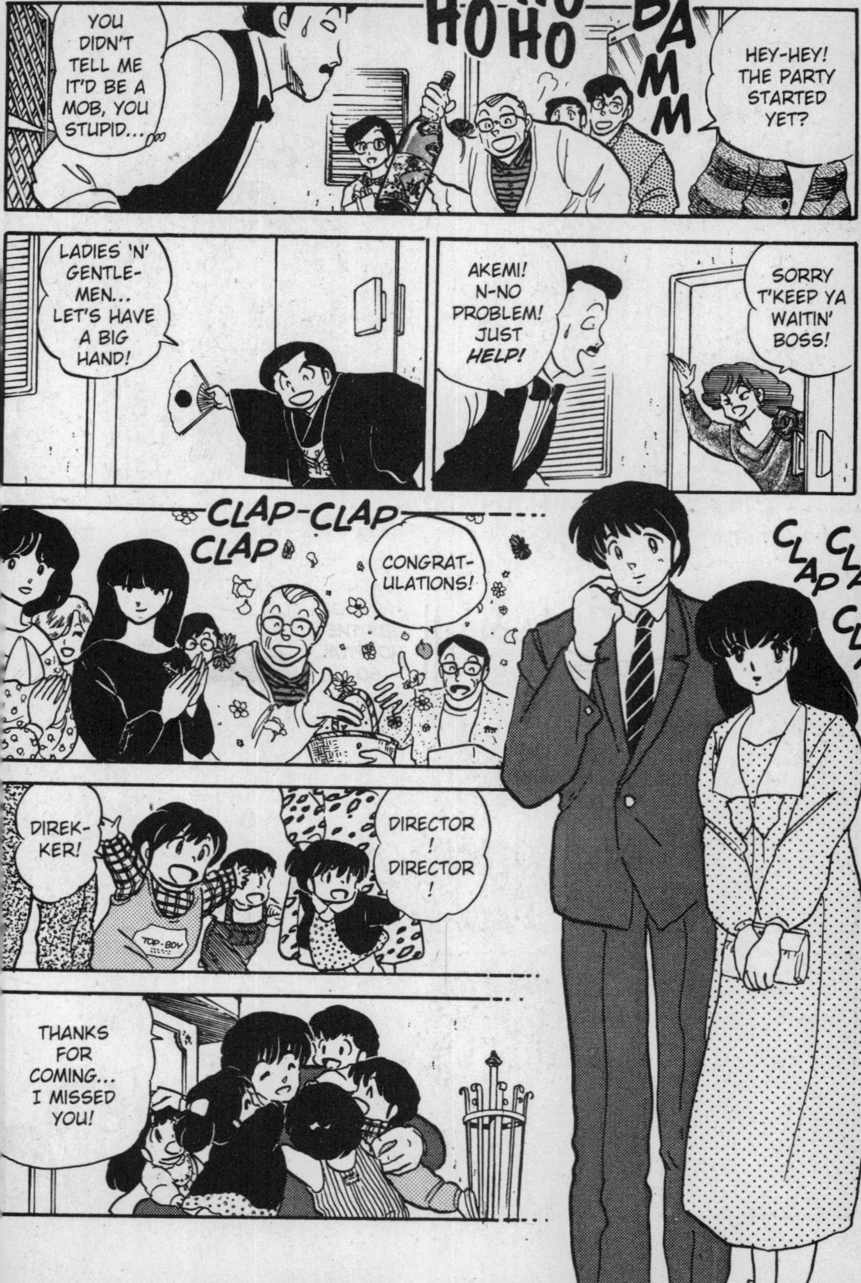
HEY-HEY! THE PARTY STARTED YET?
BAMM
HO HO HO HO
YOU DIDN'T TELL ME IT'D BE A MOB, YOU STUPID...
SORRY T'KEEP YA WAITIN' BOSS!
AKEMI! N-NO PROBLEM! JUST *HELP!*
LADIES 'N' GENTLE-MEN... LET'S HAVE A BIG HAND!
CLAP CLAP CLAP CLAP
CLAP-CLAP CLAP
CONGRAT-ULATIONS!
DIRECTOR! DIRECTOR!
DIREK-KER!
TOP-BOY
THANKS FOR COMING... I MISSED YOU!

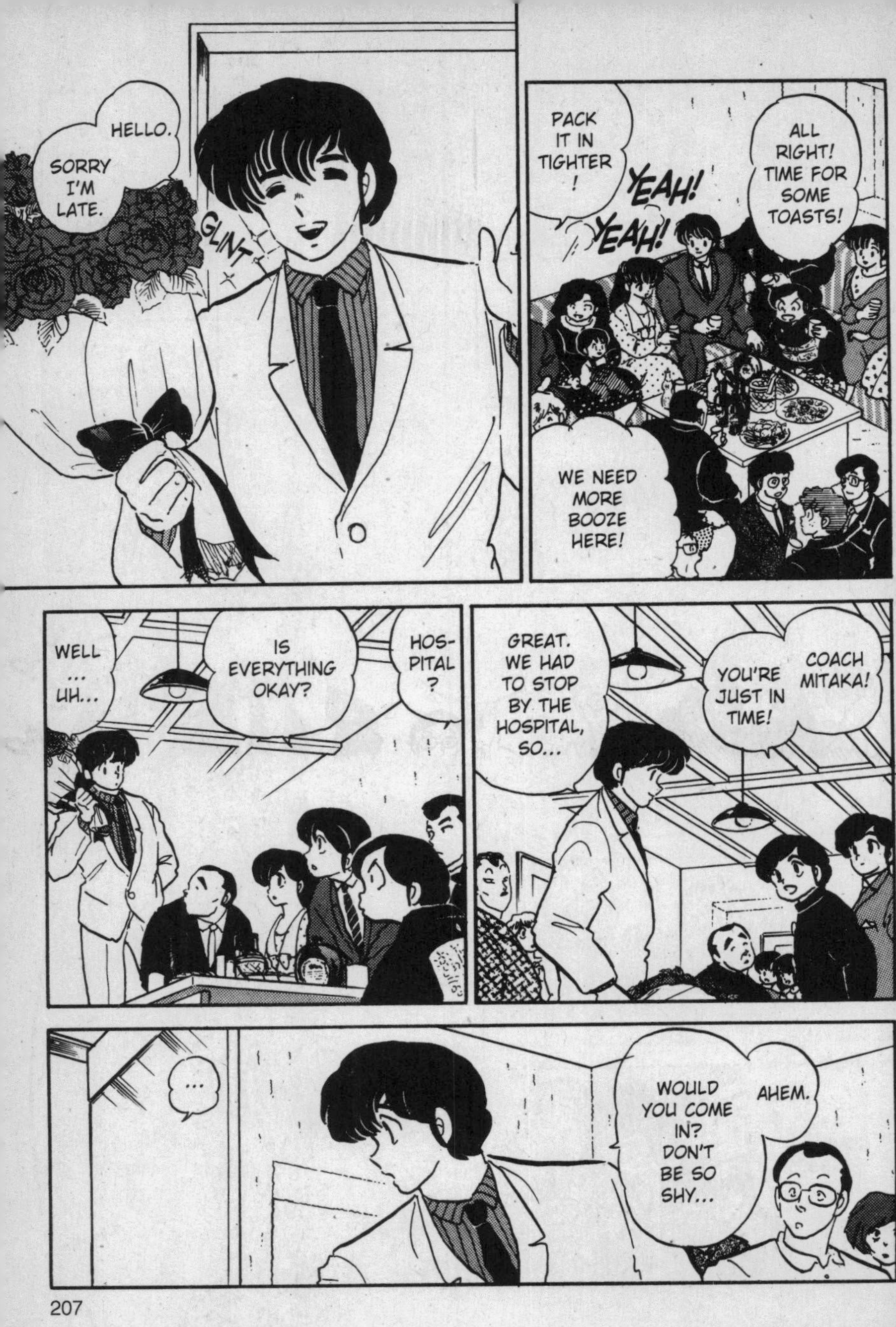
ALL RIGHT! TIME FOR SOME TOASTS!
YEAH!
YEAH!
PACK IT IN TIGHTER!
WE NEED MORE BOOZE HERE!
HELLO.
SORRY I'M LATE.
GLINT
COACH MITAKA!
YOU'RE JUST IN TIME!
GREAT. WE HAD TO STOP BY THE HOSPITAL, SO...
HOS-PITAL?
IS EVERYTHING OKAY?
WELL ... UH...
AHEM.
WOULD YOU COME IN? DON'T BE SO SHY...
...

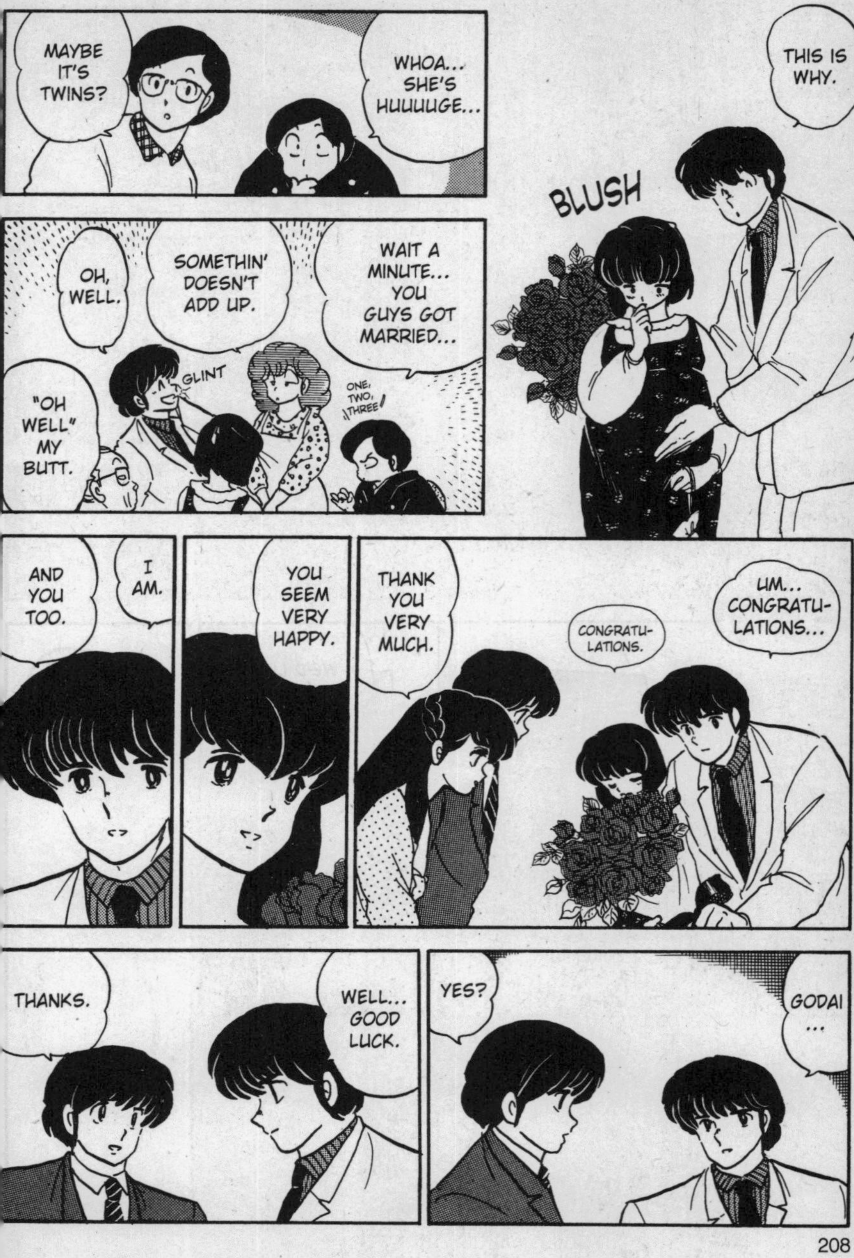
THIS IS WHY.
BLUSH
WHOA... SHE'S HUUUUGE...
MAYBE IT'S TWINS?
WAIT A MINUTE... YOU GUYS GOT MARRIED...
SOMETHIN' DOESN'T ADD UP.
ONE, TWO, THREE!
OH, WELL.
GLINT
"OH WELL" MY BUTT.
UM... CONGRATU-LATIONS...
CONGRATU-LATIONS.
THANK YOU VERY MUCH.
YOU SEEM VERY HAPPY.
I AM.
AND YOU TOO.
GODAI...
YES?
WELL... GOOD LUCK.
THANKS.

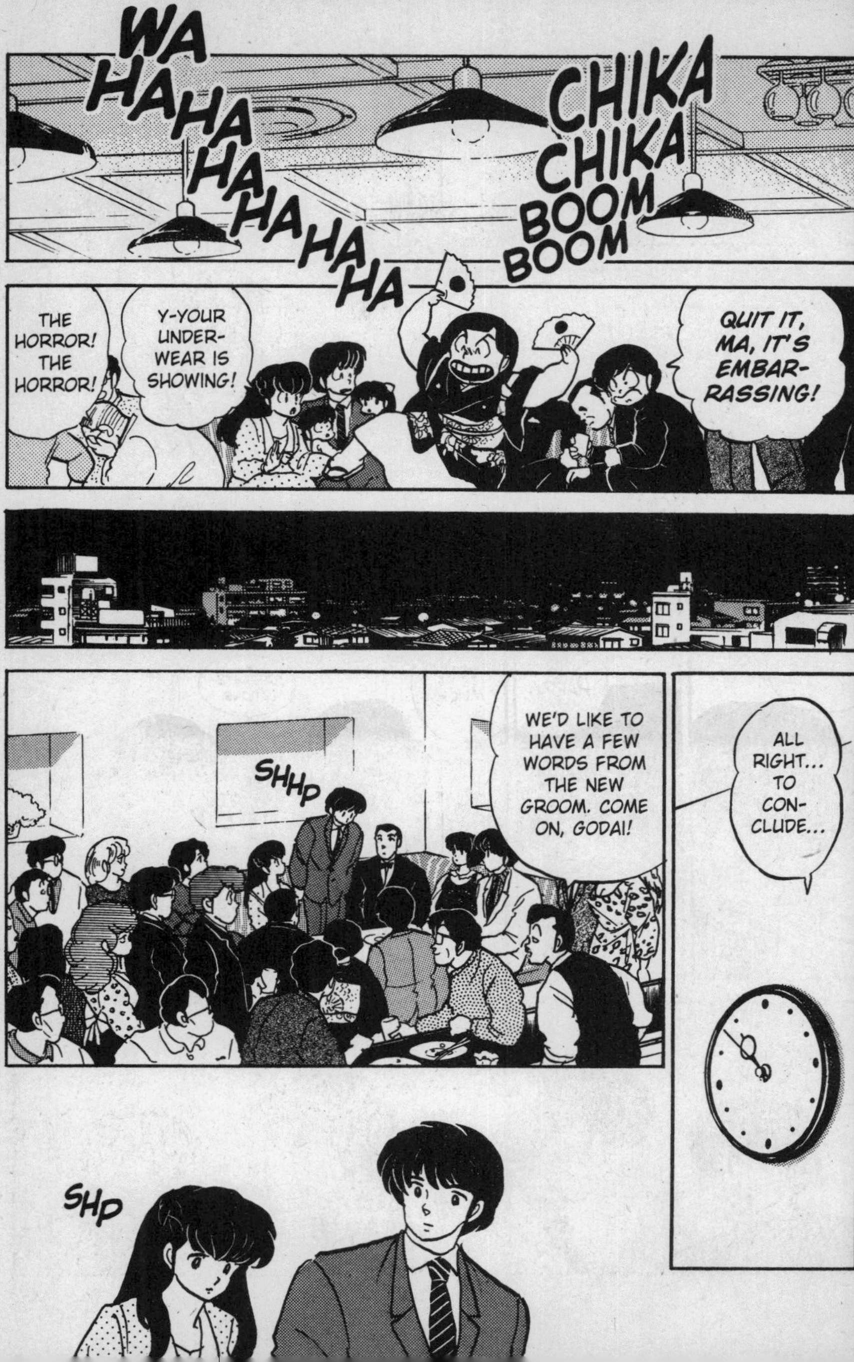
CHIKA CHIKA BOOM BOOM
WA HAHAHAHAHAHA
QUIT IT, MA, IT'S EMBARRASSING!
Y-YOUR UNDERWEAR IS SHOWING!
THE HORROR! THE HORROR!
ALL RIGHT... TO CONCLUDE...
WE'D LIKE TO HAVE A FEW WORDS FROM THE NEW GROOM. COME ON, GODAI!
SHHP
SHP

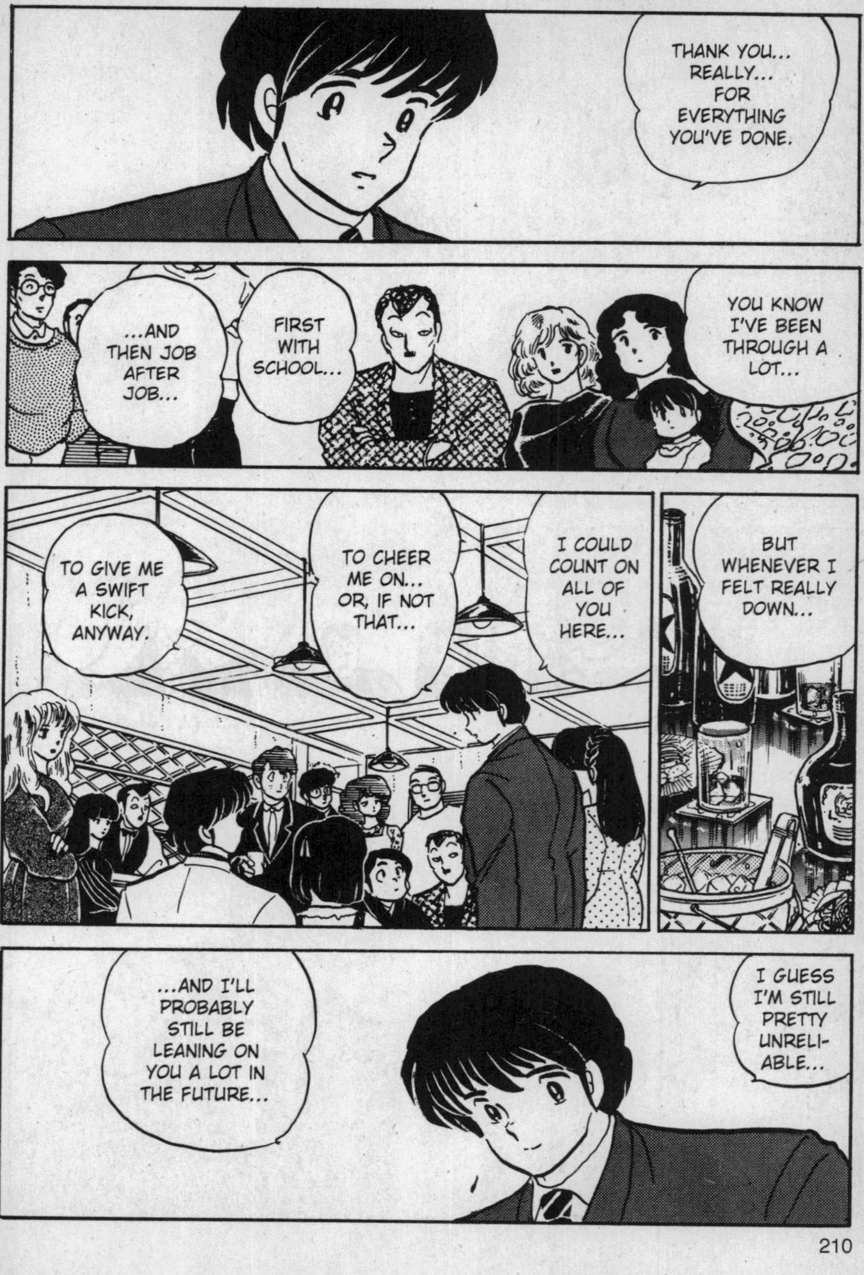
THANK YOU... REALLY... FOR EVERYTHING YOU'VE DONE.
YOU KNOW I'VE BEEN THROUGH A LOT...
FIRST WITH SCHOOL...
...AND THEN JOB AFTER JOB...
BUT WHENEVER I FELT REALLY DOWN...
I COULD COUNT ON ALL OF YOU HERE...
TO CHEER ME ON... OR, IF NOT THAT...
TO GIVE ME A SWIFT KICK, ANYWAY.
I GUESS I'M STILL PRETTY UNRELI-ABLE...
...AND I'LL PROBABLY STILL BE LEANING ON YOU A LOT IN THE FUTURE...

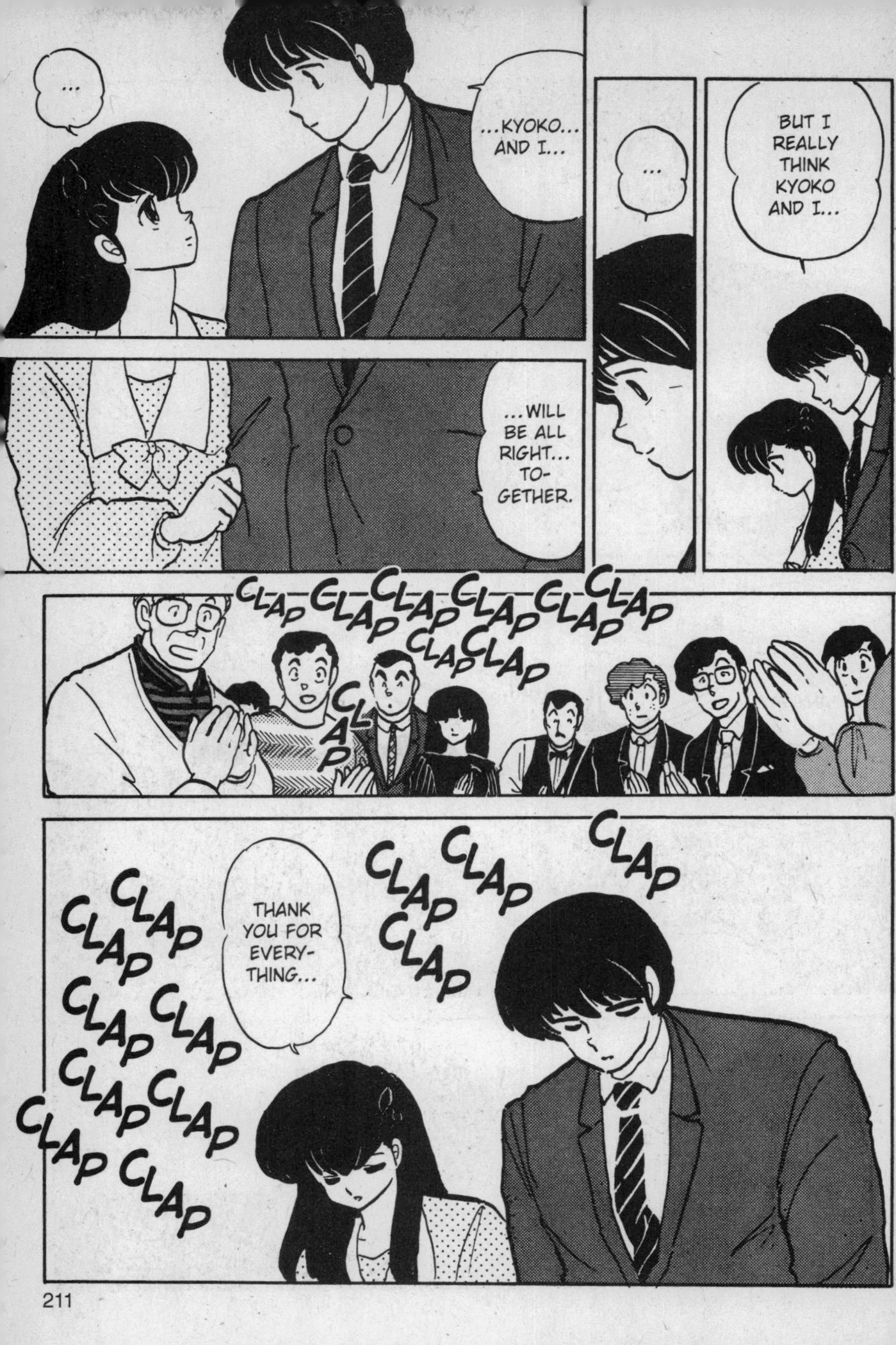

BUT I REALLY THINK KYOKO AND I...
...
...KYOKO... AND I...
...
...WILL BE ALL RIGHT... TO-GETHER.
CLAP CLAP CLAP CLAP CLAP CLAP
CLAP CLAP
CLAP
CLAP
CLAP
CLAP
CLAP
THANK YOU FOR EVERY-THING...
CLAP
CLAP
CLAP
CLAP
CLAP
CLAP
CLAP
CLAP

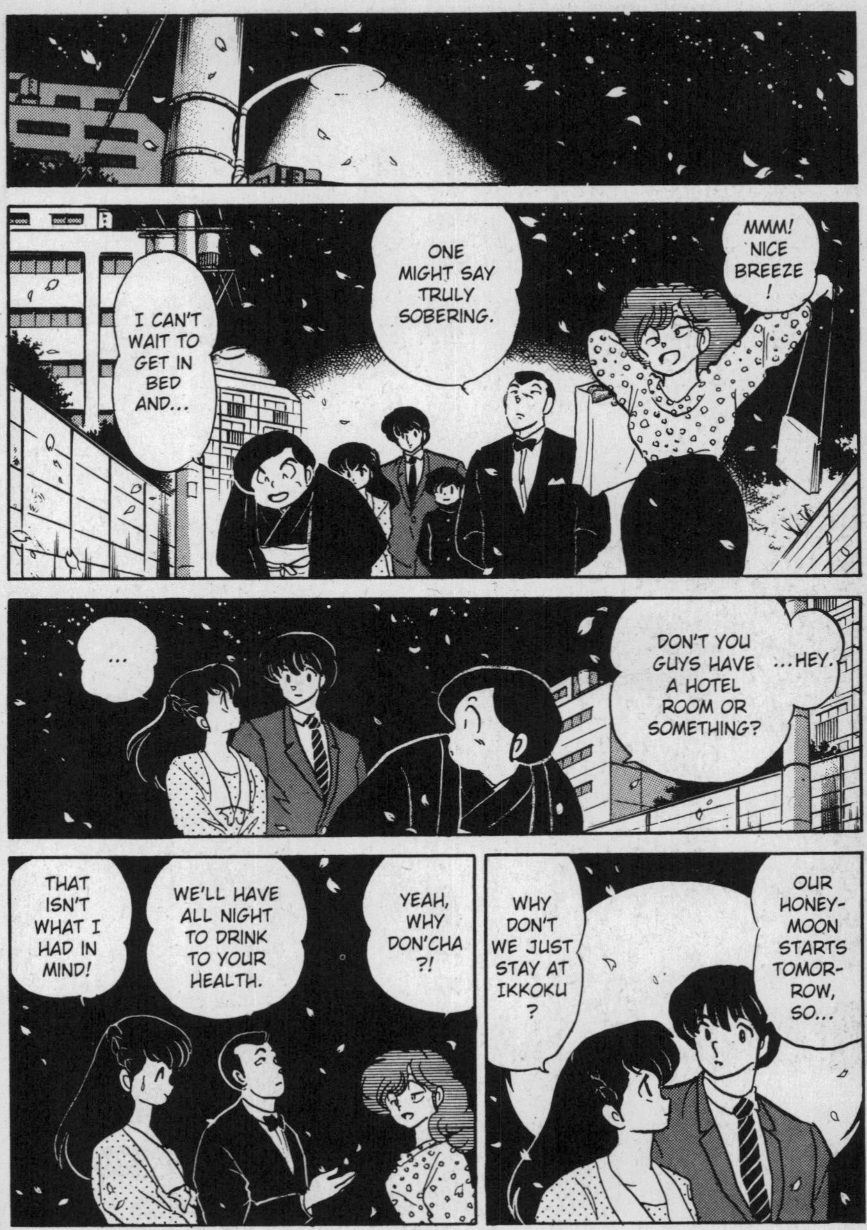
MMM! NICE BREEZE!
ONE MIGHT SAY TRULY SOBERING.
I CAN'T WAIT TO GET IN BED AND...
...HEY.
DON'T YOU GUYS HAVE A HOTEL ROOM OR SOMETHING?
...
OUR HONEY-MOON STARTS TOMOR-ROW, SO...
WHY DON'T WE JUST STAY AT IKKOKU?
YEAH, WHY DON'CHA?!
WE'LL HAVE ALL NIGHT TO DRINK TO YOUR HEALTH.
THAT ISN'T WHAT I HAD IN MIND!

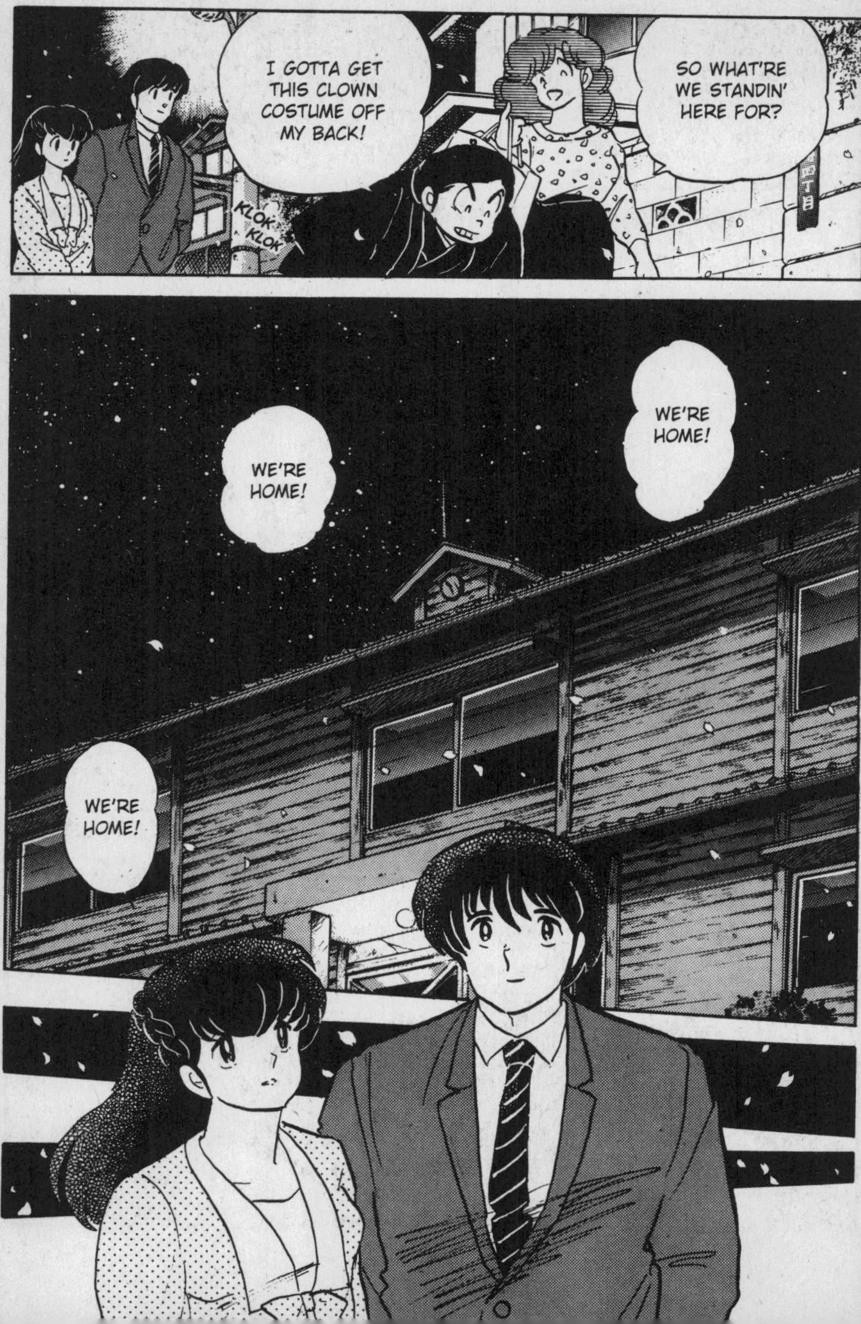
SO WHAT'RE WE STANDIN' HERE FOR?
I GOTTA GET THIS CLOWN COSTUME OFF MY BACK!
KLOK KLOK
WE'RE HOME!
WE'RE HOME!
WE'RE HOME!

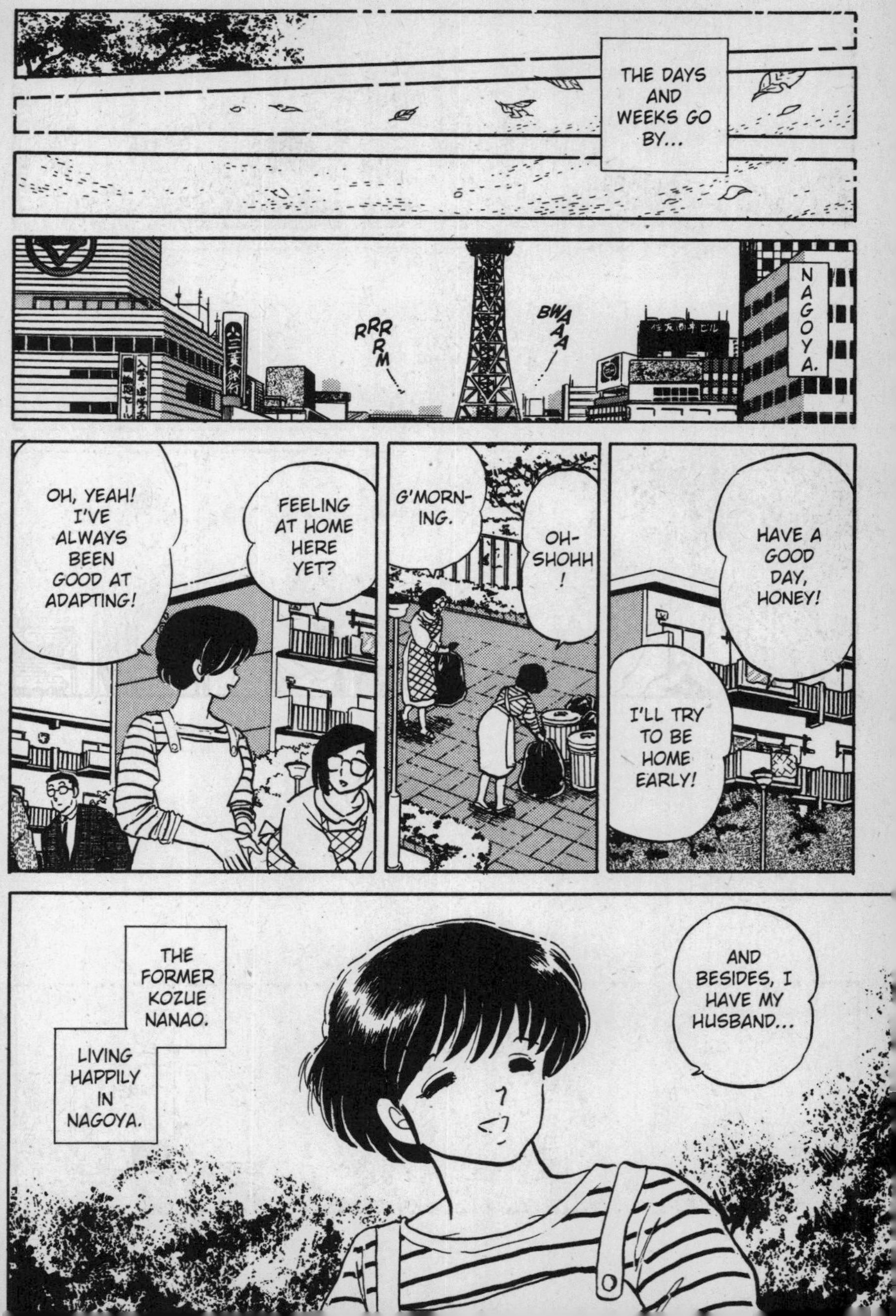
THE DAYS AND WEEKS GO BY...
NAGOYA.
BWAAA
RRRRM
HAVE A GOOD DAY, HONEY!
I'LL TRY TO BE HOME EARLY!
G'MORN-ING.
OH-SHOHH!
FEELING AT HOME HERE YET?
OH, YEAH! I'VE ALWAYS BEEN GOOD AT ADAPTING!
AND BESIDES, I HAVE MY HUSBAND...
THE FORMER KOZUE NANAO.
LIVING HAPPILY IN NAGOYA.

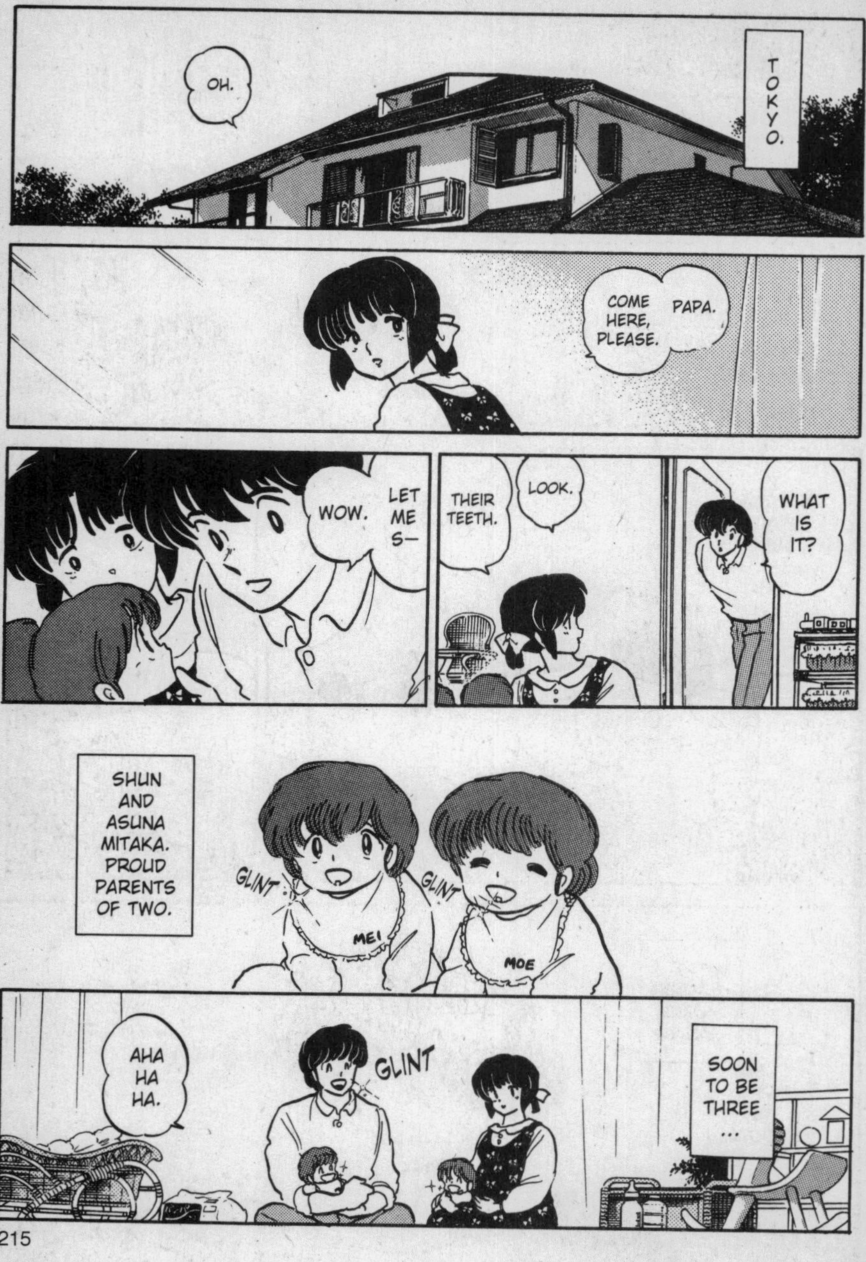

TOKYO.
OH.
COME HERE, PLEASE.
PAPA.
WHAT IS IT?
LOOK.
THEIR TEETH.
LET ME S—
WOW.
GLINT
MOE
GLINT
MEI
SHUN AND ASUNA MITAKA. PROUD PARENTS OF TWO.
SOON TO BE THREE ...
GLINT
AHA HA HA.

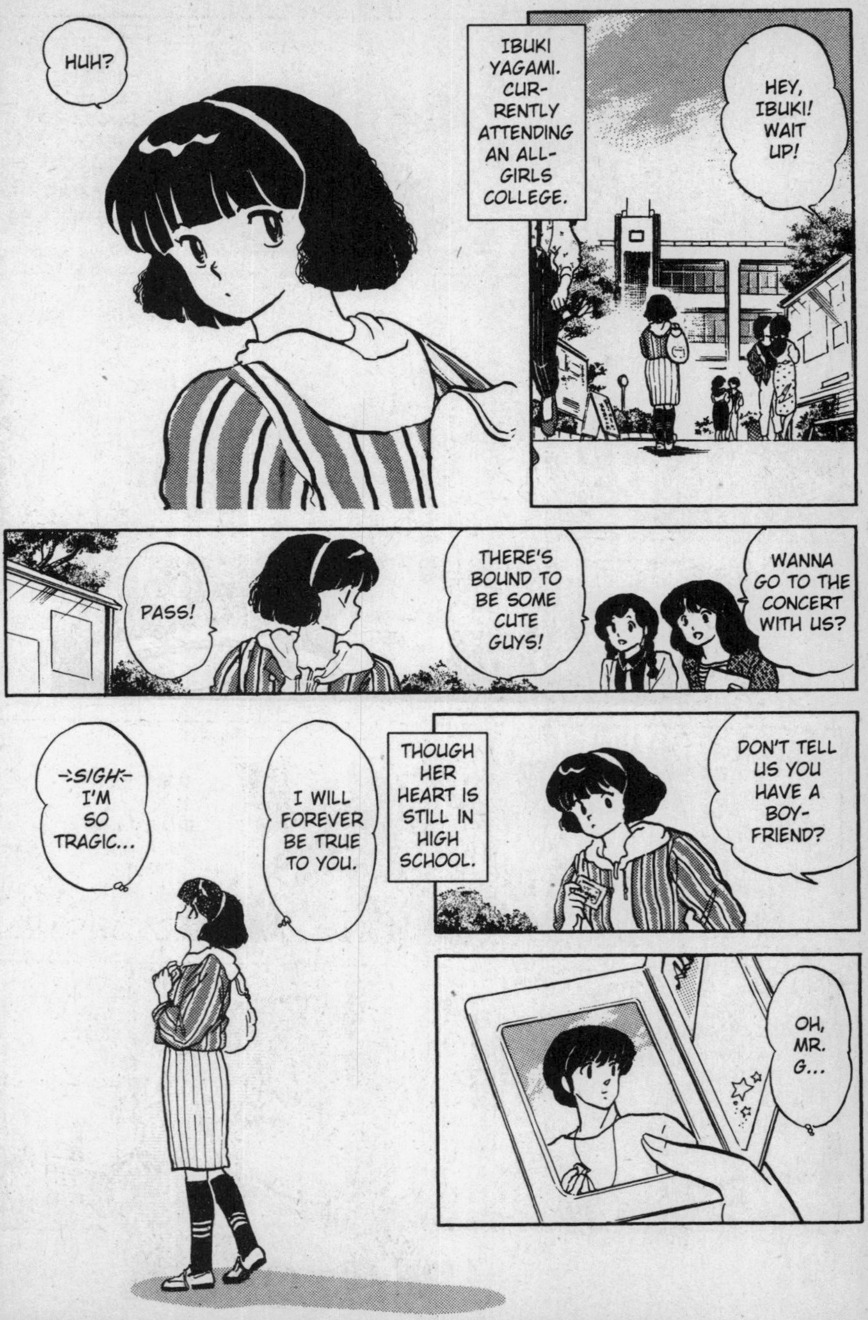
HEY, IBUKI! WAIT UP!
IBUKI YAGAMI. CUR-RENTLY ATTENDING AN ALL-GIRLS COLLEGE.
HUH?
WANNA GO TO THE CONCERT WITH US?
THERE'S BOUND TO BE SOME CUTE GUYS!
PASS!
DON'T TELL US YOU HAVE A BOY-FRIEND?
THOUGH HER HEART IS STILL IN HIGH SCHOOL.
OH, MR. G...
I WILL FOREVER BE TRUE TO YOU.
-SIGH- I'M SO TRAGIC...

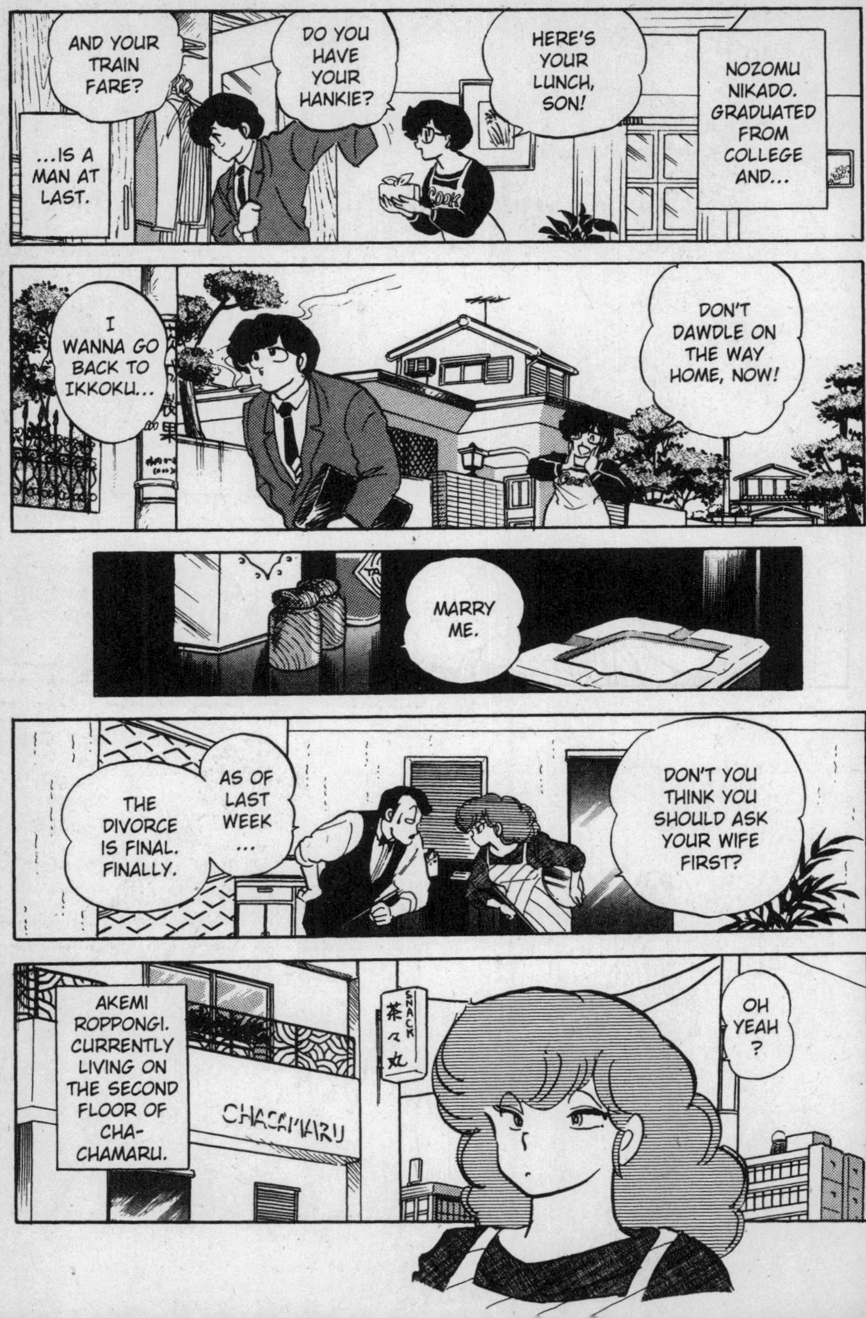
NOZOMU NIKADO. GRADUATED FROM COLLEGE AND...
HERE'S YOUR LUNCH, SON!
DO YOU HAVE YOUR HANKIE?
AND YOUR TRAIN FARE?
...IS A MAN AT LAST.
DON'T DAWDLE ON THE WAY HOME, NOW!
I WANNA GO BACK TO IKKOKU...
MARRY ME.
DON'T YOU THINK YOU SHOULD ASK YOUR WIFE FIRST?
AS OF LAST WEEK...
THE DIVORCE IS FINAL. FINALLY.
OH YEAH?
SNACK
茶々丸
CHACHAMARU
AKEMI ROPPONGI. CURRENTLY LIVING ON THE SECOND FLOOR OF CHA-CHAMARU.

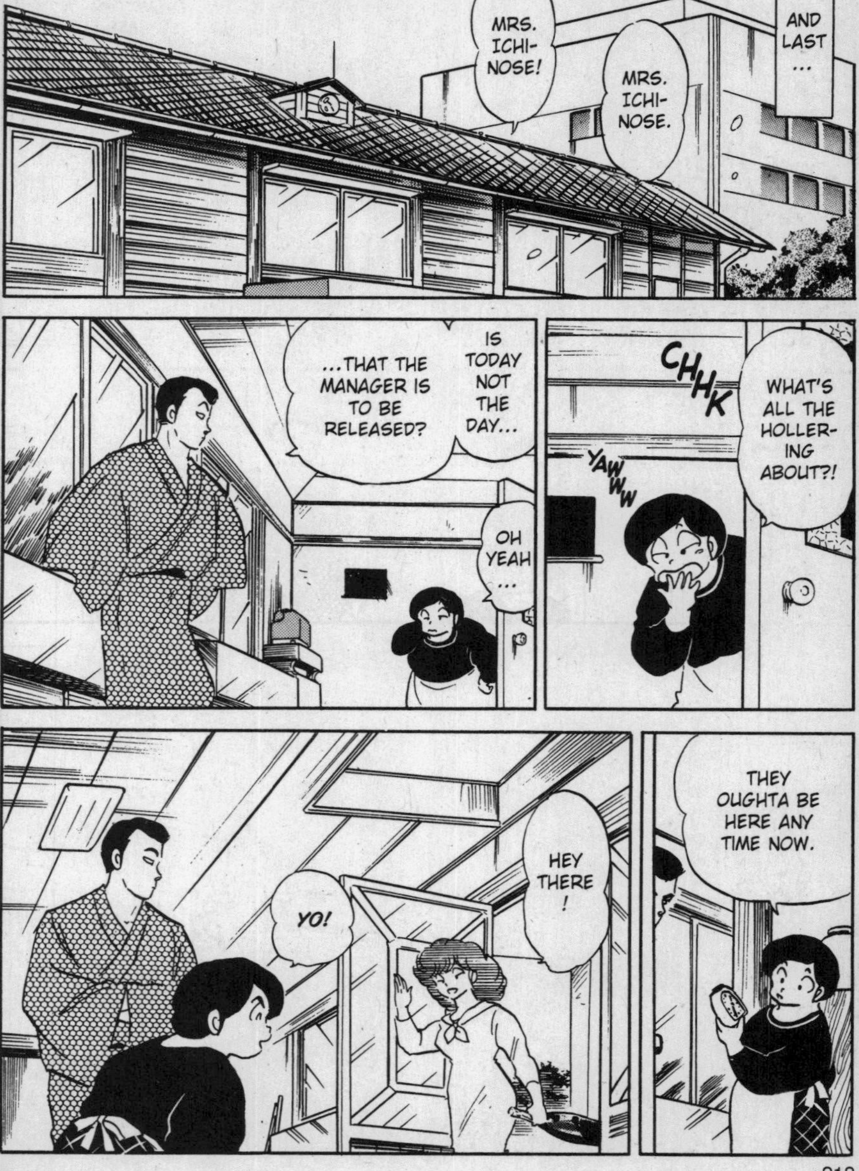
AND LAST...
MRS. ICHI-NOSE.
MRS. ICHI-NOSE!
CHHK
YAWWW
WHAT'S ALL THE HOLLER-ING ABOUT?!
IS TODAY NOT THE DAY...
...THAT THE MANAGER IS TO BE RELEASED?
OH YEAH...
THEY OUGHTA BE HERE ANY TIME NOW.
HEY THERE!
YO!

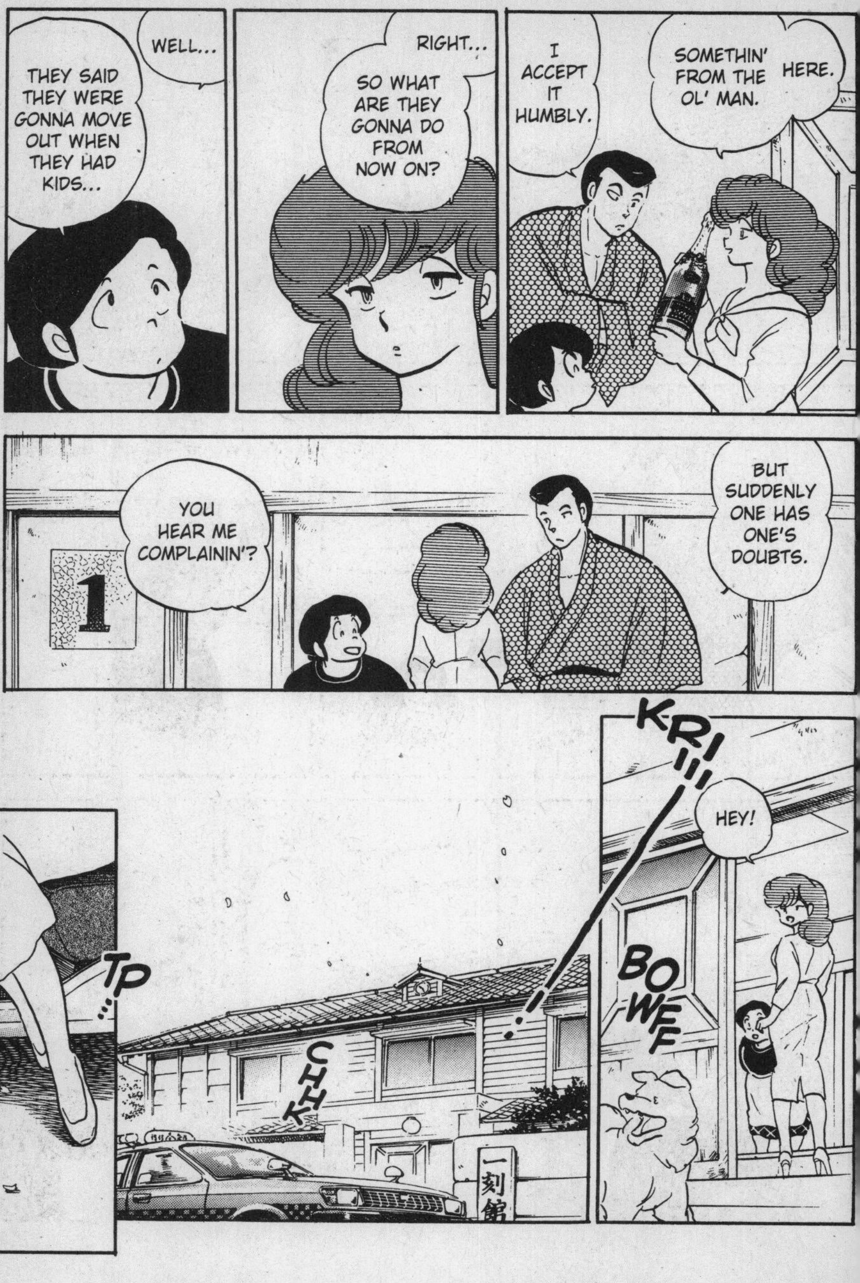
HERE.
SOMETHIN' FROM THE OL' MAN.
I ACCEPT IT HUMBLY.
RIGHT...
SO WHAT ARE THEY GONNA DO FROM NOW ON?
WELL...
THEY SAID THEY WERE GONNA MOVE OUT WHEN THEY HAD KIDS...
BUT SUDDENLY ONE HAS ONE'S DOUBTS.
YOU HEAR ME COMPLAININ'?
KRIIII
HEY!
BOWFF
一刻館
CHHK
TP...

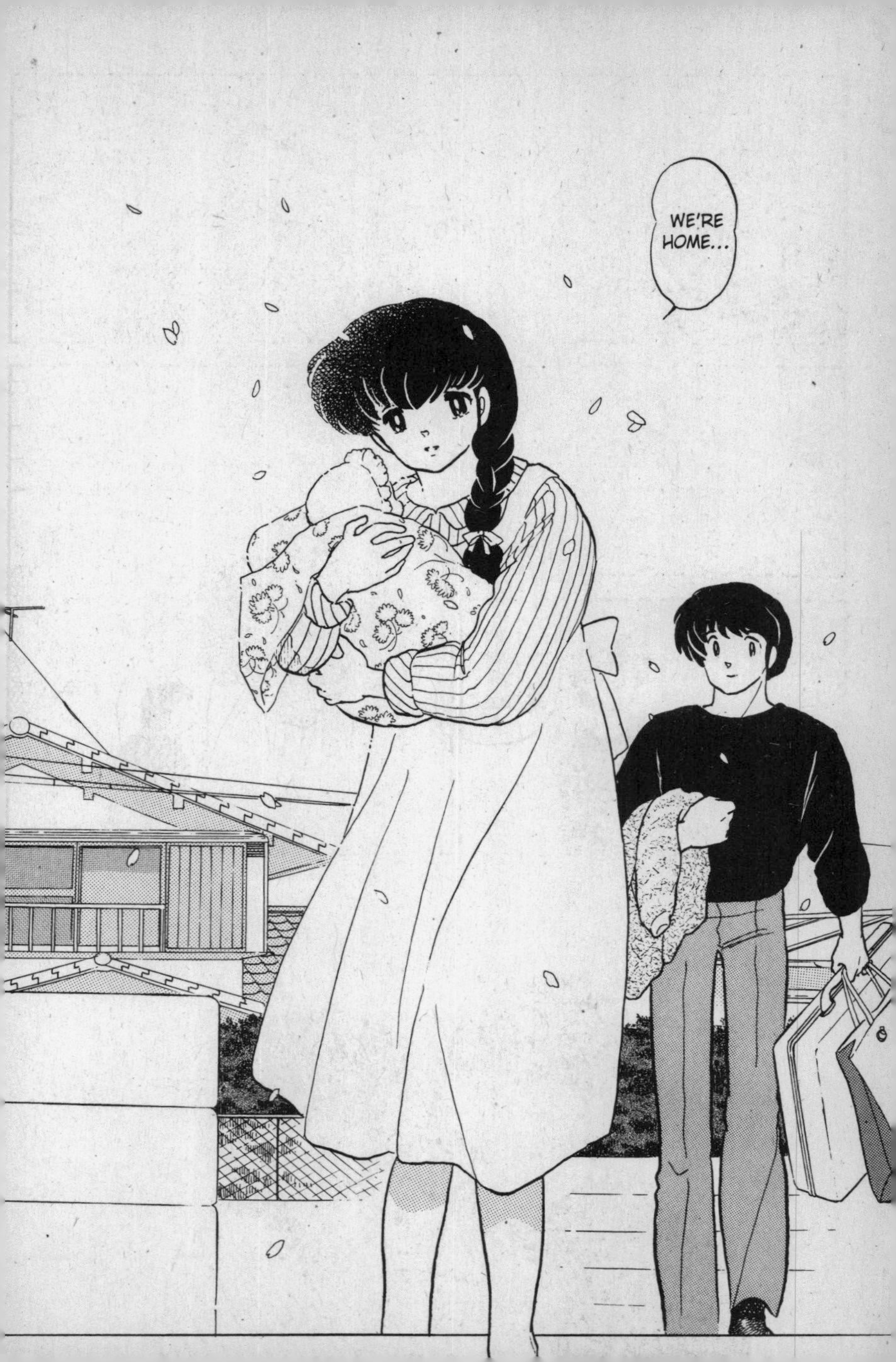
WE'RE HOME...

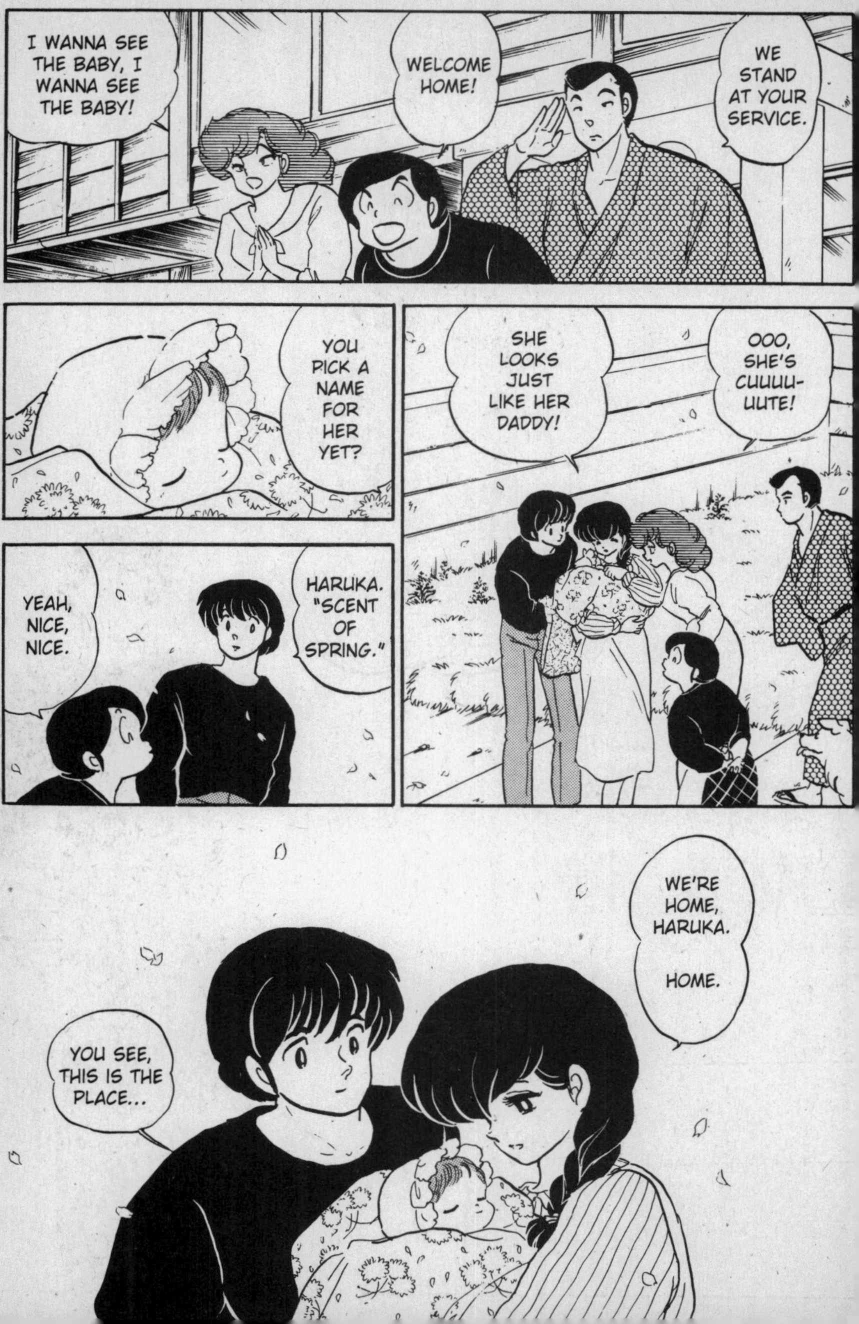
WE STAND AT YOUR SERVICE.
WELCOME HOME!
I WANNA SEE THE BABY, I WANNA SEE THE BABY!
OOO, SHE'S CUUUU-UUTE!
SHE LOOKS JUST LIKE HER DADDY!
YOU PICK A NAME FOR HER YET?
HARUKA. "SCENT OF SPRING."
YEAH, NICE, NICE.
WE'RE HOME, HARUKA.
HOME.
YOU SEE, THIS IS THE PLACE...

...WHERE
MOMMY AND
DADDY FIRST
MET.

The End

MAISON IKKOKU
VOLUME 15
Story and Art by Rumiko Takahashi

Translation/Gerard Jones & Mari Morimoto
Touch-Up Art & Lettering/Susan Daigle-Leach
Design/Nozomi Akashi
Editor – 1st Edition/Trish Ledoux
Editor – Editor's Choice Edition/Kit Fox

Managing Editor/Annette Roman
Director of Production/Noboru Watanabe
Vice President of Publishing/Alvin Lu
Sr. Director of Acquisitions/Rika Inouye
Vice President of Sales & Marketing/Liza Coppola
Publisher/Hyoe Narita

Printed in Canada

Published by VIZ Media, LLC
P.O. Box 77010
San Francisco, CA 94107

Editor's Choice Edition
10 9 8 7 6 5 4 3 2 1
First printing, February 2006
First English edition published 2000

www.viz.com

PARENTAL ADVISORY
MAISON IKKOKU is rated T+ for Older Teen and is recommended for ages 16 and up. This volume contains strong language, alcohol and tobacco use, and sexual themes.

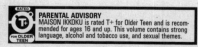

ABOUT THE ARTIST

Rumiko Takahashi, born in 1957 in Niigata, Japan, is the acclaimed creator and artist of *Maison Ikkoku, InuYasha, Ranma 1/2* and *Lum * Urusei Yatsura*.

She lived in a small student apartment in Nakano, Japan, which was the basis for the *Maison Ikkoku* series, while she attended the prestigious Nihon Joseidai (Japan Women's University). At the same time, Takahashi also began studying comics at Gekiga Sonjuku, a famous school for manga artists run by Kazuo Koike, author of *Crying Freeman* and *Lone Wolf and Cub*. In 1978, Takahashi won a prize in Shogakukan's annual New Comic Artist Contest and her boy-meets-alien comedy *Lum * Urusei Yatsura* began appearing in the weekly manga magazine *Shonen Sunday*.

Takahashi's success and critical acclaim continues to grow, with popular titles including *Ranma 1/2* and *InuYasha*. Many of her graphic novel series have also been animated, and are widely available in several languages.

EDITOR'S RECOMMENDATIONS

More manga!
More manga!

Fans of

maison ikkoku

should also read:

© 1988 Rumiko
TAKAHASHI/Shogakukan Inc.

RANMA 1/2

It's a story as old as time itself. Well, not really. Ranma Saotome, a budding martial artist, goes to China with his father to further his training. What he never expected was that a life-altering curse awaited both himself and his bumbling paterfamilias. Everyone has a secret or two to keep from their fiancé, but what happens when your secret is that you turn into a girl when splashed with water? It'll take more than marriage counseling to iron out this doozy of a domestic situation.

© 1997 Rumiko
TAKAHASHI/Shogakukan Inc.

INUYASHA

Takahashi returned to her fantasy roots with this exciting manga that combines elements of historical action, exciting horror, touching romance, and physical comedy. Modern schoolgirl Kagome is pulled into Japan's mystical past and must join forces with a scabrous half-demon named Inuyasha. This series has also spawned an immensely popular TV series as well!

© 1999 Hiroyuki
NISHIMORI/Shogakukan Inc.

CHEEKY ANGEL

Tired of wishy-washy manga heroes? Is Godai's congenital passive-aggressiveness rubbing you the wrong way? Then Megumi Amatsuka, the hero (and heroine) of *CHEEKY ANGEL*, should provide you with some much needed proactive entertainment. Long story short, although Megumi is the most gorgeous girl in school, she's not afraid to throw down on any and every punk that gets in her way. (After all, she was a little boy until a magic genie turned her into a girl. Don't you hate it when that happens?)

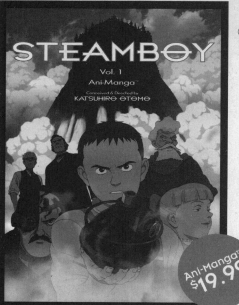
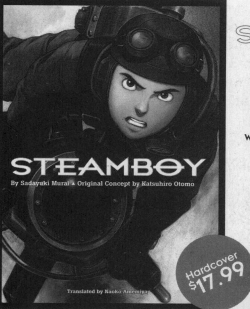

The Evolution of Science...
The Downfall of Man?

Based on the hit movie from Katsuhiro Otomo

STEAMBOY

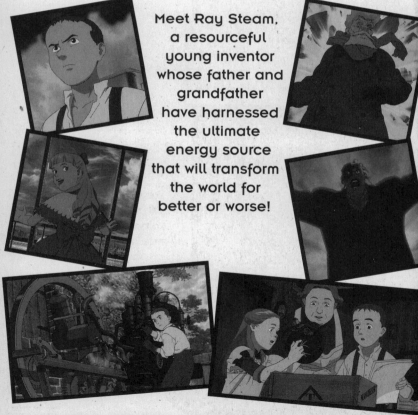

Meet Ray Steam, a resourceful young inventor whose father and grandfather have harnessed the ultimate energy source that will transform the world for better or worse!

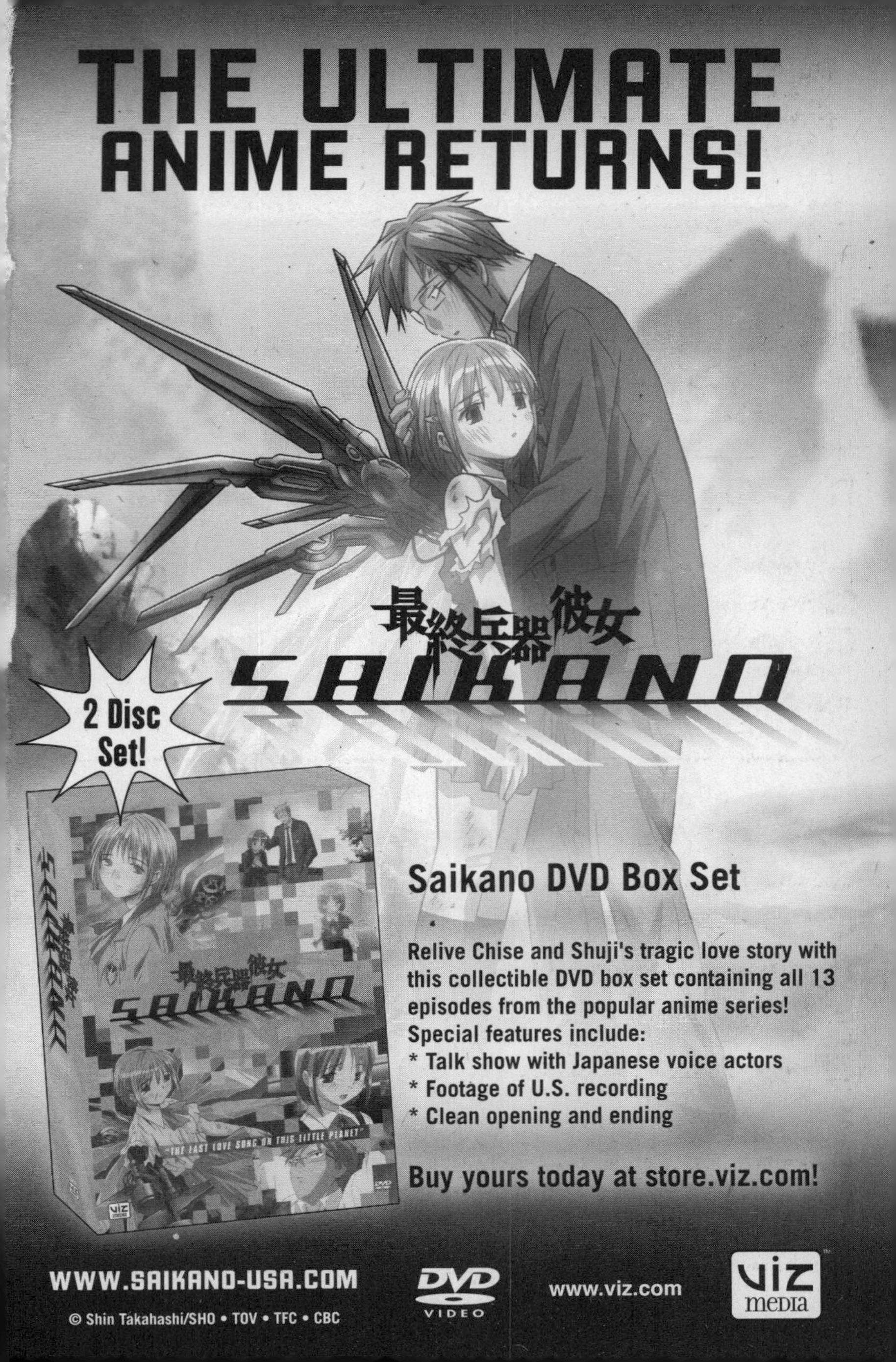
THE ULTIMATE ANIME RETURNS!
最終兵器彼女
SAIKANO
2 Disc Set!
最終兵器彼女
SAIKANO
"THE LAST LOVE SONG ON THIS LITTLE PLANET"
Saikano DVD Box Set
Relive Chise and Shuji's tragic love story with this collectible DVD box set containing all 13 episodes from the popular anime series!
Special features include:
* Talk show with Japanese voice actors
* Footage of U.S. recording
* Clean opening and ending
Buy yours today at store.viz.com!
WWW.SAIKANO-USA.COM
DVD VIDEO
www.viz.com
viz media
© Shin Takahashi/SHO • TOV • TFC • CBC

LOVE MANGA?　LET US KNOW!

☐ Please do NOT send me information about VIZ Media products, news and events, special offers, or other information.

☐ Please do NOT send me information from VIZ Media's trusted business partners.

Name: _____

Address: _____

City: _____ State: _____ Zip: _____

E-mail: _____

☐ Male　☐ Female　Date of Birth (mm/dd/yyyy): ___ / ___ / _____　(Under 13? Parental consent required)

What race/ethnicity do you consider yourself? (check all that apply)

☐ White/Caucasian　　☐ Black/African American　　☐ Hispanic/Latino

☐ Asian/Pacific Islander　　☐ Native American/Alaskan Native　　☐ Other: _____

What VIZ Media title(s) did you purchase? (indicate title(s) purchased) _____

_____

What other VIZ Media titles do you own? _____

_____

Reason for purchase: (check all that apply)

☐ Special offer　　　　☐ Favorite title / author / artist / genre

☐ Gift　　　　　　　☐ Recommendation　　☐ Collection

☐ Read excerpt in VIZ Media manga sampler　☐ Other _____

Where did you make your purchase? (please check one)

☐ Comic store　　　☐ Bookstore　　　☐ Grocery Store

☐ Convention　　　☐ Newsstand　　　☐ Video Game Store

☐ Online (site: _____)　☐ Other _____

How many manga titles have you purchased in the last year? How many were VIZ Media titles?
(please check one from each column)

MANGA	VIZ Media
☐ None	☐ None
☐ 1 – 4	☐ 1 – 4
☐ 5 – 10	☐ 5 – 10
☐ 11+	☐ 11+

How much influence do special promotions and gifts-with-purchase have on the titles you buy?
(please circle, with 5 being great influence and 1 being none)

1 2 3 4 5

Do you purchase every volume of your favorite series?

☐ Yes! Gotta have 'em as my own ☐ No. Please explain: ______________________

What kind of manga storylines do you most enjoy? (check all that apply)

☐ Action / Adventure
☐ Comedy
☐ Fighting
☐ Artistic / Alternative
☐ Science Fiction
☐ Romance (shojo)
☐ Sports
☐ Other ______________________
☐ Horror
☐ Fantasy (shojo)
☐ Historical

If you watch the anime or play a video or TCG game from a series, how likely are you to buy the manga? (please circle, with 5 being very likely and 1 being unlikely)

1 2 3 4 5

If unlikely, please explain: ______________________

Who are your favorite authors / artists? ______________________

____

What titles would like you translated and sold in English? ______________________

____

THANK YOU! Please send the completed form to:

NJW Research
42 Catharine Street
Poughkeepsie, NY 12601

Your privacy is very important to us. All information provided will be used for internal purposes only and will not be sold or otherwise divulged.